Marketing the e-Business

As effective marketing becomes increasingly tied up with the Internet and other electronic media, making the most of the Internet and other new technologies is key to a company's success – from the brand image portrayed on its Web site to the development, maintenance and enhancement of customer relationships.

But since the much-hyped dotcom crash, treading the e-Business path can be daunting. In these increasingly uncertain and cynical times, *Marketing the e-Business* unpicks the challenges of e-Marketing for many types of business. It uses topical case studies and accompanying Web material to provide an up-to-date study of effective marketing strategies, for example:

- Multi-channel marketing
- Change management
- Lessons learned from the dotcom crash
- Branding, e-Retail and relationship-building
- Digital divides, privacy and data security

Providing a new approach to the subject matter, this book analyses the benefits of e-Marketing as a tool for improving efficiency and effectiveness rather than for business revolution. Considering the practicalities of marketing in an e-Business context, it is the first book of its kind to voice such a rigorous argument for the importance of e-Marketing, and is a crucial text for anyone studying or practising e-Business in the real bricks 'n' clicks world.

Lisa Harris is a Chartered Marketer and lecturer in Marketing at Brunel University. She is founder of the University's e-Commerce Research Group and is Course Director for the B.Sc in e-Commerce.
Charles Dennis is a Chartered Marketer and lectures in Marketing and Retail Management at Brunel University. Internationally published, he is currently researching e-Retailing.

Routledge e-Business series

Routledge e-Business is a bold new series examining key aspects of the e-Business world, designed to provide students and academics with a more structured learning resource. Introducing issues of marketing, Human Resource Management, ethics, operations management, law, design, computing and the e-Business environment, it offers a broad overview of key e-Business issues from both managerial and technical perspectives.

Marketing the e-Business
Lisa Harris and Charles Dennis

e-Business Fundamentals
Edited by Paul Jackson

e-Retailing
Charles Dennis, Bill Merrilees and Tino French

Marketing the e-Business

Lisa Harris and Charles Dennis

London *and* New York

First published 2002 by Routledge
11 New Fetter Lane, London EC4P 4EE

Simultaneously published in the USA and Canada
by Routledge
29 West 35th Street, New York NY 10001

Routledge is an imprint of the Taylor & Francis Group

© 2002 Lisa Harris and Charles Dennis

Typeset in Perpetua and Bell Gothic by
Florence Production Ltd, Stoodleigh, Devon
Printed and bound in Great Britain by
St Edmundsbury Press, Bury St Edmunds, Suffolk

British Library Cataloguing in Publication Data
A catalogue record for this book is available from the British
Library

Library of Congress Cataloging in Publication Data
A catalog record for this book has been requested

ISBN 0–415–25600–3 (hbk)
ISBN 0–415–25601–1 (pbk)

Contents

Illustrations

FIGURES

TABLES

Contributors

LISA HARRIS ACIB, Dip.M., MCIM, MBA, Ph.D., Chartered Marketer

Dr Lisa Harris is a lecturer in Brunel University's School of Business and Management, and Course Director of the e-Commerce B.Sc. She worked in the banking industry for ten years and her Ph.D. research examined the management of change in the banking industry in the early days of the Internet. Lisa is currently running a research project reviewing emerging trends in the ethics of e-Commerce. She is a Chartered Marketer, Education Officer for the Royal Counties branch of the Chartered Institute of Marketing, and teaches Marketing courses for the Student Support Group and Oxford College of Marketing.

CHARLES DENNIS Dip.D.M., DMS, Ph.D., C.Eng., M.I.Chem.E., MCIM

Dr Charles Dennis is a Chartered Marketer and a lecturer in Marketing and Retail Management at Brunel University, London, where he co-ordinates the 'Marketing' pathway of the University's B.Sc. (Business and Management) degree. Originally a Chartered Chemical Engineer, he spent some years in engineering and technical posts, latterly with a 'marketing' emphasis. The industrial experience was followed by seven years with 'Marketing Methods', as an Institute of Marketing-approved consultant. He has been full time in the current post since 1993. Charles has published internationally on consumer shopping behaviour and is now researching e-Shopping and e-Retailing.

GERALDINE COHEN Dipl.Ing., MBA (INSEAD), MCIM, Chartered Marketer

Geraldine has more than twenty-five years of international business and marketing experience acquired at Fairchild Semiconductors in Germany, Cummins Engine Company in the USA, and Rank Xerox and ECI Ventures in the UK. In the 1980s and part of the 1990s, she ran her own marketing consultancy, advising industrial and commercial clients as well as non-profit organizations. Geraldine has a Diplôme Ingénieur degree in Electrical and Electronic Engineering and an MBA from INSEAD, France. She is a member of the Chartered Institute of Marketing and has been a Chartered Marketer since 1998. She has been a non-executive director of Mount Vernon and Watford NHS Trust, as well as Trust Convenor, and has chaired a number of trust management committees. Geraldine has been teaching at the Brunel School of Business and Management since 1998. Geraldine's current research interests lie in the areas of marketing for professional services and corporate branding.

Acknowledgements

The authors would like to thank the following individuals for their invaluable support, examples, explanations, patience and encouragement throughout this project:

- Stuart Newstead, General Manager, Business Partners, O2 (UK) Ltd
- Paul McAleese, Global Commercial Director, Genie Internet
- Andrew Jones, Managing Director, Aerodeon
- Jon Twomey, Director, Student Support Group
- Chris Barker, Head of Fixed Income e-Commerce, BNP Paribas, London
- Rosie Phipps, Principal, Oxford College of Marketing
- Dr Leslie Budd, Open University Business School

Thanks are also due to a number of staff and students of Brunel University:

- Dr Laura Spence
- Lefki Papacharalambou
- Yuri Gandamihardja
- Tamira King
- Glen Freeman
- Alaina Dixon
- Alan McGuinness
- Balraj Sandhu
- Simran Grewal
- Christine Chazakis
- Laura Pegg
- David McLaverty
- Gurpal Dhensa
- Ketan Makwana
- Craig Martin
- Spencer Tarring

Particular votes of thanks must go to Simran Grewal for some excellent diagrams, to Chris Barker for his diverting emails and to George the Dog for keeping us all sane!

Lisa Harris and Charles Dennis,
February 2002

Abbreviations

ADSL	Asynchronous Digital Subscriber Line
AOL	America Online
ARPA	Advanced Research Project Agency (of the US Department of Defense)
ASP	Application Service Provider
ATM	automated telling machine
B2B	business to business
B2C	business to consumer
B2G	business to government
C2B	consumer to business
C2C	consumer to consumer
CDMA	Code Division Multiple Access
CEO	chief executive officer
CMC	computer-mediated communication
CNO	Chief Net Officer
CPFR	collaborative planning, reporting and replenishment
CRM	customer relationship management
DAA	data aggregation agent
DMCA	Digital Millennium Copyright Act 1998 (USA)
EDI	Electronic Data Interchange
EFF	Electronic Frontier Foundation
EFTPOS	electronic funds transfer point of sale
EMS	Enhanced Messaging Services
EPIC	Electronic Privacy Information Centre
EPOS	electronic point-of-sale
ERP	Enterprise Resource Planning
ES	electronic shopping
ETF	Electronic Funds Transfer
EU	European Union
FAQ	frequently asked question

FMCG	fast-moving consumer goods
FOMA	Freedom of Mobile Multimedia Access
FTC	Federal Trade Commission (USA)
FTP	File Transfer Protocol
FTSE 100	Financial Times Stock Exchange 100 Index
GDP	gross domestic product
GM	General Motors
GPRS	General Packet Radio Services
GSM	Global Service for Mobile
ICANN	Internet Corporation for Assigned Names and Numbers
ICT	information and communications technology
iDTV	Interactive Digital Television
IETF	Internet Engineering Task Force
IP	Internet Protocol
IPO	initial public offering
ISOC	Internet Society
ISP	Internet Service Provider
IT	information technology
IVR	interactive voice response
JIT	Just in Time
LAN	local area network
MIS	marketing information system
MKIS	marketing information system
MMS	Multimedia Messaging Services
NPL	National Physical Laboratory (UK)
NSF	National Science Foundation (USA)
NTIA	National Telecommunications and Information Administration (USA)
P2P	peer to peer
PDA	personal digital assistant
PEST	political, economic, social and cultural, technological
PHS	Personal Handyphone System
PIMS	Profit Impact of Marketing Strategy (study)
PPC	pay-per-click
PR	public relations
RRP	recommended retail price
SALT	Speech Application Language Tags
SCIP	Society of Competitive Intelligence Professionals
SMART	specific, measurable, actionable, realistic, timed
SMEs	small and medium-sized enterprises
SMS	Short Message System
SWOT	strengths, weaknesses, opportunities, threats
TDMA	Time Division Multiple Access

URL	Uniform Resource Locator
VAN	value added network
VAT	value added tax
VOIP	Voice Over Internet Protocol
VPA	virtual personal assistant
W3C	World Wide Web Consortium
WAN	wide area network
WAP	Wireless Application Protocol
WWW	World Wide Web

Introduction

AIM

The aim of this book is to demonstrate to both marketing students and practitioners how marketing efficiency and effectiveness can be improved through the use of the Internet.

RATIONALE

Relatively few companies (with the exception of the 'pure-play' or 'dotcom' brigade) are able to start with a 'clean sheet of paper' as far as Internet operations are concerned. For most companies, setting up Internet operations involves a significant degree of cultural and structural change. It also usually means running both 'traditional' and 'new' business alongside each other, and developing an appropriate degree of integration between them to create useful synergies. Although a number of lessons can be learned from the bursting of the dotcom bubble (and these are considered where relevant), the main focus of this text is upon the challenges faced by 'bricks and mortar' organizations as they introduce and develop their online operations *alongside* their established business activities.

Kanter highlights a key theme of this book, which is that in our enthusiasm to keep up with the ways in which the world is changing, we often fail to notice just how much remains the same. In her words,

> History demonstrates that new channels tend to coexist with old ones and sometimes even join them. . . . Yes, the technology is revolutionary, network economics are different, and all the wheels must turn a lot faster, but the problems of leadership, organization and change are similar to those we have experienced for decades.
>
> (Kanter 2001: 5)

A lot has been written about the 'revolutionary' business implications of the Internet, to the extent that some authors have argued that a new business 'paradigm' has emerged, as a result of the scope of the potential applications of Internet technology. However, Palmer (2001) notes that the recent difficulties experienced by dotcom businesses indicate that there has actually been little change in the underlying beliefs and values. Such firms therefore operate within the same business environment as conventional businesses and hence are subject to the same rules. Similarly, Dutta and Biren (2001) propose that the key role of Internet technology is not to revolutionize business practices but instead to seek efficiency improvements through 'e-nabling' the current activities of the firm in a 'low-risk' approach to innovation that is consistent with existing organizational culture. In addition, Phillips (2001) calculates that the application of technology to improve the efficiency of current operations may represent as much as 72 per cent of all IT developments. Palmer (2002) supports this by noting the success enjoyed by the convergence of 'e-Businesses' and more conventional operations (such as, for example, Amazon, Waterstones and Virgin Wine) in what he terms a 'shared' rather than 'revolutionary' business paradigm.

STRUCTURE

This book adopts a methodical approach to the development, implementation and control of Internet marketing strategies. The relevance of the chapter's subject matter to that of the book as a whole, a summary of the key lessons that will be learned, and an ordered list of subtopics to be covered are set out at the start of each chapter. Feedback is provided at the end of each chapter on a number of self-assessed questions posed in the text, together with a list of specific Web-based sources and book references. The book's supporting Web site will be used to keep these chapter-by-chapter resources up to date.

A 'mindmap' depicts the structure of the book.

Chapter 1: History, definitions and frameworks

Reviews the history and early business usage of the Internet and outlines the various approaches currently available to firms in terms of the degree of commitment to Internet operations and options for structural change.

Chapter 2: Marketing research

Considers the evolving scope of the Internet to support both primary and secondary research activity.

Chapter 1
History, definitions
and frameworks

Chapter 2
Marketing research

Chapter 3
Change
management

Chapter 4
Strategy

Chapter 5
Branding

Chapter 6
Relationship
marketing

Chapter 7
Multi-channel
marketing

Chapter 8
The marketing
mix

Chapter 9
e-Retailing

Chapter 10
Marketing
planning

Chapter 11
Legal, ethical and
public policy
issues

Introductory level

Strategic level

Operational level

Big picture

Mindmap showing structure of this book

Chapter 3: Change management

Outlines key issues of innovation and change management that are particularly important for companies with an established history of 'traditional' business activity.

Chapter 4: Strategy

Examines strategic issues such as planning and the degree of integration required between 'online' and 'offline' marketing strategy. On the business-to-business side, recent developments in online strategy such as the growth of e-Marketplaces are discussed.

Chapter 5: Branding

Examines branding strategy such as the development of new online brands and also considers how the Internet can be used to raise awareness of established offline brands.

Chapter 6: Relationship marketing

Reviews the rapidly developing area of relationship marketing (CRM) strategies to key stakeholder groups, namely staff, customers and business partners.

Chapter 7: Multi-channel marketing

Reviews the increasingly diverse range of Internet access mechanisms such as digital television, radio and mobile telephones as well as the personal computer itself. The challenges of developing an integrated marketing communications strategy across a range of online and offline platforms are then outlined.

Chapter 8: The marketing mix

Examines the management of the online marketing mix, and how online and offline marketing activities can be integrated to best effect in both business to business and business to consumer scenarios.

Chapter 9: e-Retailing

Examines the growing phenomenon of e-Retailing, which is the sale of goods and services via Internet or other electronic channels for personal use by consumers.

Chapter 10: Marketing planning

Outlines practical considerations of strategy implementation, resourcing, budgets, controls and contingencies that come together to form an integrated e-Marketing plan for a range of companies covering both business-to-business and business-to-consumer situations.

Chapter 11: Legal, ethical and public policy issues

Takes a more macro-level view of the Internet trading environment, covering such diverse issues as security, ethics, globalization, data protection, governance and legislation.

History, definitions and frameworks

LISA HARRIS

MINDMAP

Chapter 1
History, definitions
and frameworks

Chapter 2
Marketing research

Chapter 3
Change
management

Chapter 4
Strategy

Chapter 5
Branding

Chapter 6
Relationship
marketing

Chapter 7
Multi-channel
marketing

Chapter 8
The marketing
mix

Chapter 9
e-Retailing

Chapter 10
Marketing
planning

Chapter 11
Legal, ethical and
public policy
issues

Introductory level

Strategic level

Operational level

Big picture

LINKS TO OTHER CHAPTERS

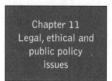

- Chapter 4 – Strategy
- Chapter 11 – Legal, ethical and public policy issues

KEY LEARNING POINTS

After completing this chapter you will have an understanding of:

- Historical context of Web developments
- Terms of reference used in the book
- An overview of the major evolving debates in Internet marketing

ORDERED LIST OF SUB TOPICS

- A brief review of the history of the Internet
- Overview of recent developments
  - Governance
  - Access
- Key definitions
- Frameworks for Internet marketing
- Lessons from history and cautionary tales
- Chapter summary
- ❖ Case study: The rise and fall of Boo.com
- ❖ Further reading
- ❖ Questions
- ❖ Web links

A BRIEF REVIEW OF THE HISTORY OF THE INTERNET

In 1969, the Internet was just a demonstration project linking up four university campuses in the USA, but it now boasts in excess of 300 million users across the world. It was supported by the US Department of Defense's Advanced Research Project Agency (ARPA). The Internet was based on an original concept developed by the Rand Corporation in the early 1960s, and added to by bodies such as the UK's National Physical Laboratory (NPL). The objective of the research was to provide the USA with a communications network that would survive in the event of a nuclear conflagration. The project was codified into a set of protocols (eventually called TCP/IP) by Vinton Cerf during the mid-1970s, and deployed across all the interlinked networks in 1983. Growth between 1980 and 1987 shows numbers of hosts in the tens of thousands.

After 1987, when the US funding body the National Science Foundation (NSF) started to work with the Internet, the number leapt into the hundreds of thousands. Many non-US academic sites and scientific and research bodies linked up at this point. It was inherent in the technology that new nodes could easily be added to the Internet, and this has permitted the exponential growth of users. Moreover, all messages are treated equally – there is no inherent prioritization of messages – so no matter what computer is being used, all messages have equal rights regardless of whether the user is an employee of a large corporation or an individual accessing the Internet from home.

No single entity owns the Internet or is wholly responsible for its functioning. It is a decentralized network whose operation is influenced by a number of bodies and forces, not least large commercial interests such as Cisco and Microsoft, which help drive information and communication technology (ICT) standards and innovation in the marketplace itself, and as members or otherwise of the various bodies. Between 1987 and 1995, however, one of the most dominant influences on the Internet and Web was the NSF, which subsidized its use along with scientific and academic institutions that paid for servers and created Web content. The ethos underpinning the Internet at this point was one of not-for-profit, and the lack of packet prioritization underpinned an essentially democratic spirit among its user communities. It was only with the emergence of the World Wide Web (WWW) that individuals with little knowledge of such protocols could participate in this electronic medium. By use of hypertext (embedded links within electronic documents) and a pointing device such as a mouse, navigation through a series of Web pages was made possible for novice users. The development of the Web browser Mosaic in 1993 meant that rapid colonization of the network by commercial interests began. It is from this point that e-Commerce dates, at least in its Internet manifestation.

Earlier forms of e-Commerce include Electronic Data Interchange (EDI). This is the exchange of information and orders by trading partners using technically defined templates. It traces its origins to 1969, when a US freight company sought to optimize its freight shipments by use of cabling alongside its tracks to link it with customers. The succeeding decades saw many large corporations taking up EDI based on value-added networks operated by private-sector organizations such as IBM to the point where by 1995 there were in excess of 30,000 EDI networks in Europe alone. Another early mechanism was Electronic Funds Transfer (EFT), and for two decades international settlements by banking interests have been undertaken via the SWIFT system. Intranational settlements have been made by BACS since 1982. As opposed to the Internet, which uses protocols that are *open* and *non-proprietary*, these EDI systems are *closed* or *proprietary* systems that are open only to invited participants.

The Internet as we know it today consists of small area networks belonging to individual organizations (local area networks, LANs), networks spread across large geographic areas (wide area networks, WANs) and individual computers. To connect to the Internet, a computer or network uses the TCP/IP protocol. The Internet itself usually utilizes an operating system called UNIX. Within the Internet there are more networks. These include:

- backbone networks (e.g. the NTSNET system);
- commercial networks (businesses with direct links to the Internet)
- service providers that offer smaller firms an Internet connection;
- non-commercial networks belonging to educational/research organizations; and
- gateway networks which allow their subscribers access to the Internet (e.g. America Online (AOL) or Compuserve).

Most Internet sites have an address or 'domain name' that acts as a telephone number for individuals wishing to reach them. Transfer of information uses File Transfer Protocol (FTP). These files can contain images, video clips, sound recording, text or graphics. In short, the Internet is capable of transmitting anything that can be put in digital form. This means that the cost of information transfer is becoming negligible, distance is increasingly irrelevant and content can be accessed almost immediately. For a relatively small outlay on a computer, a suitable telecommunications link (e.g. via a phone line and modem), and an online account provided by an Internet Service Provider (ISP), individuals located across the globe can access this massive network, which is growing at an exponential rate. The network – the Internet – hooks up the physical infrastructure of computers via cable and wireless links, enabling users to access rich informational sources and use interactive forms of communication such as email.

The latest statistics concerning Internet growth can be found at Network Wizards (see www.nw.com). It is perhaps unsurprising to note that the densest concentrations of users are in North America (60 per cent) and Europe. From being a relatively unknown medium at the beginning of the 1990s, by 2000 the Internet was heading for 100 million hosts (i.e. separate computers linked up) across the world. Compaq estimates that the number of users will grow from around 300 million in 2001 to around 1 billion in 2005. In addition to these fixed hosts that link individual desktop computers to the Internet will be mobile hosts linking up mobile phones to it using wireless technology. The implications of such new Internet access mechanisms for marketing strategy will be discussed in Chapters 4 and 7.

For more detail on the development of the Internet, Hobbe's Internet Timeline identifies a chronology of events and the individuals behind them at www.zakon.org/robert/internet/timeline Another excellent historical source by one of the key players is *Weaving the Web* by Berners-Lee (1999).

OVERVIEW OF RECENT DEVELOPMENTS

Governance

Principal among the bodies that have a prescribed influence on the ongoing development of the Internet and the Web are the Internet Engineering Task Force (IETF), the World Wide Web Consortium (W3C) and the Internet Corporation for Assigned Names and Numbers (ICANN). The IETF was created in 1986 to be responsible for drawing up the technical standards for the Internet, and comes under the aegis of the Internet Society (ISOC) – created in 1992 – which assumes overall responsibility for the organization of its development. W3C focuses on the development of the Web (a subset of the Internet) and was created in 1994. It is chaired by the Web's original creator, Tim Berners-Lee. ICANN, created in 1998, controls the accreditation of domain name registrars which undertake the business of registering Web sites. Decisions made by these bodies determine how Internet and WWW operations take place, and, by definition, what products and/or services are to be successful in the market. Internet 2 is a collaborative project involving over 100 universities that is focusing on increasing the speed of information transfer over the Internet. This is intended to drive forward collaborative use of the Web for learning purposes, for example through video conferencing and virtual laboratories, which struggle to achieve suitable transmission speeds with current technology.

The UK government is committed to extending the use of the Internet. According to the Prime Minister, Tony Blair, speaking in 2000, 'The Internet-driven knowledge economy is becoming the preserve of an elite.' He drew upon a study from technology and management consultants Booz, Allen and Hamilton, which showed that Britain is top of the e-league in Europe, in terms of Internet use and revenue from e-Commerce. The study also shows that 45 per cent of those online in the UK are aged between 15 and 24, and almost half of British users are in the top (AB) social group, but the poorer sector of the population uses the Internet very little. As a consequence, the Prime Minister pledged that 'every British citizen should be able to go online within five years'. He wants the Internet to be available to all as part of a drive to position the UK at the forefront of the 'new' economy. The government aims to ensure that people can get online via computers at home, at work, and in libraries and schools, via digital television and mobile telephones.

Access

Business demands on the Internet are for increasing speed and greater bandwidth. As a result, ADSL (Asynchronous Digital Subscriber Line) is seen as the means of facilitating e-Commerce by offering rapid transfer rates to open up multimedia delivery to small and medium-sized firms (SMEs) and individuals. Such bandwidth has so far been available only to large companies using leased lines. Attempts to 'unbundle the local loop' to competition have not yet succeeded in the UK as the ex-monopolist BT has not moved quickly enough. As a result, high-speed services are not as prevalent as proponents of e-Commerce would like. In the USA, unbundling began in the mid-1990s. For more detail on this lengthy saga, see Burton (2001).

Currently there are in excess of 300 ISPs in the UK that offer Internet access services, and their pricing reflects the relative quality of service. Some ISPs went so far as to drop charges altogether in order to attract users. Freeserve (www. freeserve.com) got large market penetration quickly when it was launched in September 1998, and within a few months had a membership in excess of 2 million. A number of other UK ISPs quickly followed suit. Though Freeserve was effectively subsidizing the cost of user access, the rationale for doing so was linked to the value of a subscriber base to which advertising could be directed. User surveys have consistently pointed to the high proportion of individuals with large disposable incomes among those with Internet access, which makes them attractive targets for advertisers. In 2000, attention in the UK ISP market moved to service offerings that levied relatively low charges for a combined service giving Internet subscription *and* unmetered telecom charges. Breathe.com, LineOne, Freeserve, LibertySurf, Tiny, NTL and AOL led the way. For a flat-rate yearly subscription of £60, an AOL user could gain unlimited access to the Internet, and as a result, AOL rapidly attracted 270,000 applicants. However, companies offering these services quickly withdrew them when it became clear that BT was responding only in part to the draft directive which insisted that incumbent national telecommunications providers (such as BT, France Telecom and Deutsche Telecom) should allow competitors access to local telephone exchanges from 1 January 2001. The objective was to promote competition and stimulate innovation in the 'local loop' market, especially in high-speed bit stream services such as ADSL.

Currently, more than 300 million people around the world have Internet access, but the distribution across countries is anything but even (see www.nua.ie for full Internet population statistics). Why does the digital economy appear to be flourishing more in some countries than others? The obvious answers concerning the health of the economy and the sophistication of the telephone infrastructure do not tell the whole story. In France, one of the wealthiest economies in the world, only 15 per cent of the population have access to the Internet, and only 5 per cent of households own a personal computer. Culture may provide the answer: the accepted language of the Web is English, which is less than popular in France. People in Scandinavian countries are known for their language skills, and Internet penetration in Sweden is 44 per cent. In Asia, the sheer diversity of languages and cultures has slowed the spread of the Internet. It may cross national borders with ease, but linguistic barriers are proving harder to negotiate. For this reason, Latin America is predicted to be a major online force in the years to come, because only two languages separate the entire continent. It is also evident that countries respecting individualism and

Table 1.1 *Internet penetration rates by country (October 2001, www.nua.ie)*

Country	Net penetration as per cent of population
Norway	50
Iceland	45
USA	45
Sweden	44
Canada	43
Finland	38
Australia	36
Denmark	36
UK	26
Italy	16
France	15
Greece	12
Spain	9
Russia	4
China	0.7
India	0.5

entrepreneurship are more likely to embrace e-Commerce. In some Middle East countries, even public access to the Internet is difficult, with systems heavily policed by the government.

The figures in Table 1.1 are taken from NUA Internet Surveys (October 2001, www.nua.ie) showing the wide variation of Internet penetration in different countries.

However, the most important ingredient for increasing Internet penetration is a modern telephone system. The imminent impact of mobile phones is also likely to be pivotal in the next generation of Web developments. Wireless transmission has brought speedy communications to countries that were too poor to build traditional telephone networks. Uruguay, for example, is not saddled with crumbling analogue cabling, and it now has one of the most advanced digital networks in the world. Another critical factor is the cost of telecommunications, as described earlier. These issues will be considered in more detail in Chapter 11.

ACTIVITY

Examine the Web site of Cyberatlas (www.cyberatlas.com), which also gives details of the level of Internet access in a number of different countries. This picture is incomplete without an understanding of the demographics that apply within each country (age, sex, income, geographical region). See www. emori.co.uk for UK demographic data. What does this add to your understanding of UK Internet users?

KEY DEFINITIONS

This section will introduce you to some of the key Internet terminology and new business frameworks that you will encounter throughout the book.

Intranets

An intranet can be defined as

> A network within a single company which enables access to company information using the familiar tools of the Internet such as web browsers and email. Only staff within a company can access the intranet, which will be password protected.

> (Chaffey *et al.* 2000: 76)

Intranets are becoming increasingly popular within organizations as a communication tool with which to collect and disseminate information. *Firewalls* (special security software applications) are necessary to prevent access to confidential information, such as employee records, which can then be accessed by password only. The use of intranets to facilitate internal marketing will be discussed in more detail in Chapter 6. Like the Internet itself, an intranet can work all over the globe for a company that has offices based in several countries, meaning that it is not constrained by geography.

The main benefits of an intranet to the organization are improved competitiveness through operational efficiency and productivity. An Intranet can also create a culture within the firm that is conducive to information sharing and collaboration. O'Keefe, Professor of Information Systems at Brunel University, is unequivocal about the potential of intranets: 'Intranets are about distributing control and management of information, reversing decades of self-serving centralization and inefficient information hiding.'

The Intranetroadmap.com (www.intranetroadmap.com) divides the benefits of intranets into tangible and intangible aspects as follows:

Tangible benefits

- They are inexpensive to implement (an intranet can be established on a company's existing network with little training needed).
- They are easy to use; just point and click. (This is because intranets work on the same technology as a Web page – thus employees already know how to navigate around sites,)
- They save time and money by providing better information faster (information which previously was locked away in cupboards or in the heads of key staff is now accessible to all at the click of a mouse).
- They are based on open standards (the key to the intranet is freedom of information).
- They are scaleable and flexible (an intranet can be managed and changed instantly).
- They connect across disparate platforms (an intranet can work for a business which has various regional offices within or outside a country).
- They put users in control of their data (an intranet can allow and enable users to update their data).

Intangible benefits

- They offer improved decision-making, owing to the fact that employees now have access to far more information at their fingertips and so can make more informed and thus better decisions.

- They empower users (if they are allowed to by management, users can edit and control their data and thus begin to become empowered).
- They build a culture of sharing and collaboration (this is created through the intranet's ability to enable documents to be shared and online collaboration of projects to happen).
- They facilitate organizational learning (developed through the culture that the intranet creates and achieved via the data that the intranet provides for everybody to see).
- They break down bureaucracy (mainly through the reduction in paper required, but also by the empowering of users).
- They offer improved quality of life at work (an intranet creates this not only through the modified culture, but by empowering the users and creating a sense of ownership for them).
- They enable improved productivity (as the sum of both the tangible and the intangible benefits described).

However, problems can also occur with the use of intranets:

- They have to be continually updated to be credible, which is a resource-intensive job.
- Intranets that merely mimic existing inefficient processes will not add much value.
- Poor design can mean that information is hard to find, and the resource will be underutilized.
- If there is no means of control over Intranet content, chaos can result through overuse.
- Responsibilities for development and maintenance must be clearly understood.

Extranets

The distinction between intranets and extranets is important:

> An extranet is formed by extending the intranet beyond a company to customers, suppliers, collaborators or even competitors. This is again password-protected to prevent access by general Internet users.
>
> (Chaffey *et al*. 2000: 76)

Extranets are a rapidly developing area and significant cost savings can be generated by companies that are linked electronically through extranets along the supply chain. They also offer the opportunity to cut out intermediaries in some cases (**disintermediation**), while introducing new types of intermediary (**reintermediation**) in others. Chapter 4 will explore the use of extranets and exchanges to facilitate communications with trading partners in more detail.

e-Commerce or e-Business?

There are many definitions of e-Commerce. The narrowest refer to it simply as the buying and selling of goods online. Chaffey treats e-Commerce as a subset of e-Business because the former does not include intra-business functions such as the processing of a purchase order. He quotes the following definition of e-Business:

> When a business has fully integrated information and communication technologies (ICTs) into its operations, potentially redesigning its business processes around ICT or completely reinventing its business model . . . e-Business, is understood to be the integration of all these activities with the internal processes of a business through ICT.
>
> (Chaffey 2002: 8)

Zwass defines e-Commerce much more broadly:

> the sharing of business information, maintaining business relationships, and conducting business transactions by means of telecommunications networks.
>
> (Zwass 1998: 157)

In its broadest form, therefore, e-Commerce can be regarded as synonymous with IBM's expression 'e-Business', which is a holistic concept covering the full range of business functions and structures effected by the Internet, and this is the approach taken in this book. Given the marketing perspective of the book, the more general terms 'Internet strategy' and 'Internet marketing' are also used extensively here. Agonizing over definitions is probably a waste of effort, because all these terms are likely to be transitory as the Internet becomes an integral part of business activity. In fact, such terms can be likened to early descriptions of the motor car as a 'horseless carriage'.

Electronic commerce has existed for some years in the form of EDI, but technical problems and restricted functionality contrived to ensure that the system never achieved widespread credibility. The lack of a common standard for document formats meant that companies tended to get locked in to one supplier. It has taken the growth of the Internet with its universal standard to project electronic trading into mainstream commercial credibility, allowing businesses to connect throughout the value chain, exchange real-time information and streamline business processes both internally and externally. The principal driver for the take-up of e-Commerce is economics. For example, the cost of processing

Table 1.2 *Zwass's hierarchical framework for e-Commerce*

Meta-level	Level	Function	Examples
Products and structures	7	Electronic marketplaces and electronic hierarchies	Electronic auctions, brokerages, dealerships and direct search markets
			Inter-organizational supply-chain management
	6	Products and systems	Remote consumer services (retailing, banking)
			Infotainment on demand (fee-based content sites, educational offerings)
			Supplier–customer linkages
			Online marketing
			Intranet/extranet-based collaboration
Services	5	Enabling services	Electronic catalogues e-Money/smart card systems
			Digital authentication services
			Copyright protection services
	4	Secure messaging	EDI, email, Electronic Funds Transfer
Infrastructure	3	Hypermedia/multimedia object management	WWW with Java
	2	Public and private communication utilities	Internet and value added networks (VANs)
	1	Wide-area telecommunications infrastructure	Guided and wireless media networks

a financial transaction on the Web can be as little as 1 per cent of doing the same at a bank branch using traditional paper methods. So once fixed costs such as equipment and telecommunications lines are covered, the marginal cost of servicing transactions on the Web can be very low. In business-to-business terms, procurement costs can be significantly reduced.

Zwass (1998) devised a hierarchical framework of e-Commerce comprising seven levels to illustrate the interrelationships between its various aspects, and help make sense of the likely impacts of e-Commerce. His framework is represented in Table 1.2. Zwass regards e-Commerce as comprising three meta-levels:

1 *infrastructure*: the hardware, software, databases and telecommunications that are deployed to deliver such functionality as the WWW over the Internet, or to support EDI and other forms of messaging over the Internet;

2 *services*: messaging and other services enabling the finding and delivery of information, including a search for potential business partners, as well as the negotiation and settlement of a business transaction;

3 *products and structures*: direct provision of commercial information-based goods and services to consumers and business partners, intra- and inter-organizational information sharing, and organization of electronic marketplaces and supply chains.

Within these meta-levels are seven distinct levels. The first three make up the technological infrastructure of e-Commerce. Levels 4 and 5 represent the business infrastructure, and levels 6 and 7 cover business-to-business transactions and business-to-consumer transactions through electronic marketplaces and intra-organizational communications through intranets. As these tools encourage the dissemination of information, reducing (and in some cases eliminating) the need for 'privileged points of contacts or gatekeepers in organizations', they are also contributing to 'the move away from centralised, hierarchical approaches and transforming traditional relationships within and between organisations' (Timmers 1999: 132).

Fischer (1999) describes the scope of e-Commerce revenue under headings that can be summarized as the '5Cs':

- *Connection*. AOL, for example (www.aol.com), as an ISP, obtains its revenues from connecting customers to the Internet.
- *Commercials*. Some companies obtain revenue from displaying advertisements for other companies. Key sites such as Yahoo! with millions of visitors can charge high fees. Smaller, more specialist Web sites can attract advertisers with relevant products or services to offer; for example, an estate agent's Web site might carry advertisements for removal companies or solicitors.
- *Commerce*. Goods or services are sold directly to customers online.
- *Content*. Some sites can charge for content that can be accessed from the site. For example, a market research firm might offer research reports for sale.
- *Community*. Specialist online community sites may be able to charge a membership fee for access and discussion participation.

19

Types of e-Commerce

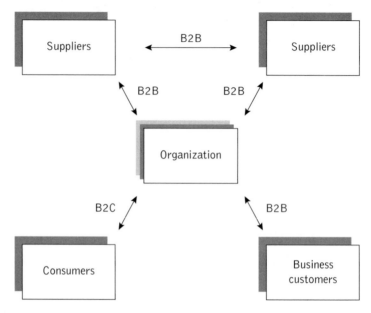

Figure 1.1 *The relationship between business to business (B2B) and business to consumer (B2C)*

As illustrated in Figure 1.1, business to consumer (B2C) refers to the selling of goods and/or services directly to consumers by businesses. The classic example is Amazon (www.amazon.com) which offers in excess of 1.5 million book titles online and has extended its sales into other products, including music CDs, videos and games.

Business to business (B2B) refers to the selling of goods and/or services by one company to another as part of their supply chain, and is likely to contribute to at least 80 per cent of the growth of e-Commerce in the next five years. An example is Marshalls (www.marshalls.com).

There are also some more recent arrangements:

- Consumer to consumer (C2C) refers to the selling of goods and/or services between individuals; see, for example, the auction house eBay (www.ebay.com).
- Consumer to business (C2B) refers to consumers generating trade with businesses. For example, www.letsbuyit.com allows consumers to come together and aggregate their purchasing power to command discounts normally reserved for large organizations. It can also cover individuals such as lawyers or accountants offering their services to businesses.

- Business to government (B2G) refers to the trade in goods and services between the private sector and local or national government.
- Peer to peer (P2P) refers to a relationship between two individuals that is electronically mediated but not conducted via any central body. For example, Freenet (www.freenet.com) is a network that promotes the digital exchange of music artefacts on a P2P basis.

ACTIVITY

New descriptors are appearing on a regular basis, can you think of any more?

Marketing orientation

A 'marketing orientation' describes a guiding management philosophy or attitude of mind throughout the organization that puts the customer first. This is a much broader view of the role of marketing than is traditionally envisaged – referring just to advertising or sales – and it cuts across a wide range of organizational functions. Successful adaptation of a marketing orientation also requires effective management of other stakeholder groups such as staff, business partners, shareholders and suppliers. As Chaffey *et al.* note, 'The marketing concept should lie at the heart of the organisation, and the actions of directors, managers and employees should be guided by its philosophy' (2000: 5).

In fact, it can be argued that in these circumstances a specific marketing department is no longer necessary. This contention is supported by Piercy (1997), who notes that the current emphasis upon the value of cross-functional teams conducting 'pan-company marketing' may obviate the need for marketing departments, especially if such project teams also cross organizational boundaries and blur the distinction between the internal and external environment.

Internet strategy or Internet marketing?

There are significant overlaps between Internet strategy and Internet marketing, particularly if a company adopts a broad perspective of marketing by engendering customer focus throughout the business, as described above. Indeed, the two terms can be regarded as synonymous. Chaffey (2002) regards Internet marketing as a subset of Internet strategy that he calls 'sell-side e-commerce', meaning that it focuses on building relationships with customers, in parallel with 'buy-side e-commerce' that focuses on supply chain management. Chen (2001) regards Internet marketing as dealing with operational rather than strategic issues, but

21

includes customer relationship management in the 'operational' category. In this book, we use the term 'Internet marketing' in a broad sense, while still distinguishing strategic aspects (Chapters 4, 5, 6 and 7) and operational aspects (Chapters 8, 9 and 10).

New business models

Timmers (1999) categorizes a number of new types of online business model, as shown in Table 1.3. In practice, many of these categories overlap, and some are just electronic versions of existing business models, but the table provides a useful demonstration of the range of e-Commerce activities, some of which are still at an early stage of development. By the time you read this, no doubt there will be more!

Table 1.3 Online business model typology

Category	Example
e-Shop/e-retailer	Usually with a B2C focus such as www.whsmith.co.uk
e-Procurement	Online business purchasing of goods (B2B) www.rswww.com
e-Malls	A grouping of e-tailers that can be compared with a traditional shopping centre; see, for example, www.indigosquare.com
e-Auctions	B2B or B2C customers bid for goods; for example, www.ebay.com
Virtual communities	Groupings of customers or businesses with similar interests; for example, www.thepetchannel.com
Collaboration platforms	Enable collaboration between customers or businesses; for example, www.egroups.com
Third-party marketplaces	Intermediaries bringing together buyers and sellers; for example, www.esteel.com
Value chain integrators	Offer a range of services across the value chain; for example, the online events booking service www.omniticket.com
Value chain service providers	Provide functions for a specific part of the value chain, for example the logistics company www.ups.com
Information brokerage	Provide information for consumers or businesses, such as price comparisons: www.moneysupermarket.com
Trust and other services	Provide kitemarks authenticating online service quality, www.truste.org, or security, www.verisign.com

Source: Timmers (1999)

FRAMEWORKS FOR INTERNET MARKETING

This topic will be covered in detail in Chapter 4, so only a brief overview is provided here. Chaffey *et al.* (2000: 122) describe how many companies have been reactive and followed a natural progression in developing a Web site to support their marketing activities:

Level 0	no Web site;
Level 1	listing in an online directory such as Yellow Pages (www.yell.co.uk);
Level 2	basic site containing contact details and product information (brochureware);
Level 3	simple interactive site allowing email queries (www.brunel.ac.uk);
Level 4	interactive site supporting transactions and customer services;
Level 5	fully interactive site providing relationship marketing and facilitating full range of marketing functions.

The amount of effort devoted to online marketing tends to be proportional to the position currently occupied by the company on this hierarchy, or, in other words, how central the Internet is to their marketing activities. An alternative way of describing the degree of Internet sophistication along similar lines is by categorization as 'first', 'second' and 'third generation'.

- First-generation sites are just 'brochureware'.
- Second-generation sites are interactive and transactional.
- Third-generation sites (very few exist at present) rely on convergence of media and are fully integrated into the business.

Chaffey *et al.* also note that at a more strategic level, alternatives for the Web can be categorized in order of increasing commitment as follows:

- information only;
- interactive communications tool;
- channel to market;
- separate online business;
- integration with traditional business;
- transformation of traditional business to the Web.

Another useful framework categorizes Internet activities in terms of organizational structure as follows. 'Dotcoms' have received considerable adverse publicity of late. These are firms established specifically for Internet trading; the classic example is Amazon.com, which has built up a massive customer base in just a few years, but has yet to make a profit. 'Clicks and mortar' firms pursue strategies that combine 'old' and 'new' business practices. The term is derived from the established expression 'bricks and mortar', which symbolizes a wholly physical presence.

LESSONS FROM HISTORY AND CAUTIONARY TALES

As noted in the Introduction, the information 'revolution' prompted by the Internet is often discussed as though it is without precedent. It can be tempting to conclude that the rate of innovation and technological change puts extraordinary and unique pressure on companies as they struggle with the demands of a '24/7' economy. Kanter provides a welcome dose of reality among the hordes of Internet evangelists. She notes:

> Many discussions of the New Economy take place in an historical vacuum. Mention the Internet, and intelligent people sometimes act as if they have had a portion of their brain removed – the memory. . . . As we search for the new and different things that occur in the wake of revolutionary communications technology, it is also important to recall what can be learned from previous waves of innovation.
>
> (Kanter 2001: 3–4)

She goes on to highlight the key theme of her book, namely that in our enthusiasm to keep up with the ways in which the world is changing, we often fail to notice just how much remains the same. In her words,

> History demonstrates that new channels tend to coexist with old ones and sometimes even join them. Yes, the technology is revolutionary, network economics are different, and all the wheels must turn a lot faster, but the problems of leadership, organization and change are similar to those we have experienced for decades.
>
> (ibid.: 5)

Hanson draws some uncanny parallels between the Internet and the growth of radio in the 1920s. He demonstrates that change is always with us, however radically we might think that the Internet is altering marketing practices at the moment. His description of radio developments highlights that they made a huge impact on the society of the 1920s. Hanson reminds us that radio 'so captured the public's imagination that commentators claimed it would revolutionise culture, education and commerce' (2000: 2). Similarly, David (1991) compares the growth of information technology to the early days of electricity, which was also labelled 'revolutionary' when first made available. He shows how it took several decades for people to learn how to make the most of the new technology and overcome their preference for 'traditional' and familiar alternatives. The same argument has been used persuasively by Simon (1987) in his study of the steam engine. Jardine (1999) looks further back into history, and claims that the emergence of the printed book in the fifteenth century was equally radical in its impact on contemporary life. Interestingly, however, she notes that it took some fifty years for the printing business to become profitable, with a number of prominent early market entrants going out of business along the way. If a common pattern from these historical examples is not yet obvious, the following quotation from Charles Fraser (written in 1880, reproduced in www.economist.com in June 2000) should clinch matters: 'An agent is at hand to bring everything into harmonious co-operation, triumphing over space and time, to subdue prejudice and unite every part of our land in rapid and friendly communication . . . and that great motive agent is *steam*.'

It is often suggested that e-Business is just about technological change, but there are greater difficulties in implementing the intellectual, cultural and structural shifts necessary to succeed in a much more interactive business environment. Firms set up specifically to operate through the Internet (the so-called dotcoms) are ideally placed to recruit suitable staff and deal with customers in the most effective way, although many are struggling with current economic conditions. Established firms, however, may have a whole history of embedded working practices and customer relationships that require significant change if e-Business is to be implemented successfully. This issue will be explored further in Chapter 3.

Some of the qualities required for success are a lack of 'baggage' (in the shape of established business processes), a deep understanding of how technology can serve business strategies, and a flair for implementing these strategies. According to Lou Gerstner, CEO of IBM, the innovations that such net pioneers (labelled the 'dotcoms') have put in place to date will pale into insignificance once established and powerful corporations such as retailers or banks gear themselves up to transform their activities using the Internet. Such organizations are taking time to work out how to adapt their multi-layered supply chains, diverse distribution channels, legacy IT systems and conservative core customers, but this situation will not last. General Motors, for example, recently introduced a new e-GM Division to pull together all the firm's different Web activities under a single chain of command that will extend to the top of the global organization. The goal is to offer its cars for sale throughout the world via a single Web transaction. The electronic relationship thus developed with customers can then be built upon in the near future when wireless Internet services become more widely available, thereby making GM an Internet service and application provider. The marketing opportunities presented by such a scenario are mind-blowing.

It is easy to get carried away about the potential of the Internet, but several problems remain:

- The sheer volume of traffic can cause delays and lockouts.
- Security breaches by hackers and viruses hit the headlines regularly.
- A large proportion of the population still do not have Internet access.
- High-speed access necessary to support the latest multimedia features is still costly and remains the preserve of large organizations.
- The performance of the technology can be patchy.
- The huge volume of users can make access and navigation slow (does WWW stand for the World Wide Wait?).

Moreover, is not always as easy as it sounds to develop an effective online presence, despite what much of the hype suggests. Throughout the book we also look at the difficulties associated with Internet marketing and suggest how the potential problems might be overcome. Even when an Internet initiative is properly organized, with appropriate leadership, its multidisciplinary demands can test an organization. This is particularly true in bureaucratic companies that are organized around traditional business functions. Internet initiatives require teams with strategic, marketing, technical, graphic design, communications, publishing and operations capabilities. The organizational challenge of assembling, managing and empowering such teams is immense.

CHAPTER SUMMARY

In this chapter, the historical background to the Internet has been outlined, and recent developments have then been incorporated to bring the story up to date. Contemporary terminology and frameworks that will be used throughout the book have also been introduced, followed by some salutary lessons from history. An unanswered question remains how an 'online' world will change the way people work with each other. An unprecedented degree of collaboration is now possible, but it is difficult to predict how far this will reach outside the boundaries of individual firms and how employees or customers will adapt to rapidly shifting business alliances. According to Bill Gates, chairman of Microsoft, in his book *The Road Ahead*,

The rise of the Internet and the increase in subscribers to these online services is a fantastic thing. But it's important to recognise that the revenue payments to contact readers in the interactive world have been

> miniscule to date, so the opportunity to really turn that into a major revenue source, that's completely in front of us and really a major theme.
>
> (1995: 5)

These questions will be returned to throughout the book. We live in exciting times, where the only constant is change. We aim to inform you about the latest developments, while also inspiring your interest and making you think about the possible implications for marketers, and indeed the very structure of society, as we move into the early years of the twenty-first century.

Case study:
THE RISE AND FALL OF BOO.COM

Between 1998 and 2000, many traditional UK and European financial institutions began a surge of investment into new high-technology business start-ups. Investment euphoria could be largely attributed to the commercial possibilities of the Internet. The Internet was regarded not only as a new channel for commerce but as an entirely new era in the retail industry. Thus ensued a huge rush of B2C 'dotcoms', supported by a pack of hungry venture capitalists determined to make millions from the 'new economy'. Unfortunately, misconstruing Internet technology as a 'cannibalistic' revolution rather than a mere complement to the traditional retail industry has meant that a lot of dotcoms have tripped at the first hurdle and many invested millions have been wasted. According to Gledhill (2001: 13), 'One by one they arrived in a blaze of publicity and then collapsed under a mountain of debt.'

Perhaps the most hyped of all the failures is that of Boo.com. This notorious company managed to launch after five failed attempts, squandered £90 million in investment capital and then went into receivership after only six months of trading. Boo was positioned as a leading site in fashion, selling premium designer sportswear collections through the concept of 'geek chic'. The site was over-ambitious, operated in various countries, including the USA, and contained ground-breaking innovations such as a virtual hostess, 3-D imaging and a virtual magazine called *Boom*. Launching a highly complex international project on time and within budget is a huge task. It takes more than entrepreneurial flare to start and maintain a business, and this is key to the failure of Boo.com.

What went wrong?

To be objective in this analysis, we must also consider the macro-environment at the time of Boo. The whole of the UK was buzzing with talk of 'net millions' and the fantastic opportunities of the new economy. 'The people behind the new internet companies were being hailed as the pioneers who could lead Britain into the information age' (Cellan-Jones 2001). As a result, the first valuations for dotcom start-ups were ridiculous, as business credibility was measured through site traffic, click-throughs and page views rather than purchases and profit (Tunick 2001). Boo's biggest mistake was to misconstrue the new economy as a 'get rich quick' scheme. This attitude meant that valuable knowledge and experience accrued in traditional 'bricks and mortar' retail were snubbed.

For example, Boo's founders, Ernst Malmsten (artist and poet) and Kajsa Leander (former model), had little business experience but were very inspirational characters. Before Boo they had demonstrated their ability to obtain finance for high-profile events and business ventures by organizing the Festival of Nordic Poetry in New York, sponsored by Ericson, Saab, Carlsberg and Absolut. They also founded a pioneering online bookstore in Sweden called Bokus. A good concept, however, is not enough in itself. Although charisma is an essential part of entrepreneurial management style, Malmsten and Leander lacked the 'the ability of the manager to perform a number of tasks including planning, organising, budgeting, staffing, controlling and coordinating' (Carr 2000: 24). They also began to consider product diversification at a very early stage: 'We had invested millions in building a global retailing platform, we had established a powerful brand name, so why stop at clothes?' (Malmsten *et al.* 2001: 101).

Although Malmsten and Leander were clearly inexperienced, the third partner Patrick Hedelin (Boo's chief financial officer), was an ex-banker. If this role had been executed professionally, then resource management should have been sensible, and proper financial forecasts should have been made. However, a kind interpretation of Patrick is 'too much of an individual to be a good financial officer' (Jackson, 2001). A less kind description is 'embarrassingly incompetent' (Cellan-Jones, 2001). Callan-Jones also notes that the highly qualified Rachel Yasee was contracted from KPMG as supporting chief financial officer, but 'she was regarded as a hired help rather than a major player in the boo hierarchy'. The job of overseeing Boo's finances was passed around 'as if it were a ticking time bomb'. No one wanted to control the founders' expenditure for fear of being ridiculed or reprimanded. Therefore, responsibility changed hands often, as no one wanted to be 'caught out' when misuse of resources was discovered.

Once Malmsten and Leander had raised enough capital to begin making strategic partnerships with headhunters, tax consultants and technology providers, they started a heavy PR strategy. Building a brand before a business platform is in place is risky, and Boo had over 230,000 registrations before the site was launched. As a result, they were unable to test their platform properly and had to invest over a million pounds just to ensure that the site did not collapse owing to high density of traffic. 'If it had been less of a high profile site the platform could have been tested quietly' (Malmsten *et al.* 2001).

The international aspect of the site's growth was also problematic, although many of the issues involved could have been resolved with careful planning. For example,

Boo discovered only through experience that Portugal required every delivery package to be hand-stamped with serial numbers, and in Canada all returns were taxed. Language translations were also a problem. A generic invitation by email was sent to all Scandinavian site members and it was described by insiders as 'gobbledygook'. Internationalization should also have been approached as part of gradual expansion, once the site was established. Progressive strategies are used by many traditional retailers when setting up overseas operations to ensure co-ordination and focus, thus increasing the chances of success.

Boo's culture was centred on the concept of youth, exuberance and creativity. The founders insisted that Boo was a lifestyle and not just a company. The company encouraged extravagant alcohol-fuelled nights out at top nightclubs and celebrity parties. This lifestyle drained capital and was not compatible with day-to-day business operations. One hundred per cent commitment was demanded: 'High living masked the reality of a company that had always expected a super-human degree of commitment' (Malmsten *et al.* 2001: 41). Many of the staff were young and inexperienced yet were expected to perform well with little guidance. For example, the founders hired an ex-club DJ to coordinate the opening of their new Paris operations. According to Malmsten, 'He didn't have much management experience but he was bright, energetic and well plugged into the youth culture of Paris' (ibid.). It would seem a ludicrous decision to employ someone with no management experience to open and coordinate overseas operations just because he fitted in with the brand image. The company culture also made it difficult to make good management decisions regarding staff. For example, the founders discovered that it was difficult to make over 300 members of staff redundant, as many were viewed as friends. Malmsten goes on to note, 'While I sat quietly at my desk, my management team had to take part in the blood-letting which made me feel even more ashamed' (ibid.: 42).

Paradoxically, however, the concept of a culture of friendship and camaraderie was heavily contradicted by political undertones. Departments seen as 'cool' such as advertising and promotions created psychological barriers with teams involved in the site's technical development or in finance, which were deemed 'uncool'. Such childish behaviour meant that important communication channels were impaired, seriously compromising the site's co-ordination and development.

If they had received proper scrutiny from their financial advisers and prospective investors, Boo's founders would have been forced to be more realistic and substantiate their amateurish business plan with suitable research, costings, checks and balances. Any business start-up needs a strong plan complete with a business and marketing strategy, objectives, financial co-ordination, and resource allocation. Full environmental, competitive and customer analyses are essential components of such a plan. It is clear from the founders' behaviour that they had no budgeting skills and seemed to concentrate their efforts on brand-building rather than careful resource planning and allocation. According to Tim Jackson, Financial Analyst of the *Financial Times* (2001), the company was holding extravagant staff parties before it even had a product. Surely, celebratory parties of self-congratulation should come after a company has made its first million, not borrowed it?

Boo managed to spend $30 million even before the site launched, five months late, in November 2000. Company finance paid for the founders' executive apartments, first-class travel, expensive business trips and hotels, holidays and living expenses. At this point it was realized that 'sales would be less than 10% of the promised target' (Malmsten *et al*. 2001: 85). This revelation meant that Boo needed another $20 million to enable it to continue trading until February 2001. It was only after investors declined to release more capital in March that Boo management started to discuss spending cuts. Despite the fact that the company managed to save $27 million in cutbacks and that its weekly revenue was higher than that of Amazon, it failed to secure further funding and Boo went into receivership.

A misunderstanding of what constituted good marketing was also a large factor in Boo's demise. Abel Harpen of Texas Pacific, one of Boo's investment contacts, said Boo had only two assets, 'brand and back-end logistics' (Malmsten *et al*. 2001). Boo's brand strength was no accident. Leander and her team went to great lengths to ensure that Boo built an extremely strong brand in only six months as a result of a dedicated and creative promotional campaign. External promotion was also complemented by *Boom*, the online fashion magazine which they hoped would transform Boo into a 'lifestyle choice' rather than just a place to shop.

Brand image was so important that the smallest detail was considered, even if it was costly. Boo's rationale for its average monthly spending of $10 million was that the expenditure was necessary to create a multinational company with the strongest brand. For example, Boo paid for the world's most famous hairstylist, Eugene Souleman, to sit with a graphics designer for a day and design the hairstyle of the site's virtual hostess, Miss Boo. This seems like an expensive extravagance that served no purpose, especially as the hairstyle was changed at a later date.

One of the most important aspects of marketing for a new business is market research. Boo's founders felt that 'old economy' rules no longer applied: 'Market Research? That was something Colgate did before it launched a new toothpaste' (Malmsten *et al*. 2001: 15–16) Market research might actually have prevented one of Boo's biggest mistakes, which was to overestimate the technical capabilities of its potential customers. The site was so technically advanced that to view the graphics customers had to use special software (plug-ins). Malmsten had to admit, 'Our technologically sophisticated site has expected too much of its users' (ibid.). Not being able to view the site gave many potential customers a rational reason not to revisit it. The founders believed that after six months of trading they would have a loyal customer base of 50,000. This figure had no validity and seemed to have been plucked from thin air. Boo also relied on groundless estimates of the amount of supplier discounts that could be obtained, which impacted adversely on pricing policy.

Boo was a good concept, but the project too ambitious because the market, systems and customers were not sophisticated enough to maximize the potential of the technology. The strategy might have been more successful if its founders had started small, building the brand more slowly over time. The virtual magazine *Boom*, the virtual shop assistant Miss Boo and the 3-D imaging should have been introduced gradually as the site developed a loyal customer base. If Boo is compared with successful fashion Web sites there are many differences. For example, zoom.com has managed to survive, because of its unique positioning and a strong strategy. The site is trendy yet accessible, and manages to combine simple navigation and shopping processes with desirable products. Lessons about tight budgeting, gradual development in a climate of uncertainty, and substantial customer research can also be learned from traditional retailers' commercial sites such as Next.com and Debenhams.com.

It can also be argued that Boo's experienced investors and contractors could have helped control the company rather than watch it head rapidly towards destruction. Unfortunately, in line with the spirit of the times, the venture capitalists concentrated on getting a high valuation for a company that was no more than a creative concept, with the hope of selling it on at a huge profit. Therefore, they were concerned with short-term profit rather than long-term success.

What next for Boo?

Under new management, Boo has become a content-only site used as an advertising platform for established fashion-brand home sites. Fashionmall.com bought the Boo brand and has sold its assets (state-of-the-art technology in which millions had been invested) for just £250,000 (Fraser 2001). Boo's return has been positively received, and the new Chief Executive, Ben Nassin, is confident that it is a good investment: 'Miss Boo's fans are not put off by her past.' He hopes that Boo's original 'hard-to-reach customer' will be directed to fashion sites linked to Fashionmall. Although Boo may still have a strong brand, a content-only site may not be the best choice. It is unlikely that an information site will be as popular as a transactional one, unless its offering is unique. This is especially true if fashion advice is readily available from sites such as Zoom.com, which is both informative and transactional. The site is in competition with other, more accessible forms of media offering the same service, such as established fashion magazines like *Vogue* and *Cosmopolitan*.

Source: This case study was kindly contributed by Alaina Dixon, Brunel University.

FURTHER READING

Berners-Lee, T. (1999) *Weaving the Web: The Past, Present and Future of the World Wide Web by Its Inventor*, London: Orion.

Cairncross, F. (1998) *The Death of Distance*, London: Orion Business Books.

Kuo, J. D. (2001) '*Dot.Bomb: Inside an Internet Goliath from Lunatic Optimism to Panic and Crash*', London: Little, Brown (an insider's salutary story of the rise and fall of a dotcom company).

QUESTIONS

Question 1.1
What do you see as a major danger for societies inherent in the Internet access scenario described above?
Feedback – Evidence is mounting that the world may be dividing along the lines of the 'information haves' and the 'information have-nots', meaning that people without Internet access become increasingly disadvantaged and disenfranchised.

Question 1.2
Despite the benefits listed above, why do you think companies might still be reluctant to make full use of an intranet?
Feedback – A cynic might claim that 'information is power' and that individuals in possession of certain important information have a vested interest in keeping such data to themselves. Senior management may be reluctant to disclose details of strategy in the belief that it is a mark of status to have access to privileged information. Fortunately, attitudes like this appear to be less common these days, as traditional hierarchies of management are being broken down in many firms.

Question 1.3
Can you anticipate any problems associated with operating through extranets?
Feedback – The issue of exactly who should be allowed access to data could be problematic. Imagine, for example, a situation where customer email addresses have been collected and each partner company wants to make use of them to implement an email marketing campaign.

Question 1.4
What particular benefits does e-Commerce offer the business customer?
Feedback – Lower purchasing overheads; greater choice; faster fulfilment cycle time; greater ability to supply information; lower cost than EDI; ease of swapping between suppliers.

Question 1.5
What particular benefits does e-Commerce offer the consumer?
Feedback – Demands for increased choice; demands for information; demands for interactive, online support; avoidance of travel and search costs; 24-hour availability.

Question 1.6

What are the implications of e-GM for the firm's more traditional business operations?

Feedback — From the company's point of view, this new strategy places the Internet at the centre of its activities, making it no longer a mere adjunct to existing business practices. GM is attempting to 'harmonize' its channels by integrating electronic trading effectively with current traditional trading methods. All this entails a radical restructuring of operations and a reordering of business priorities. The size of the costs and practical difficulties associated with such integration should not be underestimated. Other firms are sidestepping this problem by developing entirely separate Internet operations, or have chosen to network with other firms or contract out the necessary tasks to specialists.

Question 1.7

From your reading of the Boo case study, can you think of a better way of adapting the original Boo package for the relaunch?

Feedback — It would probably have been wiser to sell the business as a package to an established retailer looking to sell its products online. For example, Boo's brand and offering are in keeping with those of Selfridges, which has yet to launch a transactional site. A successful example of this acquisition strategy was used in the case of failed dotcom Letsbuyit.com, which was recently acquired by John Lewis as a means of extending its online presence. Boo is currently restricted by its use as a mere information site and could face oblivion if it does not attract the number or calibre of customers need to substantiate its sponsorship.

 WEB LINKS

www.nw.com and www.cyberatlas.com
Latest statistics concerning worldwide Internet growth.

www.durlacher.co.uk
Quarterly research reports on Internet usage from a UK perspective.

www.intranetroadmap.com
Useful student resource with definitions, links and examples.

www.ebusinessroadmap.org
Useful student resource with definitions, links and examples.

www.whatis.com
Directory of Internet terminology.

www.whatis.com/tour.htm
An introduction to how the Internet works.

www.butlergroup.co.uk
Reports on latest developments in electronic commerce from a UK perspective.

www.kpmg.co.uk
Produces regular free reports on the latest trends in e-Commerce.

www.ebusiness.uk.com
Allows subscription to a new monthly paper-based magazine containing up-to-date case studies and updates on latest trends.

www.w3.org
An organization responsible for defining worldwide standards for the Internet.

www.isi.gov.uk
The Information Society site, with details of government projects, White Papers and pending legislation.

Marketing research

LISA HARRIS

MINDMAP

Chapter 1
History, definitions
and frameworks

Chapter 2
Marketing research

Chapter 3
Change
management

Chapter 4
Strategy

Chapter 5
Branding

Chapter 6
Relationship
marketing

Chapter 7
Multi-channel
marketing

Chapter 8
The marketing
mix

Chapter 9
e-Retailing

Chapter 10
Marketing
planning

Chapter 11
Legal, ethical and
public policy
issues

Introductory level

Strategic level

Operational level

Big picture

LINKS TO OTHER CHAPTERS

Chapter 6 Relationship marketing	Chapter 10 Marketing planning	Chapter 11 Legal, ethical and public policy issues

- Chapter 6 – Relationship marketing
- Chapter 10 – Marketing planning
- Chapter 11 – Legal, ethical and public policy issues

KEY LEARNING POINTS

After completing this chapter you will have an understanding of:

- The basic principles of marketing research
- How to choose the most appropriate method to address a particular research task
- The increasingly central role and scope of research in effective marketing
- How the Internet can be applied to add value to the research process
- The legal and ethical issues raised by online research in terms of data protection and privacy

ORDERED LIST OF SUB TOPICS

- Introduction to research
  - The importance of research
  - The research process
  - Sources of data
  - Data collection methods
  - Sampling methods
  - Problems with research data
- Using the Internet for marketing research
  - How research drives new forms of online marketing strategy
  - The Internet as a source of secondary data
  - The Internet as a means of collecting primary data
  - Problems with Internet research

- Ethics of online research
- ESOMAR guide to conducting marketing and opinion research using the Internet
■ Chapter summary
❖ Case study: DoubleClick
❖ Case study: 'Exposing the myths of online buyer behaviour' by Accenture
❖ Further reading
❖ Questions
❖ Web links

INTRODUCTION TO RESEARCH

The importance of research

Research is conducted to aid understanding of a particular problem, and to identify what actions can be taken to bring about improvement. It plays two critical roles in the marketing process:

- It provides managers with feedback on the effectiveness of current marketing strategy or tactics and indicates the nature of any changes that might need to be made
- It allows new market opportunities to be identified and evaluated.

McDaniel and Gates define marketing research as

the planning, collection and analysis of data relevant to marketing decision-making and the communication of the results of this analysis to management.
(2002: 6)

The choice of research method is critical to structure an understanding of the problem situation, help collect relevant information about it, and provide analysis to aid decision-making. An understanding of research methods can ensure that:

■ the work is carried out systematically – in that it is planned and executed in a clear and well-thought-out way;
■ the data collected are reliable. In other words, they:
  - reflect the (subjective) views and meanings of people interviewed, and/or
  - describe the (objective) phenomena that have been examined
  - consistently measure the same thing;

37

■ the resulting knowledge claims are valid – meaning that the arguments and statements are actually supported by the data and theory covered in the research.

A good way of illustrating the difference between reliability and validity is to think about the example of a thermometer. One which consistently informed you that water boiled at 80 degrees Celsius (at sea level) would be reliable, but not valid. One which gave a temperature reading for the boiling point of water as 99 degrees one day but 101 degrees the next would be more valid but not very reliable.

The research process

- Research objectives and plans need to be set. Setting them will help to focus the research, sharpen the questions and problems to be examined, and possibly also derive hypotheses that the research will set out to test.
- Appropriate data collection and sampling methods should be chosen.
- The questions or problems are then pursued by going out and obtaining relevant data.
- Depending on the methods used, data will be produced in a number of forms (for example, interview transcripts, statistics, archive papers).
- The data are then examined using suitable analytical techniques such as 'data mining'.
- An account of the findings is then produced.

But this is not necessarily the end of the research. The analysis may well lead to new questions or problems, or suggest that existing ones need to be refined. We can see, then, that the research process is likely to be iterative rather than linear. It may involve several circuits before the research is complete. It might also be that a number of stages are executed simultaneously (for example, data may still be being collected while analysis and a review of theory takes place). The research process is summarized in Figure 2.1.

Research is often interpreted very narrowly by organizations, some of which may operate with just a small 'research' section within a marketing department, or contract out specific research tasks to agencies as required and undertake no in-house research at all. To companies using this approach, only data collection and moments of insight based on those data are thought of as research. This approach can be likened to the core of an apple.

Thinking of research in terms of an onion illustrates a broader approach. An onion has many layers which are all integral constituents, but no core as such. Likewise, in a piece of research, all the activities involved are important and have a bearing on success. A researcher must be skilled at all of them – from persuading

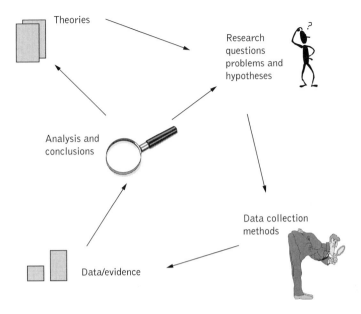

Figure 2.1 *The research process*

people to take part in interviews, to setting goals and targets and making sure they are met. In this concept, the very nature of what actually constitutes research is also much more inclusive. For example, as will be described in the next section, ongoing research is critical to the development and maintenance of relationship marketing strategies where all employees are expected to take responsibility for identifying and meeting customer needs. Here, research becomes part of an individual's normal way of working rather than an isolated task.

Sources of data

Secondary data are information that has been collected earlier for a different purpose, but which may still be useful to the research project under consideration. Census data are a good example of secondary data, and of course the Internet can be searched by key words entered in search engines to obtain secondary data on a huge range of subjects. Finding the information needed to answer a particular research question from secondary data avoids the need to spend time and money on primary research, but the likelihood of an ideal match is remote.

Primary data are information that is being collected for the first time in order to address a specific research problem. This means that it is likely to be directly relevant to the research, unlike secondary data, which may be out of date or collected for a totally different purpose. Ideally, an effective research project should incorporate both primary and secondary data.

Data collection methods

- Questionnaires can be used. They can be self-administered (as with postal or email questionnaires), or done by telephone or face to face.
- Structured interviews are interviews in which the interviewer asks a standard set of questions, often by phone but also face to face, but with some opportunities for open-ended discussion.
- In-depth interviews allow for a more open-ended discussion, perhaps based around broad themes or questions (such interviews are commonly referred to as 'semi-structured').
- Observation is a technique in which the researchers engage directly with the phenomenon under study (for example, by watching and recording group processes in a product development team). Observation can be done as either a 'participant' or a 'non-participant' in the real-world activity, and is the method that gets 'closest' to the object under study.
- Focus groups are unstructured, free-flowing interviews with a small group of people. The supermarkets are big users of focus groups, for example to canvass the opinion of customers concerning proposed changes to store layouts. The approach is flexible, and a skilled group moderator can draw in all the participants and allow the critical issues to arise from the discussions to create synergies.

Gummesson (1991) contrasts common research methods in terms of their 'access to reality'. His concern is how close they get to the real-world phenomenon under study. The key challenge is to choose methods of research that gain insights into how the world 'really is'. Often, he notes, researchers focus on issues they think are important, but because they have relied too heavily on second-hand accounts, they gain a false impression of the phenomenon under study and focus on issues that might not be the most pertinent to the research. Gummesson likens the problem to the exploration of an iceberg, in that certain research projects will require methods that 'get beneath the surface' of the phenomenon, as illustrated in Figure 2.2.

By flying over, sailing by or landing on the iceberg, you are going to get only basic facts, and may simply achieve a superficial impression of what the iceberg is like. This may be fine, of course, where you are clear about the things you are interested in, and their dynamics are well known. This is akin, we could say, to the use of questionnaires and structured interviews. The presumption here is that the phenomenon under study is reasonably understood and that deep investigation is not required. For that reason, a structured set of closed questions is sufficient to gain insight into the issues at hand. These methods are useful, therefore, when researchers do not want to look at something in depth, and instead wish to compare a set of characteristics across a large sample. This might be the

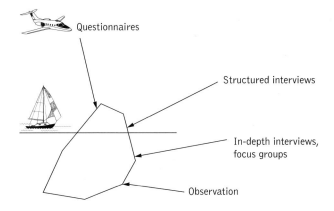

Questionnaires

Structured interviews

In-depth interviews,
focus groups

Observation

Figure 2.2 'Getting beneath the surface'

case if you were to examine the relationship between marketing priorities in
small firms and the industry in which those firms are located. In this case, the
questions would be reasonably straightforward and 'objective'. They might only
ask about:

● the range of marketing activities undertaken;
● the number of employees in marketing roles;
● the total number of employees;
● the products and services produced;
● the industry sector to which the firm belongs.

Such information could easily be obtained over the phone. And because the study
might be seeking to establish the picture across a broad population (say, all small
firms in London), the sample of firms contacted could run into the hundreds
or thousands. In this case, then, the methods used are an efficient way of finding out a 'little' (just those five data items) about a 'lot' (a large sample size).
Data in these studies tend to be reasonably *quantitative*. In other words,
phenomena are defined so they can be measured or counted, with the data then
collated so that items can be compared and contrasted across the data set as a
whole. This is quite different from research carried out using in-depth interviews, focus groups or observation.

In-depth interviews, focus groups or observation are used when the researchers
want to approach research phenomena in a more *qualitative* way. They lead to a
'richer' understanding of the things under study and thus – to use the iceberg
metaphor – help to get beneath the surface. You often need to do this in research

41

when a superficial grasp will not do; the thing under study needs to be examined in depth. Accordingly, you need to do the research in a way that tells you 'a lot' (something rich and detailed) about a 'little' (a few instances or cases). Qualitative approaches to research make fewer assumptions about research phenomena. They require you to observe people in action and capture their experiences and meanings. As a result, you are able to conceptualize what is happening and provide a new way of thinking about and describing it. For example, a study into 'the difficulties of implementing relationship marketing strategies at the shop-floor level' may work best where you can get close up to the people who do this kind of work and find out, first hand, what sort of problems they face. You could then explore how they solve these problems and examine the sources of invention that allow them to do this. By observing people and asking them to reflect, in depth, on the way they work, you may even provide an account of their working practices about which they themselves are only tacitly aware. Such an account could then be generalized to these situations more broadly.

As can be seen, then, no one method is superior to another. It really depends on the context of use. Indeed, it is common for projects to involve both qualitative and quantitative methods. For example, qualitative methods may be used to look – in depth – at issues that have arisen from the exploration of quantitative data. In contrast, qualitative methods may be used first – to sharpen the issues and problems (providing a better conceptualization of the phenomenon under study) – with quantitative methods then being employed to explore these in a broader population.

Sampling methods

It is rarely possible to interview or survey the entire target population (the UK's national census, conducted just once every ten years, is a famous exception). For most research projects, a compromise needs to be reached between, on the one hand, obtaining the number of respondents necessary for accuracy and, on the other, the time and cost involved in dealing with them.

The terminology of different sampling methods is confusing, so a brief explanation will be given. **Probability sampling** is where individual respondents are drawn at random from the population. The key alternatives are:

- **simple random sampling**, in which individuals are randomly selected from the population at large;
- **stratified random sampling**, which first divides the population into groups based on criteria such as age or gender. Individuals are then randomly selected from within these groups.

Non-probability sampling is where individuals are selected by the researcher on the basis of predefined criteria. The key alternatives are:

- **judgement sampling**, in which the researcher uses their judgement to select individuals that they feel are representative of the population or have a particularly useful expertise which should be drawn upon;
- **convenience sampling**, where time and resources are saved by choosing respondents on the basis of convenience (a very common method!);
- **quota sampling**, in which the researcher selects a predetermined number of individuals from groups based on gender, age etc

For a detailed discussion of sampling methods, see McDaniel and Gates (2002).

Problems with research data

So far we have concentrated upon the benefits of research, but of course there could also be a number of disadvantages:

- The research might not be objective. For example, if it were seeking to save money by cutting back on online activities, a company might be tempted to present the results of research into the contribution made by online trading in as negative a light as possible.
- Research may be used to justify a decision that has already been taken. This means that a company may have a predetermined 'result' established and then takes steps to 'influence' the results of the research to ensure that the findings reflect the required position.
- Some types of research might not be ethical. Think, for example, of the practice of 'mystery shopping', whereby the performance of sales staff is assessed by researchers posing as customers. This controversial research method is now also spreading to the Internet; see, for example, www.emysteryshopping.com.
- It is possible to 'over-research' so that decision-making is stifled by a perceived need to check out everything first – a situation known as 'analysis paralysis'.
- The cost of conducting the research may exceed the benefits obtained from it.
- The results might be unexpected, and unwelcome! For example, research conducted into the failure of a new product launch might point the finger of blame at certain individuals.

USING THE INTERNET FOR MARKETING RESEARCH

How research drives new forms of online marketing strategy

It was mentioned earlier in the chapter that research, in a broad sense, is becoming increasingly central to marketing strategy. Think of the trend towards mass customization, in which customers can specify their exact requirements and the production process is customized accordingly. See www.levi.com for a classic example. Detailed knowledge of customer needs is essential here if the goods are to be produced on an individual basis. Another example concerns permission marketing (which will be described in detail in Chapter 6), where specific services are provided to customers based entirely on 'permission' that the customer has given the company. This means that a travel company may be given permission by a customer to send them promotions that relate only to self-catering holidays in Florida in the month of October – and nothing else. The company will need to be able to process and act upon this information (which of course is research data about customer preferences) and not just send the customer a general brochure that includes all of the company's holidays.

Loyalty, and hence customer retention, is based upon a thorough understanding of customer needs that can be established and maintained only by research. The economic benefits of customer retention are obvious: revenues and market share grow through repeat business and referrals, while costs fall through economies of scale and the reduced amount of effort that needs to be spent on customer acquisition and the servicing of familiar customers. McDaniel and Gates (2002) describe the example of British Airways, which researched the preferences of first-class passengers and found them to be – sleep. So, as an alternative to receiving a series of intrusive services during the flight, such passengers can now have dinner in the lounge before take-off and then enjoy an uninterrupted flight.

The Internet is becoming an increasingly important *source* of research data (known as secondary data) as well as providing a cost-effective new *medium* for the research process itself, for example as an alternative means of collecting data by completion of an online questionnaire rather than from telephone or face-to-face interviewing (known as primary data).

The Internet as a source of secondary data

The best way to find information on the Internet is to key in the unique Uniform Resource Locator (URL) which will take you directly to the page required, without the need to rely upon search engines. Organizations can promote their URL address on company stationery, on the side of vehicles or buildings, or in other increasingly innovative ways.

If you are looking for information without knowing the exact source, then a key word search on one of the many search engines is the best strategy to adopt.

The exponential growth of the Web is making the task of search engines increasingly difficult because of the sheer volume of new sites and information being placed on the Web. McDaniel and Gates (2002) provide a comprehensive table in chapter 4 of their book explaining the features of the major search engines, as well as a list of sites that are of specific relevance to market researchers. You might also like to try www.netskills.ac.uk for an online tutorial guide to searching the Internet, or www.researchbuzz.com, which has news on new information sources and search engines, or www.searchenginewatch.com, which explains how search engines work.

Information available online is increasingly diverse. For example, exporters now have the opportunity to resolve historical information gaps when contemplating trading internationally that previously may have dissuaded firms from pursuing such strategies. Details of market access, exchange control regulations, costs of import duties, etc. are now much more transparent on the Web. Some organizations are competing to offer quality content online, thereby enhancing their brand image and encouraging repeat visits and recommendations for research purposes. Many of the traditional sources of market information are now available online, for example annual reports, large-scale market surveys, government reports and economic data. While there are valuable data freely available, care needs to be taken because the Internet also carries vast amounts of poor-quality data. As with traditional market research, appropriate questions to ask are:

- Are the data relevant?
- Are the data accurate?
- Are they up to date?
- What sampling techniques have been used to collect the data?

ACTIVITY

Compare the information that is available from the following market research agencies and consider the questions beneath:

www.forrester.com   www.mori.co.uk

www.nielsen.com   www.euromonitor.com

www.durlacher.co.uk

Do you notice any similarity in terms of the way in which research data are made available by the respective companies? Are some more generous than others in terms of what they give away? Which sites are easiest to navigate and find what you are looking for? Why is this?

The Internet as a means of collecting primary data

Possible research topics

There are a number of primary research tasks that can be effectively carried out online; for example:

- measuring the effectiveness of a firm's Internet strategy;
- measuring customer satisfaction levels;
- obtaining customer feedback on new product/service ideas;
- polling consumers for information about any subject you can think of (see mini case study 'The Internet survey industry' on p. 51.)

Undertaking primary research to measure the effectiveness of a company's Web site is a critical aspect of the evaluation of online marketing strategy. This topic will be considered in more detail in Chapter 10, so only a brief overview is provided here. The following questions may be asked:

- Are the objectives of the site being met?
- Is the corporate message getting across?
- How effective are the various promotional techniques used to attract visitors to the site?
- What changes need to be made to improve the quality of customer service offered?
- Is the site easy to use?
- How many sales are resulting from online contacts?
- How many visitors are coming back to the site?
- How much new business has resulted from the Web site (as opposed to its merely offering an additional channel to existing customers)?
- How does the site compare with those of competitors?

Chaffey (2002) recommends five specific categories of measurement:

1 Channel promotion measures assess why customers visit a site:
   - Which sites have they been referred from? (What was the electronic link?)
   - Which offline adverts did they see?
   From this analysis it should be possible to measure the percentage of customers whose enquiry was prompted by online and offline means respectively, thereby guiding the nature of future promotional campaigns.
2 Channel buyer behaviour measures assess which aspects of the Web site content are visited, the times of day and the duration of the visit. This

analysis enables 'stickiness' to be measured, for example the average length of a visit, and the proportion of first-time to repeat visitors. It can also suggest changes to site structure and content.

3 Channel satisfaction measures evaluate customers' perception of online service quality issues such as email response times. It is also possible to use services such as Gomez (www.gomez.com) to benchmark service quality against the competition.

4 Channel outcome measures compare the number of site visitors to the number of actual purchases made; in other words, how many visitors leave the site without buying anything. For example, if 10 purchases result from 100 visits, the conversion rate is 10 per cent.

5 Channel profitability measures are a critical test of success. How much does the online channel contribute to business profit after taking account of the costs incurred?

In addition to evaluating existing marketing strategy, research can also play a more proactive role through identifying changes in the market and customer needs, thereby suggesting future strategic directions for the firm. Asking customers what they expect from a company's site and obtaining feedback on current promotions can provide important information to aid market segmentation and other marketing applications. For example, Honda now has different sites for male and female customers, following a research exercise that established how men preferred detailed graphics emphasizing different aspects of car performance, while women preferred brief factual information.

Company intranets can also be used effectively to gather research data from staff, a key group of stakeholders whose importance is now increasingly recognized by the designation 'internal customers' (see Chapter 6 for detailed discussion of managing stakeholder relationships). Staff opinions are a valuable source of research data that can be sought and collated through an online questionnaire.

Methods of primary data collection

SPECIALIST SOFTWARE

To measure Web site effectiveness, increasingly sophisticated software is now available to assess the number of visitors to the Web site by measuring site visits (where one or many pages may be viewed) or page impressions (one person viewing one page). It is now also possible to assess:

- which parts of the site are most popular;
- what times of the day people visit the site;
- which search engines people are using to find the site;

- the route people take through the site;
- how long they spend there (a measure of the so-called 'stickiness' of the site).

Also, a number of ISPs such as www.hitbox.com or www.webtrends.com are being established to capitalize on this technological capability. Firms can install a free link to Hitbox.com and it will calculate how many times their pages are viewed, and offer a real-time display of this information in a password-protected area on the firm's site. Hitbox also provides information about:

- visitor domains;
- country of origin;
- URL of referring sites;
- browser type;
- operating system;
- visitor frequency;
- entry and exit pages;
- session duration.

Information about the configuration of visitors' browsers can be very useful in guiding a company's site design parameters. For example, there would be no point in building in elaborate graphics into a Web site if analysis of visitors showed that few had the technical capacity to appreciate their full glory. There is no charge for the Hitbox service because the company now has animated links to itself on over 350,000 Web sites that have taken advantage of the service, so it gets plenty of visitor traffic to attract advertisers and build banner advertising revenue.

WEB SITE REGISTRATION

In order to identify and assess *individual* visitors to the Web site, a firm can request registration details. If a company knows the identity of visitors who are browsing the site, they can be contacted directly through other means, for example to arrange a sales visit. Persuading visitors to register their interests by supplying their email address and personal information requires a suitable incentive, such as useful free information, and sufficient trust on the part of the visitor that the information supplied will not be misused. The danger is that a site visitor may be put off by the request to register before accessing the site and look elsewhere to resolve their query.

SURVEYS/QUESTIONNAIRES

Questionnaires distributed via email or over the Web are quick, inexpensive, have a broad geographical reach and the data received can be input directly into a database for purposes of recording and analysis. There are two major ways of conducting such research:

- Email customers, quoting a URL in the text of the message that customers can click on at their own convenience to link to an online questionnaire.
- Include a 'pop-up' box on the Web site that customers can complete while they are actually viewing the site online. DealerNet (www.dealernet.com) offered customers the chance to win a free car if they answered a few short questions asking about the year, make and model of their current car and signed up to receive a free monthly email newsletter. Processing this small amount of information enabled the company to customize subsequent email newsletters sent to these customers very specifically and effectively.

Companies now exist which allow researchers to design and administer an online survey without the need to purchase expensive software. Take a look at www.websurveyor.com, which allows a survey to be created, published on a Web site, data collected, results analysed and then printed out as a report.

Internet surveys have a number of specific advantages over more traditional data collection methods:

- The results can be broadcast quickly and cheaply to a large number of respondents on a global basis.
- Increasing the number of respondents does not necessarily add to costs or the time taken to conduct the research.
- Messages can be personalized to increase the chances of response.
- 'Hard to reach' groups can be accessed.
- Surveys can be completed and returned at the respondent's convenience.
- Because it is a relatively new data collection medium, people tend to be more tolerant of online research than they are of telephone or postal surveys, although of course the novelty may not last too long!

e-Satisfy's (www.e-satisfy.co.uk) Site Monitor (Figure 2.3) allows companies to interview Web site visitors when they enter or leave the Web site. It uses survey modules to gather general, commerce or visitor profile information. Try the demonstration – by answering the questions posed, you are giving e-Satisfy feedback on its products in the same way that a company could use the service on its own Web site to collect data from visitors. When a visitor arrives at or leaves a page, Site Monitor pops up and asks if they would answer a few questions about the site. If the visitor agrees to answer questions by clicking 'Continue', they are informed that it will take only a few minutes to complete the survey. A series of

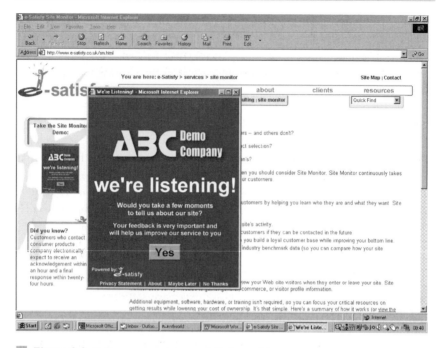

Figure 2.3 Online surveys (www.e-satisfy.co.uk)

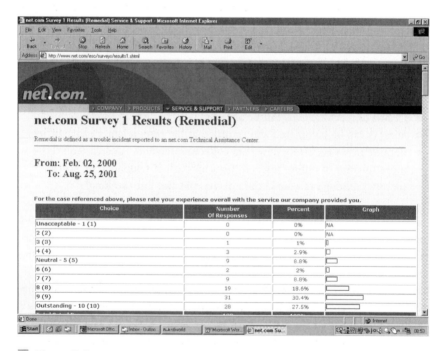

Figure 2.4 Displaying research results to build trust (www.net.com)

questions is then asked in short sets, and the visitor clicks on the 'Next' button when they have completed each set. The final page thanks the respondent, then asks for additional comments and an (optional) email address. Survey information is automatically captured into e-Satisfy's secure database where the company can:

- review aggregated reports of visitors' and customers' responses;
- review trends to monitor activity/service/opinion over the course of the survey's project life;
- download the raw data and visitor's comments to analyse/review using its own software/reporting methods.

Added value in terms of building trust and brand equity can then be achieved by displaying the results of the survey on the site, as in Figure 2.4.

Mini case study:
THE INTERNET SURVEY INDUSTRY

The Internet survey industry that sprang up during the boom to satisfy an endless thirst for Web statistics (and cheap publicity) is getting beyond a joke. In the search for original material, the Internet service provider AOL resorted to a poll of what people wear when they are online. The answer: they wear the same clothes as they would for any other daily chore, but why let the facts get in the way of the stats? Apparently 8 per cent of Yorkshire Internet users have surfed naked ... so the hundreds of surveys churned out each month can be entertaining and, very occasionally, useful. But just as advertising agencies made a killing from dotcom budgets before the bubble burst, the winners from the survey glut are the polling companies that can always find another '1,000 home internet users' to badger about their habits.

Source: Adapted from Grande (2001)

Mini case study:
WEB MARKETING TODAY

Web Marketing Today (www.wilsonweb.com) is a free monthly email newsletter distributed to some 90,000 people worldwide. From the Web site, potential subscribers can sign up without supplying vast amounts of data about themselves. While this customer-friendly policy may encourage visitors to request the newsletter, it means that the Web site owner had little idea of who his customers are or why they are reading his newsletter. So a few basic questions were posted on the site, along the lines of 'What is your job?' and 'Why do you find the newsletter useful?' Analysis of the results allowed the owner to segment his customers and redesign the site around the needs of the five major segments identified, creating several different versions of the same newsletter. Subsequently, a customer who was identified as a student would receive the next newsletter in a very different style and focus compared with a customer identified as a consultant. Subscription rates improved significantly as a result.

ONLINE FOCUS GROUPS

Online focus groups are still rare in the UK but increasingly popular in the USA. There, bulletin board discussion groups on the company Web site are used to collect real-time feedback from a selected group of customers in response to questions from the focus group leaders. Customers may be asked to comment on particular aspects of the company's business and respond to points made by other members of the group in an online version of a 'round-table' discussion. One of the leading companies offering this service is www.w3focus.com.

The respective merits of online and offline focus groups are currently the subject of much debate. The advantages of online focus groups are:

- There is a lack of geographic barriers.
- Costs are lower.
- They can be administered quickly.
- Respondents less likely to be intimidated by more opinionated group members or the discussion moderator than when groups meet face to face.
- They provide access to 'hard-to-reach' market segments such as time-pressed professionals who would not make the effort to attend a face-to-face session.
- It is hard for one overbearing individual to dominate an online group.
- People tend to be more direct and honest in their responses.
- Unrelated small talk and time-wasting are unusual.
- 'Emoticons' (for example '☺') can be used to convey emotions (albeit in a rather primitive way!).
- www.vrroom.com has an ejection feature to remove participants who try to sabotage the online discussions.

There are, however, also a number of disadvantages:

- It is difficult to create group dynamics when participants are not interacting face to face.

- Non-verbal input such as facial expression and body language is impossible to detect.
- Participants may not give the session their full attention for the required timespan.
- The ability of the moderator to draw in all group members is limited online.

For a detailed discussion of online focus groups, see Sweet (2001).

KIOSK-BASED COMPUTER INTERVIEWING

Kiosk-based computer interviewing is an innovative way of gathering data about customers' buying experiences. Multimedia touch-screen computers are set up in kiosks and can be programmed to administer surveys, show images, and play sound and video clips in order to ascertain and capture customer feedback. They are becoming increasingly common in new retail shopping centres (see Chapter 9 for more detail in this area, and www.modalis.com/english/technologies/cati. html for an example).

FEEDBACK BUTTONS TO EMAIL COMMENTS

You can see from the screenshot in Figure 2.5 that Southwest Airlines does not accept email feedback. Sterne (2001) notes that a version of this message has

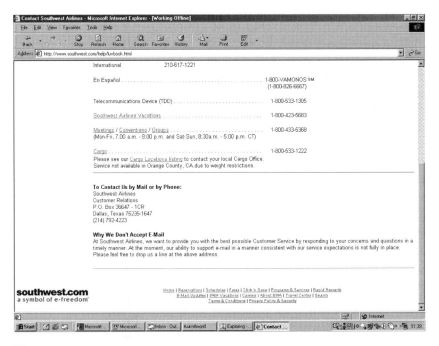

Figure 2.5 Southwest Airlines' Web site (www.southwest.com)

been displayed on the company's Web site for the past four years, forcing customers to use more traditional methods of contact. It seems that Southwest Airlines is missing a valuable research opportunity – what do you think? We will return to this example when discussing customer communications in Chapter 6.

INTERNET PANELS

The use of TV panels as a method of analysing viewer behaviour has been common for many years. Panels such as those operated by Nielsen/NetRatings (www. nielsen.netratings.com) provide the firm's customers with online access to comprehensive Internet audience information. The Internet population is profiled by NetRatings on a regular basis using random sampling techniques that ensure that representative sampling can be generalized to the entire Internet user population. Households are recruited to the panel through analysis of census data, and they are then given a 'box' to attach to their computers that tracks and stores their online behaviour. NetRatings customers can then interrogate the data to answer such questions as 'Which banner advertisement best reached my target audience in October?' or 'Where are my competitors advertising?'

COOKIES

A cookie is a text file that contains a unique user identifier. When a visitor accesses a Web site, the site's server can place a cookie in the user's browser. As the visitor navigates the site, the cookie transmits the path taken back to the server so that the movement of the visitor through the site can be tracked. The cookie is associated with the browser rather than the individual user, so, for example, if you access www.amazon.co.uk from a different computer, you may find that the usual personalized 'welcome' greeting is missing. There are, of course, ethical issues here regarding invasion of privacy in the collection of such data, and these will be discussed in more detail in Chapter 11.

The European Parliament has recently outlawed the use of cookies without *explicit* prior consent. Until now, many businesses have relied mainly upon *implied* consent by using privacy statements to inform visitors that cookies are being used to collect personal data, but this will no longer be sufficient. Explicit consent requires the user to agree in advance to the gathering and use of information. This means being informed as to what information is going to be gathered and exactly how it will be used. The consent process would need to take place on each occasion when data are collected, meaning for example that the whole buying experience will be slowed down and complicated, whereas for most people the attraction of online shopping is speed and simplicity. The implications for advertising companies such as DoubleClick may well be considerable (see the case study on pp. 60–62).

Problems with Internet research

Earlier in the chapter we discussed some of the problems that can occur when conducting research, and these issues are just as pertinent for Web-based research. There are, however, a number of new problems that are specific to online research:

- Web sites requiring a lengthy registration procedure may provide excellent research data, but only if visitors can be bothered to complete the process.
- Customers may be reluctant to supply their e-Mail address for fear of such personal details being sold to third parties and a deluge of 'junk e-mails' set in motion.
- Access to the Web is still frequently slow or interrupted.
- A sample of customers surveyed online may well be representative only of that section of the company's online customers who have the time and the inclination to respond to surveys. This approach can lead to what is called 'selection bias' in the data. The respondents are in any case very unlikely to be representative of the entire customer base, because not everyone has Internet access, or indeed, a willingness to respond to surveys.

Nancarrow *et al.* (2001) warn of what they call the seven deadly Internet research sins:

1 *excess* – leading to respondent burn-out if 'over-surveyed';
2 *omission* – failure to take note of the shortcomings of online research;
3 *exposure* – innovative research techniques or market insights falling into the hands of competitors;
4 *intrusion of privacy* – through use of cookies, as discussed above;
5 *negligence* – in protecting the confidentiality of data;
6 *off-loading costs* – expecting respondents to pay for the cost of completing a survey online;
7 *complacency* – in failing to take the consequences of the above sins seriously.

Ethics of online research

Gaining respondents' confidence is crucial for research to go ahead with any kind of openness. Assuring people that their comments can remain confidential will be an important starting point. It will also be important to discuss issues of 'anonymity' with respondents. For example, where their words might subsequently appear in print, they might be promised that a pseudonym will be used, thus ensuring that their comments will not be attributed to them as individuals. It is therefore crucial that researchers:

- respect confidentiality, whether explicitly or implicitly promised;
- do not misuse data and other findings – in other words, do not use them for (potentially damaging) purposes for which the data were not provided in the first instance;
- recognize the 'wider implications' of actions taken, for both individuals and organizations – does your report, for example, recommend changes that may cost people their jobs?;
- abide by both the large and the small print of privacy policies.

The Web site of the Market Research Society (www.marketresearch.org.uk) contains useful information on ethical standards and codes of conduct for research practice, as does ESOMAR (its guidelines are reproduced below). These issues will be explored further in Chapter 11.

ESOMAR guide to conducting marketing and opinion research using the Internet

ESOMAR (www.esomar.nl) is the World Association of Opinion and Marketing Research Professionals. Its guidelines for online marketing research are as follows:

Basic principles

Marketing and opinion research is the professional activity of collecting and interpreting consumer, business, and social data so that decision makers can make better and more efficient marketing and social decisions.

All research carried out on the Internet must conform to the rules and spirit of the main ICC/ESOMAR International Code of Marketing and Social Research Practice and also to Data Protection and other relevant legislation (both international and national). ICC/ESOMAR Codes and Guidelines are always subordinate to existing national law. There is currently no international unanimity as to whether country of origin or country of destination applies to research on the Internet.

Such marketing and opinion research must always respect the rights of respondents and other Internet users. It must be carried out in ways which are acceptable to them, to the general public and in accordance with national and international self regulation. Researchers must avoid any actions which might bring Internet research into disrepute or reduce confidence in its findings.

Introduction

The rapid growth of the Internet has opened dramatic new opportunities for collecting and disseminating research information worldwide. At the same time it raises a number of ethical and technical issues which must be addressed if the medium is to be used effectively and responsibly for marketing and opinion research purposes.

The fact that the Internet is inexpensive to use and difficult to regulate means that it can be open to misuse by less experienced or less scrupulous organisations, often based outside the research industry. Any Internet surveys which fall seriously below the high standards promoted by ESOMAR and other leading professional bodies will make it more difficult to use the medium for research and could seriously damage the credibility of such research, as well as being an abuse of the goodwill of Internet users generally.

ESOMAR has issued this Guideline to protect the interests both of Internet respondents and of the users of Internet research findings. Because information technology and the Internet are evolving and changing so rapidly it is not practicable to discuss in detail all the technical features of Internet research in such a Guideline. This therefore concentrates on the main principles which must be followed in carrying out research on (or about) the Internet and in reporting the findings of such research.

Co-operation is voluntary

1 Researchers must avoid intruding unnecessarily on the privacy of Internet respondents. Survey respondents' co-operation must at all times be voluntary. No personal information which is additional to that already available from other sources should be sought from, or about, respondents without their prior knowledge and agreement.

2 In obtaining the necessary agreement from respondents the researcher must not mislead them about the nature of the research or the uses which will be made of the findings. It is however recognised that there are occasions on which in order to prevent biased responses, the purpose of the research cannot be fully disclosed to respondents at the beginning of the interview. In particular, the researcher should avoid deceptive statements that would be harmful or create a nuisance to the respondent – for example, about the likely length of the interview or about the possibilities of being re-interviewed on a later occasion. Respondents should also be alerted when appropriate to any costs that they may incur (eg of on-line time) if they co-operate in the survey. They are entitled at any stage of the interview, or subsequently, to ask that part or all of the record of their interview be destroyed or deleted and the researcher must conform to any such request where reasonable.

The researcher's identity must be disclosed

3 Respondents must be told the identity of the researcher carrying out the project and the address at which they can without difficulty re-contact the latter should they wish to do so.

Respondents' rights to anonymity must be safeguarded

4 The anonymity of respondents must always be preserved unless they have given their informed consent to the contrary. If respondents have given permission for data to be passed on in a form which allows them to be personally identified, the researcher must ensure that the information will be used for research purposes only. No such personally identified information may be used for subsequent non-research purposes such as direct marketing, list-building, credit rating, fund-raising or other marketing activities relating to those individual respondents.

Privacy policy statements

5 Researchers are encouraged to post their privacy policy statement on their online site. When such privacy policy statements exist, they should be easy to find, easy to use and comprehensible.

Data security

6 Researchers should take adequate precautions to protect the security of sensitive data. Researchers must also reasonably ensure that any confidential information provided to them by clients or others is protected (eg by firewall) against unauthorised access.

Reliability and validity

7 Users of research and the general public must not be in any way misled about the reliability and validity of Internet research findings. It is therefore essential that the researcher:
   (a) follows scientifically sound sampling methods consistent with the purpose of the research;
   (b) publishes a clear statement of the sample universe definition used in a given survey, the research approach adopted, the response rate achieved and the method of calculating this where possible;

(c) publishes any appropriate reservations about the possible lack of projectability or other limitations of the research findings for instance resulting from non-response and other factors.

It is equally important that any research *about* the Internet (e.g. to measure penetration, usage etc.) which employs other data collection methods, such as telephone or mail, also clearly refers to any sampling, or other, limitations on the data collected.

Interviewing children and young people

8 It is incumbent on the researcher to observe all relevant laws specifically relating to children and young people although it is recognised that the identification of children and young people is not possible with certainty on the Internet at this time. ESOMAR requirements about the precautions to be taken are set out in the ESOMAR Guideline on Interviewing Children and Young People. According to the ESOMAR Guideline, permission of a responsible adult must be obtained before interviewing children aged under 14 and asking questions on topics generally regarded as sensitive should be avoided wherever possible and in any case handled with extreme care. Researchers must use their best endeavours to ensure that they conform to the requirements of the Guideline referred to, for example by introducing special contacting procedures to secure the permission of a parent before carrying out an interview with children under 14. Where necessary researchers should consult ESOMAR or their national society for advice.

Unsolicited e-mail

9 Researchers should not send unsolicited messages on line to respondents who have indicated that they do not wish to receive such messages relating to a research project or to any follow-up research resulting directly from it. Researchers will reduce any inconvenience or irritation such e-mail might cause to the recipient by clearly stating its purpose in the subject heading and keeping the total message as brief as possible.

ESOMAR
Vondelstraat 172
1054 GV Amsterdam
The Netherlands

Tel: +31–20–664 2141
Fax: +31–20–664 2922
e-Mail: email@esomar.nl

CHAPTER SUMMARY

In this chapter, we have considered the basic principles of marketing research and how to choose the most appropriate method to address a particular research task. We have emphasised the increasingly central role played by research in evolving online marketing activities such as one-to-one marketing and permission marketing, topics which will be considered in more detail in Chapter 6. It should also now be clear to you how the Internet can add value to marketing research more generally through such innovations as online questionnaires and focus groups. Finally, it is important to bear in mind the legal and ethical issues raised by online research in terms of data protection and privacy, and these issues will be considered in more detail in Chapter 11.

Case study: DOUBLECLICK

There has been a lot of negative publicity surrounding the activities of DoubleClick, currently the Internet's largest advertising company. The firm is based in New York and has thirty-seven offices around the world. According to its online publicity material, 'DoubleClick makes marketing work in the digital world. By combining media, data, research and technological expertise, DoubleClick allows marketers to deliver the right message, to the right person, at the right time, while helping Web publishers maximize their revenue and build their business online' (December 2001, www.doubleclick.net).

In the early days, DoubleClick grew by checking the Internet addresses of people visiting participating Web sites and targeting advertisements, for example so that consumers received promotions different from those received by business users. Each time a viewer clicked on a banner, DoubleClick was able to build up its dossier of personal information by adding a cookie to the user's hard drive. In 2000, the firm stepped up a gear and began tracking Web users by name and address as they moved from one Web site to the next. This practice gives it the ability to know the household, and in many cases the precise identity, of the person visiting any of the thousands of sites that use DoubleClick's ad-tracking cookies. What made such detailed profiling possible was the firm's purchase of Abacus, a direct marketing company that had a database of the names, addresses and purchasing habits of 90 per cent of US households. DoubleClick could now correlate this information with people's Internet activities, allowing online advertisements to be targeted at specific viewers and hence made more useful to advertisers, who of course would pay handsomely for such access. From DoubleClick's perspective, it is personalizing consumers' online experiences for mutual benefit. However, many people saw it as a blatant invasion of privacy.

Exactly how does this work? If a network of sites conspire together, they can share cookies. For example, when you visit the search engine AltaVista, AltaVista loads in a small image from DoubleClick, setting a cookie on your hard drive. This either updates or creates a user profile on you. One of the cookies that DoubleClick sets is the search that you performed on AltaVista. If you now want to visit Sporting News Online (also part of the DoubleClick network of sites), another image from DoubleClick is loaded. DoubleClick checks the cookie it previously set, sees that you were searching for car information on AltaVista, and gives you a banner for an Internet car dealership along with the Sporting News Online page. When you perform a search on Sporting News Online or some other action, DoubleClick might set another cookie based on what you did. Before you know it, DoubleClick can have quite a profile on you, along with over 10 million others. The DoubleClick Network covers sixty-three sites, including such major players as:

- AltaVista Search;
- The Dilbert Zone;
- Sporting News Online;
- Travelocity;

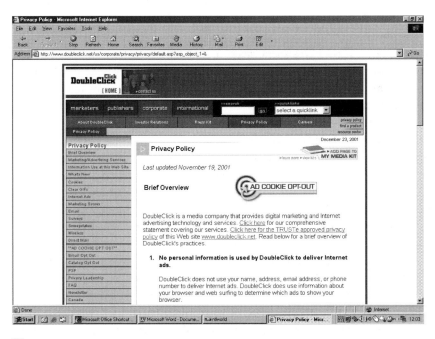

Figure 2.6 *Web site of DoubleClick (www.doubleclick.net)*

- US News Online;
- Blockbuster.

Users who do not want to be tracked are able to 'opt out', but that chance may be buried in the small print of participating sites' privacy policies. Interestingly, 'opt out' is actioned by setting a cookie. After a Federal Trade Commission investigation, DoubleClick (and its partner firms) now spell out very clearly and prominently what type of information is collected, who has access to it and how individuals can opt out. Also, PricewaterhouseCoopers has been appointed to perform privacy audits.

ACTIVITY

How do you feel about companies like DoubleClick tracking your Internet activities?

Case study:
'EXPOSING THE MYTHS OF ONLINE BUYER BEHAVIOUR' BY ACCENTURE (WWW.ACCENTURE.COM)

Accenture conducted a Web-based survey of 2,000 US consumers in February 2001 across seventeen industry segments. Respondents were segmented into the categories and characteristics shown in Table 2.1 (note: each segment contains representatives from all demographic groups).

The results of the survey were surprising, and a number of online 'facts' may actually appear to be 'myths':

1 It is generally assumed that online shoppers are price sensitive. Accenture found that price was only a minor consideration (never constituting more than 13 per cent of the total needs of any segment, and unimportant to 'variety seekers' and 'Netizens'). Lowering price may build some volume, but the pay-off from investing in brand selection, site speed and other performance dimensions is greater. It is worth asking whether this information might have made a difference to the dotcom sector, where a number of companies struggled to establish profitability while keeping their prices artificially low.

2 Another Web 'fact' is that most frequent online shoppers are young and trendy. This research found that most frequent purchasers are actually 35–44 years old, and 44 per cent of heavy online spenders are over 35.

Table 2.1 *'Exposing the myths of online buyer behaviour' by Accenture (www.accenture.com)*

Category	Characteristics
Cherry pickers	26% of online consumers; bargain hunters, seek wide range of reputable brands, tend to be younger and better educated than average
Brand reliants	22% of online consumers; while they value competitive pricing, they are equally concerned with brand reputation, brand familiarity and privacy of personal information
Time savers	21% of online consumers; while price is the most important single factor, speed, functionality and ease of use are given high ratings. Convenience is more important than brand reputation
Variety seekers	16% of the online market; they want a comprehensive selection of reputable brands, and speed is far more important than price
Netizens	15% of online consumers; are primarily concerned with privacy of information. Site speed, interactivity and personalization are also important. Price is not

3 Many companies assume that shoppers are impressed by technical wizardry, but here the research established that speed and convenience are preferred by customers. Only 'Netizens' rank interactivity in the top five buying needs.

4 Does site personalization help to build relationships? Not according to these findings. Customers are alienated by concerns over privacy. Only 'Netizens' place any importance on personalization.

5 Is building online brand awareness through expensive advertising really worth the cost, as assumed by many dotcoms that spent huge sums promoting new brands? Perhaps not; Accenture found that brand familiarity ranked only tenth among the buying needs for the total market, and in some segments even lower.

6 It is often assumed that an established 'bricks and mortar' reputation makes it easier to build an online relationship. Accenture found, however, that online consumers are all but indifferent to a brand's presence offline.

7 Finally, many companies focus on providing a consistent customer experience, but one of Accenture's most interesting research findings was that individual consumers behave differently depending on what they are buying. Companies operating in multiple categories do not achieve uniformly high levels of brand reputation (for example, Expedia scores highly for hotel reservations, but poorly for car rental). Accenture's message for e-Brand Managers: 'Think like duck hunters; pick a target for each shot, don't blast away at the whole flock.'

63

FURTHER READING

Mann, C. and Stewart, F. (2000) *Internet Communication and Qualitative Research: A Handbook for Researching Online*, London: Sage.

QUESTIONS

Question 2.1

What sources of secondary data can you think of, from both inside and outside an organization?

Feedback – Internally published data sources include financial records, sales records, customer database, production records, internally conducted research projects, customer complaints and staff suggestions. Externally published data sources include market research reports, government statistics, trade journals, newspapers, CD ROM databases, the Internet and company annual reports.

Question 2.2

List the advantages and disadvantages of secondary data in comparison with primary data.

Feedback

Advantages	Disadvantages
Save time and money	As it has been collected for a different purpose, the formats and categories used may differ from what is now required
Time series studies are possible (examining the history of a particular problem to highlight changes over time)	Data may be out of date
Data is easy to access	Data may be inaccurate
Can tell in advance whether the data is going to be useful or not	There may be information overload, particularly if the Internet is used

Question 2.3

What method of data collection would most suited to the following research projects:

2.3.1 Finding answers to 'closed' questions about customer satisfaction levels in order to test a set of hypotheses about service quality in high-tech businesses.

Feedback – Closed questions and hypothesis-testing involve a quantitative approach, and the search for 'objective', 'factual' data. For that reason, questionnaires would be the most efficient method to use. Structured interviews might also be appropriate.

2.3.2 Investigating how cabin crew maintain service quality while having to deal with drunk and difficult passengers on airlines.
Feedback – Observation, ideally as a 'participant' (i.e. as another member of the cabin crew), would be most appropriate here. It would allow you to get close to the action and see how problems are dealt with in the context of action. Slightly less effective, though more straightforward to earth-bound researchers, would be in-depth interviews. Questionnaires or structured interviews would not be appropriate because this method is usually used to collect quantitative data, and the situation here calls for 'richness': understanding the dynamics of practice, as well as the experiences of the cabin crew involved.

2.3.3 Exploring the difficulties established companies face when introducing online channels to market.
Feedback – The challenge here is to get managers to reflect on, and contrast, their experiences of online and offline marketing. They might not always be conscious of the greatest difficulties they face, and are even less likely to be conscious of why they face them. In-depth interviews would give you the freedom to explore the richness of these issues. Observation would be less effective because the data needed stretch across domains of experience (in time and space). You could observe what someone is doing here and now, but this would not help you to make connections with their earlier experiences in previous jobs.

Question 2.4
Which method of online primary data collection do you think is most likely to be successful? Why?
Feedback – Emailing customers gives a broader reach, but the recipient then has to go online to complete the survey, which they might not have the time or inclination to do.

Question 2.5
Why might data collected from an online questionnaire not be representative of the population as a whole?
Feedback – The obvious answer is because not everyone has access to the Internet, but there are more subtle problems as well. The type of person inclined to respond to an online questionnaire is likely to be technology literate and have time on their hands. Such individuals may make up only a small segment of a firm's customer base, and their views may well differ from those of more mainstream customers. The problem can be addressed by the use of screened Internet samples when collecting data. This means that quotas based upon particular sample

characteristics such as age or income bracket are imposed on self-selected sample groups. Alternatively, panels of respondents may be drawn upon who have agreed in advance to participate and therefore have been pre-selected and categorized into demographic segments.

Question 2.6

Can you think of any other problems in connection with Internet survey research?
Feedback – As will be demonstrated in Chapter 11, there are increasing concerns about privacy and security on the Internet. People are concerned that the personal details they supply when responding to surveys may be misused. It is also possible that survey results may be skewed by individuals submitting multiple replies to a questionnaire which is posted on the Web for anyone to see. To get around this problem, unique passwords can be supplied to participants that will access the survey form only once.

Question 2.7

Can you think of a way in which the arguments for and against online focus groups can be resolved?
Feedback – Perhaps a combination of methods might be a suitable compromise. For example, offline group sessions can be recorded and then broadcast to senior management over the Internet.

Question 2.8

How significant do you consider the Accenture research findings to be?
Feedback – It is always dangerous to generalize from one piece of research. However, the results are interesting because they demonstrate that a number of online shopping behaviours seem to have acquired 'fact' status without being based upon thorough research. For example, many companies have based their entire marketing strategy on the notion that prices on the Web have to be low. More research needs to be done to build upon and validate the Accenture results.

 WEB LINKS

www.busreslab.com
Useful specimen online questionnaires to measure customer satisfaction levels, and tips on effective Internet marketing research.

www.marketresearch.org.uk
The Market Research Society. Contains useful material on the nature of research, choosing an agency, ethical standards and codes of conduct for research practice.

www.statistics.gov.uk
Detailed information on a variety of consumer demographics from the Government Statistics Office.

www.privacy.net
Useful information and demonstrations of online privacy issues.

www.esomar.nl
The World Association of Opinion and Marketing Research Professionals site; it contains detailed guidelines on conducting online research and managing privacy policies, plus a useful glossary of marketing research terminology.

Chapter 3

Change management

LISA HARRIS

MINDMAP

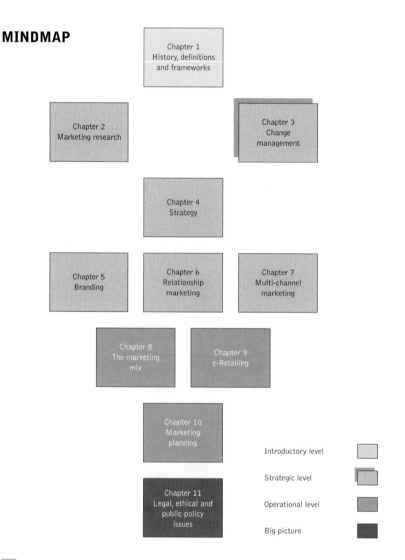

LINKS TO OTHER CHAPTERS

Chapter 4 Strategy	Chapter 6 Relationship marketing	Chapter 7 Multi-channel marketing

Chapter 10 Marketing planning

- Chapter 4 – Strategy
- Chapter 6 – Relationship marketing
- Chapter 7 – Multi-channel marketing
- Chapter 10 – Marketing planning

KEY LEARNING POINTS

After completing this chapter you will have an understanding of:

- The importance of change to established companies in developing effective online operations
- The technical and organizational challenges associated with managing change and how they might be addressed
- The central role played by leaders and change agents in the effective implementation of change

ORDERED LIST OF SUB TOPICS

- The need for organizational change in the e-Business era
- Barriers to change
- Challenges of change
  - Technology
  - Resistance to change
  - Leadership

- ● Relationship-building and communications
- ● Role of the change agent
- ● Adapting organizational culture
- ■ A framework for implementing change
- ■ Chapter summary
- ❖ Case study: 'Practise what you preach?'
- ❖ Case study: Debenhams.com
- ❖ Case study: Kanga Bank
- ❖ Further reading
- ❖ Questions
- ❖ Web links

THE NEED FOR ORGANIZATIONAL CHANGE IN THE E-BUSINESS ERA

As described in Chapter 1, the commercialization of the Internet has given rise to a range of new business concepts, and the popular imagination has been captured by the rise and fall of Internet start-ups – the dotcoms. This was particularly the case where the companies involved demonstrated new business models and offered customers novel value propositions. The great 'e-Pioneers' are certainly worthy of attention and analysis. All businesses can learn much from their birth pangs and their experiences of the early days of the Internet era. But for most companies, online operations are not matters of innovation from scratch, but of organizational change and adaptation – even corporate transformation. As Kalakota and Robinson note. 'In the e-business world, companies must anticipate the need for transformation and be ready to re-examine their organisations to the core' (1999: 8).

Quite apart from the dotcom saga, the Internet continues to have an enormous impact on established organizations. It is affecting how they operate and how they do business; it provides new opportunities for businesses of all sizes and has created a new sales channel. Figure 3.1 illustrates the ever-increasing scope of e-business change. Furthermore, even such radical restructuring cannot be regarded as just a one-off activity. As Butler *et al.* (1999) state, the network technologies that support this are built on silicon – i.e. *sand* – and 'as the sand shifts so does an e-business'. In other words, companies have to be prepared to reorganize and restructure themselves continuously. For this reason, understanding how to manage change effectively becomes essential. As Stroud notes, 'The benefits that the Internet is expected to deliver will not be realised unless a company adapts its organisational structure and methods to meet the radical new ways of working that this new technology makes possible' (1998: 225). It is worth noting, however, that some companies have embraced the need for

70

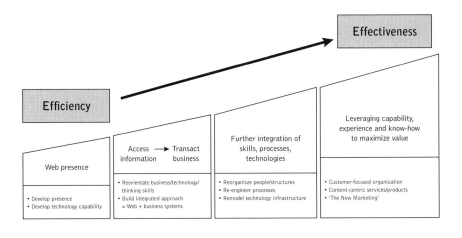

Figure 3.1 *Moving to e-Business*

Source: Adapted from Willcocks and Sauer (2000)

change perhaps *too* enthusiastically. One manager of a software company re-marked, 'We start to get worried if change is not taking place every week even; the question is, will we get left behind? We must change something. But often it's change for change's sake' (private conversation).

At the other end of the scale, some companies remain reluctant to grapple with the opportunities offered by the Internet. In a piece of research conducted by Jupiter Communications in 2000, only 24 per cent of the US CEOs surveyed actu-ally viewed their Web initiatives as an integrated part of their core business. The US experience, according to Cohan (2000), is that companies generally fall into two broad camps with their e-Initiatives: being 'self-reinventing' in order to maintain market leadership, or else 'change-avoiding' by persevering with existing ways of doing business. As the Jupiter study implies, the self-reinventors are still in the minority, but these companies, according to Cohan, have the following characteristics:

- They believe it is better to attack their existing business models than allow competitors to do so.
- They are led by CEOs who are very concerned about keeping competitors from gaining access to their customers.
- Their CEOs have a financial incentive to reinvent the company in order to sustain rapid profit growth.
- Their CEOs are personally open to learning more about e-Commerce if that is what is necessary to maintain the strategic initiative in the industry.

71

Similarly, Siegel (2000) recommends that in developing e-Business strategies, self-reinventors spend time sharpening the 'big questions'. These include:

- Which business areas are we open to exploring, and which are we going to avoid?
- Which parts of our business are going online fastest?
- What changes do we expect from competitors?
- Which start-ups are going to put us out of business?
- Which of our competitors would make good partners?

These questions suggest a radical or transformational view of e-Business-related change, rather than an incremental one. This has major implications so far as the process of change management is concerned, as well as the likely successes and difficulties it will involve.

BARRIERS TO CHANGE

It is worth reporting here the recent findings of Rosabeth Moss Kanter (2001), who undertook a survey of 785 companies to investigate the barriers to e-Business change. The results are listed below in overall descending order of importance from 1 (most important) to 17 (least important). Bear in mind that companies more than 20 years old face fewer marketplace and technology barriers than younger ones do, but they face many more internal barriers – from decision-making uncertainty to divisional rivalries.

1 The unit does not have staff with adequate technical or Web-specific skills.
2 Customers and key markets do not want to change their behaviour.
3 There are more important projects that require existing resources and time.
4 Technology and tools are inadequate, unavailable or unreliable.
5 It is hard to find the right partners to work with.
6 Suppliers are not co-operative or not ready for e-Business.
7 Employees are not comfortable with change.
8 Leaders are not sure where to begin: they do not understand how to make the right choices.
9 Top executives do not personally use computers and are not personally familiar with the Internet.
10 Rivalries or conflicts between internal divisions get in the way.
11 It is hard to find the capital for new investment.
12 Managers fear a loss of status or privileged positions.
13 Employees fear loss of jobs, or unions and employee groups fear loss of membership.

14 Government rules and regulations get in the way.
15 The company is successful as it is: leaders see no need for change.
16 The company had a bad previous experience with new technology.
17 It is a waste of time or money: it is not relevant to the business.

It is evident that there are a number of difficulties in implementing the intellectual, cultural and structural shifts necessary to succeed in a much more interactive business environment that requires a diverse range of skills. Drobik (2000) notes that 'organisations need to wake up to the complications of being an e-business', but he claims that one of the biggest mistakes organisations make when implementing an e-business strategy is that they 'completely redesign the business in order to become an e-business'. In other words, organisations cannot simply 'switch' to e-business. He explains that success depends on 'mix management' – a mix in which traditional and e-business models coexist, which supports the central theme of this book.

CHALLENGES OF E-BUSINESS CHANGE

Technology

One of the first challenges companies face when attempting to develop online channels is to consider how such a strategy will impact upon their 'bricks and mortar' organization. Developing a 'clicks and mortar' operation may result in a more 'virtual' form of organization in which traditional ways of working are mixed with electronic communications. It is here that a company encounters its first problem, which is usually one of technology. The particular difficulty relates to the attempt to evolve 'legacy' systems (i.e. the technical infrastructure that has accumulated to support the business over time) to an infrastructure that will support e-Business. Few businesses find themselves in the position where they can 'throw away' the old and introduce new, customized computer systems. Legacy systems often perform essential activities upon which daily business processes depend.

While start-up companies can leapfrog these problems, established ones face some difficult challenges. Effective e-Business solutions demand integrated front- and back-end systems, a process which may demand close co-operation between two groups (or even subcultures) with the organization. As Nigel Waterson of Gemini puts it, 'The front end has quite often been built by guys in ponytails, while the people who understand the back end are often grey haired' (Conway 2000: 63). System integration means that when customers interact via the Web, placing orders and purchasing goods, the stock control and financial systems also speak the same language and carry out their part of the transactions. The problem is that many such back-end systems are unlikely to be based on open Internet protocols and may even have been custom built. Nonetheless, such systems may be critical to a company's business, and include such details as bank account data and stock rotation information. As Conway points out,

> IT managers are loath to replace them with something new and untested. They may not even fully understand how their legacies work any longer. The people who built the systems may well have left the company, leaving present IT experts reluctant to tinker.
>
> (2000: 62)

Replacing or upgrading such systems also takes time, which may slow up Web developments critical to speedy e-Commerce innovation.

Over and above the technological matters identified above, major *organizational* change issues must be recognized and addressed for online strategies to be realized successfully. This is because of the need to redesign business processes and structures, change organizational culture, and engage in education and training. A wide range of stakeholders may be affected, with many personnel needing to 'buy in' to the change. As Siegel puts it,

> There is only one way to do e-Business: fully committed. Everyone in the company must be dedicated to the effort. You can't have ten people for every thousand working on it. You can't delegate it. You have to encourage everyone to jump into the water and support them in teaching each other to swim. I'm asking for the biggest cultural change in your company's history.
>
> (2000: 35)

These issues will now be considered in turn.

Resistance to change

There are a number of reasons why people may be unwilling to accept organizational change, as summarized below:

- Stability and security are threatened.
- Coping strategies and comfort zones are affected.
- The uncertainty of change creates anxiety.
- Imposed change reduces perceived autonomy and control.
- Job content is changed and new skills are demanded.
- Authority structures and reporting lines are altered.
- Work groups and other relationships are disrupted.
- Established routines and practices are abandoned.
- An individual's power and authority is threatened.

74

According to Markus (1999), workers' reactions to change vary greatly. She suggests that while some workers readily embrace new technologies, some can be hostile, and the reason for this hostility can often be attributed to poor communication and shifts in organizational power. Effective internal marketing is important here in order to segment employees into 'supporters', 'neutrals' and 'opponents' of change, and then develop appropriately customized communications in order to deal with the differing priorities of each of these groups. This issue will be expanded upon in Chapter 6.

Nadler and Tushman (1997) explain that implementation of change involves the disruptive transition from a current state to a future state, as a result individuals or groups can resist change. They claim that there are three types of problems encountered when an organization goes through a significant change:

- *Power.* Change can be viewed as a threat to existing power structures and it creates uncertainties, so the struggle for power escalates as individuals and groups attempt to control their environment by resisting change.
- *Uncertainty.* Anxiety is created as individuals are not sure where they stand and whether at the end of the change process they will still have a role within the organization. As a result, individuals can act irrationally, as they find it difficult to understand and interpret clearly information related to the change.
- *Control.* During the change period, it becomes difficult to maintain control because goals are changing, as are structures and roles, and certain control systems become irrelevant.

These authors also highlight the important point that within large organizations individuals usually do not openly resist change; instead, they 'subtly or passively' resist. The degree of employee involvement and participation can significantly affect the success of change. Markus claims that workers' reaction to change is dependent on

> whether they have had a say in selecting the technology or the way it is introduced and used, how the new technology is communicated, how much training and support are provided, and how carefully the roll out is planned and executed.
>
> (1999: 11)

Involving employees fully means that they become responsible for the success of the change, becoming 'owners' of the change process. IBM Global Services recommends that in order to build a successful e-Business, organizations need to challenge their employees to:

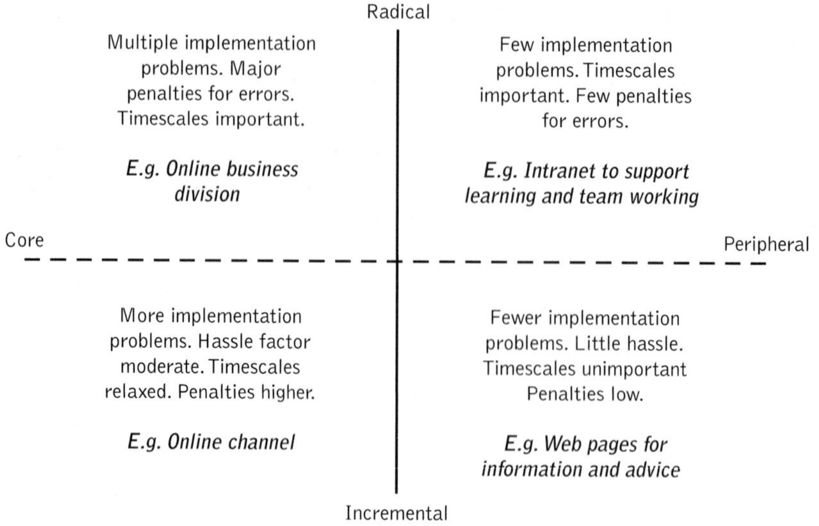

Radical

Multiple implementation
problems. Major
penalties for errors.
Timescales important.

*E.g. Online business
division*

Few implementation
problems. Timescales
important. Few penalties
for errors.

*E.g. Intranet to support
learning and team working*

Core — Peripheral

More implementation
problems. Hassle factor
moderate. Timescales
relaxed. Penalties higher.

E.g. Online channel

Fewer implementation
problems. Little hassle.
Timescales unimportant
Penalties low.

*E.g. Web pages for
information and advice*

Incremental

Figure 3.2 *Assessing the extent to which employees may resist change*

identify the cultural changes that will also be needed and to shape the processes, the linked education, learning and competency development that will be required to deliver real value in the new ways of doing business that they are proposing.

(1999: 14)

Another critical point is that organizations are bound to encounter complications in asking individuals to make changes that they are incapable of implementing. Adequate investments in training and development programmes are therefore essential, particularly, for example, if new skills in Web design are required. If individuals do not possess the skills and capability necessary to introduced planned changes, the likelihood of success is significantly reduced.

According to Buchanan and Boddy (1992), the more radical change projects are, the more open they are to organizational disruption and failure. Badham *et al.* (1997) point out that there are two aspects to radical change, as illustrated with examples in Figure 3.2. The first concerns the issue of 'breadth' – the degree to which change is central to the organization's strategy – and demands radical as opposed to incremental modifications throughout the organization. The second relates to the degree to which such modifications mark a significant departure from existing ways of doing things. Both of these certainly apply to e-Business. For example, such changes point to business process redesign, the development of cross-functional team working, and the move towards a customer-focused (instead of management-led) culture. These changes are likely to be politically controversial and threaten the interests of a wide range of stakeholders. Unlike routine change, such initiatives are also likely to be highly complex. As Badham *et al.* note, there may be a high degree of uncertainty as to what to do and how to do it; objectives may be less clear, and resource requirements will be less well known. In addition, it may be less easy to create shared perceptions of goals and build and maintain necessary commitment. For this reason, these authors suggest that more time will need to be spent ensuring effective communication to encourage flexibility, address perceptions, and generate and regenerate involvement. To illustrate the problems that can ensue in such a situation, the authors describe Merrill Lynch's move into online trading:

> At the core of the change process was conflict at many levels within Merrill Lynch. There was conflict between the defenders of the brokers and their commissions and proponents of online investing. There was conflict between Merrill brokers who were concerned about losing customers to online brokers and Merrill brokers who were concerned about losing commissions. There was even conflict among Merrill executives between who favoured setting up a separate online unit to compete with the brokers and those who favoured keeping the online unit under the same executive.
>
> (1997: 151)

Leadership

Leadership plays a crucial role in effective change management. Hunt (1998) claims that change is a learning process because people have to learn to behave differently, but in order for this process to work and for change to be successful, individuals need to be encouraged, and it is here that leadership becomes very important. Carnall (1999: 32) also expresses the need for strong leadership; that is, 'the ability to maintain progress and a facilitative and supportive approach', and suggests that for this to happen, the leader needs to have knowledge of the change area and appropriate skills to encourage learning and change.

Some leaders use 'coercive persuasion' to force change; in other words, 'employees have no alternative but to accept the new reality because they have nowhere else to go' (Brown 1998: 114). Although individuals may not like the change, they have no choice, so will accept the change and accommodate the new ideas. He goes on to state that leaders need to be able to 'manipulate people's understandings of what is going on, and who are able to deliver the results quickly' (ibid.: 5). The role of the leader can be to create conditions under which success can visibly be achieved, even if only in a limited and partial way, and to rationalize and capitalize upon positive events after they have happened. Managers will instead need to be skilled in the art of leadership and corporate politics. The need to enrol and re-enrol support, neutralize dissent and resistance, and secure

77

resources will demand networking skills and the ability to build consensus and support (Buchanan and Boddy 1992). They must start by gaining buy-in at the top. As Siegel puts it, 'You can have the world's greatest web strategy, but it won't work unless managers have a stake in the outcome' (2000: 82). To make sure they do, Siegel recommends the formation of a change team, headed by a Chief Net Officer (CNO). Furthermore, he suggests that businesses should 'Strengthen the team with managers who have good relationships with people in other divisions. The CNO will need a lot of favours, so make sure the team is credible in the eyes of the rest of the company' (2000: 83). If leaders recognize the type of change they are faced with, and are familiar with the sort of skills and tactics that may be employed to deal with it, the management of change is more likely to be successful.

Relationship-building and communications

Earlier in this chapter, the importance of effective internal marketing to engage staff in the change process was emphasized. Increasingly, such communications are a critical aspect of external relationship building too. According to Symonds (1999a), a crucial misconception is that any business is a 'free-standing entity'. For example, in order to participate in a new development such as e-Procurement or customer relationship management, it is essential that companies involve their suppliers, partners and customers in their processes and allow each party to become familiar with each other's processes. This degree of openness and transparency is new to most organizations, and it requires significant change and high levels of trust between participants.

A genuine e-Business strategy provides electronic links in order to 'foster conversations' with staff, customers and partners. Such 'customer-led' approaches involve listening to customers in a strategic way, deepening relationships and loyalty. The importance of engaging in rich customer conversations is underpinned by a number of recent works on e-Business. The highly influential *Cluetrain Manifesto* (Levine *et al.*, 2000), for instance, asserts in the first of its ninety-five theses on the new economy that 'markets are conversations'. Newell's *Loyalty.com* (2000) underlines this point, and highlights the way companies must 'leverage customer information' for the effective management of customer relationships on the Internet. Seybold's *Customers.com* (1998) makes similar points, again focusing on the need for customer-focused strategies that engage customers as parts of a community based around a company's products and personnel. Such strategies suggest something much more radical in terms of change than the mere 'bolt-on' approach of adding an online channel to market, which is often proposed as a straightforward and simple process. It calls for a re-engineering of processes and structures focused around key customer groups, rather than product or service divisions. It also implies cross-functional, team-based working. As Siegel puts it,

78

The customer-led company has a broad interface across which all employees can get to know their customers. Employees invite customers in to collaborate on new products, support systems, and methodologies. Facilitating those interactions will take new communication skills, new tools, and the ability to move people in and out of product teams easily.

(1999: 107)

At Dell Computers, for instance (www.dell.com), customers are brought into the product planning and manufacturing processes, with all employees encouraged to have contact with customers. Through effective collaboration across boundaries, ideas can be shared about product designs and value propositions. The result is faster and more customer-focused product and service innovation. To produce the capacity for this, considerable attention must be placed on organizational structures, processes, skills and culture – elements that may need a radical overhaul in established companies. Relationship-building will be discussed in more detail in Chapter 6.

Role of the change agent

Buchanan and Boddy (1992) emphasize the importance of having an appropriate 'change agent' or 'project champion' in the successful implementation of change. The change agent should be someone who is committed to the success of the project and prepared to 'go the extra mile' in order to motivate, bully or cajole other participants as required. There is a diverse range of skills associated with performing this role; for example:

- influencing;
- negotiating;
- selling;
- inspiring;
- commanding respect;
- political;
- magic and miracle working!

It is a tall order for any one individual to have all of these skills, and some will be more important than others at different stages of the project. In practice, therefore, more than one change agent may be required.

Adapting organizational culture

There are many ways in which the terms 'culture' and 'organizational culture' can be understood, but for our purposes we have chosen the following:

79

the system of meanings which are shared by members of a human grouping and which define what is good and bad, right and wrong and what are the appropriate ways for members of that group to think and behave.

(Watson 1994: 111–112)

the pattern of learned basic assumptions that has worked well enough to be considered valid and, therefore, to be taught to new members as the correct way to perceive, think, and feel in relation to the problems of survival and integration.

(Schein 1985: 8)

Schein (1985) suggested that employee acceptance of technological change required a change in organizational culture, because practices and values tend to be built around existing technologies that have contributed to the successful development and self image of the organization. One of the strongest elements of culture he identified was the status system attached to these traditions, and the possession by individuals of critical skills. Schein claimed that innovation was a property of culture, and the potential of information technology as a competitive and strategic weapon would not be fulfilled unless innovative cultures were present or developed, enabling the organization to learn and adapt. This attitude was also noted by Piore and Sabel (1984), whose theory of 'flexible specialization' emerged from their observations that technological progress could be self-blocking, and new products were generally designed to fit existing equipment and procedures. The importance of culture was also emphasized in a study of video disk development by Graham (1986), who found that prevailing cultural values and attitudes in the firm, based upon past experience, were inadequate when it came to dealing with an innovative product in a new market.

Although these studies pre-date the Internet era, they illustrate quite clearly how a change in organizational culture is often necessary for full advantage to be taken of the opportunities presented by new technologies. A vast literature now exists on the subject of how to change culture. As early as 1952, Lewin identified three phases of culture change, namely 'unfreezing', 'change' and 'refreezing'. 'Unfreezing' results from the questioning of norms that have led to a specific failure, thereby sensitizing employees to the need for change, which is then consolidated into new procedures or behaviours during the 'refreezing' phase. This theory seems overly simplistic and linear in its classification of the technological change process, which in practice appears invariably to be a more dynamic and turbulent series of events. Mintzberg (1979) advocated the development of a culture of 'adhocracy' that is organic and decentralized in structure, thereby avoiding the pitfalls that are usually associated with bureaucracy. He claimed that in search of innovation, such organizations minimize planning, control and the division of labour.

80

In practice, however, while examples do exist of individual companies, such as British Airways, that have 'created' a new corporate culture (Brown 1998), these success stories appear to be few and far between. March and Simon (1994), in their revised edition of a seminal text that introduced the concept of 'bounded rationality' (referring to the limited cognition of organizational members), maintained that their theory still holds true today. Despite the vastly increased resources available to the modern organization, these authors believed that potential for change would always be constrained by the conflicting agendas of employees. Green also questioned the ability of organizations to manage culture in a prescriptive way:

> If culture could be levered into shape then, by now, someone would have discovered the method. The metaphors of fine-tuning and fit which abound in much of the literature on culture and strategy are altogether inappropriate for something as complex as human social systems.
>
> (1994: 427)

He noted that while corporate cultures appear to be stable and static when studied at a particular point in time, applying a longitudinal perspective reveals that they are in fact too multidimensional and dynamic to be susceptible to manipulation by management. The key point about culture change, therefore, is that it is rarely as simple a process as is sometimes suggested when recommended as a tool for implementing projects involving new technology.

A FRAMEWORK FOR IMPLEMENTING CHANGE

If we bear the above discussion in mind, the implementation of a change project such as the development of a new online sales channel can be summarized as follows:

1 Definition and initiation phase
   - Clarify goals:
     - What should the project achieve?
     - What are the priorities?
   - Identify risks and constraints:
     - What resources and time are available?
     - What might go wrong?
   - Work out project assumptions.
   - Build the project team.
2 Planning phase:
   - What needs to be done?
     - What are the tasks that make up the project?

- What are the task-dependencies and critical paths?
  - When must they be done?
    - What are the deadlines ?
    - When should we start/finish?
  - How should they be done?
    - With what equipment/techniques?
    - By which people/organizations?
  - What budgets should be allocated?
  - What responsibilities should be assigned?
3 Execution and control phase:
  - Get started with a bang:
    - Build team spirit.
    - Symbolize the start.
    - Communicate the vision.
  - Set up the organization:
    - Establish lines of authority and responsibility.
    - Set up communication channels.
    - Clarify guidelines and procedures.
  - Keep things on schedule:
    - Monitor whether tasks are on time.
    - Solve problems or assign more resources.
    - Co-ordinate changes with other activities.
4 Closing phase:
  - Decide on the formal end of the project.
  - Symbolize the ending.
  - Disband the team.
  - Undertake evaluation.
  - Establish review mechanisms.
  - Ensure that learning is shared and passed on.

CHAPTER SUMMARY

In this chapter, we have shown that the Internet has the potential to trigger a seismic shift in the way business is conducted. The changing business environment is creating both challenges and opportunities, but facing the challenges and taking advantage of the opportunities for most businesses requires change. It should now be clear that over and above the techno-logical matters, major organizational change issues must be recognized and addressed for e-Business solutions to be realized successfully. This is because of the need to redesign business processes and structures, change organizational culture, demonstrate effective leadership, overcome employee resistance, and engage in the necessary education and training. Internal marketing plays an important communication role in many of these issues.

Case study:
'PRACTISE WHAT YOU PREACH?'

This case study concerns the implementation of e-Business strategies within a large international technology company that is itself at the forefront of providing Internet and e-Business solutions. Despite this level of expertise, the adoption of e-Business strategies within the firm has been fraught with difficulties, as is explained below. The case focuses upon the Financial Services Division. It is described as a 'matrix organization', with instructions flowing from headquarters in New York and the Geographical Team at the European headquarters in Paris. There is a hierarchical structure in that information flow is 'top-down'. According to one interviewee, a major problem with the matrix organization is 'conflicting instructions', in that worldwide headquarters says one thing and the European headquarters says another. Time is then wasted arguing about how to proceed, which means that decision-making can be quite slow, despite the fact that the matrix organization is supposed to encourage cross-functional teamwork and facilitate better communication.

The firm consists of a top layer of vice presidents, chief financial officers and the chairman. This top layer is then surrounded by a 'camouflage' layer, which controls both the information that flows into the top layer and that which filters to the bottom layers of the organization. Control and power truly lies within the camouflage layer, as it is these people who have control of the flow of information. Below this are numerous networks that have a mixture of hierarchical and matrix structure. The matrix organization is supposed to encourage cross-functional teamwork and facilitate better communications, especially with e-Business tools such as email and an intranet in place. Most employees are members of at least four or five networks, each of which has one main sponsor or mentor.

Even though the firm is trying to shed its 'traditional' image and has become more customer focused, in some ways it is still very old-fashioned. In fact, one interviewee claimed that it operates on a 'feudal system'. Such 'mechanistic' organizations are better suited to stable conditions and find it more difficult to cope with change. Since the e-Business environment is constantly changing and no one truly knows what the future holds, an 'organic' structure would appear to be more logical. All the interviewees agreed that the pace of e-Business adoption in the firm had been slower than

83

expected. A senior manager suggested that top management were more concerned with 'selling the solutions' than implementing them internally and that the changes that had been made so far were superficial – done merely to illustrate to customers and potential customers that the firm was taking a dose of its own medicine. As one employee put it, 'We are often the last to practise what we preach; we can use the Internet for communications, we can use it to look up news, or buy and sell shares, but our finance system is not Web-enabled.'

The most common reasons given by staff for the slow pace of change were:

- resources being concentrated upon converting customers into e-Businesses;
- so much information still needing to be on paper;
- little integration between processes;
- the fact that e-Business is not just about technology, and that other organizational issues have to be addressed.

One of the staff interviewed thought that the pace of adoption of e-Business had been slow because 'Employees are now expected to do and track everything themselves – too much time now gets spent accessing intranets to find out what is going on in the department.' She went on to say that a lot of people were suffering from 'adoption fatigue', with too many new tools available to use, which were also slow to access on the servers. Server overload and system failures discouraged employees from using the technology. However, one employee questioned whether speed was necessarily such a good thing anyway: 'If we are all totally honest, we would admit that we do not know where e-Business is leading or whether it has a long-term future. At the same time, however, we have no choice but to adopt e-Business or be left behind by the competition.'

The major problems encountered when managing change typically relate to organizational issues such as culture, strategy and structure. The firm's e-Business strategy is one that is 'customer facing'; in other words, directed at the external market. It could therefore be said that internal system integration is a secondary priority. This order of priorities was reflected by one employee who claimed, 'The customer comes first, then the company, and lastly the employees.' One senior manager also noted that although the firm had embraced e-Business because of the potential revenues and the market pressures, it also recognized that cost reductions and efficiency gains could result from becoming an e-Business. The danger is that a focus on revenue does not allow 'people' to be taken into consideration, and could go some way towards explaining the slow uptake of the e-Business philosophy within the firm. This rather negative attitude contrasts with the positive disposition of employees, who noted how the clear e-Business strategy has given the firm direction, describing it as 'a banner under which the whole organization could unite'. All the employees interviewed agreed that in order for change to be successful, everyone should be involved and the change should not merely be 'bolted on'. One went on to say, 'You do not just have to change the process but also the behaviour, the people, their aspirations, the brand image . . . and in established organizations these can be deeply rooted.' This, of course, reflects the need for a 'hearts and minds' approach to change, with culture – and therefore people – at the centre of attention.

Critical to success, of course, is visible and credible change leadership. However, one senior manager admitted that the firm does not have an e-Business leader. He claimed,

> There are hardware, software and services leaders but there are no e-Business leaders. There is no one writing the strategy or calling the shots. Some people think they are, but they are not. If they are, they are definitely not driving the individual components towards integration.

Research suggests that the process of e-Business integration would be greatly helped if management led by example. A non-managerial interviewee believed that the bottom layers of the organization are the real e-Business people in the firm, noting that 'The higher up in senior management we go, the less access they seem to have to the e-Business tools. They talk about it with their team but they don't necessarily do anything with it.' One problem is that use of these tools demands a change in behaviour, involving greater openness and co-operation. But the sort of communication and knowledge-sharing this demands is seen by some middle managers as a threat to their position. Their power base is often viewed to result from 'the knowledge they have, the people they know and the position they hold'. They therefore do not want information to flow freely across the organization, which would effectively render their roles as gatekeepers obsolete. In the words of one interviewee,

> Top management can have the commitment to change, people on the floor can see the market changing and the need to change with it, but the middle managers who see their job threatened are only interested in keeping the status quo, where they feel comfortable and powerful, thus hindering the process of change.

The firm is defined as having a 'high-performance culture'. One of the senior managers suggested that this culture has taken some of the pain out of change, especially when compared to the past, where the culture was more paternalistic, meaning that change was difficult. Within this high-performance culture, change is easier, because the goal is what is important, so if change is necessary to achieve this goal, then it is more quickly accommodated. However, some of the 'relics' from the past are still there to resist the changes. Although these employees have worked for a technology company most of their working lives, new technologies are seen as 'foreign' and they are neither confident nor comfortable using the latest technology. It seems, therefore, that the culture of the company has not changed as much as the staff would like to think it has, and this misconception is currently holding back e-Business developments.

Source: This case study was kindly contributed by Delphine Thompson, Brunel University.

Case study:
DEBENHAMS.COM

Early days

Debenham's separation from the Burton Group in the early 1990s prompted the beginning of a holistic reinvention of its corporate strategy. In order to progress from a stagnant position in the retail market, Debenhams focused on a complete reversal of the company's mentality by setting long-term goals, aims and objectives, changing organizational behaviour, and, most importantly, reviewing its strategic positioning. It was widely recognized within the company that complete redevelopment of the business was necessary if Debenhams was going to stay competitive in the long term. The advent of e-Commerce as a new channel to market was to play a critical role in the repositioning of the business. This case study describes the evolution of Debenhams.com since 1996 and demonstrates how the company as a whole has changed alongside the Internet developments.

Debenhams.co.uk was set up in 1996 when the Internet was first recognized as a method of improving customer experience and increasing the number of shopping channels available to the customer. The site, developed by Condé Nast, was at first content only and presented in the style of a glossy magazine containing features such as 'What's New' and 'Competitions', as well as 'magazine-influenced' points of interest, for example recipes, horoscopes and children's games. Although the site was promoted to all the major search engines, it was launched with no specific advertising, as it was merely an exploratory venture at this stage to test the level of Internet awareness among Debenhams' customers.

Three years of subsequent planning and research led to the launch of Debenham's first commercial Web site (Debenhams.com) in October 1999. This development was viewed as an opportunity to extend in-store and catalogue product ranges on a selective basis, rather than attempt to cover all the company's products. In keeping with Debenham's careful approach to new launch initiatives and preference for incremental rather than radical changes to the business model, it was decided that Debenhams.com should be introduced to the Internet through 'soft' launch. Although many competitor sites utilized extensive multi-channel marketing requiring huge advertising budgets, Debenhams.com primarily created awareness in-store, with the URL being placed on shopping bags, till receipts and posters. Unlike many of the 'pure plays' established between 1998 and 2000, Debenhams.com already had the advantage of an established brand. This factor was significant in the success of the launch. Over 10,000 casual browsers sought Debenham's web presence by using the chosen URL before the site was even launched. These browsers and existing customers were the initial target consumers.

Web site managers Conchango designed and maintained the Debenhams.com functionality and content. Site marketing and promotion, product selection and merchandise management, customer services and site development were all managed in-house. Outsourcing content management was necessary to combat the limited specialist skills in this area within the company at that time. Owing to the infancy of Internet retailing at the time of launch, an 'out-of-the-box' solution was not available to Debenhams, and addressing individual business requirements would create extensive integration issues. Therefore, even though a 'bespoke' technology platform was perhaps not the most cost-effective solution, it was the only one available at launch. The site was a compilation of in-store product areas and unique online business opportunities. In-store fashion, gifts and wedding services were also offered online. The Flower Delivery service was unique to the site, and indeed unique among the UK's high street department stores in 1999. The service is an example of how the site enabled Debenhams to respond to consumer expectation and exploit gaps in the marketplace in an efficient and cost-effective manner. The site also served to strengthen Debenham's multi-channel focus, offering the 'express purchase', which was an online purchasing facility for all Debenhams Direct (catalogue) products.

Debenhams.com is closely integrated with both store and catalogue operations to maintain consistency of branding throughout the company. Integration is achieved on many levels through merchandising, customer services and integrated marketing. In-store promotions are extended online; online competitions often feature in-store products, relate to in-store themes and support in-store campaigns. In-store activity is also featured on promotional emails tailored to Debenhams.com customers. Similarly, general store marketing and card marketing feature Debenhams.com promotions, products, campaigns and competitions in their mail-outs and direct marketing methods. The online wedding service has a strong presence within store. Wedding service customers are encouraged to use online facilities as a matter of protocol. As integration has developed, the service appears seamless, and it is difficult to distinguish the two channels, which are often perceived as a complete package. The Debenhams.com flower service is also currently building in-store presence with prominent displays in windows and on concession stands as well as subtle marketing through table talkers, posters, and promotional brochures located at till points. These efforts demonstrate the extent to which Internet developments were linked with the repositioning of the business as a whole.

Challenges of change

It was always apparent that Debenhams.com would have to develop rapidly in order to stay competitive. The main challenge caused by the speed of change in e-Commerce was that the technology platform could not keep up with the marketing demands placed upon it; for example:

- Affiliate partnerships could not be taken advantage of because site technology was incompatible. As 'deep linking' was not possible, customers had to purchase goods advertised through partner merchants separately from Debenhams goods, causing much customer dissatisfaction.

- Banner and button marketing were also restricted, as links were only capable of directing customers to the site or to a particular area, rather than to the specific product advertised in the banner.
- Affiliate management and analysis proved difficult, as the supporting affiliate management agency could not integrate its software with that of the site, causing additional work, communication problems and extra costs.
- Day-to-day marketing efforts could not be developed quickly enough in order to be sufficiently distinctive, new and creative. For example, the set promotional email formats for 'What's New' and 'What's Hot' limited creativity and potential.
- Perhaps the most important problem was the missed opportunity to record and track individual customer purchases and the most-visited areas of the site. These data could have been linked with registration preferences to create opportunities for personalized marketing campaigns.

Outdated technology therefore caused serious problems for site profitability, credibility and market position. As an expensive new e-Commerce channel, there was always significant pressure on Debenhams.com to exceed expectations and prove its worth. Many sites experienced this type of pressure because of the difficulty of measuring the profitability and potential of a unique new platform. It was recognized at an early stage that customer expectations of the site needed to be met as comparative competitor sites were already utilizing personalization and customer relationship management (CRM) solutions in a more sophisticated fashion. However, the purchase of software consumed a large proportion of the budget, as there was no way of managing the technology in-house because the necessary skills were not available. The obvious solution is a more user-friendly package that could reduce maintenance costs in the long term while simultaneously integrating marketing functionality with content templates and content databases.

As the market has developed, so have visitor numbers. The software could not accommodate increasing numbers of users, resulting in longer page download times, purchasing difficulties and navigation problems. During the period June–August 2001 this was particularly true of the Wedding List service. The number of couples who signed up their wedding list with Debenhams during this period far exceeded all predictions. During peak months, the site was forced to increase its phone order service as the site's user capacity paralysed functionality. This in turn affected all other areas of the site, including the flowers order service, fashion and gifts, whose predicted sales were all affected by slow page download and payment execution problems.

In June 2000, eighty-seven of the UK's top 100 retailers had Web sites, but only thirty-six had transactional capabilities (Verdict research, June 2000). In all, 12 to 15 million people in the UK had home Internet access, with 3 to 4 million people shopping online, spending a total of £1.3 billion. By September 2001, not only had the Internet retail market developed significantly, but so had the number of people using the Internet. It is predicted that in 2005, 30 to 35 million people in the UK will have home Internet access, with 15 to 18 million shopping online, spending a total of £12 billion (Debenhams.com IADS report, 2001). As online spend increases and online shopper demographics change, it is more important than ever to stay competitive and maintain and develop a significant proportion of market share.

By 1999–2000, Next, John Lewis, Allders, Marks and Spencers, and Debenhams were all operating 'phase 2' sites offering transactional capability but limited customer experience and high-cost maintenance. However, in 2001, John Lewis, Allders, Marks and Spencers, and Next upgraded to 'phase 3'. At this level, sites offer personalized services, advanced product management techniques and 'leading data analysis tools' (Hawkes, 2001). Not only do these direct competitors pose a threat to Debenham's market share and Web presence, but sites such as Well-being and Argos.com have also entered the market for the first time at this level of development, bypassing the preliminary stages. All these sites have credible branding and are established Web traders with growing market share.

The future

Debenhams.com 'phase 3' was launched in October 2001. The new 'look and feel' of the site was developed by Internet software providers Blue Martini, which also manages sites such as Sacs (US). The new platform has allowed Debenhams.com to:

- increase functionality within the site and portal/affiliate presence;
- fine-tune customer profiling;
- create new data-mining opportunities;
- personalize the customer's shopping experience;
- free up limited merchandising capabilities through cross-sell, up-sell and combination facilities;
- deepen customer service;
- aid business development;
- increase efficiency and cost-effectiveness.

The aim of 'phase 3' is to improve the shopping experience by improving site navigation functions while learning about customer preferences and buying habits in order to drive loyalty by targeting people with the right products at the right time. New software has simultaneously brought much content management capability in-house, thereby reducing maintenance costs. Simplification and integrated information databases have allowed Debenhams.com to transfer much of its operational customer service function to the call centre with the aim of improving customer service through faster response times. With the launch of stage 3, a new business has been developed

89

within the site, called Health and Beauty. This section has a unique proposition by offering Internet sales of top cosmetics brands such as Clarins and Estée Lauder, currently an underdeveloped niche in Internet retailing.

The company is now almost unrecognizable from the struggling traditional retailer that launched a basic Web site in 1996, but it cannot afford to stand still. After this radical rejuvenation, emphasis is now directed at developing the core areas of the site to maintain customer retention, with personalized experience being a key development task. Debenhams.com, like many multi-channel retailers, is now hoping to strengthen its position and multi-channel goals by providing direct site access in-store via Internet kiosks. Kiosks will provide customers with a greater opportunity to shop from the site while in the store environment. In the world of e-Commerce, the only constant is change.

Source: This case study was kindly contributed by Alaina Dixon, Brunel University.

Case study:
KANGA BANK

Kanga Bank (real name disguised by request) initiated a major change programme in 1995 in response to increasing competition in the financial services industry. The aim was to improve business performance and enable profitability levels to be increased by £200 million within five years. Although the project was centred around IT, it involved and impacted upon every part of the bank, as all banking services were to be integrated within one IT network.

It was intended that customers would be able to gain electronic access to all their accounts throughout the country from any terminal (to transfer funds, arrange a loan, pension or mortgage, for example), without the need for specialist knowledge and functions to be maintained in individual branches. The entire structure and image of the bank was to be altered, removing a traditional emphasis upon geographical splits and making the layout of branches more efficient and welcoming. More than £100 million was invested in the technology required to effect this transformation.

In the course of the change programme, problems began to surface as the bank tried to reconcile planned job losses with a severe skills shortage in the area of new technology development and management, and the often conflicting aims of business and technical personnel. It appeared that staff felt their skills were being devalued, or their jobs put under threat. There was little commitment to the change process, and morale suffered. Technically, it was difficult to integrate the new client server technologies (written in SQL Windows) with the mainframe programs written many years before in COBOL. The mainframe system was also account based and could not easily be changed into a customer-based system. This meant that data concerning customers with more than one account could not be linked together, and this caused administrative problems, duplication of work and low service quality.

A number of people in this project formed part of a team within the Technology Division, which was developing and implementing 'middleware' – new technology that enables disparate systems to be integrated. For example, the bank wanted to have a global view of the loan arrears management. Under the old system, customer data would be held in different areas of the bank depending on the particular products involved, and it was a technically difficult and time-consuming job to integrate the data and provide a single figure representing the total outstanding funds owed by an individual customer. Once the systems were upgraded and middleware installed, remote sites across the country could access and assimilate data held in core systems.

This work formed part of the bank-wide systems integration objective of the project. The Technology Division expanded rapidly as the project progressed, with staff numbers increasing by over 300 per cent between 1995 and 1997. Many of these newcomers were temporary, employed by consultancies or by the bank as short-term contractors, to meet what was perceived as a growing knowledge gap between the skills of the original staff and the new technological requirements of the project.

Significant difficulties were encountered from a managerial perspective in terms of group morale, as many individuals found their skills to be obsolete and their hitherto secure jobs under threat from the new entrants. These staff had been used to a stable and undemanding environment, looking after an established and well-known computer system on behalf of user departments. They now had to acquire new skills as new technologies were introduced, and to deal with unforeseen problems in interfacing the new systems with the old mainframe, while coping with increasing demands and tight deadlines from user departments. In effect, the old working environment and culture was overturned in a short space of time.

Uncertainty about the future encouraged rumour, speculation and confusion. In addition, there was no managerial infrastructure in place to co-ordinate each element of the project, which was under the control of different project teams, in line with overall company strategy. As a result, different sub-projects imposed their own procedures and standards. For example, within the same office, some groups were working with Microsoft Access version 1 software, and others with version 2, which was fundamentally different in terms of its usage and capacity. As a result of these difficulties, the project began to exceed its budget and timescales.

A decision was taken to compromise the original objectives of the programme in order to keep within the allocated schedules. Consequently, the radical change programme was abandoned in favour of a more incremental adjustment. Despite the level of investment made in the project, no attempt was made to analyse and address the reasons for the project failure.

FURTHER READING

Buchanan, D. and Badham, R. (1999) *Power, Politics and Organisational Change: Winning the Turf Game*, London: Sage.

Burnes, B. (2000) *Managing Change: A Strategic Approach to Organisational Dynamics*, 3rd edition, London: Pitman.

Cairncross, F. (2002) *The Company of the Future: Meeting the Management Challenges of the Communications Revolution*, London: Profile Books.

Kanter, R. M. (2001) *Evolve! Succeeding in the Digital Culture of Tomorrow*, Boston: Harvard Business School Press.

QUESTIONS

Question 3.1

Do you think it is possible to be *too* focused upon change management?

Feedback – We are told that 'the only constant is change', but it is possible to be too enthusiastic, and embrace change for its own sake, even if the status quo is still valid. Some firms appear to be obsessed with the idea that they need to change their strategies each week in order to remain competitive. Is this too extreme in today's environment? What do you think?

Question 3.2

How might a project manager's communications with 'supporters', 'neutrals' and 'opponents' of a proposed change in marketing strategy differ in style and approach?

Feedback – Supporters do not need to be convinced about the value of a project, but instead need to be encouraged to communicate their commitment to others. Neutrals need to be persuaded of the merits of a project in order to convert them into supporters, and the concerns of opponents need to be listened to and addressed, or further explanations of the need for change given and the potential benefits of supporting the change highlighted.

Question 3.3

What do you learn from the case studies about the nature of change-management challenges in the Internet environment?

Feedback – It is evident from the Debenhams case that change is an ongoing process because no sooner has a new strategy been implemented than competitor activity moves the goalposts again. For a company with no established history of technical expertise, Debenhams seems to be doing rather better than the technology company that is struggling to implement e-Business internally. The most surprising feature of the Kanga Bank example is the senior management's refusal to commission a post-project review to evaluate why the change project had failed so dismally. This was because particular individuals feared that the finger of blame might be laid at their door, and this consideration outweighed the need to learn from the mistakes made.

WEB LINKS

www.dell.com
A good example of a firm that has made good use of the Web to develop effective interactive relationships with customers that have helped to transform the business model.

Strategy

LISA HARRIS

MINDMAP

Chapter 1
History, definitions
and frameworks

Chapter 2
Marketing research

Chapter 3
Change
management

Chapter 4
Strategy

Chapter 5
Branding

Chapter 6
Relationship
marketing

Chapter 7
Multi-channel
marketing

Chapter 8
The marketing
mix

Chapter 9
e-Retailing

Chapter 10
Marketing
planning

Chapter 11
Legal, ethical and
public policy
issues

Introductory level

Strategic level

Operational level

Big picture

LINKS TO OTHER CHAPTERS

Chapter 3
Change
management

Chapter 5
Branding

Chapter 6
Relationship
marketing

Chapter 8
The marketing
mix

Chapter 10
Marketing
planning

- Chapter 3 – Change management
- Chapter 5 – Branding
- Chapter 6 – Relationship marketing
- Chapter 8 – The marketing mix
- Chapter 10 – Marketing planning

KEY LEARNING POINTS

After completing this chapter you will have an understanding of:

- Emerging models of Internet strategy for both B2C and B2B operations
- The importance of developing the appropriate balance between 'bricks' and 'clicks'
- The variety of ways in which organizations are restructuring themselves for effective e-Business

ORDERED LIST OF SUB TOPICS

- Strategic planning in an Internet context
- Alternative approaches to Internet strategy
  - 'The mix of clicks and bricks'
  - Models of Internet strategy
  - New Internet channels

- New organizational structures for Internet strategy:
  - Virtual organizations
  - Networked organizations: the importance of business partnerships
  - Separation or integration of online operations?
- Key differences between B2B and B2C strategies
  - Building customer relationships
  - The marketing mix
  - Emerging e-Marketplaces
- Chapter summary
- ❖ Case study: Internet banking strategies
- ❖ Further reading
- ❖ Questions
- ❖ Web links

STRATEGIC PLANNING IN AN INTERNET CONTEXT

A detailed model to guide the planning process has been developed by McDonald (1999) and it is illustrated in an Internet context by Chaston (2001: 12), as shown in Figure 4.1.

The traditional emphasis upon marketing planning should not be forgotten when it comes to developing Internet marketing strategies, although, as will be discussed below, adaptations may be required. Planning issues will be discussed in more detail in Chapter 10, which draws together all the topics covered in the book through the development of an Internet marketing plan. A proactive planning-based approach involves defining goals, assessing the operating environment, reviewing alternatives and then selecting the best approach, based upon effective matching of skills and resources with identified market opportunities. By setting realistic goals and assessing whether they have been achieved, a firm can evaluate the contribution its online marketing is making, and then use this information to guide the choice of future strategy and its implementation.

Historically, writers have distinguished 'prescriptive' and 'emergent' approaches to strategic planning. The two forms are differentiated by Lynch (2000) as follows:

- Prescriptive models regard strategic planning as a predetermined, sequential process moving from analysis to development and finally to implementation
- Emergent models view the process as more chaotic, with considerable overlap and reiteration between the various stages.

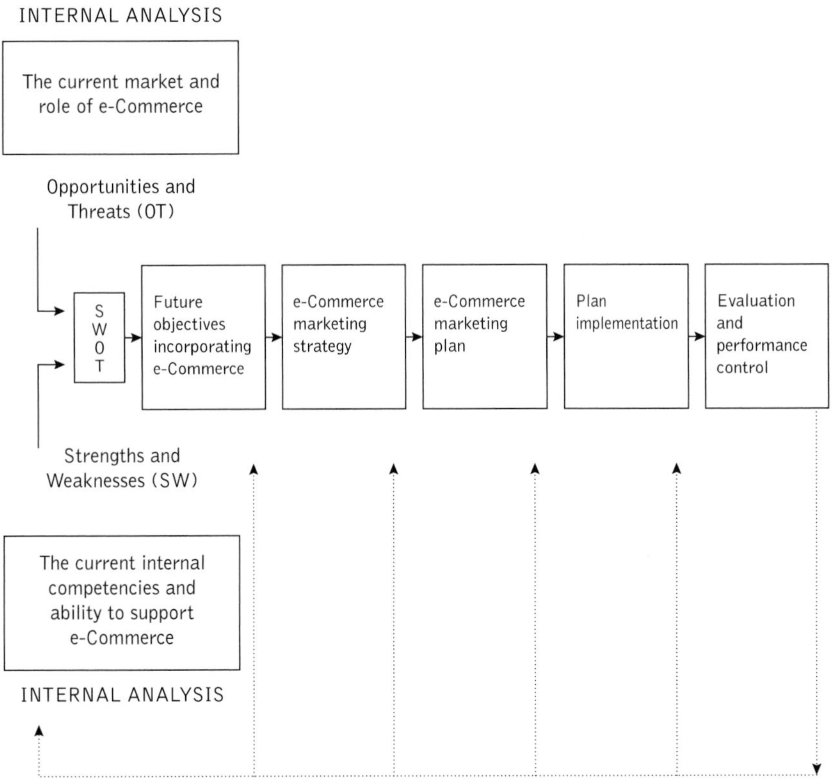

INTERNAL ANALYSIS

```
┌─────────────────────────┐
│ The current market and  │
│   role of e-Commerce    │
└─────────────────────────┘
```

Opportunities and
Threats (OT)

```
        ┌───┐  ┌──────────┐  ┌──────────┐  ┌──────────┐  ┌──────────────┐  ┌────────────┐
        │ S │  │ Future   │  │e-Commerce│  │e-Commerce│  │ Plan         │  │ Evaluation │
   ────▶│ W │─▶│objectives│─▶│marketing │─▶│marketing │─▶│implementation│─▶│ and        │
        │ O │  │incorpo-  │  │strategy  │  │plan      │  │              │  │ performance│
   ────▶│ T │  │rating    │  │          │  │          │  │              │  │ control    │
        └───┘  │e-Commerce│  └──────────┘  └──────────┘  └──────────────┘  └────────────┘
               └──────────┘
```

Strengths and
Weaknesses (SW)

```
┌─────────────────────────┐
│ The current internal    │
│ competencies and        │
│ ability to support      │
│ e-Commerce              │
└─────────────────────────┘
```

INTERNAL ANALYSIS

Figure 4.1 *Internal marketing planning model*

Source: Adapted from Chaston, (2002: 12)

The latter would appear to be most appropriate in a dynamic business environment. However, there has been criticism of traditional planning models since well before the Internet era. For example, Mintzberg (1994) argued that his extensive research involving observation of actual management practices found little correlation between the degree of planning and business profitability. Now, of course, it can be very tempting to abandon traditional planning models altogether in order to move at Internet speed. Bicknell (2000) claims that the business environment is changing so rapidly that any planning would have to be revised too regularly to obtain any value from the exercise, an observation supported by Venkatram: 'We need to abandon calendar-driven models of strategy perfected under the predictable conditions of the Industrial Age. We should embrace the philosophy of experimentation since the shape of future business models is not obvious' (2000: 21).

Chaston (2001: 14) confirms that Internet entrepreneurs are particularly reluctant to spend time on the strategic planning process, despite the possible benefits, which he lists as follows:

- It forces an assessment of the external environment.
- It forces an assessment of the organization's internal competencies.
- It quantifies the expected performance goals for the new venture.
- It identifies the scale of the required resources and the degree to which these will have to be met through the attraction of external funds.
- It creates a 'road map' that can be used to monitor actual performance against expectations at the launch of the venture.

Chaston also notes that the planning model can be entered at any point, and hence does not have to be followed as a sequential process. As shown in Figure 4.1, the critical aspect is the feedback loop whereby new information can be incorporated into the plan and the impact on earlier stages reassessed if appropriate. For example, the entry of a new competitor into the market may necessitate another look at the firm's market positioning as identified in the market analysis, which in turn could influence marketing mix decisions such as price or promotion. The marketing planning process will be considered further in Chapter 10. This chapter will focus on the choice of Internet strategy and appropriate business structures.

ALTERNATIVE APPROACHES TO INTERNET STRATEGY

'The mix of clicks and bricks'

As introduced in Chapter 1, a number of frameworks can be drawn upon to examine the range of alternative Internet strategies that firms are currently pursuing. At a corporate level, alternatives for the Web can be categorized in order of increasing commitment as follows:

- information only;
- interactive communications tool;
- channel to market (e-Commerce);
- separate online business;
- integration with traditional business strategy;
- transformation of traditional business to the Web.

As the degree of commitment increases, issues concerning organizational structure become more important. In this section, the basic structures considered are:

- *'bricks and mortar'* – traditional business model; the Web site is brochureware only;
- *'clicks and mortar'* – the company pursues online and offline marketing and transactions;
- *'clicks only'* – the entire business model is online, with little or no physical presence (such companies are also known as 'dotcoms' or 'pureplays').

See Figure 4.2 for an illustration of these key points. Other new ways of organizing, namely virtual and networked organizations, are considered later in the chapter.

Gulati and Garino (2000) discuss the need for a company to get 'the right mix of bricks and clicks'. 'Bricks and mortar' firms obtain all their revenue from traditional means, and the Web site is used purely for providing information (Figure 4.2), hence little change to established strategy is required. At the other end of the scale, 'pureplay' Internet firms obtain the majority of their revenue online and in some cases may need no physical presence at all. For an established firm, this strategy requires radical change and offers little flexibility to customers, so it is more likely that the intermediary category of 'clicks and mortar' – combining online and offline strategies – will apply. Companies such as Easyrentacar (www.easyrentacar.com) have tried to reduce costs and hence prices by providing an 'Internet only' car hire service, but a number of well-publicized customer service disasters caused by technical hitches have led to an upgrading of the more 'traditional' telephone call centre.

Kumar (1999) suggests that a firm should decide whether the Internet will primarily *replace* ('clicks' only, or pureplay) or alternatively *complement* other channels to market ('clicks and mortar'). If the former, it is important that sufficient investment is made in the necessary infrastructure to achieve this. It is a critical decision because it forces the firm to think about whether the Internet is just another channel to market, operating alongside traditional methods, or whether it will fundamentally change the way in which the firm interacts with its customers, as it is transformed into an Internet 'pureplay'. He suggests that replacement is most likely to happen when:

- Customer access to the Internet is high.
- The Internet offers a better value proposition than other media.
- The product can be standardized, and ideally also delivered over the Internet.

The attitude of the senior management team will be critical in establishing the degree of commitment to the Internet, and therefore in choosing the most appropriate strategy given the resources available. In many cases, firms are reluctant to commit to providing Internet channels to market because of a fear of 'cannibalizing' their existing business. This means that they fear that providing alternative channels to customers will add to costs, as existing customers take advantage of the ability to switch at will between different ways of dealing with the firm, without any new business being generated by the existence of the new channel. This is undoubtedly a risk, but the alternative of not providing the channel at all may mean that customers go elsewhere, where competitors do provide the choice.

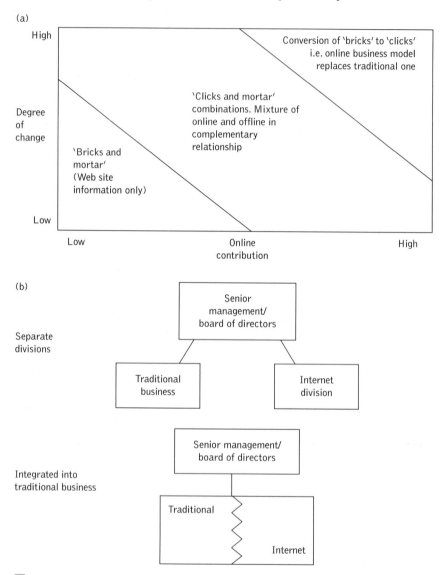

Figure 4.2 *Progressive transformation from 'bricks' to 'clicks', and structural alternatives for 'clicks and mortar' organizations*

So while the Internet channel may not generate additional business (at least in the short term), it should at least help to ensure that existing customers do not defect.

'Bricks and mortar'

Brochureware Web sites, a novelty and hence a distinct competitive advantage in the mid-1990s, are now often derided as reflecting an unimaginative approach to Internet strategy, as the company concerned continues to rely largely on an established 'bricks and mortar' business model. When dotcom fever was at its height early in 2000, the fear among established firms was that new, flexible online business models would render 'old-economy' firms obsolete. Many organizations that felt threatened in this way rushed to catch up and develop their own online strategies. Little more than a year later, the dotcom threat had receded, and firms that adopted a 'wait and see' approach are reaping the benefits of learning from their competitors' mistakes before testing the online waters. Indeed, for some types of business, maintaining a 'bricks and mortar' approach with online brochureware may well turn out to be a viable long-term strategy as well. For others, a combination of online and offline will be more effective.

Dotcoms

Dotcoms have received considerable adverse publicity of late, owing to a number of spectacular failures. (See, for example, David Kuo's book *Dot.bomb* for a fascinating story of boom and bust at www.valueamerica.com, or an even better one with the same title by Rory Cellan-Jones). They are firms established specifically for Internet trading. The classic example is Amazon.com, which has built up a massive customer base in just a few years, but has yet to make a profit.

As mentioned above, the dangers of Internet-only structures are highlighted by recent adverse publicity surrounding Easyrentacar.com. Cope (2000), writing for *The Independent*, is scathing about the standard of customer service offered by the company. Easyrentacar prides itself on the low prices it is able to charge through focusing solely on its Internet service, meaning that there is not even so much as a telephone helpline to handle customer queries. This approach means that even email responses are standardized by computers sending pre-prepared replies generated by key words in the text, which may well not exactly conform to the enquirer's request.

As traditional companies such as W. H. Smith begin to offer a multi-channel service to incorporate online business, and leverage their established competencies such as customer service at the same time, it would make sense for online-only operations to offer some services that are also rooted in the physical world. W. H. Smith allows local store return and exchange facilities that 'online-only' stores cannot offer. Lastminute.com bowed to market trends and launched a paper-based Christmas 2000 catalogue, and Amazon has recently announced an alliance with the international retailer Walmart. A lesson perhaps for the much-maligned 'dotcoms' is that a little flexibility of 'Internet-only' structures might now be somewhat overdue.

'Clicks and mortar'

'Clicks and mortar' represents a combination of 'old' and 'new' business practices. The term is derived from the established expression 'bricks and mortar', which symbolizes a wholly physical presence. Firms such as W. H. Smith (www.whsmith.co.uk) exemplify the trend towards 'clicks and mortar' operations whereby synergies can be generated by the availability of a choice of delivery mechanisms through both traditional and Internet channels. Stores in prime high street locations throughout the country can promote special Internet dealing offers, provide terminal access to online ordering for products not held in store, and also act as a collection point for returned goods that were delivered direct to the home. W. H. Smith is also experimenting with WAP and iDTV platforms (which will be discussed in more detail in Chapter 7).

Nadler and Tushman (1997) note how the current business environment will increasingly require organizations to develop different kinds of structures in order to manage different channels of distribution simultaneously. Many firms are struggling with the concept of channel 'cannibalization' whereby adding Internet-based channels to market merely adds to costs by offering more choice to existing customers instead of attracting additional business. For example, RS Components has won many awards for the significant investment made in its innovative and highly successful Web site, but the firm admits that the volume of paper catalogues it produces has merely stabilized, and not decreased as might be expected. RS Components' strategy is based on the premise that 'If *you* don't cannibalize your own customer base, then your competitors will be happy to do it for you' (private conversation, January 2000).

Kumar (1999) reports that companies tend to use existing distribution networks for too long, fearing the wrath of powerful resellers within the channel. The temptation of course is not to 'rock the boat', but the opportunities for firms that are proactive in their consideration of electronic routes to market are considerable.

Debenhams is a good example of a 'clicks and mortar' currently devoting considerable attention to its Internet channel (as demonstrated in the case study in Chapter 3). The firm has set up a separate Internet division that is known internally as the 'pressure cooker', a reference to the prevailing frantic office atmosphere. Kleindl (2001) notes that such separate divisions allow the firm to avoid conflicts between existing entrenched cultures and the new 'knowledge' mindset necessary for Internet success. By functioning as a totally separate unit, the new division is 'ring-fenced' from the established, slow-moving and inflexible bureaucracy of its parent, while still benefiting from association with a trusted brand image. In the current climate of dotcom failures, the reputation and values associated with the traditional Debenhams brand are a powerful strategic asset.

There are other practical marketing issues to consider:

- Customer expectations are rising. People expect an immediate response to queries at any time of the day or night, and are unimpressed if a Web site does not display the most up-to-date product information and availability. This puts pressure on firms to ensure that customer service centres are adequately staffed and that their sites are easy to navigate and contain the information that the customer seeks.
- For 'clicks and mortar' firms that are still also committed to customer interaction either face to face or by telephone, there can be a significant additional cost burden associated with providing an extra channel to market in terms of the allocation of 'online' and 'offline' duties and additional training requirements.
- The traditional organization of marketing departments is by means of geography (which of course is limited in importance on the Web) or by product. In either case, it is difficult to implement strategies of personalization and cross-selling which cross geographical or product-line boundaries. Organization by customer group makes the most sense in terms of personalizing interactions and assessing lifetime customer value, strategies that Internet developments are rapidly facilitating.
- Individual customers can now be tracked regardless of their physical location or specific product choices. Firms such as Amazon can track wide-ranging purchases back to a single customer account, and customize future promotional campaigns and cross-selling opportunities accordingly. But for 'clicks and mortar' firms, which often lack a sophisticated and integrated computer system, these developments require a feel for the whole product range and geographic spread of the business that challenges internal communication effectiveness. Imagine a case where a customer makes contact by WAP phone one minute, by iDTV the next, then telephones the retail store and all the while expects the company to have a unified view of his or her business, updated in real time . . . These issues will be explored further in Chapter 6 and 7.

Sawhney and Zabin (2001) note that there are certain products and services (an obvious example being the refuelling of vehicles) that will always rely on physical delivery. Others will vary in the degree to which the Internet channel can contribute to delivery. They suggest a number of factors that influence the extent of online contribution:

- the complexity of the exchange;
- the degree of asset specialization (for example, certain chemicals may require low-pressure transportation);
- the level of reseller fragmentation (powerful distributors may be able to resist manufacturer efforts to sell direct to customers);
- the knowledge of customer needs (if this largely resides with channel partners, they will be difficult to circumvent successfully).

Sawhney and Zabin quote the example of the furniture maker Herman Miller, which introduced a direct selling channel while maintaining the co-operation of its retail partners. The company is a market leader and 90 per cent of its sales are still made through the traditional channel, which is relied upon by the retailers. The mutual dependence means that both producer and retailer are prepared to be flexible.

Mini case study:
3M CORPORATION

3M sells 50,000 different products in 200 countries through forty separate divisions that function as separate companies with their own independent sales staff, IT systems and customer databases. Until recently, this meant that it was impossible to tell how much business the company did with any individual customer. Each division had its own Web site requiring separate registration if a customer wanted to buy products crossing divisional boundaries. There was no integration of data, so that records of earlier transactions by a customer were not available to other divisions. Each Web site also had a different design and navigation procedure. The company decided to address the mounting problem in 1997 with a $20 million initiative to create a global data warehouse storing and co-ordinating customer, product, stock and financial data across the whole company, encompassing 250,000 customer relationships and 500,000 product configurations. Just one registration is required and the whole site is consistent in style. Employees and business partners can access the database and ascertain a global picture of each customer account. Resource allocation can be optimized by analysing customer, partner and product profitability. Physically, 3M remains organized by product divisions, but the unified online 'face' allows customer-centric aggregation of the company's products in a radically different way, facilitating segmentation and promotional campaigns.

Source: Adapted from Sawhney and Zabin (2001)

Models of Internet strategy

Michael Porter has updated his classic model of industry structure and competitive forces influencing company strategy to consider the impact of the Internet. He argues:

> The Internet has created some new industries, such as on-line auctions and digital marketplaces . . . its greatest impact has been to enable the reconfiguration of existing industries that have been constrained by high costs for communicating, gathering information or accomplishing transactions.
>
> (2001: 66)

Porter predicts that successful companies will be those viewing the Internet as a complement to existing operations and not as a separate means of doing business. He provides a useful generic framework to understand the changes in industry structure inspired by the Internet, as illustrated in Table 4.1.

Downes and Mui (1998) identify three significant additional forces at the macro level that have come to prominence in recent years:

- globalization;
- digitization;
- deregulation.

These issues will be considered further in Chapter 11.

Table 4.1 *Impact of the Internet on Porter's Five Forces*

Competitive threat	Example
New market entrants	Low market entry barriers online have allowed companies such as Amazon to achieve market-leading positions in a short space of time
Bargaining power of suppliers	Companies with significant buying power can insist that their suppliers are linked to them electronically and enjoy considerable efficiency gains and cost savings as a result
Bargaining power of customers	Greatly increased as customers use the Web to evaluate competing products and compare prices
Substitutes	A new product becomes available with the same functionality as the incumbent; for example, emails as substitutes for letters
Industry rivalry	Competition between existing firms becomes more intense as efficiencies of the supply chain are increased and costs saved

Source: Porter (2001: 66)

Hackbarth and Kettinger (2000) distinguish three levels of Internet strategy:

Level 1   Individual departments develop isolated applications serving parochial interests that are not co-ordinated into corporate strategy.

Level 2   Functional departments integrate Internet resources to support existing business strategies. Electronic links are also established with customers and suppliers to reduce costs and enhance relationships across the network.

Level 3   Internet strategy drives corporate strategy. New revenue streams are developed as partners (including competitors) are incorporated into a seamless network generating 'win-win' opportunities.

Many organizations will recognize themselves as being at level 1. Some, for example the supermarket chain Tesco (www.tesco.co.uk), are now reaping the benefits of committing the resources necessary to reach level 2. To date, very few have reached level 3. Chapter 2 of the book by Sawhney and Zabin (2001) describes how the evolution of such online initiatives works in practice, using the diverse examples of human resource development, knowledge-sharing and the insurance industry. These authors' ideal of the 'seamless company' is illustrated in Figure 4.3.

The implication from all these models is that organizations should progress over time towards more and more integration of their Internet activities. However, the priorities will vary depending on the type of business model. For example, a consultancy firm will place more emphasis on building online customer relationships or recruitment of staff than the procurement of its own supplies. A firm operating through a reseller network will focus primarily on developing electronic links with its partners, whereas an industrial manufacturer will be more concerned with sourcing raw materials online. These priorities will dictate the direction and emphasis of online developments and not necessarily lead to a 'complete' solution as implied by stage models. Examples of varying Internet strategy priorities within different industries will be demonstrated in more detail in the sample marketing plans in Chapter 10.

The traditional Ansoff Matrix is also useful for considering alternative Internet strategies. Its categories may be summarized as follows:

- market penetration;
- market development;
- product development;
- diversification.

Market penetration, whereby the firm focuses on selling existing products in existing markets, is the 'safest' strategy, but does not maximize the potential of

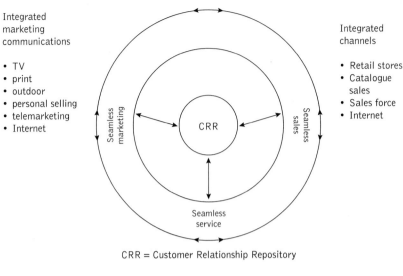

Integrated marketing communications

- TV
- print
- outdoor
- personal selling
- telemarketing
- Internet

Seamless marketing

CRR

Seamless sales

Seamless service

Integrated channels

- Retail stores
- Catalogue sales
- Sales force
- Internet

CRR = Customer Relationship Repository

Unified contact management

- Inperson
- Telephone
- Fax
- Email
- Live chat
- Voice-over IP

Figure 4.3 *The seamless company*

Source: Adapted from Sawhney and Zabin (2001: 139)

the medium. For example, added value can be offered to existing customers by providing online contact options.

Because of its global reach, the Internet is ideal for market development strategies, where existing products can be offered in new markets without the need to establish an expensive physical presence in the country concerned. Chaffey (2002) notes that new market segments may also be drawn in if products are offered online. He quotes the examples of consumer retailer Argos (www. argos.co.uk), which has also attracted business customers, and the business-focused RS Components (www.rswww.com), which is now attracting individual consumers online. It may also be possible to develop new information-based products that provide added value to existing customers (product development). A common application here is the development of free 'white papers' or case studies providing useful information while also promoting the activities of the company itself (see www.rightnowtechnologies.com). Online diversification is unusual because it carries the most risk. Unlike the other categories, both product and market are unknown quantities.

As we saw in Chapter 1, Chaffey *et al.* (2000) note that the degree of Internet marketing sophistication can be categorized in terms of three 'generations'. It is worth repeating their classification here:

First generation	'brochureware';
Second generation	interactive and transactional;
Third generation	rely on convergence of media and are fully integrated into the business (very few exist at present).

These authors also describe how many companies have merely been reactive and have followed a natural progression over time in developing a Web site to support their marketing activities:

Level 0	no Web site;
Level 1	listing in an online directory such as Yellow Pages (www.yell.co.uk);
Level 2	basic 'brochureware' site containing contact details and product information;
Level 3	simple interactive site allowing email queries (www.brunel.ac.uk);
Level 4	interactive site supporting transactions and customer services (www.whsmith.co.uk);
Level 5	fully interactive site providing relationship marketing and facilitating the full range of marketing functions (www.amazon.co.uk).

The amount of effort devoted to Internet marketing strategy tends to be proportional to the position currently occupied by the company on this hierarchy, or, in other words, how central the Internet is considered to be to its marketing activities. This categorization applies to what Chaffey (2002) terms 'sell-side' e-Commerce, the process of selling to customers and collecting money for goods or services rendered. He notes that a similar progression based on levels can be applied to 'buy-side' e-Commerce, which is the sourcing of a firm's products through the supply chain (sometimes called 'procurement'):

Level 1	No use of the Web for product sourcing or electronic integration with suppliers.
Level 2	Review and selection from competing suppliers using intermediary sites, B2B exchanges and supplier Web sites. Orders placed by conventional means.
Level 3	Orders placed electronically through EDI, intermediary sites, exchanges or supplier sites. No integration with supplier's systems. Rekeying of orders needed into procurement or accounting systems.

Level 4   Orders placed electronically, with integration of company's procurement systems.

Level 5   Orders placed electronically, with full integration of procurement, planning and stock control systems.

Chaffey bases this chronology on the results of an international benchmarking study by the UK's Department of Trade and Industry (DTI 2000), where the staged process is likened to climbing a ladder, as illustrated in Figure 4.4.

As was noted earlier in the chapter, while many firms have undoubtedly progressed along these stages in developing both online marketing and procurement strategies, it would be a mistake to assume that such a linear and logical

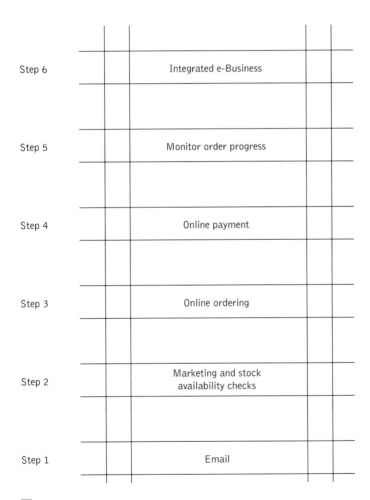

Step 6	Integrated e-Business
Step 5	Monitor order progress
Step 4	Online payment
Step 3	Online ordering
Step 2	Marketing and stock availability checks
Step 1	Email

Figure 4.4 *The e-Business ladder*

Source: Adapted from Department of Trade and Industry (2000)

process has widespread applicability. The models illustrated above are most appropriate for transactional Web sites such as www.debenhams.com, but Chaffey points out that it is important to remember there are several other types of online presence in which collecting payment is not a direct priority:

- Service-oriented relationship-building Web sites such as those operated by PricewaterhouseCoopers (www.pwcglobal.com) and other major consultancy firms focus on the provision of information rather than online transactions.
- Brand-building sites such as www.guinness.com focus on supporting the offline brand.
- Portal sites such as www.yahoo.com provide gateways to a wide range of content across the Web that can be customized to individual preferences.

ACTIVITY

Study the example sites above and then see if you can find other examples where the primary function of the site is not to sell goods or services and collect payment online. For each example you identify, consider whether it focuses on relationship-building, brand-building, information provision, or perhaps something else entirely.

Chaston (2001) provides another perspective for categorizing Internet strategy options:

Product performance – customization of products online (see, for example, www.levi.com);

Transactional excellence – makes it easy to source and buy products, and track progress of delivery (see Amazon's 'one-click' ordering service at www.amazon.co.uk);

Relationship excellence – focuses on personalization based on order history to engender loyalty (again, see Amazon's 'recommendations' based on knowledge of reading habits gleaned from past purchases);

Price performance – special offers for online transactions to maximize the cost-effectiveness of the technology (see www.easyjet.com).

These categories are not mutually exclusive, as the inclusion of Amazon in two categories demonstrates.

ACTIVITY

Look up www.gomez.com and examine the results of the company's ranking of so-called e-tailers according to customer perception of use of use, confidence, site resources, relationship-building initiatives and cost. Try out the leading sites for yourself. Do you agree with the published rankings?

New Internet channels

As was pointed out in Chapter 1, recent technological developments mean that the choice for businesses is no longer merely 'online' versus 'offline'. Increasingly, multiple platforms need to be supported. For example, as mentioned earlier in the chapter, W. H. Smith Online (www.whsmith.co.uk) offers PC, mobile and digital television access. As Chaffey (2002) notes, possible benefits of this strategy include:

- enhanced brand image;
- early-mover advantage;
- learning about the technology from experience;
- customer acquisition;
- customer retention.

Other access platforms at early stages of development include home appliances (Electrolux), vending machines (Maytag) and cars (General Motors' Onstar). Recent developments and their marketing applications will be considered in detail in Chapter 7.

NEW ORGANIZATIONAL STRUCTURES FOR INTERNET STRATEGY

Since the pioneering work of Burns and Stalker (1961), it has been accepted that unpredictable market and technological environments may require 'organic' organizational structures rather than the more traditional 'mechanistic' forms best suited to more stable conditions.

- An example of a 'mechanistic' structure would be the hierarchical and functionally divided arrangements still common in long-established organizations such as banks.
- An example of an 'organic' structure would be the creation of flexible cross-functional project teams within a firm to develop specific new products as the occasion demands.

The assumption is that organic structures can generate a high degree of 'fit' between the external environment and the internal organizational form. However, the scenario of organic structures enabling 'matching' to take place with changing external conditions is increasingly problematic for several reasons:

- The capacity to 'read' the requirements of the external environment is seen as relatively straightforward.
- The boundary between the external environment and the organization is assumed to be clear and distinct.
- The achievement of optimum 'fit' is regarded as a stable and sustainable configuration.

Miles and Snow (1986) criticized this model by noting how the external environment is becoming an increasingly dynamic, complex and 'difficult to read' phenomenon. Even in the 1980s, boundaries between the organization and its environment were becoming increasingly blurred, and further change has taken place since then!

Organizational structure was once the way in which companies could control the flow of information within the firm. Clear hierarchies of responsibility meant that information flowed up and down functional areas (if slowly), but was often not made available to other parts of the organization, or could be excluded from certain individuals. An individual's position in the management hierarchy could be ascertained by the degree of access they held to important information about company strategy, for example. Powerful fiefdoms could be established by individuals who controlled access to such information. With the recent development of the Internet and internal company intranets, such barriers to information access can now be transcended. Real-time access to information may be available to any employee with Internet access, and the activities of diverse functional areas become transparent to employees at all hierarchical levels. On the other hand, the sheer volume of information now available to organizations creates problems of its own. These developments have major implications for marketers seeking opportunities to generate competitive advantage.

As was discussed in Chapter 3, Internet developments therefore provide a powerful incentive for established firms to experiment with new ways of structuring their operations, in order to compete with more flexible new market players such as dotcoms that are not burdened by legacy computer systems and entrenched operational routines. For example, Kalakota and Robinson put consideration of new forms of organizational structure at the heart of Internet strategy:

Maintaining the status quo is not a viable option. Unfortunately too many companies develop a pathology of reasoning, learning and attempting to innovate only in their comfort zones. The first step to seeing differently is to understand that eBusiness is about structural transformation.

(1999: 5)

Day (1998) notes that many firms try to maintain traditional structures when developing their online strategies, and hence become victims of new firms with better alignments of structure and strategy. Effective Internet strategy, however, calls for a re-engineering of processes and structures in order to focus on key customer groups, rather than product or service divisions. It is essential that firms understand how to manage change effectively in order to sustain competitive advantage.

Virtual organizations

Information technology is the catalyst for many recent changes in the structure of organizations. When this critical feature is taken together with general business trends towards reduced management hierarchies, debureaucratization, team-based working and inter-organizational collaboration, then opportunities for entirely new ways of working across both time and space are created. One such innovation is the 'virtual' organization.

For example, some software development companies have considerably enhanced their productivity by creating new product development teams with representatives in the Far East, the Middle East, Europe and North America. Development tasks can thus be passed electronically around the world on a twenty-four-hour basis; as the working day comes to an end in one particular centre, it will still be lunchtime in the next! Taking the degree of 'virtuality' to new extremes, some organizations now outsource all non-core activities and may require no physical presence at all. Amazon.com revolutionized the bookselling market by linking directly with customers through an extensive and interactive Web site, with no physical store presence.

Networked organizations: the importance of business partnerships

An increasingly common type of structure is the 'networked' organization. It may in fact be a 'hybrid' of several firms working together for mutual benefit. The rationale for network formation is that synergies can be created by collaboration that would not be available to any one partner firm acting alone. Networked structures permit organizational flexibility in the face of rapidly changing environmental conditions, and therefore represent a more viable response to the current business operating conditions than the 'organic' structures described earlier. In its simplest form, one party to a collaborative network may obtain access to particular skills that it does not maintain in-house, while the other party is able to 'piggyback' access to new markets that it would otherwise have found difficult to penetrate. In more complex cases, it may be difficult to ascertain the position of organizational boundaries, particularly if an organization is involved in a number of different networks that change composition and evolve over time. In some industries, customers may be attracted to the network on the basis of the quality of the partner organizations involved (note, for example, the often proudly displayed logo 'IBM Business Partner'). Such desirability can lead to the somewhat bizarre situation of firms 'competing to collaborate'.

There are a number of challenges:

- Networked organizations do not just 'happen' by themselves. Even if a 'win–win' situation such as the one described above is evident, the relationship between the partners still has to be developed, nurtured and managed over time if the firms are to work together effectively. Formal legal agreements are often deemed necessary to set out the respective obligations of the partners, especially in the early stages of a relationship. Over time, formal arrangements may be relaxed as trust becomes established. On the other hand, the costs associated with managing the network may counteract the benefits of participation.

- In some cases, an independent 'network broker' may play a critical role in finding suitable partners, reconciling vested interests within the network and negotiating how network benefits are to be shared between the participants. While IBM now talks of the need for 'triple hybrid' managers to manage collaborative relationships effectively, the skills of the network broker can extend even further to encompass those of an entrepreneur, technician, sociologist, businessperson and politician!

- Another challenge concerns how best to deal with collaborators that may also be competitors in other contexts. Although collaborating with competitors does not come naturally for UK firms, research has shown that companies involved in successful inter-organizational networking may become 'strategic collaborators' by internalizing these networking skills and applying them in entirely new contexts in the future. Seth and Sisodia (1999) use the term 'co-opetition' to describe such arrangements. Traditional marketing relationships focus upon five key groups, namely shareholders, employees, customers, suppliers and the community at large (see, for example, McIntosh et al. 1998) Competitors are usually conspicuous by their absence from such lists of potential stakeholders. A wider definition of stakeholders would include 'any group or individual who can affect or is affected by the corporation' (Freeman 1997: 24). According to this definition, a competitor would clearly be a stakeholder of the firm, but the assumption of a competitive rather than collaborative environment remains the norm. In an influential early article, Hamel et al.

(1989) advocated strategic alliances and networking between firms with their proposal that collaboration rather than competition was a winning strategy. They concluded that firms benefiting from competitive collaboration see it as competition in a different form, regarding harmony as the most important measure of success, co-operation as limited and learning from partners as paramount. Key challenges for marketers here include the ability to define the boundary between competition and collaboration, in other words being able to ascertain where the 'internal environment' becomes the 'external environment'.

● At the operational level, another challenge for marketers with regard to Web-based inter-organizational networks is that customer communications do not necessarily involve just one customer talking to one enterprise. Decisions need to be taken on where responsibility lies for particular tasks, to avoid duplication and customer confusion. To provide the kind of service that improves the chance of customer loyalty, companies need to co-ordinate their partners and vendors and customers through extranets that facilitate the sharing of information across company boundaries. Kalakota and Robinson (1999) suggest considering partners and vendors to be part of the firm's extended enterprise, and this means sharing customer communication issues with everyone in contact with the customer through *integrated applications* such as customer service, field service, sales and marketing. This is the most critical issue currently facing 'clicks and mortar' firms in developing a successful Internet strategy. Such open policies of information sharing mean that a whole host of issues have to be addressed concerning the 'ownership' of customer data, notwithstanding the technical difficulties inherent in integrating computer systems belonging to different organizations through an extranet.

While there are undoubtedly many firms that have an established tradition of successful inter-organizational networking, recent Internet developments have made such initiatives increasingly central to e-Business strategy. According to a special report on business and the Internet in *The Economist*,

> The first and most crucial shift in thinking is to get away from the idea that any business is more or less a free-standing entity. The objective for large companies must be to become e-business hubs and for smaller ones to ensure they are vital spokes. The companies involved must be willing to bring suppliers and customers deep into their processes and to develop a similar understanding of their business partners' processes. That implies a degree of openness and transparency which is new to most commercial organisations.
>
> (1999: 98)

115

This warning is endorsed in the same publication by Symonds:

> The ability to collaborate with others may be just as much of a competitive advantage as the ability to deploy the technology. Certainly the technology matters, but getting the business strategy right matters even more. And that may mean not just re-engineering your company, but reinventing it.
>
> (1999b: 112)

Kalakota and Robinson believe that the business design of the future will consist of a flexible network of relationships between firms, customers and suppliers creating 'a unique business organism' (1999: 18). Such structures enable resources to be pooled and hence generate economies of scale, with each network member contributing its particular expertise. It might be argued that these strategies are not new, and represent little more than the outsourcing of non-core activities to reduce costs. Kalakota and Robinson, however, argue that enthusiastic protagonists are going much further: changing corporate cultures, accessing key skills and implementing sophisticated technological systems in a manner that no individual firm could achieve alone.

At an early stage of the Internet era, Tapscott (1995) predicted the creation of competitive advantage in a digital world through collaboration, as networks of enterprises generate efficiencies for the benefit of all parties. In his most recent work he is unequivocal about the value of such networks, which he terms 'Business webs' or 'B-webs':

> Business webs are inventing new value propositions, transforming the rules of competition, and mobilising people and resources to unprecedented levels of performance. Managers must master a new agenda for B-web strategy if they intend to win in the new economy.
>
> (Tapscott *et al.* 2000: 17)

Turner (2000) also emphasizes how the development of the information economy (in particular, the transition from 'market-places' to 'market spaces' without the need for physical contact) is pushing firms towards organizational structures based on networks. As a final example of how networking strategies are transforming organizational structures, Anders (2000) describes how Wells Fargo Bank is creating synergies by teaming with a number of small Internet firms. The bank prefers to learn from the new mindsets and high energy levels of such enterprises, rather than smothering creativity by trying to foster innovation within its own bureaucratic structures and the associated slow decision-making systems. It is a 'win–win' situation, because from an Internet firm's perspective, valuable credibility can be obtained through association with a trusted brand in the banking world.

The main point to take away from this section on partnerships is that the commercial benefits of the Internet go far beyond speeding up and automating a company's own internal processes. It is the ability to spread efficiency gains to the business systems of suppliers and customers that is becoming critical. The ability to collaborate effectively with others may be just as much of a competitive advantage as the ability to deploy the technology.

Separation or integration of online operations?

For 'clicks and mortar' companies, one of the key debates about Internet strategy concerns the implications for organizational structure. The question is whether it should be 'a detailed strategy that is part of the broader strategic marketing planning process . . . or a separate strategy for a company for which the Internet is a significant communications or sales channel' (Chaffey *et al.* 2000: 121).

It is important to distinguish *structure* from operational marketing *activities*. As will be demonstrated in Chapters 8 and 9, regardless of the degree of online/offline structure, actually promoting the company through a combination of online and offline means can generate valuable synergies.

According to Gulati and Garino (2000), the advantages of creating of a separate Internet division are that it provides more focus and flexibility for innovation, it avoids having to integrate legacy systems, and it offers opportunities to float as a separate business. The Abbey National Bank has pursued this strategy in the UK with the development of Cahoot (www.cahoot.co.uk). On the other hand, the advantages of integration include leverage of existing brands, generation of economies of scale, and sharing of information.

Sawhney and Zabin recommend that Internet operations should initially be separated from the rest of the organization, but over the longer term there should be a clear integration plan. They note: 'Remember that e-business is a crutch, not a leg. It is useful to separate it from the lines of business when you are learning to walk, but eventually it needs to become an integral part of the business' (2001: 27). They describe how in 1999 Bank One launched WingspanBank.com in an early example of separating out online business activities. The new venture was promoted under the tag line 'If your bank could start over, this is what it would be.' In practice, while the parent bank offered both online and offline access to its customers, WingspanBank's customers were not allowed to use Bank One branches in order to keep the new venture completely separate from the parent. As a result, the parent bank gained more 'online' customers than its 'Internet only' venture did, despite huge promotional spending. A U-turn was performed and Wingspan brought back into the core business.

KEY DIFFERENCES BETWEEN B2B AND B2C STRATEGIES

Building customer relationships

Although these issues will be explored further in Chapter 6, it is worth noting here the following key differences between B2B and B2C strategies in terms of building relationships with customers, as summarized by Peppers and Rogers (2001).

Relationships within relationships

While a consumer is a single decision-making unit, a business may contain many people with an influence on the decision whether or not to buy a product because of financial control procedures. Questions that need to be addressed include:

- Who has the authority to make the purchase decision?
- How do the purchasing procedures differ from department to department?
- Which individuals might be willing to try a new product?
- Which individuals are the 'gatekeepers' who aim to maintain traditional buying behaviour?
- Are the users of the product the same people who are responsible for purchasing it?

Few, but large, customers

It is difficult for a B2B company to generalize its clients into distinct segments because there may well be far fewer of them than in a B2C context, but still too many to treat individually. This means it can be difficult to focus marketing strategy in an appropriate manner.

Account development selling

Particularly in high-technology markets, customers and suppliers have to exchange detailed information about product design, operation and service. There may be a long period of supplier comparison and evaluation. Because of these timescales and complexity, a B2B company is likely to focus on selling a broader range of products or services to existing customers rather than expanding the total volume of customers.

Channel complexity

The means by which a B2B company connects with its customers through channel partners tend to be more complex than for a B2C company. Distribution channels might well be multi-tiered and global in scope.

Knowledge-based selling

A B2B company may well need to focus on training its business customers on how to use the product most effectively, and indeed even convince them that they have a need for the product at all. A good example here is Dell Computers' 'Premier Pages', which are managed within an extranet and customized according to the needs of individual business customers (www.dell.com).

Infrequent purchases

Actual purchase events by business customers may be rare, particularly if the products are of high value, so maintaining customer relationships in between purchases can be quite a challenge.

Helping clients manage themselves

The complexity of B2B interactions means that providing added value beyond the actual product or service itself in terms of online information or support can help to differentiate a B2B company from its competitors. Cisco (www.cisco.com) has had considerable success with its online technical support functions because not only could customers easily find the information they were seeking, but they soon began to share experiences and answer each other's queries without the need for intervention by Cisco staff.

Thus developing relationships in a B2B context is very different from in a B2C one.

The marketing mix

The application of the marketing mix will be considered in more detail in Chapter 8. In this section, we focus briefly upon the different priorities in B2B and B2C scenarios:

- The composition of the B2B marketing communications mix is likely to place more emphasis on personal selling than on advertising and promotion.

119

- High-value B2B purchases are unlikely to be actually processed online. Instead, the Internet aids the purchase decision by providing easy access to technical information or support rather than transactional capability.
- Internet access is now almost guaranteed in the UK B2B sector, but still decidedly patchy for B2C. These differences will influence the relative degree of overlap between online and offline communications in the two sectors.
- There has been significant interest in the potential of new intermediaries to bring together B2B buyers and sellers in order to reduce costs and inefficiencies in the supply chain. These e-Marketplaces will be considered in the next subsection.

Emerging e-Marketplaces

In its traditional sense, a 'marketplace' allows information to be disseminated and activity between buyers and suppliers to be co-ordinated. Before the slump in 2000, many firms took a huge 'leap of faith', investing large sums of money into new forms of technology and the associated business practices, without always fully realizing the implications of doing so. In the B2B electronic marketplace arena in particular, new exchanges appeared overnight, and from a peak of some 8,000 the inevitable shake-out reduced the number to about 2,000 in early 2002 (according to www.ebusiness.uk.com, February 2002). The e-Marketplace industry is therefore only just beginning to evolve, and a wealth of confusion currently exists as to the optimal strategy for companies to adopt. Many commentators see it as the next wave of the IT/information revolution (as illustrated in Figure 4.5).

The division of markets by spatial competition is now evaporating because of the scalability and virtual geographical nature of the Internet. The emergence of B2B e-Marketplaces is leading to more open collaboration among buyers and suppliers, and the rise in information-based products and services on the Internet has led to the circumvention of traditional intermediary business and information brokers. As evidenced by the travel industry, traditional market structures are being transformed and are giving rise to new forms of intermediaries and business models. With the introduction of new technologies that take advantage of this e-Marketplace phenomenon, markets can perform transactions on a global scale, and thus grow exponentially.

Some of the most notable early impacts on market structure have been in the financial services industry, where online brokerage services such as E*Trade have stolen market share away from many of the established brokerage firms such as Goldman Sachs. Each user of E*Trade benefits from a larger network, since online booking enables a larger number of transactions to be made. It also

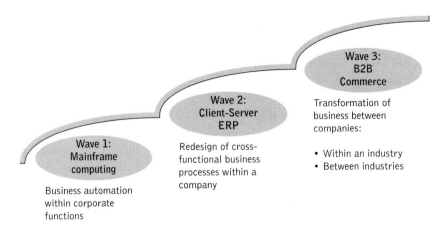

Figure 4.5 *Business to business: the next wave of the information revolution?*
Source: ICG document, 2001

facilitates the exchange of 'investor tips' and the usage of discussion forums on the membership Web pages. As a result, more and more traders are willing to join the E*Trade 'community' and thus use the E*Trade platform for trading.

An optimum e-Marketplace entry strategy must take into consideration a number of factors:

- the estimated lifespan of the market;
- the degree of change required to existing business processes;
- the costs of imitating the pioneer;
- the extent of financial resources available;
- the likely cost of customer acquisition.

At present, despite the ongoing shake-out, many e-Marketplaces are striving to reach critical mass. The initial focus has been on transactions, with only a long-term view taken towards collaboration. Some, particularly independent e-Marketplaces such as Chemdex (chemicals) and Opitmark (equities), have already been forced to close down. Transactions are limited and costly at this stage, and there is little incentive for many industry participants to take advantage of what is currently available. Moreover, creating an online catalogue remains a complex process, and the willingness of many companies to use e-Marketplaces as a medium of exchange has been less than enthusiastic. Some prefer to keep prices confidential and negotiate closely with their customers. In addition, most of the FTSE 100 and Fortune 500 companies are locked in to existing electronic technologies such as EDI, which represents an expensive point-to-point trading network.

121

Despite current low usage levels, the potential for e-Marketplaces is evidenced by many recent studies. For example in a research report conducted by Forrester Research (2001), more than 75 per cent of companies envisaged trading online by 2004, and at least 50 per cent expect to participate in four or more e-Marketplaces by 2004. According to Durlacher (2000), B2B e-Commerce is estimated to account for almost 20 per cent of GDP in the UK and approximately 12 per cent of GDP in all of Europe by 2004. Forrester Research (2001) notes that while industries are moving at different speeds in order to take advantage of B2B initiatives, the automobile industry is leading the way with a forecast spend of almost 200,000 million euros by 2005. For example, Covisint, owned by Ford Motor Co., DaimlerChrysler AG, General Motors Corp., Renault SA, Nissan Motor Co., Commerce One Inc. and Oracle, plans to reduce supply chain costs and bring efficiencies to its owners' business operations. As a result, many B2B e-Marketplaces are incorporating a variety of value-added services in their offering in order to attract participants and differentiate themselves from competitors, and thus create a sustainable revenue model that is also profitable. These services vary across different industries and products, but some of the most common features include:

- auctioning;
- collaborative planning, forecasting and replenishment (CPFR);
- improved knowledge management, reporting and visibility;
- e-Procurement;
- supply-chain management;
- e-Logistics services.

 CHAPTER SUMMARY

To conclude this chapter investigating online strategy, it is worth noting Sawhney and Zabin's comments about the 'tyranny of opposites' (2001: 142). They discuss the folly of 'boundary-focused thinking' as evidenced by such notions as 'old economy versus new economy' and 'business versus e-Business':

> In understanding a dual concept, we tend to focus on the boundaries that define the end points, causing the pendulum of our understanding to swing violently between the extremes of black and white. Upon deeper reflection, the pendulum usually settles in the middle, with the emergence of a unifying principle that merges the opposites.
>
> (2001: 145)

The emerging frameworks discussed in this chapter demonstrate that as far as the Internet is concerned, we are still some way off the 'unifying principle'. It should now be clear to you that already the boundaries between the so-called old and new economies are blurring in the emphasis on integration of online and offline strategies to add value.

Case study:
INTERNET BANKING STRATEGIES

Background

More than a third of the UK's internet population now use the Web to visit banking sites, according to a survey from the Internet monitoring company Netvalue (Figure 4.6). Overall, the number of visitors to e-Banks has grown 27 per cent in the first half of 2001 to top 5 million visitors in July, proving that customers are not being deterred by a run of embarrassing technology glitches.

Gandy (2000) notes that while Internet banking currently attracts just 5–10 per cent of the population, demographic trends dictate that the number will naturally increase over time as more people grow up accustomed to using internet technology. It is also predicted that by 2003, 25 million households will use Internet banking, with 6–10 million of them earning at least $65,000 per annum (Boss et al. 2000). In addition, average revenues generated on the Internet from banking services are projected to grow from 2 to 10 per cent in the USA by the end of 2002 (Daranvala 2000).

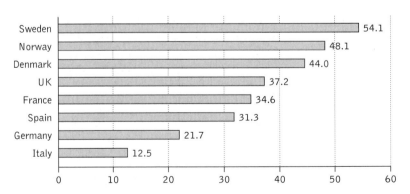

Figure 4.6 *Percentage of Internet users visiting banking sites*

Source: NetValue

123

According to Murphy and Berg (1999), electronic banking strategies are particularly attractive to banks because:

- There is no need to establish a physical presence in new areas, since growth can be accommodated centrally.
- The time-to-market for new products and services is reduced.
- Partnership arrangements (e.g. with retailers) can provide added value for customers at little cost.
- Transactions and updates can occur daily.
- Customers can have access whenever and wherever it is convenient for them.

Consumer behaviour

The Internet revolution is changing consumer behaviour, redefining the role of intermediaries and creating new economic models for business. This sea change poses serious issues for banks, as it places emphasis on two factors: branding and customer satisfaction, neither of which the banks have been particularly good at providing. Banks will have to understand their products and their customers' needs if they are to survive the onslaught of the new competition.

(Timewell and Young 1999: 27)

Retail banking customers are more sophisticated and demanding today than they were twenty years ago. Sophistication has come from a greater awareness of financial matters following saturation coverage in the media. Consumers are more demanding as they seek to maximize precious leisure time by leveraging technology in the pursuit of speedy and effective service. Today's customers require multiple products, a range of channels, seamless service and sound advice from a bank they can trust. But segmenting a customer base in a meaningful way by clustering behavioural and attitudinal traits, lifestyle, familiarity with technology and levels of financial awareness reveals a marked difference in needs. Segmentation and targeting by wealth has revealed that affluent customer groups are more likely to hold a greater number of complex financial products with higher expectations of service excellence and seamless delivery across all channels. This segment is also taking up new technologies faster than the general population and is more active online, leading many banks to create 'high net worth' offerings. In addition, many offline purchases are actually driven by prior online research, so that the benefit of building a 'virtual showcase' for financial products is greater than take-up statistics would suggest, albeit difficult to quantify accurately.

'Bricks' or 'Clicks'?

Around 1998, many banks hoped that online banking would allow them to cut costs dramatically by closing branches. They are now becoming increasingly aware that because customers expect a choice of channels, *absolute* customer numbers are not a reliable indicator of the success of an online offering; rather, the number of *active* online customers is a more meaningful measure. Recognizing that it will take much longer to realize the anticipated cost savings, banks are adopting various strategies to push customers online:

- using branches to educate customers in how to use online services;
- providing reassurances over security;
- offering lower fees and higher interest rates;
- giving staff incentives to encourage customers to use online banking services.

The 'bricks and mortar' bank branch, therefore, is unlikely to become redundant in the near future.

Generally speaking, traditional banks have not adapted products and prices or developed customized propositions for their online operations. 'Pure plays' (new Internet-only banks) have competed so far on the basis of products with aggressive pricing, innovative offerings and investments in new technologies. However, their efforts to win market share have been costly and will not be sustainable in the long term. In a very crowded marketplace, banks will increasingly try to 'poach' other online customers, which is a potentially more profitable strategy than encouraging existing customers to migrate to the Internet.

Some authors are now pointing out the irony that virtual banks are seeking to set up physical operations just as traditional banks create online ones. Gandy argues that competition is not about 'bricks' versus 'clicks': 'It's about integrating both – pulling together the best of what is available through the physical distribution with the best of the Web world' (2000: 122). Yakhlef (2001) examined four dominant banks in the Swedish banking sector to ascertain whether Internet banking was causing the importance of bricks and mortar locations to diminish. The results indicated that banks have achieved better communications with their customers and lowered transaction costs whether they have used the Internet as a complement to or a substitute for their existing operations.

A further structural dilemma for banks is to determine whether their online operations should be integrated into the existing business or 'ring-fenced' as a separate division. Gulati and Garino note that the issue of integration or separation is not a zero-sum game, and that companies should 'strike a balance between the freedom, flexibility, and creativity that come with separation and the operating, marketing, and information economies that come with integration' (2001: 113). In December 2001, the Bank of Ireland decided to merge its previously separate Internet bank, called F. Sharp, into its main operations after attracting just 2,000 customers. The rationale was that the online operation could not offer the high level of customer service on its own that is necessary to support high-net-worth customers (*e.business magazine,* January 2002). Other banks with separate Internet operations such as the Abbey

125

National (www.cahoot.co.uk) and the Co-op Bank (www.smile.co.uk) have focused on less exclusive segments of the market with considerable success in terms of customer numbers, but also at significant cost to the bottom line.

As well as achieving optimum balance between 'bricks' and 'clicks', effective Internet banking calls for customer-based data grouping in order to obtain a unified view of customer activity across a range of product areas (Williams 2000). Up until recently, banks have gathered their data according to particular product lines, so this imperative may also call for significant organizational restructuring to improve internal communications.

FURTHER READING

Cellan-Jones, R. (2001) *Dot.bomb: The Rise and Fall of Dot.com Britain*, London: Aurum.

Hagel, J. and Singer, M. (1999) 'Unbundling the corporation', *Harvard Business Review*, March–April: 133–141.

Lindstrom, M. (2001) *Clicks, Bricks and Brands*, London: Kogan Page.

Peppers, D. and Rogers, M. (2001) *One to One B2B*, New York: Doubleday.

QUESTIONS

Question 4.1

Can you think of any other examples of well-known companies that have established separate Internet divisions?

Feedback – British Airways is another high-profile organization that recently set up a separate division. The objective was to mimic the speedy decision-making and organizational flexibility of an Internet start-up company without the constraints of established business structures and practices.

Question 4.2

Can you think of specific examples of companies for which business priorities or industry structure dictate a more 'unusual' approach to Internet strategy?

Feedback – Companies in the fast-moving consumer goods (FMCG) sector, for example, will tend to focus on brand-building rather than customer relationships, because the mundane nature of many such products is unlikely to stimulate significant consumer interest. However, Procter & Gamble (www.pg.com) has a section for Crest toothpaste that attempts to engage customers by advising on dental hygiene. Pharmaceutical companies can focus on innovation management by sponsorship of health-related online communities to learn more about rare diseases and add considerable value to research and development activities. See Sawhney and Zabin (2001: ch. 2) for more detail.

Question 4.3

Can you think of other examples of virtual organizations? What do you consider to be the particular characteristics that make them successful?

Feedback – Another enormously successful virtual organization is Edmunds.com, which acts as a 'one stop shop' for the automobile market. The firm has redrawn market boundaries by grouping together related services online such as spare parts, leasing facilities, insurance and car dealerships in 'seamless bundles' with a customer perspective. In the 'real' world, such organizations may inhabit different industry groups, and sources of information are consequently fragmented. Edmunds collects referral fees from the connections made between customers and service providers, and, with 80,000 'hits' per day, can provide a highly targeted audience for advertisers. The firm maintains its central position in the webs that it creates by broking connections between buyers (for example, by setting up special interest groups for classic cars) and also between sellers (for example, by linking finance companies with car dealerships). Thus it can also be regarded as a classic example of a 'networked' organization.

Question 4.4

Are networked organizations really a new phenomenon? Can you think of examples of types of business that have always been conducted in this way?

Feedback – Such arrangements have been around for a long time. One practical example concerns building firms that draw upon a network of architects, electricians, plasterers and plumbers as required, on a project-by-project basis.

Question 4.5

Do you think 'networked' or 'virtual' organizations are more likely to develop from established organizations or be entirely new set-ups? Give reasons for your answer.

Feedback – It is much easier for a newly formed organization to devise an innovative organizational structure than it is for an established business to initiate a major structural change. Employees may prefer to maintain a tried and tested formula rather than learn new skills. Jobs may be put under threat. Business processes could be closely tied to 'legacy' computer systems that would be extremely costly to redesign. When Midland Bank designed First Direct, its telephone banking operation, the decision was taken to set up a new operation, with customized new technology and newly recruited staff, rather than attempt to instigate major change within its traditional banking operations.

Question 4.6

In view of the difficulties discussed in the case study at the end of this chapter, why do you think traditional banks are so keen to invest in online banking services?

Feedback – If one bank does not offer its customers the choice, then a competitor will be only too pleased to do so. In addition, competition in the banking and financial sector now does not come only from other bank institutions. Non-bank competitors use smart cards, Internet and software cryptography to reduce their market entry costs and steal a march on traditional banks. One should also consider that programs like Quicken and Digicash were not developed from banks but from the software industry. Retailers such as Tesco have more recent technological infrastructures and their engagement with e-Commerce keeps them ahead (Classe 1997). A survey conducted by the Centre for the Study of Financial Innovation predicted that winning firms in the banking sector within ten years will be those banks with strong brand names, reputed for their customer service, along with supermarkets, insurance companies and telecommunications providers (CFSI 1999).

 WEB LINKS

www.amazon.co.uk
An innovator in online trading and customer relationship-building.

www.argos.co.uk
Traditionally catalogue based, but now offers products through a range of online channels.

www.cahoot.co.uk
The Internet-only bank owned by Abbey National.

www.cisco.com
A market leader in online community-building.

www.dell.com
The leading e-Commerce company Dell Computers, which provides custom-built computers to consumer specification.

www.easyjet.com
A low-cost airline that has migrated its business model to the Web.

www.easyrentacar.com
An Internet-only car hire service that has been forced to upgrade its offline channels to improve service quality and provide customer choice.

www.ebusiness.co.uk
Allows subscription to a new monthly paper-based magazine containing up-to-date case studies and updates on latest trends.

www.e4m.biz
Some good case studies on both B2B and B2C Internet marketing strategies.

www.gomez.com
Ranks online retailers in terms of the quality of service provided.

www.guinness.com
The Web site supports the offline brand image.

www.levi.com
Uses technology to provide customized jeans.

www.open24.gr.
Portal site developed by Greek bank Ergobank.

www.pg.com
An example of an FMCG product Web site. A section on Crest toothpaste provides dental hygiene advice.

www.pwcglobal.com
Leading consultancy PricewaterhouseCoopers focuses on information provision online.

www.righnowtechnologies.com
Provide free white papers and case studies to build the brand and generate goodwill among potential customers.

www.rswww.com
RS Components traditionally offered products via paper-based catalogues, but now has award-winning Internet channels.

www.smile.co.uk
The Internet-only bank owned by the Co-operative Bank

www.tesco.co.uk
Successful retailing site that integrates Internet resources to support offline business strategies.

www.whsmith.co.uk
An excellent example of a 'clicks and mortar' company now offering multi-channel services.

www.yahoo.com
Yahoo!, a major Internet portal site.

www.yell.co.uk
Online directory version of Yellow Pages.

Chapter 5

Branding

GERALDINE COHEN AND LISA HARRIS

MINDMAP

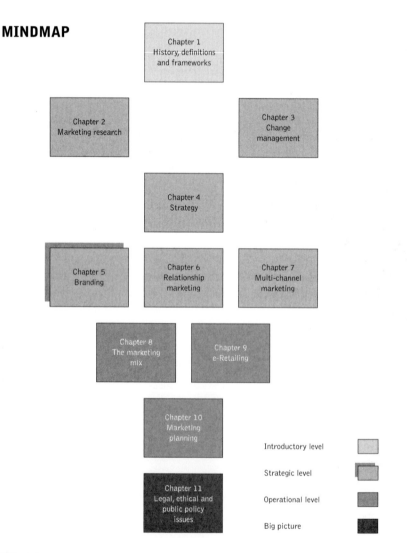

LINKS TO OTHER CHAPTERS

Chapter 4 Strategy	Chapter 6 Relationship marketing	Chapter 7 Multi-channel marketing

- Chapter 4 – Strategy
- Chapter 6 – Relationship marketing
- Chapter 7 – Multi-channel marketing

KEY LEARNING POINTS

After completing this chapter you will have an understanding of:

- The increasingly broad scope of branding which can encompass whole corporations or even business partnerships as well as specific products
- The range of branding strategies available to companies seeking to establish their brands online
- The emerging challenges inherent in multi-channel branding

ORDERED LIST OF SUB TOPICS

- What is a brand?
- The scope of branding
- Global v. local branding
- Key trends in branding
- Online branding strategies
  - Offline brand reinforcement
  - Brand creation
  - Brand followers
  - Brand repositioning
  - Co-branding
- Building brand awareness
- Brand convergence

■ Chapter summary
❖ Case study: Ergobank
❖ Further reading
❖ Questions
❖ Web links

WHAT IS A BRAND?

Kotler *et al.* provide the following rather pragmatic definition of a brand:

> A brand is a name, term, sign, symbol, design, or a combination of these which is used to identify the goods or services of one seller or group of sellers and to differentiate them from those of the competitors.
>
> (2001: 469)

Olins is rather more emotive with this description:

> Branding reaches beyond immediate commercial objectives and touches the soul.
>
> (1999: 128)

Consumers are surrounded by brands in all walks of life, so what makes a successful brand among the clutter? According to Aldisert, 'Branding is not about getting your prospect to choose you over the competition; it's about getting your prospect to see you as the only solution' (1999: 36).

Large sums of money are invested each year in order to create and maintain the awareness of and the preference for a brand. Powerful brands command unwavering consumer loyalty and provide strong competitive advantage in the marketplace:

> The wealth of an organisation is, to a not insignificant extent, judged by the strength of its brands – be it in consumer or business-to-business markets, with brands that have either a high product or a high services component.
>
> (Pickton and Broderick 2001: 22)

The immediate association with a brand tends to be a product name. However, treating a brand only as a name misses the main point of branding. The brand is a complex symbol and can be applied to specific products, whole corporations or even countries. Think, for example, of the Silk Cut brand; the imagery of the crumpled and slashed silk is so strong in its own right that the company was able to circumvent UK legislation preventing cigarette advertising by merely omitting the company name and continuing to advertise.

According to a recent Marketing Trends survey (February 2002) by the Chartered Institute of Marketing (www.cim.co.uk), the key attribute of a strong brand is 'value for money'. This feature was nominated by 69 per cent of marketers from a range of industry sectors who were asked to rank their brands' attributes in order of importance. In comparison, 38 per cent of firms selected 'reliability' as the top attribute, 11 per cent chose 'ethics' and only 3 per cent nominated 'long life'. Strong brands can command consumer loyalty, which means that a sufficient number of consumers will demand these brands in preference to unbranded substitutes, even if the latter are offered with comparable quality and at lower prices. Such brands are said to have **consumer franchise** providing the companies who own them with 'competitive advantage and insulation over their competitors' promotional strategies' (Kotler *et al.* 2001: 469).

According to Kotler *et al.*, a brand can deliver up to four levels of meaning:

1 *Attributes*. A powerful brand will be able to conjure certain product attributes in the minds of the consumer. For example, the Audi brand would suggest such attributes as 'well engineered', 'technologically advanced', 'well built', 'durable', 'high prestige', 'fast' and 'expensive'. The company might use any combination of these attributes to promote its products. In fact, Audi used its slogan 'Vorsprung durch Technik' (progress through technology) for many years.

2 *Benefits*. Customers do not buy product attributes; they buy benefits. In order to have strong brands, companies have to translate attributes into functional and emotional benefits. For example, the attribute 'durable' could translate into the benefit of not having to buy another car for many years. The attributes 'technologically advanced' and 'well built' might translate into the functional and emotional benefits of driving a safe and prestigious car.

3 *Values*. A brand also conveys something of the buyer's values. An Audi customer would value high performance, safety and prestige. The skill of the brand marketer would lie in matching the values of the targeted group of buyers with the brand benefits.

4 *Personality*. A brand also projects a certain personality. This association is often used by motivation researchers when asking, 'If this brand were a person, what personality trait would it have?' The consumers might visualize the brand as having a certain personality with which they might want to be associated. For example, an Audi car might project the personality of a young, successful executive. This brand would attract potential buyers whose actual or desired self-image would match the brand's image.

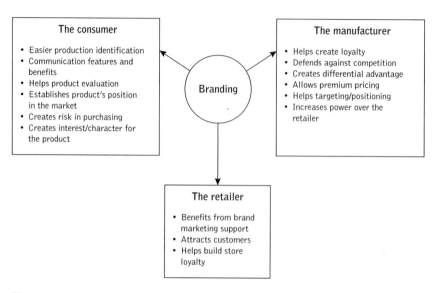

The consumer

- Easier production identification
- Communication features and benefits
- Helps product evaluation
- Establishes product's position in the market
- Creates risk in purchasing
- Creates interest/character for the product

Branding

The manufacturer

- Helps create loyalty
- Defends against competition
- Creates differential advantage
- Allows premium pricing
- Helps targeting/positioning
- Increases power over the retailer

The retailer

- Benefits from brand marketing support
- Attracts customers
- Helps build store loyalty

Figure 5.1 *The benefits of branding to different stakeholder groups*
Source: Adapted from Brassington and Pettitt (2000)

The benefits of branding to a number of different stakeholder groups are summarized in Figure 5.1.

Brands vary in the marketplace according to the level of consumer awareness and loyalty. According to Kotler *et al.*, 'the most lasting and sustainable meanings of the brand are its core values and personality. They define the **brand essence** (2001: 470). Some brands are largely unknown to most consumers except for those closely involved with them. Others enjoy a higher degree of consumer **brand awareness**, whereas brands which are consistently chosen over their competitors are said to have **brand preference**. The most powerful brands can command a high degree of brand loyalty. Such a brand has high **brand equity**, defined by Kotler *et al.* as:

> the value of a brand, based on the extent to which it has high brand loyalty, name awareness, perceived quality, strong brand associations and other assets such as patents, trademarks and channel relationships.
>
> (2001: 470)

As noted by Grassl (1999), some theories see brand equity as being anchored in consumer awareness. Consumers perceive brand equity as the value added to a product by associating it with a brand name and other distinctive characteristics. Brand equity has been recognized as a major dynamic in the business world, owing to the importance of brands, which extends beyond their simple role as

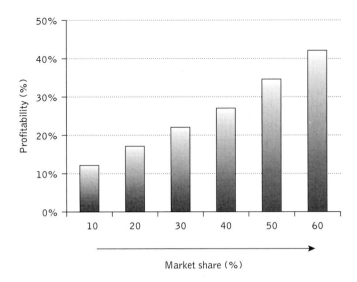

Figure 5.2 *The relationship between profitability and market share*
Source: Cranfield School of Management (2000)

marketing tools. Companies founded on strong brands are often acquired for multiples of their book value. Paul Polman, of Procter & Gamble, once asserted that the difference between the company's market value (*c.* £37 billion) and the accountants' estimate of the value of its assets (*c.* £8 billion) was largely made up by the value of its brands (Pickton and Broderick 2001). Most successful companies have thriving brands and also a coherent, company-wide understanding of the unique benefits of their brands that makes a company worth more than the sum of its parts.

The famous PIMS study (Profit Impact of Marketing Strategy) established that the brand with the highest market share is always more profitable. Specifically, a brand with a 40 per cent market share is three times as profitable as a brand with only a 10 per cent market share. This important relationship between profitability and market share identified in the PIMS study is shown in Figure 5.2.

What are the world's most powerful and valuable brands? Interbrand, (www.interbrand.com), a global branding consultancy, has identified seventy-five 'billion-dollar' brands. The brand valuation calculation is based on analyses of economic earning forecasts for the world's best-known brands. At the top of the 'billion-dollar brand league' are Coca-Cola and Microsoft (Table 5.1). According to Interbrand's valuations, some of the more 'traditional' brands such as Kodak, Heinz, Xerox, Hertz, Burger King, Johnnie Walker, Guinness and Pampers have lost their brand value recently, while representatives from the 'up and coming' industries have gained. Although Ericsson's value is estimated to

Table 5.1 Brand league table

Rank 2000	Rank 1999	Brand	Country	Brand value 2000 ($bn)	Brand value 1999 ($bn)	percent- age change
1	1	Coca-Cola	USA	72.5	83.8	−13
2	2	Microsoft	USA	70.2	56.7	24
3	3	IBM	USA	53.2	43.8	21
4	7	Intel	USA	39.0	30.0	30
5	11	Nokia	Finland	38.5	20.7	86
6	4	General Electric	USA	38.1	33.5	14
7	5	Ford	USA	36.4	33.2	10
8	6	Disney	USA	33.6	32.8	4
9	8	McDonald's	USA	27.9	26.2	6
10	9	AT&T	USA	25.5	24.2	6
11	10	Marlboro	USA	22.1	21.0	5
12	12	Mercedes	Germany	21.1	17.8	19
13	14	Hewlett-Packard	USA	20.6	17.1	20
14	—	Cisco Systems	USA	20.0	*	*
15	20	Toyota	Japan	18.9	12.3	53
16	25	Citibank	USA	18.9	**	**
17	15	Gillette	USA	17.4	15.9	9
18	18	Sony	Japan	16.4	14.2	15
19	19	American Express	USA	16.1	12.6	28
20	24	Honda	Japan	15.2	11.1	37
21	—	Compaq	USA	14.6	*	*
22	13	Nescafé	Switzerland	13.7	**	**
23	22	BMW	Germany	13.0	11.3	15
24	16	Kodak	USA	11.9	14.8	−20
25	21	Heinz	USA	11.8	11.8	−1
26	27	Budweiser	USA	10.7	8.5	26
27	23	Xerox	USA	9.7	11.2	−14
28	26	Dell	USA	9.5	9.0	5
29	29	Gap	USA	9.3	7.9	18
30	28	Nike	USA	8.0	8.2	−2

Source: Adapted from Kotler *et al.* (2001)

Notes: * New entry ** Not comparable, owing to change in availability data

have plunged by 47 per cent between 2000 and 2001, its arch-rival Nokia surged forward a staggering 86 per cent over the same timescale. The only online brands currently in the Interbrand league table are AOL, Yahoo! and Amazon.com, with the latter two showing remarkably rapid growth in brand value (Kotler *et al.* 2001: 472).

The following criteria were used by Interbrand to estimate the financial value of the leading brands:

- brand weight, defined as measure of influence in the market;
- brand length, meaning the extent to which the brand can be extended to cover a range of products;
- brand breadth, meaning the extent of the brand's appeal to diverse age groups or geographical markets;
- brand depth, defined as the degree of loyalty that the brand has inspired in its customers;

THE SCOPE OF BRANDING

Knox (2000) summarizes the potential rewards associated with successful branding as shown in Table 5.2. These issues demonstrate the broad scope of branding and will be discussed in more detail throughout the chapter.

Pickton and Broderick (2001) argue that commodity-type products such as metal tubing or screws, which in the past have been perceived as 'non-branded', should be considered as branded through their packaging, labelling or logos.

Table 5.2 *The scope of branding*

Supplier/alliance markets	Value-managed relationships Co-branding
Recruitment markets	Enhanced recruitment opportunities
Influencer markets	Share prices Safe investment
Referral markets	Channel co-operation Word of mouth endorsement
Customer markets	Brand loyalty Market penetration Brand awareness Brand stretching Price premium
Internal markets	Employee retention and loyalty Customer orientation

Source: Adapted from Knox (2000)

137

Companies are creating brands through the consistent use of names, logos, a form of packaging, colours, shapes, typography, short descriptions or slogans. Branding can be provided through a variety of mechanisms, such as brand names, brand logos, trade names or trade marks.

Brand name

A brand name is the part of a brand that can be spoken and which includes letters, numbers or symbols, such as Coca-Cola, VW, or Yahoo. This might be different from the legal name of the company; think, for example, of the use of initials such as AA or RAC, or numbers such as 7-Up or 3M, which have created enduring brands. Brand names can be reinforced through the use of a distinctive colour or typography. The classic example is the Coca-Cola brand name, which has a strong visual appeal and is recognized anywhere in the world through the design rather than the words. Coca-Cola is easily identifiable whether the name is written in English, Arabic, Russian or Chinese because the look is always the same.

Trade name

The trade name is the legal name of an organization, which might or might not be related to its other branded products. For example, the organization with the full trade name of National Westminster Bank Plc is branded as NatWest Bank. Some companies, such as Lever Brothers or Procter & Gamble, will underplay the corporate brand, concentrating all their promotional efforts on their product brands such as Persil, Surf and Radion. Few consumers will realize that these apparently competitive brands come from the same manufacturer.

Trade mark

A trade mark is a brand name, symbol or logo that is registered and legally protected for the owner's sole use. In line with EU trademark legislation, the 1994 Trade Marks Act allows organizations to register not only brand names and logos but also product shapes and packaging, smells and sounds. This means that the Coca-Cola bottle, the Toblerone chocolate bar and the Heinz tomato ketchup bottle are as protected as their respective brand names (Brassington and Pettitt 2000). Trade marks are valuable assets, and organizations invest large sums of money in creating them and maintaining consumer awareness. Because of their value in the eyes of the consumer, they often became prey to counterfeiters and the illegal counterfeit trade. Manufacturers of luxury branded goods such as perfumes, watches or Nike trainers are fighting to try to stem the growing flow of low-cost copies of their branded goods.

Table 5.3 *Brand logos*

Visual brand logo	Brand name	% Correctly identified
Golden arches	McDonald's	90
Crossed fingers	National Lottery (UK)	83
Piper	BT	82
Tyre man	Michelin	76
Badge logo	BMW	73

Source: *Marketing* (February 1998: 24)

Brand logo or brand mark

A logo is the element of a brand. It only infrequently includes words or letters, being more usually made of symbols or pictures. The logo can also be termed a brand mark; examples include the golden arches known the world over as the symbol of McDonald's, or the four coloured squares that have come to symbolize Microsoft Windows.

A survey reported in *Marketing* magazine (February 1998) asked 300 people to correctly identify twelve visual brand logos. Table 5.3 shows the high percentage of logos that were correctly identified, thereby illustrating the enduring nature of the images created by these logos (Pickton and Broderick 2001: 30).

Some companies have successfully 'stretched' their brands to encompass product variations. Think, for example of Galaxy chocolate bars, muffins, small wrapped sweets, selection boxes . . . Eventually, the brand might be stretched into completely new product categories, in which case it becomes known as a **brand extension**. For example, Mars, a company with well-established confectionery brands, has recently extended its brands (Snickers, Twix, etc.) into the ice-cream market. Brand extensions represent an opportunity for firms to use the equity inherent in the names of existing brands to enhance marketing productivity and attract new customer segments.

As mentioned at the beginning of the chapter, branding need not just apply to specific products. It also takes place at the corporate, partnership, geographical region or even national level. In Chapter 6, we will discuss **employer branding**, which refers to the image that a company seeks to put across to prospective employees in order to brand the organization as a 'good place to work'. **Corporate branding** can encompass a range of products, services and their associated image which together form part of the benefits 'package' offered to consumers, who want to know that they can trust the company they are doing business with. Corporations that are branded in this way offer reduced risk. This is especially important in online transactions, which can compound consumers' concerns over transaction security and privacy.

Mini case study:
REINFORCEMENT OF CORPORATE E-BRANDING IN THE CHEMICAL SECTOR

Despite the present economic uncertainty and the anticlimax of the dotcom debacle, B2B commerce is set for significant growth. 'Old-economy' industries such as the chemical sector are increasingly using branding strategies more associated with consumer branding giants like Unilever, and Procter & Gamble. Although Dow Chemical, DuPont and BP are well-established B2B brands using sophisticated marketing strategies, the industry in general is perceived as environmentally benign at best and insensitive at worst. It is often misunderstood by its end users, the public, who tend to be unaware of its impact on everyday life. That is why the chemical giants are intensifying their branding efforts in order to reach and shape the perception of their customers, shareholders, employees, investors and the media. There is mounting pressure on 'old-economy' companies just like those in the chemical industry to be more transparent in terms of corporate behaviour. They are using corporate branding as a fundamental communication vehicle through television and radio, and, increasingly, through the Internet.

A recent survey by Accenture on purchasing decision-makers across several industries, including the chemical sector, examined the value of B2B brands in the 'new economy' and the impact of the Internet on the total customer experience. The findings revealed that, contrary to popular opinion, marketing and branding are more critical to B2B than to B2C. B2B buyers say that their single most important preference is a strong brand, followed by service; price is third and variety last.

Source: Adapted from Bartels and Hoffmann (2001: 18–19)

GLOBAL V. LOCAL BRANDING

In this section, we will examine the arguments for and against global branding. The decision whether to standardize or adapt the brand by varying the marketing mix elements is a major one for any organization operating outside its home environment. Standardization through global branding allows the organization to maintain a consistent image and identity throughout the world. It provides economies of scale and is particularly valuable for maximizing impact with the internationally mobile customer. It works best within an identified international segment and with a product of well-defined complexity. However, few brands can be regarded as genuinely global in this sense, and many companies have made some costly mistakes by ignoring the often significant cultural differences between markets around the world.

140

The process of **globalization** involves the transfer of an existing business system to other countries or the management of another business system in other countries. The terms 'international', 'multinational', 'global' and 'transnational' have been used to describe different stages in the globalization ladder of business development. The decision for a nationally based business to 'go global' will depend on certain factors such as demography, entry modes, socio-cultural diversity, as well as the approach and management style to be used when entering new markets. The USA today represents the largest national market in the world, with roughly 25 per cent of the total world market for all products and services. The fact that 75 per cent of the world market potential is outside US national territory has been the driving factor for many US companies to 'go international', and even to extend further and 'go global'. With three-quarters of its revenues generated by its soft drink business outside the USA, Coca-Cola, acknowledged as the most successful global brand, has driven the message of globalization further than anybody else.

In Europe in the early 1990s, 'pan-European' advertising was all the rage among direct marketing companies in the UK. A precursor of global communications, it was based on a simple idea, namely that consumers in various countries fall into the same socio-demographic categories, with similar, if not identical, buying habits and tastes brought about by low-cost cross-border travel. The same imagery, messages, product and brand positioning are used across all campaigns and all markets. Economies of scale could be achieved and global brands built as campaigns were extended from one country to another. This philosophy has worked well in some cases. A good example is basic office software such as Microsoft Word, which works equally well in most countries, once it has been localized for language characteristics. Other examples are soft drinks like Coca-Cola or imaging products like Kodak, which need only minimal changes to adapt global campaigns to suit local tastes.

However, it is a different story for cars, which are more of a 'lifestyle' purchase. Consumer tastes in cars vary more widely between countries, and achieving substantial economies of scale in either product development or advertising is more difficult. Ford has been one of the manufacturers most successful in using a modular approach to car manufacturing and marketing. Recognizing that there are strong differences in consumer preferences, Ford has reduced the number of components – and thereby has achieved economies of scale – without affecting the number of options available to customers in each of the seventy-five different national markets in which it sells cars. Ford manages to use a modular approach also in its advertising messages, emphasizing safety in Scandinavia, performance in Italy, design in France and handling in Germany. The Ford brand may be global, but the product and its supporting marketing effort are very much local.

While the Internet could be argued to support global branding because of its worldwide scope, in practice few brands have been extended across national boundaries successfully. Lindstrom (2001) notes that a global branding strategy should actually be a local plan for each component market, as to apply a standard approach worldwide without considering local preferences and cultural differences is doomed to failure. Yahoo! is an example of a brand that is recognized worldwide, but the company still has had to adapt its approach by partnering with a local company with detailed knowledge of the Japanese marketplace in order to be accepted. Even companies like Coca-Cola and McDonald's localize their marketing communications to suit specific occasions such as sporting events despite the global appeal of their brands. The positioning and branding of American Express is consistent throughout the world, but elements of the marketing mix such as advertising are varied to suit local conditions. Chapter 8 will consider the management of the marketing mix in more detail.

Both online and offline branding strategies need to be localized in terms not only of meaning, but also of relevancy. Almost certainly the editorial content will have to be adapted in terms of products and services relevant to the population targeted and in the dialects used with the idioms and colloquialisms used locally. For example, a Web site in Spanish has to be made specific to Spanish-speaking users in Spain, Mexico, Argentina or the south of France. Similarly, colours must be chosen with care when a brand is aimed at a global audience. Some colours such as black, white and red have different symbolic or religious meanings throughout the world. A black background can appear 'cool' and 'sophisticated' to an American audience, but black is linked to death and bad luck in Chinese culture. Purple has religious significance in Catholicism, as has green in the Islamic world. Customer feedback is necessary when designing promotional activities in order to avoid culturally insensitive choices. Consultancy companies such as Mainspring (www.mainspring.com) perform 'cultural audits' on sites destined for global audiences, to make sure mistakes like these do not damage the brand.

Mini case study:
GLOBALIZATION CAN GO BADLY WRONG ...

Translations

- Thai dry cleaner: 'Drop your trousers here for best results.'
- Sign in a Hong Kong tailor: 'Ladies may have a fit upstairs.'
- Moscow guide to a Russian Orthodox monastery: 'You are welcome to visit the cemetery where famous Russian and Soviet composers, artists and writers are buried daily, except Thursdays.'

- Spanish sports shop called 'The Athlete's Foot'.
- French dress shop advertising: 'Dresses for street walking.'
- Back of a jacket in Japan: 'Vigorous throw up. Go on a journey.'

Hotel signs across the world

- Paris: 'Please leave your values at the front desk.'
- Japan: 'You are invited to take advantage of the chamber maid.'
- Zurich: 'Because of the impropriety of entertaining guests of the opposite sex in the bedroom, it is suggested that the lobby be used for this purpose.'
- Romania: 'The lift is being fixed for the next day. During that time we regret that you will be unbearable.'

Badly translated adverts

- 'Come alive with Pepsi' – 'Rise from the grave with Pepsi' (German)
- 'Avoid embarrassment, use Parker pens' – 'Avoid pregnancy, use Parker pens' (Spanish)
- 'Body by Fisher' – 'Corpse by Fisher' (Flemish)
- 'Chrysler for Power' – 'Chrysler is an aphrodisiac' (Spanish)
- 'Tropicana orange juice' – 'Tropicana Chinese juice' (Spanish in Cuba)
- 'Tomato paste' – 'Tomato glue' (Arabic)
- 'Drinking coffee provides a relaxing break and takes the load off your chest' – 'Ease your bosoms. This coffee has carefully selected high-quality beans and roasted by our all the experience' (Japanese)

Sources: Jobber (2001); Keegan and Green (1997).

KEY TRENDS IN BRANDING

According to Knox (2000), there are a number of important branding issues that demonstrate how branding strategy is currently evolving and growing in sophistication:

1 The focus of brand trust is shifting from products to people and processes. To focus on product excellence is not enough if the overall package is let down by poor customer service. As many product characteristics are easy to copy, what is often the only differentiator between companies is the value added to the brand image by the people and processes behind the product. These issues will be considered further in Chapter 6.

2 Brands no longer close the sale. Customers are increasingly expecting a complete 'package' and not just a 'one-off' product. For example, for

someone deciding to buy a new car, it is not just the vehicle itself but the service elements that come with it that form a critical part of the purchase decision, such as regular servicing, courtesy cars, insurance and finance packages, etc.

3 Brands are strategic management tools. As the scope of branding becomes increasingly broad and encompasses not only the product and associated services but the entire corporate ethos in many cases, then branding becomes ever more strategic and central to business success.

4 The price of a brand is not what customers pay for it. From the customer's perspective, the price of the brand includes search costs, peace of mind if needs are met, and time-saving through familiarity with people and processes. This means that customers tend to seek a longer-term relationship rather than a one-off transaction in order to leverage maximum value from the buying experience.

5 Branding moves beyond marketing. As branding becomes ever more strategic in scope, then brand management starts to involve the whole organization and is no longer merely regarded as a promotional task for the marketing department. In Chapter 1, we introduced the concept of the 'marketing orientation', which holds that the entire company is responsible for adopting a customer focus; marketing therefore becomes an attitude of mind rather than an operational business function. This issue will be explored further in Chapter 6.

6 Brands are spreading beyond corporate boundaries. Branding has already spread from the product to the corporate level, and is now crossing organizational boundaries. In the next section, we will examine innovative branding strategies, whereby companies add value by operating as part of a network of firms in order to add value by each contributing particular expertise or service features.

ONLINE BRANDING STRATEGIES

In the 1990s, online brands evolved with amazing speed. Yahoo! took just five years to become a global brand, whereas Coca-Cola took fifty. Now that the online market has matured, the degree of clutter means that brands find it harder to stand out from the crowd. In addition, the anonymity of the Internet medium means that companies have to assert their brand identity more strongly online (Bartels and Hoffmann 2001). Many leading organizations are currently grappling with the challenge of translating their brands to the online context. According to Lou Gerstner, chief executive of IBM, 'Branding in a network world will dominate business thinking for a decade or more' (Willcocks and Sauer 2000: 28).

One aspect of branding that has developed significant online momentum is **viral marketing.** The low-budget horror movie *The Blair Witch Project* owed its worldwide success to a vast volume of 'word-of-mouth' recommendations passed around Internet chat rooms. Hotmail account holders send an advertising message that is attached to the bottom of every email. Email newsletters offer an opportunity to raise brand awareness and generate goodwill through dissemination of useful free content, and many contain the plea to 'forward to a friend'.

Corporate branding is an important factor in building up reputation, Web traffic and, ultimately, revenues online. Reputation is one aspect of branding that is often highlighted as an intangible asset: very difficult to create, imitate or substitute, but extremely important as a source of competitive advantage. Research by Kotha *et al.* (2001) showed that companies with an established reputation are more likely to attract attention online than new Web-based firms. Brand-building features such as community groups provided on the Web site allow customers to interact and share information with others, which helps in building up a degree of trust that can partly compensate for the absence of an established retail presence and then result in increased revenues. For a good example, see the book reviews posted at Amazon. It should be noted, however, that such facilities can also be used by disgruntled customers to humiliate a brand publicly, and the way in which a company responds to such complaints can make it a laughing stock if the task is handled badly. Special sites have also sprung up to allow customers to vent their frustrations; see, for example, www.sucks500.com, which features a long list of complaints against a range of companies.

There are a number of questions facing companies in respect to online branding strategy, for example:

- Should a company leverage its existing offline brands on the Internet or should new e-Brands be created?
- What kind of service is it offering online? Does it enhance the offline service offering, or is it something entirely new?
- Is the matter of reaching the market quickly important? In this case, it is speedier to leverage an existing brand than to launch a new one.
- Is the online strategy fraught with the risk of failure? Then it may be better to create a new online brand than to decrease the traditional brand equity by associating with a failure.

Alternative online branding strategies have been summarized by Willcocks and Sauer (2000) (see Figure 5.3, overleaf) as follows.

Offline brand reinforcement

Many well-established companies are using the Internet as an additional channel to reinforce brand awareness rather than focus on transactional e-Commerce capabilities. Migrating existing brand names from the real world into the virtual

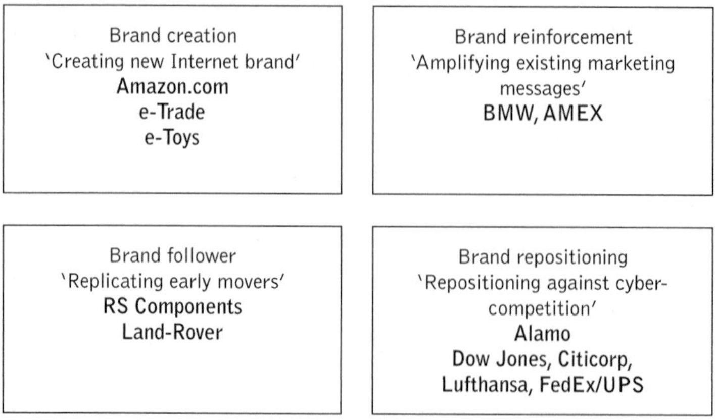

Brand creation 'Creating new Internet brand' **Amazon.com** e-Trade e-Toys	Brand reinforcement 'Amplifying existing marketing messages' **BMW, AMEX**
Brand follower 'Replicating early movers' **RS Components** Land-Rover	Brand repositioning 'Repositioning against cyber- competition' Alamo **Dow Jones, Citicorp, Lufthansa, FedEx/UPS**

Figure 5.3 *Brand strategies on the Internet*

Source: Adapted from Willcocks and Sauer (2000)

one is the simplest and most common approach. The best chances of success are those companies with strong, established brands, such as, for example, BMW. The company's mission was to make its site 'drive and feel like a BMW' by offering users the opportunity to experience the brand. In 2000, BMW allowed its customers to build their own dream cars online and even to hear the sound of its M-series engine in the Z3 Roadster (www.bmw.com). The success of this campaign posed a dilemma for BMW: how far should it go towards selling through the Internet? Traditionally, the company has tended to prefer the face-to-face interaction and bonding offered by the potential customer's visit to a BMW dealership.

Richard Branson's Virgin Group spans 170 businesses, from airlines and railways to music stores, financial services and even bridal wear. www.virgin.com achieved 1.9 million visitors in its first year, making the Web site the twelfth most popular destination online in the UK. Now Branson is trying to build it into one of the world's top portals and has spent more than $225 million developing Net businesses and services, ranging from a global mobile phone company to a sister site called www.radiofreevirgin.com offering software that turns a PC into a digital radio. Branson believes that the Virgin name, known for its hip, consumer-friendly image, will translate well across his Web businesses. 'Virgin.com isn't a company, it's a brand,' says a Virgin director who is overseeing the company's e-Commerce activities. The red-and-white Virgin logo is a big attraction for potential partners too. Following in the footsteps of easyJet, the logo and the Web site address are being splashed on everything, from shopping bags in Virgin Megastores to the sides of trains and the tails of planes, saving a fortune on advertising. 'Considering the brand recognition that Virgin has wherever it operates, they've got the right strategy in place: an online marketplace for offline products,' says Jamie Wood, head of European equity research at J. P. Morgan. 'The Web works best when a brand aggregates a variety of services into one place with a guaranteed level of service' (Capell, 2001).

Debenhams is another good example of a 'clicks and mortar' company that has successfully migrated its brand online (as demonstrated in the case study in Chapter 3). The firm has set up a separate Internet division that is 'ring-fenced' from the parent, but which still benefits from association with a trusted brand image. In the current climate of dotcom failures, the reputation and values associated with the traditional Debenhams brand are a powerful strategic asset. In fact, many staff who left the company in the rush to set up dotcoms in 1999 have since sought to return to Debenhams, seeking the security of working for an established brand name in the retailing sector.

Brand creation

Some companies, particularly in the financial services sector, have established new online brands rather than use the Internet to reinforce existing brands. In the UK, examples include Egg (www.egg.com), which is owned by the Prudential, and Smile (www.smile.co.uk), which is owned by the Co-operative Bank. Egg has been particularly successful in attracting customers, and enjoys high levels of brand awareness, but the attractive rates of interest that it offers to savers and the high level of advertising expenditure have resulted in a perilous financial position. The bank hopes to achieve profitability by cross-selling more lucrative products to its savings account customers. Establishing new brands for online activity offers traditional banks – which often have a rather staid image – the opportunity to 'start again' and develop a more modern style to appeal to new customer segments online. However, one drawback is the increasingly high cost of establishing an online brand as the marketplace gets ever more crowded. Another is the increasing tendency for customers to expect a choice of channels, and not be forced to conduct all their banking online. Consequently, it is rumoured that Egg is now looking to set up a physical branch network. It has also been suggested that in the early days of the Internet, the strategy of brand creation was a 'safety net' so that if the online venture failed, the established brand would not suffer by association with it.

Brand followers

Brand followers copy successful 'early adopters' of online marketing. The high degree of visibility online means that this strategy is increasingly easy to achieve, as innovations can be easily copied. Many traditional booksellers have attempted to follow Amazon's approach to online trading, and while this might be a low-risk strategy, it sends a clear signal to the market that the company is just a 'me too'. Such companies, by making no attempt to distinguish their offering from competitors', make it appear that they are not really committed to Internet channels.

Brand repositioning

Developing an Internet presence can be a timely opportunity to reposition the brand. The courier company UPS (www.ups.com) took advantage of Internet technology to add value to its brand by including a tracking service so that customers could tell whereabouts their package was in the delivery schedule at any time. Willcocks and Sauer (2000) note that such new features enabled the company to reposition itself in the marketplace as an information provider rather than as a courier company.

Co-branding

According to Strauss and Frost (2001), **co-branding** occurs when two different companies put their brand name on the same product. This is done in the competitive chase for innovation offline as well as online. Banks, for example, are under strong pressure to capture customer lifetime value as new technology and varying distribution channels enable online market entrants to gain ground. One solution has been strategic alliances such as that between British Airways and the Royal Bank of Canada in 1999. The companies teamed up to provide financial services to frequent travellers, expatriates and members of the British Airways Executive Club. According to *The Banker*, 'For both bank and airline there is a win–win situation in which the strategic alliance helps expand the bank's customer base and both brand values can be reinforced' (1999: 72).

Co-branding is quite a common practice on the Internet as it is a good way for firms to build synergy through expertise and brand recognition. An excellent example was the barter arrangement between Yahoo! and Pepsi, whereby Pepsi plastered the portal's address on 1.5 million cans. In return, Yahoo! took Pepsi's already established loyalty programme 'Pepsi Stuff' online. www.PepsiStuff.com is a co-branded Web site that lets consumers collect points from bottle caps. The loyalty points are redeemable for prizes ranging from electronic goods to concert tickets. Three million consumers logged on and registered on the Pepsi Stuff Web site, providing Pepsi with detailed consumer information that would have been very difficult and expensive to obtain through market research or from focus groups. According to Neuborne (2001), information was available in days that once took months to get. Sales rose by 5 per cent during the online promotion and the cost was 20 per cent of what it had been as a mail-in project. From this experience, Pepsi learned that while banner advertisements and other more traditional advertising have had some success, it is the creation of creative and interactively engaging Web sites like this that has given the brand the most impetus online.

BUILDING BRAND AWARENESS

Powerful companies with large promotional budgets are reinforcing their competitive advantage through strong advertising offline as well as online. In 1998, the average cost of building a national online brand was about $5–10 million. In 2000, it cost $50–100 million, a tenfold increase. In 1999, 40 per cent of web development budget was going on towards marketing, with more than 80 per cent of all television commercials in the USA featuring a Web address and 30 per cent promoting an individual Web site (Lindstrom, 1999). Excessive spending on brand-building without compensating revenues can be blamed for the downfall of many dotcoms (see the Boo case study in Chapter 1 for a classic example). Many of those that survive have incurred significant cost. According to Haigh (2000), AOL has so far spent $2 billion on building its brand identity and Yahoo! $300 million.

Web site promotion is becoming more sophisticated, but there is always the danger of targeting the wrong audience, which was estimated to be the case in as many as 70 per cent of 1999 campaigns. This has led to a quest for a more effective way. Some companies have been quite creative. For example, Orange Technologies, during the launch of a special youth product, offered to repaint all its customers' cars free of charge. The only condition was that Orange would choose the colour. (Guess which one!) After just one day, 24 cars had been painted, at the cost to Orange of $4,200. Even giants like Yahoo! have resorted to creative, inexpensive offline promotions. Chauffeurs holding signs at airports to pick up 'Mr Yahoo!' have actually been corporate promotions (Lindstrom 1999). Gimmicks like this resulted in extensive free publicity for such companies in the media in the early days of the Internet. Small companies have found it hard to compete with these levels of expenditure, and hence need to be particularly creative in order to maximize the value of small promotional budgets.

Many advertisers have adopted the now widespread use of banner advertisements as branding tools rather than transactional tools. 'There is absolutely a branding opportunity for advertisers on the Web,' says Jim Nail, senior analyst at Forrester Research, in Cambridge, Massachusetts (Heim, 2001). A good example is the Visa credit card company (www.visa.com), which in the past has blanketed the Web with banner advertisements. The consistency of the Visa brand has been likened to a reader consistently seeing the same advertisement on the back of a magazine. This in effect is helping Visa to solidify its brand image. Nevertheless, research undertaken by Dahlen (2001) on banner effectiveness has found that there are major differences between the performances of banner advertisements for familiar and unfamiliar brands. Unfamiliar brands initially perform badly, with very low click-through rates, but with repeated exposures the response rate increases. Familiar brands initially attract interest but customers quickly get bored with their campaigns, and response rates fall. Moreover, major differences were found between novice and expert Internet users with regard to their relative susceptibility to Web advertising. Dahlen therefore recommends that unfamiliar brand banner advertisements should have long-term goals, allowing multiple advertising exposures. For familiar brands, on the other hand, there should not be a long-term goal, as the advertisements quickly 'wear out'.

BRAND CONVERGENCE

Creating a strong brand both online and offline involves far more than the 'look and feel' of the Web home page, the logo or the new brochure. The very essence of a strong brand philosophy is the way in which the staff serve customers – a key part of creating **brand convergence**. Whether the customers are surfing the Web site or using the service offline, the organization must ensure consistency of all 'customer touch points' to create a single, comprehensive and memorable brand. This involves significant management and staff training, motivation and constant follow-up. Striking the right balance between online and offline delivery systems to satisfy and deepen customers' relationships and maintain the uniqueness of the brand has to be the key to success. This issue will be expanded upon further in Chapters 6 and 7. A convergent brand strategy has to address some or all of the following issues:

- Which are the channels that the customers find best suited for delivery of each service: a branch, telephone or online?
- Are the marketing strategic plans adequate to support integrated delivery through all the channels?
- Are the staff motivated and appropriately trained? Remember, a 'convergent brand' will have an impact on all areas of the organization.

Ensuring integration of high-touch/high-tech delivery channels, creating a consistent, differentiated brand and maintaining acceptable operating costs per customer will be essential for survival. Offering customers relevant services and building a strong brand image in this way are seen as vital for the future of industries such as banking (Weber and Seibert 2001).

Mini case study:
E-COMMERCE BRANDING AS PART OF INTEGRATED MARKETING COMMUNICATION STRATEGY

In the 'post-dotcom' era, one of the most important lessons learned by the survivors is that it takes more than a flashy Web site to succeed. It depends on a good business plan, promotion, focused customer service and an efficient distribution system. It also helps to be connected to a strong and trusted brand. When famous designer Ralph Lauren decided to launch his Polo brand on the Internet (www.polo.com), he joined forces with NBC (the National Broadcasting Co.), NBC.com and ValueVision Fulfilment services. Each of the partners brought its own specialism to the venture: Ralph Lauren supplies the product and the name recognition, NBC provides promotion on its networks and the Internet, and ValueVision handles distribution and customer service. The new venture went from birth to fulfilment in nine months and distributes a wide range of products, including clothing for men, women and children, as well as Ralph Lauren's home collection. The state-of-the-art distribution centre was designed with versatility in mind, down to the last detail. Even the packaging design has a strong emphasis on customer care and branding.

As explained by Howard Fox, Senior Vice President of ValueVision, 'This isn't just a normal pick-pack operation; Ralph Lauren takes a lot of pride in its packaging. It's part of their imaging and branding.' An efficient returns system is an important component to any dotcom. Polo.com is recognizing that the returns process is an extension of its customer care. Only about 10 per cent of all ordered items are actually returned. This is about half the average industry percentage for clothing-based distributors. It is also less than Polo.com originally expected.

Source: Adapted from Maloney (2001)

CHAPTER SUMMARY

In this chapter, we have emphasized the increasingly broad scope of branding, which can encompass whole corporations or even partnerships as well as specific products. The Internet poses a number of branding challenges that centre upon the extent to which an offline brand can be translated to the online environment, or whether it is best to develop new online brands. The increasing tendency for companies to offer multi-channel options to their customers highlights the need for consistency of branding and integration of business processes across a range of online and offline channels, in order to provide a uniform and seamless customer experience. These issues will be explored further in Chapter 7.

Case study:
ERGOBANK

Ergobank has a network of over 300 branches, employs 7,500 people and is one of the largest banking groups in Greece. It has recently expanded its activities outside the Greek borders to the neighbouring Balkan states of Bulgaria and Romania. The bank's business areas cover retail, asset and private banking, where it has achieved leading positions, as well as the SME sector. It has been rated A3 by Moody's financial strength C, the highest in Greece, in a Company Profile during 2001.

Ergobank's strategy is to focus on organic growth and operational cost reduction through investments in infrastructure and innovative products in order to brand the bank as an early adopter of new technologies. In particular, this means developing 'new-economy' business activities and alternative distribution channels such as PC-based Internet, digital TV and mobile phone via SMS and WAP. It has been a first mover in Greek e-Banking activities. Early electronic transactions centred upon telephone banking, and Internet banking operations commenced in February 2000. Gradually, mobile banking was developed, along with digital television, and in 2001 *netBiz* rated the service the 'easiest and most user-friendly' site providing both banking transactions and navigational information. A portal named Open24 was launched in March 2001, providing news, information, entertainment and search facilities. Interestingly, in contrast to the well-publicized branch closure programme in the UK, small physical branches of Open24 (staffed by real people!) have also been opened to provide express face-to-face services to customers. A proof of Ergobank's success is that it was recently voted 'Bank of the Year' for Greece by *The Banker*, which nominated it the market leader in terms of 'quality, dynamism, innovation and provision of financial services'.

The bank currently has an Internet division but this is seen as an inseparable, integrated part of the overall business. Since it recognizes that competition derives not only from traditional players but from new entrants too, it has tried to offer a complete Internet banking package within a short period of time. Online operations have acted as a complement to the current activities and distribution channels, and have been an integrated part of the business strategy. The need for symbiosis of 'clicks' and 'bricks' operations is also seen from its www.open24.gr service and new 'Open24' branches. The bank offers choice to its customers to conduct banking transactions and also provide them with other non-financial products. Since brands are considered the asset that will distinguish the winners in the Internet era, Ergobank has adopted a customer-led strategy and formed partnerships with other brand retailers to offer an information, services and shopping experience that combines both Internet and physical operations.

Source: This case study was kindly contributed by Christine Chazakis, Brunel University.

FURTHER READING

Ind, N. (2001) *Living the Brand*, London: Kogan Page.
Kochan, N. (1996) *The World's Greatest Brands*, London: Macmillan Business.
Lindstrom, M. (2001) *Clicks, Bricks and Brands*, London: Kogan Page.

QUESTIONS

Question 5.1

Why are many 'traditional' brands losing their brand value in comparison with online brands such as AOL, Amazon and Yahoo!?

Feedback – Brands vary in the amount of power and value they have in the marketplace. According to Interbrand, the branding consultancy, some 'old-economy' brands have lost their brand value in 2000 compared to 1999, as 'new-economy' brands have gained. Kodak, Xerox, Nike and even Coca-Cola have all shown declines in comparison with many 'new-economy' brands such as Nokia and Intel, which have showed double-digit percentage gains. This is possibly due to the 'dotcom' hype of 2000, which pushed up the brand image of online brands such as AOL, Amazon and Yahoo!. It remains to be seen if these companies will continue to make an impact, because very few have yet reached a stable financial position.

Question 5.2

Using an example of your choice, discuss how companies are reinforcing their traditional brands online.

Feedback – Many 'old-economy' companies are reinforcing their brands online because they want to shape the perception of their stakeholders. There is also mounting pressure for some industries, such as chemicals, to be more transparent in terms of corporate behaviour. So, some of these companies are using corporate branding on the Internet as a communication vehicle. Powerful traditional companies such as BMW use online brand reinforcement in order to increase their competitive advantage. BMW is pursuing a 'brand focus' online whose mission is to make its site 'drive and feel' like a BMW car.

Online brand reinforcement is also used to increase reputation, which in turn will increase online traffic and hence revenues for e-Commerce operators. Following the example of dominant Web companies such as Amazon, AOL and Yahoo!, many companies are embarking on expensive offline branding through television advertising, radio, newspapers, or events sponsorships.

Question 5.3

Building brand awareness online is an expensive exercise. Explain why this is so and what options are available to smaller businesses.

Feedback – Building brand awareness online is rarely sufficient in itself. It needs to be supplemented with substantial offline branding, which is very expensive as it involves television advertising, radio, newspapers, or events sponsorships. Smaller companies with limited offline advertising budgets need to demonstrate increased creativity. Even large companies are adopting this tactic (see the examples of Orange and Yahoo!).

 WEB LINKS

www.bmw.com
A good example of a site that reinforces the traditional offline brand image.

www.egg.com
The online banking brand of the Prudential.

www.interbrand.com
A branding consultancy that has developed a league table of global brand valuations. The site contains a wealth of information about online branding issues, including a free newsletter.

www.open24.gr
The site established by Ergobank in partnership with other brand retailers to offer an information, services and shopping experience that combines both online and express branch operations.

www.pepsistuff.com
A site set up as a result of an alliance between Pepsi and Yahoo! that allowed each company to add value to customers by combining their key competencies.

www.polo.com
A venture by Ralph Lauren to take a traditional brand online. It combines the expertise of a number of key organizations working in partnership.

www.smile.co.uk
The online banking arm of the Co-operative bank.

www.sucks500.com
A good example of how the Internet allows dissatisfied customers to post their concerns for the world to read, with potentially damaging consequences for the brands involved.

www.virgin.com
A good example of a corporate brand that incorporates a diverse product range.

www.visa.com
A good example of a company that has invested a considerable proportion of its promotional budget on building brand awareness online.

Relationship marketing

LISA HARRIS

MINDMAP

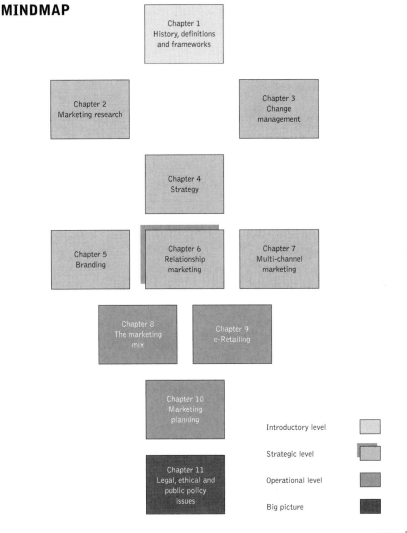

Chapter 1
History, definitions
and frameworks

Chapter 2
Marketing research

Chapter 3
Change
management

Chapter 4
Strategy

Chapter 5
Branding

Chapter 6
Relationship
marketing

Chapter 7
Multi-channel
marketing

Chapter 8
The marketing
mix

Chapter 9
e-Retailing

Chapter 10
Marketing
planning

Chapter 11
Legal, ethical and
public policy
issues

Introductory level

Strategic level

Operational level

Big picture

LINKS TO OTHER CHAPTERS

Chapter 2 Marketing research	Chapter 4 Strategy	Chapter 3 Change management

Chapter 7 Multi-channel marketing

- Chapter 2 – Marketing research
- Chapter 4 – Strategy
- Chapter 3 – Managing change
- Chapter 7 – Multi-channel marketing

KEY LEARNING POINTS

After completing this chapter you will have an understanding of:

■ The interrelationships between internal (staff) and external (customer) relationship building
■ The role of online marketing in effective relationship building
■ The difficulty of reconciling the marketer's need for information with customer concerns over privacy
■ How rising customer expectations are prompting the development of integrated multi-channel operations

ORDERED LIST OF SUB TOPICS

■ Managing stakeholder relationships
■ What is relationship marketing?
■ A 'new marketing paradigm'?
■ Business-to-business relationship marketing
■ Loyalty programmes and personalization

MANAGING STAKEHOLDER RELATIONSHIPS

A key role of modern marketing is that of a management 'mindset' implemented *throughout* an organization rather than confined to a particular department (Payne 1995). This viewpoint regards marketing as a guiding management philosophy or 'attitude of mind' that puts the customer first, and it is commonly described as a 'marketing orientation'. It is a much broader view of the role of marketing than has been envisaged in the past, and it cuts across a wide range of organizational functions. Successful adaptation of a marketing orientation requires effective management of all stakeholder groups (this means people with a particular – although not necessarily the same – interest in the activities of the company) such as staff, business partners, shareholders and suppliers, as well as customers. As Chaffey *et al.* note, 'The marketing concept should lie at the heart of the organisation, and the actions of directors, managers and employees should be guided by its philosophy' (2000: 3).

The Internet supports the concept of the marketing orientation because it provides a powerful interactive communications medium both within the organization (through the use of an intranet) and externally with other key stakeholder groups (through the use of an extranet). The characteristics of intranets and extranets were discussed in Chapter 1 (p. 15). The Internet also facilitates the gathering and management of data necessary to formulate and implement marketing strategies.

BT, for example, is using its Intranet to develop a competencies database of employee IT skills, thereby opening up a pool of potential labour for jobs that come up and highlighting training needs. Adopting relationship marketing principles within the organization in this way is known as **internal marketing**. The basic premise behind internal marketing is that a company's communications with its customers and other external stakeholders are unlikely to be effective unless

157

employees within the firm are aware of (and – more critically – prepared to 'buy into' on an individual basis) the message that the firm is trying to put across. It has been estimated that more than 20 per cent of a firm's communications are actually with itself rather than with external stakeholders, yet internal communications are rarely accorded the same degree of attention and resources as external communications.

Sometimes, very basic errors are made. For example, if the person responsible for mailing out corporate brochures is not told that a facility for customers to email such requests to the firm has been implemented, incoming messages may well be ignored by that person in the mistaken assumption that someone else is dealing with them. It is currently fashionable to refer to employees as 'internal customers'. If all employees are clear about the company's mission, objectives and strategy, then there is a much better chance that customers will get the same message. Research has shown that firms where employees understand organizational goals have considerably higher returns on capital than those where employees feel excluded or uninformed.

While press attention has focused on the achievements (and, more recently, the struggles) of Internet entrepreneurs in dotcom companies, comparatively little mention has been made of the increasing numbers of service workers who make up the bulk of the demand for labour in new technology industries. Leibovich, in an article appropriately entitled 'Service workers without a smile', provides an interesting account of employment conditions at Amazon, world famous for its ground-breaking policies of online customer relationship-building. He notes how staff are pressured to work as quickly as possible in order to achieve customer satisfaction targets, particularly those who earn low wages packing books at the firm's distribution centres or answering emails from customers, and goes on to observe the irony of the Amazon geography: 'Customer service employees work in a patchwork of cubicles scattered over three downtown Seattle buildings. The quarters have an old industrial feel, with gritty exteriors that belie the company's sleek online identity' (1999: 3). Many other 'new economy' employees work in call centres that have been dubbed 'the new sweatshops' because of pressure to work as quickly as possible under electronic surveillance that monitors, for example, the number of customer emails responded to per hour (see Chapter 11 for more detail in this area). In these service-intensive organizations, the power is in the hands of lower-level, front-line employees, upon whose handling of customer services managers must depend for the achievement of organizational objectives. As Piercy notes, 'Too many employees who deal directly with customers are damaging the product, service or corporate brand every time they open their mouths' (2000: 187). This means that internal marketing needs to play a critical role in ensuring that staff are well informed and motivated if a quality service is to be provided to customers. However, this is frequently not the case. For example, the technique of 'mystery shopping' (discussed in Chapter 2), in which researchers anonymously check out the quality of service provided by staff, may well be feared and resented. Dissatisfied or demotivated staff can try to sabotage enforced customer service policies in subtle ways, for example by wearing their name badges upside down. One major UK DIY retailer implemented a customer care programme that required shop-floor staff to be much more proactive in serving customers and suggesting suitable products. It failed because management failed to note the limited extent of employee commitment and willingness to accept the extra pressures associated with such responsibility. Instead of feeling empowered and motivated by the 'upgrading' of their jobs, many staff resented the interference and preferred the security and predictability of sitting at the till all day.

The principles of internal marketing can also be extended to *prospective* employees with the notion of employer branding (see Chapter 5), in recognition that employees are a significant source of competitive advantage in a marketplace where products and services are easily copied. Employer branding involves treating both staff and potential staff as internal customers. The aim is to acquire a reputation as a 'good firm to work for', thereby attracting and retaining the brightest and most dedicated employees, enabling the firm to stand out from its competitors. 'Forward looking companies are working on the assumption that they have to do a continuous selling job on the employee' (Grimes 2000: 13). In an age where people expect to work for a number of firms (or indeed for themselves) during the course of their career, retaining key staff is becoming more and more difficult. Some firms are experimenting with a number of benefits in order to be seen as a 'good employer'; for example:

- paternity leave;
- extended unpaid leave of absence;
- flexible work arrangements (e.g. working from home or 'child-friendly' hours);
- job sharing;
- empowerment of staff;
- open communications through simplified management hierarchies.

It is often suggested that relationships with both staff and customers can be enhanced through induction programmes, training courses, benefits, the use of intranets or through working in cross-functional teams. However, while all these are useful, things are rarely that simple. Too often, customer care programmes are instigated as a 'quick fix', without making any changes in entrenched management behaviour, or without attempting to evaluate the success of the programme implemented.

Payne regards a supportive organizational culture as a key ingredient in the success of internal marketing:

> Internal marketing involves creating, developing and maintaining an organisational service culture that will lead to the right service personnel performing the service in the right way. It tells employees how to respond to new, unforeseen and even awkward situations. Service culture has a vital impact on how service-oriented employees act and thus how well they perform their tasks as 'part-time marketers'.
>
> (1995: 48–9)

Payne goes on to note that management needs to be customer orientated in order to lead by example and instil a market-focused attitude lower down the organizational hierarchy. This may require significant organizational change. (The complexity of change management was discussed in Chapter 3.)

In what may be regarded as the ultimate integration of internal marketing and customer relationship marketing, Ulrich (1989) advises giving customers a major role in staff recruitment, promotion and development, and appraisal and reward systems. While this policy may be too radical for many organizations, it can be seen from this discussion that a suitable internal climate is a necessary first step in the development of a customer orientation. This is rarely a simple task for an established organization that has become used to operating in a particular way.

WHAT IS RELATIONSHIP MARKETING?

Having established the role of employees as a key stakeholder group in the development of effective customer service, we will now go on to examine the subject of customer relationship marketing (CRM) in more detail. There are many definitions of relationship marketing. Here are just a few:

> attracting, maintaining, and – in multi-service organisations – enhancing customer relationships.
>
> (Berry *et al*. 1983: 25)

> establishing, developing and maintaining successful relational exchanges.
>
> (Morgan and Hunt, 1994: 20)

> a business strategy which pro-actively builds a bias or preference for an organisation with its individual employees, channels and customers resulting in increased retention and increased performance.
>
> (Newell 2000: 182)

Key to successful relationship marketing is quality service. As Bolton claims,

> In ongoing service relationships, customers subjectively assess the future value of the relationship relative to the expected benefits, costs of continuing and costs of discontinuing the relationship. From this viewpoint, a significant part of the value assessment in a retention decision rests on service performance.
>
> (1998: 48)

Relationship marketing, therefore, is based on retaining *existing* customers rather than acquiring *new* ones. For the company, relationship marketing can enhance customer retention rates. This impacts directly on profitability because it can cost much more to attract a new customer than it does to retain an existing customer. For example, Bain and Co. found that a 5 per cent increase in the number of retained customers could lead to increased profitability of 25–85 per cent (Payne 1995). Retained customers become more profitable over time as the relationship between them and the supplier develops. Payne's ladder of customer loyalty (Figure 6.1) illustrates this notion well.

By focusing on the provision of a quality service to a customer, a company is increasing the chance that the customer will return. If that customer is subsequently treated in an individual way in accordance with what the company has learned about his or her preferences, then the customer starts to move further up the ladder. If customers are so pleased with the attention and service received that they start recommending the company to others, then marketing costs begin to fall, as word-of-mouth recommendations are completely free. From the customer's perspective, developing a long-term relationship with a company can also help to reduce the perceived risk associated with the purchase of goods or services. It is not feasible, of course, for a company to try to develop a relationship with all its customers. The key is to focus on those customers with the greatest profit potential. The Pareto principle applies here because just 20 per cent of customers may account for 80 per cent of profit generation. The key is to work out which particular customers make up the lucrative 20 per cent!

Traditionally, the majority of marketing resources have been expended on the more costly activity of acquiring new customers, without any significant effort at retaining customers once the transaction has been completed. This can lead to disenfranchisement among existing customers, who feel neglected and undervalued when potential customers are offered better deals (Rosenfield 1999). This problem is clearly evidenced in the UK mortgage market at the time of writing, where a plethora of special deals are offered only to prospective rather than existing customers. Reichheld (1993) notes that segmentation based on the degree of potential customer profitability is vital to focus resource expenditure on the most lucrative customers. This important feature of relationship marketing is also emphasized by Newell (2000) in the context of online relationship-building.

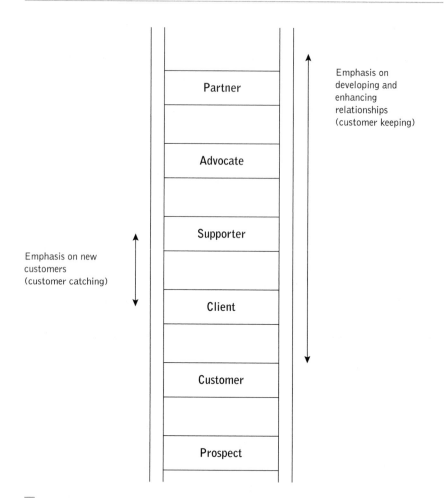

Partner

Advocate

Supporter

Client

Customer

Prospect

Emphasis on developing and enhancing relationships (customer keeping)

Emphasis on new customers (customer catching)

Figure 6.1 *The relationship marketing ladder of customer loyalty*

Source: Payne (2000)

A 'NEW MARKETING PARADIGM'?

Some theorists argue that 'traditional' marketing (based merely on managing the marketing mix) is actually defunct and relationship marketing principles represent a dramatic change in marketing focus over the past two decades. For example, Gummesson (1997) describes relationship marketing as a 'panacea' that is applicable to all organization types. Although the *practice* of relationship-building in business is accepted as an old phenomenon (Gronroos 1997), some writers (such as Gruen 1997) are criticized for presenting this fact in a distorted manner, or even not acknowledging it. This gives the impression that the importance of building relationships is a relatively *new* discovery (Petrof 1998).

Certainly, in the business world, relationship marketing is currently a highly topical area, with the prolific use of 'relationship' terminology in company literature, corporate announcements, advertisements and even job titles. From this perspective, the claim of its status as a 'new marketing paradigm' with universal applicability may seem more realistic. In recent years, speculation about the potential of the Internet in facilitating the development of relationships has ensured that the debate about the role of relationship marketing remains prominent in both theoretical and practitioner circles (see, for example, Newell 2000; Parker 2000).

The differences between 'traditional' (sometimes called transactional) marketing and relationship marketing are highlighted in Table 6.1. Relationship marketing supporters criticize 'traditional' marketing as a 'narrow, transactional, one-sale-at-a-time view of marketing' (Payne 1995: 24). They claim that an overly short-term orientation towards marketing activity is taken, and 'the unit of analysis is a single market transaction' with 'profits expected to follow from today's exchanges, although sometimes some long-term image development occurs' (Gronroos 1997: 15). In contrast, relationship marketing adopts a more longitudinal perspective, in which any short-term losses are mitigated over time by the return on investment from lasting customer relationships and their ensuing profitability. Hence its supporters advocate relationship marketing as the 'new' prescription for achieving success in today's highly competitive and dynamic marketplace.

Table 6.1 *Transaction marketing versus relationship marketing*

Transaction marketing	Relationship marketing
Focus on single sales	Focus on customer retention and building loyalty
Short timescales	Long-term timescales recognizing that short-term costs will be higher, but so will long-term profitability
Emphasis upon product features	Emphasis upon product benefits that are meaningful to the customer
Limited customer commitment	High customer commitment
Little emphasis upon customer retention	Emphasis upon higher levels of service tailored to individual customers
Quality is the concern of production	Quality is the concern of all, and failure to recognize this stores up problems for the future
Moderate customer contact	High customer contact, with each contact being used to gain information and build the relationship

Are the criticisms of 'traditional' marketing justified? Although supporters of relationship marketing are dismissive of the short-term focus of much 'traditional' marketing activity, concerns about short-termism were expressed in classic marketing papers as long ago as the 1960s. For example, Keith (1960) articulated the need for a longer-term perspective to be taken when planning marketing activity in order that customer retention be achieved. In addition, marketers may not always have an explicit choice in adopting longer time horizons because of the inherent short-termism in the reporting systems of organizations. It seems that relationship marketing supporters, in their critique of 'traditional' marketing's near-sightedness, have ignored the fundamental principles of some main 'marketing' activities and their long-term benefits. Advertising, sponsorship and public relations are used for longer-term corporate and product brand awareness, and to increase market share over time. It is really only the promotional aspect of the marketing mix (such as coupons and special offers) that is used primarily for short-term gains. (See Chapter 8 for a detailed discussion of the marketing mix.)

To summarize the discussion so far, much academic literature advocates relationship marketing as a new field of study within the marketing domain, or even as the central body of knowledge upon which incremental marketing theories should be developed. Traditional marketing is hence relegated to a sub-field of the relationship marketing school of thought. The rather sudden realization of the change in status is explained with a seemingly frequent justification nowadays: a 'paradigm shift'. 'Traditional' marketing, comprising a narrow view of explicit transactional exchange with a 'distinct beginning, short duration and sharp-ending performance', is argued to have been replaced by relationship marketing, which, in contrast, 'traces to previous agreements and is longer in duration, reflecting an ongoing process' (Dwyer et al. 1987: 13). The contention is based on relationship marketing's long-term view, customer orientation, means of differentiation and the economics of customer retention, as discussed in the previous section.

However, some writers argue that relationship marketing is just a case of 'reinventing the wheel'. They claim the term has been misinterpreted as new by those who wish to be recognized (unjustly) as the 'originators' of a new field. Petrof (1998) notes that 'Many concepts appear to be new only because their authors did not search back beyond the very recent past', and cites a number of classical works that proffer values similar to those found in contemporary relationship marketing contributions. Palmer (1997) argues that the practice of building relationships is not a new concept, but is one that came to be discounted in the second half of the last century owing to economic development that allowed economies of scale to speed up the exchange process. Branding replaced the need for close proximity and personal knowledge of consumers and suppliers to build trust in personal relationships. Relational exchange processes are still prevalent in the Far East and other countries that are at lower levels of industrialization,

164

or those in which trust-inducing relational exchanges are ingrained within the cultural context. However, the popularity of relationship marketing has now been regained in the West with advances in information technology such as the Internet, allowing relational exchanges to be combined with the benefits of branding and thereby leveraging the advantages associated with each.

Payne (1995) criticizes those companies that do not aggressively pursue customer retention, and therefore fails to note that in some business contexts a relationship-building strategy may not be relevant to, or indeed wanted by, the customer. Palmer argues that relationship marketing should not be normatively prescribed and that 'marketers should be as wary of prescribing universal solutions for exchange bases as they are of developing universal product and promotion policies for all markets' (1997: 321). Fournier *et al.* also question the universal applicability of relationship marketing strategies:

> Some of the very things we are doing to build relationships with customers are often the things that are destroying those relationships. Too often we are skimming over the fundamentals of relationship building in our rush to cash in on the potential rewards of creating close connections with our customers.
>
> (1998: 46)

It can also be questioned whether managers are actually willing to empower (that is, dilute some of their own power) lower-level employees in order to encourage them to build relationships with customers, as this may conflict with an individual's notion of power and status. The issue of employee commitment and willingness to accept the extra pressures of responsibility for customer inter-action is another critical factor, as is the question of whether punitive action should be taken against the employee if a key customer is lost. Such critical human resource management factors, encompassing issues of pay, status, symbols, working environment and managerial attitude, have been well documented in the organizational behaviour literature, but are often ignored by proponents of relationship marketing.

What if the customer never wished to be in a 'relationship' with the organi-zation in the first place? Just because an organization has decided to change to a relationship marketing strategy, this does not mean that customers will also make the shift to the same extent, if at all. Customers may actually desire a one-way marketing relationship in which they do not have to expend any effort in building and maintaining the relationship, believing that it is up to the supplying organi-zation if it wants to retain their custom. Price-sensitive customers may simply take the benefits or savings offered from a number of firms in turn. A company may then find itself in the uneconomic position of having to run with *both* transactional and relationship-building policies for different customer groups. Research by Synesis reported in *Marketing* (28 September 2000) concluded that

165

relationship marketing strategies as currently practised were more likely to alienate than impress customers. The authors note: 'while the industry is focusing on customisation and one-to-one marketing, consumers are feeling bombarded by marketing messages and just want companies to fulfil their promises on the basis of products and services'. O'Malley and Tynan (2001) confirm this viewpoint with their observation that customers may well tolerate relationship-building initiatives only for as long as it suits them because of self-interest and convenience, rather than build up the trust and commitment that the company might expect. On the Internet, of course, it is very easy for customers to compare the offerings of different suppliers and switch allegiance with the click of a mouse.

It was mentioned earlier that only a small percentage of customer relationships will have serious profit potential. A difficult issue to manage in this situation is the 'firing' of unprofitable customers that are *not* deemed suitable (meaning potentially profitable) candidates for building relationships with. Banks face this dilemma with their loss-making current account business. They hope to cross-sell more lucrative products to these customers so that the overall customer relationship is profitable, but many customers are happy to take the free service and then shop around for other suppliers to purchase other financial products from. What should a bank do in this situation? It risks adding to the already high level of negative publicity that has been generated by branch closure programmes, for example. At the other end of the scale, it should also be noted that powerful customers can decide to end a relationship and 'fire' suppliers, as has been recently exemplified by the food and clothing retailer Marks and Spencer, which ended its relationship with one of its long-term suppliers, William Baird.

Despite the challenges described above, implementing relationship marketing is often portrayed as a straightforward process (particularly by suppliers of technical 'solutions'!). There are a number of steps that can be taken in order to facilitate the process:

- Identify key customers (i.e. the sources of highest potential profit over the long term).
- Examine the expectations of both sides.
- Identify ways in which you can work more closely with these customers.
- Think about how operating procedures may need to be changed in order to facilitate closer communication.
- Appoint a relationship manager as a natural focal point.
- Be satisfied with small gains in the early stages; build over time.
- Recognize from the outset that different customers have different needs, and this should be reflected in the way the relationship is developed.

The Gartner Group describes the level of customer relationship marketing in most organizations as 'fantasy', claiming that fewer than 3 per cent have implemented projects successfully.

So-called 'CRM solutions' that purport to 'do' a company's relationship marketing can be purchased from technology vendors. According to Gartner (www.gartner.com), new licence revenue for CRM technology vendors reached $3.7 billion in 2000, and continued annual growth of 30–35 per cent is forecast for the next few years. However, true relationship marketing is a company-wide process and philosophy, not a piece of kit. According to Peppers and Rogers, as many as 80 per cent of CRM implementations fail to deliver. They blame 'inadequate vision, focus and implementation' (2001: 1), and note some common mistakes:

- 'Paving the cow path.' Here the new CRM strategy merely automates the company's existing ineffectiveness by maintaining the same business processes.
- Buying an 'off-the-shelf' solution. In this case, the buyer has to adapt the company's business processes to fit in with the standards built into the new system. Technical imperatives therefore come before customer focus.
- Failure to translate plans that seem reasonable on paper into practical action. For example, employees may not be trained or motivated, or legacy computer systems not properly integrated.

So, companies face a number of challenges in developing effective relationship marketing strategies. These can be summarized as follows:

- Customers not singled out for special treatment may have long memories!
- Relationship marketing does not appear to have universal applicability.
- Cultural norms may inhibit effective implementation, hence a significant culture change is required.
- Staff may not be prepared to take on relationship-building responsibilities.
- Managers may not be prepared to dilute their power base by delegating relationship-building tasks to shop-floor employees.
- Customers may not be interested in establishing a relationship and resent intrusive approaches.
- Companies are assumed to pursue *either* 'traditional' *or* relationship marketing strategies, which appears to be an oversimplification of what actually goes on in practice.
- The process may lead to unacceptable levels of cost.
- One firm's 'best' customer may also be a competitor's 'best' customer.
- Maintaining the necessary accurate and up-to-date databases is costly, time-consuming and subject to stringent legislation.

167

BUSINESS-TO-BUSINESS (B2B) RELATIONSHIP MARKETING

As has already been mentioned, relationship marketing is not new in reality, and this is particularly true for B2B. For example, Marks and Spencer used to have a policy of dealing with a small number of 'partner' suppliers, some of which had been involved for many decades. When Marks and Spencer personnel visited a supplier, it was referred to as a 'royal visit'; 'Factories may be repainted . . . and machinery cleaned: this reflects the exacting standards' (Jobber 2001: 106). Marks and Spencer may have moved away from that policy in recent years, but it has to be noted that the change did not coincide with a major improvement in the company's fortunes.

In this type of relationship management, there are increased pressures put on to suppliers to maintain high levels of service and reliability. Customers, though, often provide increased technical support and expertise to suppliers. Because such partnerships are long term, the partners can invest in systems that ensure good communication, reduced risks and efficiency, such as Just in Time (JIT) and EDI (considered further in Chapter 8). For the supplier, such systems have the advantage of increasing switching costs; that is, making it expensive for the customer to change supplier. This is the sort of system used, for example, by Nissan in Sunderland (UK) in car production. The seats and upholstery are ordered from the supplier only forty minutes before they are required on the production line. In that time, they are assembled and delivered to where they are required. With such tight restraints on efficiency, reliability is enforced.

Mini case study: CISCO

Cisco Corporation is a world leader in integrated information exchanges based on Internet technology and a major provider of the infrastructure that makes the World Wide Web work. Its customer relationship systems include:

- an online customer enquiry and ordering system taking 80 per cent of the company's orders;
- a Web site on which customers can design and price-switch and router products;
- an online customer care service so that customers can identify solutions from the data warehouse of technical information and download software directly. Cisco estimates that this has saved $250 million per year in distributing software plus $75 million in staffing customer care.

Source: Adapted from Jobber (2001), based on Pollack (1999)

LOYALTY PROGRAMMES AND PERSONALIZATION

Despite the problems listed above, it does seem that relationship marketing at least has the potential to enhance customer satisfaction. Although it is easy to be cynical, a satisfied customer is more likely to be loyal than one who is not. A loyal customer base has a number of benefits to a company:

- Higher returns will accrue, from repeat sales over time.
- Increasing levels of competition means that service quality may be the only differentiating factor between otherwise similar companies.
- Higher costs are associated with recruiting new customers than with managing existing ones (because of the need to conduct credit checks, take up references and other administrative tasks).
- It provides scope for cross-selling.
- It creates possibilities for strategic partnerships.
- Loyal customers will recommend the company to others by word of mouth.
- Promotional costs to acquire new business are reduced.

Loyalty programmes (also known as 'reward schemes') can be introduced to increase loyalty. For example, successful programmes have been introduced in recent years by airlines such as BA and supermarkets such as Tesco. The costs of the rewards given away can be more than offset by the additional business gained through repeat or additional purchases. For example, Tesco's Clubcard loyalty programme now covers more than 14 million customers, and special offers can be customized, based upon analysis of transactional data in order to enhance the brand image and build trust. By 1996, 200 million in-store purchases per day were being tracked by the programme, and over 5,000 distinct customer segments identified, each receiving personalized coupons. Profits have grown from £500 million in 1995 to nearly £1 billion in 2000 (www.1to1.com). When Tesco began selling goods online (admittedly after a shaky start, when the company's computer systems were not sufficiently integrated and orders had to be rekeyed manually!), the company was a 'known quantity' in comparison with the unproven Internet 'pureplays' that were setting themselves up in competition. Additional Clubcard points were awarded for online purchases, and Tesco now has over 1 million online customers. In 2000 it sold half of all online groceries in the UK (www.datamonitor.com). It dominates the home delivery market to such an extent that many competitors have accepted defeat. Safeway, for example, decided in 2001 to stop selling its goods online and concentrated instead on refurbishing and upgrading its retail outlets.

Another popular method of boosting loyalty is **personalization**. Tesco is moving in this direction with its online service, which is now becoming more sophisticated in its analytical capabilities in terms of suggesting particular products or special offers that might appeal to individual customers based upon their purchase history. Personalization software allows the name of the user to be incorporated into the Web pages, any previous transaction details to be displayed, and related areas of interest to be flagged. Personalized email messages can be distributed to highly targeted groups of customers at a very low cost. This type of marketing is also being driven by research such as that by Cyber Atlas (www.cyberatlas.com), which established that Web users who configure, personalize or register on Web sites are more than twice as likely to buy online as those who do not. A combination of a reward scheme and personalization can therefore be a powerful tool to drive loyalty. Such mechanisms are of course ideally suited to online transactions, and this aspect will be considered in more detail in the next section.

ACTIVITY

Read the personalization case studies and try the demonstrations on www.broad vision.com. How do such personalization techniques allow value to be added to customers?

As with relationship marketing as a whole, there has been a lot of hype recently claiming that personalization is a panacea for success. This ignores the fact that in many circumstances, customers are quite happy to receive a 'mass market' approach, and find any degree of personalization an intrusive invasion of privacy. Examine the mini case study below and make up your own mind – do you find such approaches valuable or intrusive? Why?

Mini case study:
ADAPTED FROM 'ARE PERSONALIZATION AND PRIVACY REALLY AT ODDS?'

Today's companies treat different customers differently for one basic reason: because they can. The technologies that enable personalisation have only recently become practical, but the fact that personalisation can occur now means that it must occur because customers demand it. As a result, companies everywhere are incorporating personalisation into their business models in order to build loyalty and generate revenue. Bruce Kasanoff, privacy expert and author of 'Making it personal: how to profit from personalization without invading privacy' (www.makingitpersonal.net), says the widespread adoption of personalization is inevitable: 'You will no more think of ignoring the differences between customers than you would think of charging a customer for a product you never delivered.'

Yet we've also heard the frequently repeated maxim that protecting your customers' privacy must be the centrepiece of any effort to profit from personalization strategies. For many executives, this poses a conundrum: How do I acquire and utilize customer data – and personalization – to generate business while protecting my customers' privacy at the same time? Why is it that personalization and privacy seem to be at odds? Kasanoff argues the conflict exists because most companies ignore the personal side of one-to-one relationships. They collect personal information solely in order to sell whatever products happen to be in their marketing plan.

The truth is that personalization, when applied in the context of a genuinely effective one-to-one programme, should not conflict with individual privacy protection. This is because relationships, to be effective, must be built on trust, but a customer's trust cannot be secured if he has any doubts at all about whether their privacy will be protected. The conflict between personalization and privacy only arises when companies view it from the 'wrong end of the telescope'. If you start by asking how you can use personalization to sell your customers more stuff, then privacy abuse is one likely outcome. But this is the wrong philosophical approach to relationship-building. The right question to ask is how you can use personalization technologies to add value for your customers, by saving them time or money, or creating a better-fitting or more appropriate product.

That said, there are several issues executives must be prepared to address when jumping into the personalization game. Just as different customers have different needs, different people have different levels of sensitivity with respect to protecting their privacy. In fact, just agreeing on a definition of privacy protection can be problematic. For example:

- Do you partner with other companies to render services to your customer? If so, are you accountable for a partner's privacy policies?
- If you give a customer's personal information to an outside company, is that a violation of the customer's privacy?
- What if you give it to another division within your own firm?
- Just what is the damage of a privacy violation, anyway?

Getting to the bottom of these issues is critical to making personalization and privacy click. For those companies that do, the secret is out: privacy and personalization are in.

Source: Adapted from Martha Rogers and Don Peppers (www.1to1.com)

GETTING STARTED WITH A DATABASE

When setting up a database for the first time, the best advice is to start simple. If possible, it is preferable to use proprietary software initially, rather than custom-designed systems. The first step is to decide how, when and where you want to use the data – and implement the simplest system possible that will achieve your objectives. Once the limitations of a basic system have been reached, you will be much clearer about requirements and specifications for upgrading. Specialist systems will readily accept an existing database such as, say, Microsoft Access or Excel formats.

Achieving the real benefits of the database entails implementing the 'Three Graces'. First, of course, customers must be identified as individuals. Basic data include 'who' the customers or prospects are – name, title, job title (if business) – and 'where' they are – address, phone, fax, email and so on. Also essential in a marketing database is the purchase and complaint history. Second, database benefits come from building continuing relationships – and in particular, segmenting the 'special customers' and making them really special; for example, e.g. with invitations to special events. Keep in touch with customers with frequent newsletters and offers. Third, test and measure – continually targeting, testing, measuring and improving performance.

Mini case study:
PREVIEW TRAVEL

The e-Business has an advantage in database-building: the Internet is a medium for both customer acquisition and customer retention. For example, US-based Preview Travel (www.previewtravel.com) attracts customers to its Web site from carefully selected banner sites. Once the customer is at the site, content is integrated with transactions. Devices such as the shopping basket, plus close-dated and exclusive offers are used to translate the customer's interest into action. Email is then used to build loyalty – responding to customer preferences and simulating the one-to-one relationship with a local travel agent. The programme is carefully tailored, including event-driven emails and seasonal messages – all on a 'permission' basis. Success measures include:

- clickthroughs;
- cost per new customer;
- look-to-book ratio;
- repeat customers;

- share of wallet;
- customer quality and cloning;
- customer retention;
- brand awareness;

Average transaction cost has been reduced from $36 to under $11.

Source: Adapted from the Institute of Direct
Marketing Educational Programme

ONLINE RELATIONSHIP MARKETING

Overview

Peppers and Rogers (1997) highlight how effective use of the Internet can greatly facilitate the following relationship marketing issues:

- Using the technology to achieve mass customization of the marketing message – and even the product itself. Mass customization can range from minor cosmetic choices (e.g. the choice of car colour, trim and specification online) to a collaborative process facilitated by ongoing dialogue (e.g. Motorola can manufacture pagers to 11 million different specifications).
- Developing the learning relationship. By this, Peppers and Rogers mean a continuous two-way dialogue which allows the offering to be adapted to meet specific needs. It can be achieved by means of online feedback forms, analysis of queries to customer service facilities, or through use of increasingly sophisticated software that analyses customer site-searching behaviour before purchase.
- Offering an incentive for the customer to engage in the dialogue. It must also be easy and convenient for the customer to engage with the company, so lengthy registration forms are often counter-productive. The best incentive is good, free, up-to-date content.
- Acknowledging the privacy of the customer and the other demands upon their time. This means communicating only with customers who have requested information, and making it easy for customers to 'opt out' if they wish. It also means guaranteeing not to pass on customer details to other companies in the form of online mailing lists.

Gathering data for personalization

Rowley (2001) notes the following methods of collecting data:

- The customer provides information in response to a request.
- If you want to find out what motivates your customers to buy from you, just ask! Tried and tested research techniques such as questionnaires or focus groups can be administered online (see Chapter 2 for full details).
- The practice of registration can be adopted, whereby access to certain sites (or parts of sites) is permitted only to individuals who have completed an initial registration form.
- Customers provide information about themselves during engagement in an online community. Building relationships through online communities is covered later in the chapter, but it is worth noting here that transcripts of community dialogues can be analysed for research information.
- The customer provides information as a by-product of a transaction. This can be as basic as contact telephone numbers and postal addresses, but also enables a profile of the customer's purchase choices to be built up over time. Amazon uses this technique to good effect by providing recommendations of books based on analysis of order history.
- The customer search path through the Web site can be tracked. Even if an actual purchase does not take place, the server log file can be analysed to determine the sites that a user from a specific Internet Protocol (IP) address has visited. This enables the attractiveness of the site to be assessed based upon where referrals are coming from.
- The merchant uses cookies to keep track of the customer's actions. The use of cookies to identify returning customers was also discussed in Chapter 2. One of the more benign uses of cookies lies in the personalization of Web pages so that individual customer greetings can be set up.

Rowley goes on to note that while the Web allows the collection of a vast amount of data by the methods listed above, this is merely the starting point. The raw data need to be stored (in a data warehouse) and then converted into knowledge (through data mining techniques) before they can actually be useful for decision-making purposes. Different sources of data may also need to be integrated before they can add value. This is therefore the core of a company's marketing information system (MIS or MKIS). As will be described in Chapter 7, these difficulties are compounded when a company relies on a number of different channels (shop, mobile, PC, iDTV, etc.) through which to interact with its customers.

Email permission marketing campaigns

According to Godin (1999), **permission marketing** is marketing in which the customer (or prospect):

- clearly consents to having an online relationship with a company;
- is able to state clear preferences for the type, frequency and context of those communications;
- has a high degree of control over the relationship: 'As new forms of media develop and clutter becomes ever more intense, it's the asset of *permission* that will generate profits for marketers' (Godin 1999: 52).

Godin (ibid.) notes that by focusing only on individuals who have indicated an interest in a product, trust can be built, brand awareness can be improved and long-term relationships can be developed. In contrast, he regards traditional marketing as 'interruption marketing', because people are bombarded with messages that in most cases they have no interest in and which actually stop them from doing something else (think, for example of how annoying it is when advertisements interrupt a good film).

It is important not to get too carried away with the concept of permission marketing. Ross, for example, is critical; he claims that the approach is not new:

The large number of direct marketers who start the selling process with an ad offering information, and take it from there with a graduated programme of data collection and follow ups will wonder how it is that they have been practising permission marketing for all this time without knowing.

(2001: 14)

However, despite the argument over the origins of the permission marketing concept, email is an ideal medium for putting such principles into action because it is:

- fast and efficient;
- simple to track, evaluate and make changes if necessary;
- a cost-effective method of raising brand awareness (see Chapter 4);
- easily integrated into the marketing mix (see Chapter 7).

The basic principles of managing an email marketing campaign can be listed sequentially as follows:

- Acquire email addresses (and permission!).
- Target audience for an email marketing campaign.

175

- Develop content and personalization of the message.
- Execute and administer the campaign (in co-ordination with other channels).
- Respond to customer replies (in co-ordination with other channels).
- Maintain and clean email lists.
- Track and measure campaign performance.

However, in 2000, US corporations spent $1.4 billion with over 200 email 'solution' providers to support their email marketing programmes. For every dollar spent externally, two dollars was spent on internal support such as:

- campaign management;
- permission policy management;
- database development;
- systems integration.

So, buying the necessary technology to conduct permission marketing campaigns is merely the starting point. The costs become much greater when the challenges of managing the entire process effectively are factored in. For example, consider the cross-functional journey of an email relationship:

- A customer may register on a Web site, perhaps to receive a copy of a free white paper.
- The registration information will then be stored in a centralized marketing database.
- The email address might be selected for a forthcoming promotional campaign.
- In response to this email, the customer may (a) telephone a call centre to place an order, or perhaps (b) telephone to complain about receiving unsolicited emails.
- Ideally, the call will be passed on to sales to arrange a sales visit, or to customer services to issue an apology . . . but in practice, many organizations have not integrated their online and offline operations sufficiently for this process to be smooth, or indeed to happen at all.

In view of these difficulties, it is not surprising that so many companies characterized their email marketing campaigns as 'out of control' (as shown in Figure 6.2)

A further problem in terms of managing permission marketing campaigns is that the definition of what actually constitutes 'permission' is a moving feast. Just because a customer agreed to participate at one point in time, this does not necessarily mean they will still be interested six months later. So today's permission is tomorrow's spam (see below).

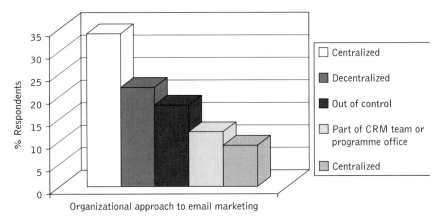

Figure 6.2 *Organizing for email marketing*

Source: IMT Strategies (2001)

There are a number of ways in which customer permission can be established, outlined here in increasing order of thoroughness:

1 'Opt-out' lists assume permission by forcing people to take action to remove themselves from future mailings. An individual may be automatically added to the mailing list if they register at a Web site and fail to notice the 'tick here if you do *not* want to receive future communications' box. This practice is now illegal in the UK.

2 'Opt-in' lists require a box to be ticked saying 'yes, please send me future communications'. However, the problem here is that people can sign others up for these services because there is no check as to the *ownership* of the email address entered.

3 'Confirmed opt-in' also means 'yes please', but before action is taken a confirmation email is sent to the customer asking them to *confirm* their wish to be added to the list for future communications. In other words, customers are given the chance to change their mind.

4 'Double opt-in' still means 'yes please', but then an email is sent back requesting the customer to say 'yes please' *again* before their name is actually added to the list.

The final category of 'double opt-in' is becoming increasingly common in a business climate where people are less and less tolerant of 'spamming', as illustrated in Figure 6.3. Spamming is the process of bombarding customers with unsolicited promotional messages without seeking their permission (spam stands for 'sending persistent annoying messages'). The privacy issues surrounding spam will be covered in Chapter 11.

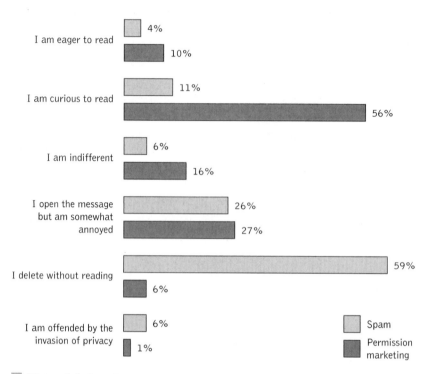

Figure 6.3 *Reactions to permission marketing as compared with those to spam*
Source: DTI (2000), in Chaffey (2002)

Building online communities

In Chapter 1, we considered some of the new business models that are developing online. One of these was the consumer-to-consumer (C2C) model, upon which online communities are based.

These communities have evolved considerably since the early days of news groups and chat rooms. They offer a simple means of overcoming the lack of human contact online and hence can meet consumers' social activity needs. Consequently, online communities can now represent a significant commercial opportunity. According to Kozinets,

Online social interaction is therefore a unique public–private hybrid never before encountered in human history. Changes in capitalism, social thought and new technologies have imploded the boundaries between home and workplace (and production and consumption). CMC [computer-mediated communication] offers ordinary people access to a mass medium, a stage before a global audience. . . . Opportunities abound not only to broadcast one's own private information, but also to partake publicly in the private information of others, and also to commoditise and commercialise these relationships.

(1999: 263)

Cisco (www.cisco.com) is a successful example of a company that has fostered customer communities and saved in excess of $550 million per year in customer support costs by letting customers help themselves to technical support information via Web communities. Seybold (1999) describes how putting the technical support function online led to the creation of a 'self-inflating balloon of knowledge' as customers competed with each other to answer queries that had been posted by others.

Even in the early days of the Web, Hoffman and Novak noted the extent to which the online community model (based on the communication principle of 'many to many') differed from traditional marketing communications (based on the principle of 'one to many'):

In this mediated model, the primary relationships are not between sender and receiver, but rather with the computer-mediated environment with which they interact. In this new model, information or content is not merely transmitted from a sender to a receiver, but instead, mediated environments are created by participants and then experienced.

(1997: 50)

There are a number of different types of C2C interaction through online communities emerging. For example, they may be based on:

- *Purpose* (e.g. www.autotrader.co.uk). For example, people with a common interest in purchasing cars can swop information on best buys, problems with particular models, garages providing high levels of customer service, etc.
- *Position* (e.g. www.bhf.org.uk). In this example, for the British Heart Foundation, the common ground is the medical condition, but various stakeholder groups such as patients, families, researchers and care providers can exchange relevant information, perhaps related to new drugs or the existence of support networks.
- *Interest* (e.g. www.thepetchannel.com). Interest-based community sites bring together people with shared hobbies. There is an increasingly diverse range of such interest groups ranging from the predictable to the bizarre to the downright dangerous . . .
- *Profession* (e.g. www.esteel.com). B2B communities such as eSteel bring together a wide range of professionals with a specialist interest in the steel industry.

179

- *Criticism* (e.g. www.untied.com). Untied is a vigilante site devoted to criticism of the customer service provided by United Airlines. Originally established by one disgruntled passenger, the site developed momentum as others contributed their own horror stories and the company presented a series of textbook examples of how not to handle complaints.

Another interesting example is the community site www.eggfreezone.com, which was set up by the online bank Egg for customers to comment on the services provided by the company. Some customers, however, were persistent in their criticism, and the site was closed. The official reason given by Egg was that the way the site was structured did not allow for individual responses to be made to customer comments. It is easy for a cynic to believe that Egg was trying to protect its reputation here, seeing the comments on the site as a threat rather than an opportunity. What do you think?

Research by Evans *et al.* (2001) that explored consumer attitudes towards online communities concluded that successful commercial communities must offer:

- quality content;
- 'added value' interactions;
- efficient use of participants' time;
- simple site design that can be navigated quickly;
- integrated contact channels (meaning that the site cannot stand alone);
- minimal requirements for registering personal details.

As was noted in Chapter 2, the information posted on relevant community sites can provide companies with valuable research data. Most online communities are currently at a relatively early evolutionary stage and have yet to be subjected to serious study.

Challenges of building online customer relationships

Multi-channel strategies to drive loyalty

As noted above, multi-channel strategies can put severe strain on a company's data collection and analysis processes in order to get a unified view of customer activity through which to personalize its marketing campaigns. The benefits of getting it right, however, are considerable in terms of the competitive advantage that could be gained.

For example, Peppers and Rogers (2001) describe the 'unprecedented' opportunities presented by the combination of mobile technologies and one-to-one marketing strategies. They use the scenario of a travelling customer looking for a hotel room who enables his or her mobile to locate a convenient room at the right price. The hotel then responds with a tailored offer based upon the traveller's previously expressed needs and preferences. Services like this are just the tip of the iceberg. The authors believe that today's reliance on proprietary mobile networks will soon evolve into a more open architecture enabling customers to pick and choose specific features at will from many service providers, intensifying competition and stimulating further innovation in this dynamic area. Chapter 7 will cover this topic in more detail.

Peppers and Rogers (ibid.) claim that in such an environment, the demands for customer information are bound to raise concerns over privacy. This topic was briefly mentioned in an earlier section and will be dealt with in detail in Chapter 11. Here it is worth noting that these authors predict the emergence of new entities called data aggregation agents (DAAs) that will address the privacy issue by consolidating and controlling outside access to a customer's personal information. In order for this to work, a customer would choose a DAA when signing up for a mobile service, then register basic profile and preference information to receive customized content. Each time new services are added, they can be linked to the original DAA without the customer needing to resupply personal data. The DAA is therefore continually learning more and more about the customer, who becomes locked in by the convenience. So for companies seeking to build customer relationships, the information held by the DAA can be drawn upon to anticipate the needs of favoured customers and hence offer customized products and services. The ability to do so will increase loyalty while ensuring that marketing resources are targeted on the 'best' customers, meaning of course those deemed to offer most potential for profit.

Partnerships for online relationship marketing

In order for relationship marketing to be effective, companies cannot rely upon departmental solutions that address only one part of the customer account relationship. Increasingly, with the growth of inter-organizational networks on the Web, customer communication is no longer just one customer talking to one enterprise. To provide the kind of service that improves the chance of customer loyalty, companies need to co-ordinate their partners and vendors through extranets that facilitate the sharing of information across company boundaries. Associated data warehousing and data mining tools facilitate the gathering, analysis and management of information necessary to formulate and implement marketing strategies. Kalakota and Robinson (1999) suggest considering partners and vendors to be part of the firm's extended enterprise, and this means sharing customer communication issues with everyone in contact with the customer through integrated applications such as customer service, field service, sales and marketing. They note that the practical organization of marketing functions and activities within such inter-firm networks may be complex. Decisions need to be taken on where responsibility lies for particular tasks, to avoid duplication and customer confusion. Open policies of information-sharing mean that a whole host of issues have to be addressed concerning the 'ownership' of customer data, notwithstanding the technical difficulties inherent in integrating computer systems belonging to different organizations. The approach is referred to as 'all-to-one' marketing by Luengo-Jones (2001). Such integration is often the most critical issue currently facing 'clicks and mortar' firms in developing a successful online strategy.

Building loyalty online: an exploratory study

The following findings, kindly supplied by Gurpal Dhensa, Brunel University, are based on an exploratory study into the nature of loyalty which was conducted by means of face-to-face interviews with managers from both dotcom companies and a traditional high street retailer in September 2001.

In earlier times, marketers could understand consumers well through the daily experience of selling to them. But as firms and markets have grown in size, many marketing decision-makers have lost direct contact with their customers and must now turn to consumer research for enlightenment. Organizations now spend more money than ever to study consumers and develop strategies that meet individual needs. Organizations that understand their consumers and can elicit loyalty from them are those that are best placed to succeed in today's highly competitive market. However, according to Newell (2000), customers are becoming cynical about loyalty schemes such as those operated by the major supermarkets. They do not want to be treated *equally*, they want to be treated *individually*. In fact, some of the very things organizations are doing to build relationships with customers are often the things that are destroying these relationships. In a multichannel environment, a company needs a unified view of customer activity in order to obtain an accurate picture of that customer's interactions with it across a range of different online and offline platforms. If the information is incomplete or inaccurate, then the customer will be suspicious of relationship-building initiatives and trust will not be developed.

The marketer's rationale behind loyalty programmes is that customers can be offered special services, discounts, increased communications and attention beyond the core product or service in exchange for the development of loyalty to the firm that will pay dividends over the longer term (Schiffman and Kanuk 1997). Schiffman and Kanuk go on to explain that placing emphasis on developing a long-term bond with customers allows them to feel some kind of 'personal connection' to the business. But retailers and e-Retailers have noted that consumers do not always act or react as marketing theory suggests they will. Marketing researchers studying the buying behaviour of consumers soon realized that many consumers balked at using exactly the same products as everyone else.

Instead, they preferred differentiated products that reflected their own special needs, personalities and lifestyle. Customers have become more sophisticated and expect companies to provide them with targeted and value-added service (Whitehead 1999). If retailers and e-Retailers do not take on board changing customer needs, then the customer will simply go elsewhere. It is very easy to walk into another retail outlet or click into a new Internet site.

What is meant by the term 'loyalty' anyway? A satisfied customer is not necessarily a loyal one. Another consideration is the extent to which the online environment differs from the retail one in terms of developing customer loyalty. What seems to be needed is for retailers and e-Retailers to start at the beginning and try to understand the parameters of loyalty and how it has changed, before developing specific programmes. As Reichheld *et al.* (2000) state, 'before you can build a relationship with a customer you need to show that you deserve the consumer's trust'. Without that trust, the highest levels of customer service will not necessarily engender loyalty. Primary data from an exploratory study by Dhensa (2001) have highlighted that respondents want 'something else' instead of points from e-Retailers. Even though the sample of respondents was small, this is still important information for e-Retailers and the future of their businesses. Reichheld *et al.* (2000) have stated that there is no difference between online and offline consumer behaviour in terms of how loyalty can be developed, but how many companies have actually *asked* their customers how they can *earn* their loyalty? This policy must surely represent the future of successful loyalty programmes. Here is one example.

Hyundai, the car manufacturer, asked customers to contribute ideas to help develop the a new model of car, the Santa Fe. According to McLuhan (2001), loyalty is considered by Hyundai to be vitally important to the bottom line. In October 2000, 20,000 Hyundai car-owners were mailed a letter inviting them to help develop the company's first sports utility vehicle. The campaign targeted customers who it believed would be interested in the vehicle itself, as well as those who were likely to change their car within two years. The 1,800 respondents were then mailed with instructions on how to offer their views, which would guide the marketing strategy for the model. The mail pack was presented in a large tube, containing a covering letter, detailed questionnaire and a product guide. Also included were four collages depicting possible user groups, two sample newspaper advertisements and an invitation to 'write your own ad' headline. Customers would be able to see to what extent their responses had influenced Hyundai's thinking when they received feedback results before the vehicle's launch. The campaign met Hyundai's objectives of promoting customer loyalty, as seen in the success of the overall marketing activity, which achieved a response rate of over 50 per cent.

CHAPTER SUMMARY

In this chapter, we have examined the interrelationships between internal (staff) and external (customer and business partner) relationship-building in adding value to a product or service, and considered how online marketing can support effective relationship-building. The key issue is to reconcile the marketer's enhanced ability to acquire information with increasing levels of concern on the part of customers over the privacy of their data. In order to meet ever-increasing customer expectations, many companies are now focusing on the difficult challenge of integrating a range of online and offline channels in order to build relationships by offering a seamless service to the customer, regardless of the access mechanism chosen.

Case study:
DELL COMPUTERS

Dell, based in Round Rock, Texas, sells its products and services in more than 140 countries to customers ranging from major corporations, government agencies, medical and educational institutions, to small businesses and individuals. The firm employs 36,500 people from offices in thirty-four different countries. Dell is commonly quoted as one of the success stories of e-Commerce, given that it achieves average daily sales through the Internet of $35 million (43 per cent of its total turnover). It sells both via its traditional sales force and over the phone, as well as via the Internet, but always direct to computer users rather than through distributors and retailers. It was also one of the first companies to realize the potential of the Internet in building direct, one-to-one relationships with customers.

Dell pioneered direct telephone sales of computers after noticing the increased sophistication of the consumer towards buying computers 'sight unseen'. The CEO, Michael Dell, was quick to grasp the power of e-Commerce since the company already had a direct sales model in place. This history has enabled it to migrate to e-Commerce more readily than companies such as Compaq that have relied heavily upon well-developed traditional marketing channels. Competitors are now following this example, but no other PC manufacturer has taken as aggressive an approach to selling over the Internet.

Beyond creating an online catalogue, Dell allows customers to configure PCs to fit individual requirements. All its machines are built to order, thereby increasing customer satisfaction and avoiding the need to keep an inventory of finished machines. The company also produces customized Web pages for its largest corporate customers, enabling them to incorporate Dell's products directly into online procurement systems. It is also using the Internet to improve the efficiency of its own procurement, manufacturing and distribution operations. In November 1999, Dell launched 'e-Support direct', a system for resolving customers' computer problems via the Internet. The site is divided into sections for corporate, small business and individual customers, and the language, content and layout of each part of the site is customized according to the needs of each of these customer groups.

Dell has also moved a significant part of its support activity online. According to Michael Dell,

Through Premier Pages, our support activities, online commerce, auctions and other offerings, we are creating a set of properties that are changing our relationships with customers to an online context. We are essentially moving every process in our business online, whether it's things we do with our suppliers, our internal operations, or our customers. Everything is moving online, and www.dell.com is at the core of that.

What really distinguishes dell.com from other sites is the sheer enormity of all the things it can do for customers. It is one of the largest Web sites in the world, with 2.5 million visitors per week, 160,000 pages of content, $30 million of daily revenue and 25,000 personalized Premier pages for large accounts. Customers can configure computers in thousands of different ways, buy 40,000 different types of peripherals and software, access a massive knowledge base of customer support information, and track their order through shipping.

Dell's online support offerings extend the company's unique direct relationship with its customers. Intuitive, comprehensive and customized, these offerings include Dell Online Knowledge Base, the 'Ask Dudley' area, file library downloads and an entire suite of customized capabilities based on system service tags. By entering a systems service tag number, customers can get support information unique to their systems. Dells' order status system enables customers to track their orders from submission to the point of delivery. For any order, customers can see where their order is in Dell's exclusive build-to-order process. For orders that have been shipped, customers can see detailed shipping status information.

Richard Owens, Vice President of Dell Online Worldwide, points out that the dell.com seen by the public is only the tip of the iceberg. 'It's a pretty large tip, but beneath it is all of the business to business e-Commerce transactions with our largest customers. About 70 per cent of our online business is happening below that waterline through extranet relationships.' He continues, 'What makes you nervous when running a large e-Commerce business is that you are showing everything to your customers. There really is nowhere to hide.'

Pioneering the ultimate customer-driven e-Service, Dell provides more than 25,000 customized Premier Pages, dedicated extranet pages designed specifically for large

185

corporate customers. These customized support pages include order information, order history, system configurations that have been approved by that company, even account contact information. Premier Pages help Dell provide better service to corporate customers while cutting down on the load to its call centres. They also help the company extend its market reach around the globe through Premier Pages for International customers.

In March 2000, Dell unveiled its plan to sell computers that manage networks and data storage technology online. By adding 'back-office' technology to its offerings, Dell is hoping to cash in on one of the fastest-growing segments of business computing in the new economy. Industry analysts expect that it will soon add a range of products for small and medium-sized businesses that are only just beginning to build their Internet infrastructures.

There have, however, been some well-publicized problems. In November, a virus forced Dell to stop production at its Irish plant – which normally produces 12,000 computers a day for the European market – for five days. Some customers complained that they were not informed about the problem and only found out when they telephoned to ask why their systems had not arrived. Many were kept waiting on premium-rate telephone lines to customer service representatives.

Other customer complaints centre upon the way in which the company has concentrated its resources upon online transactions, and neglected other channels. For customers uncomfortable with keying their credit card details into the Internet, the site offers an option to speak to a telephone operator instead when making a purchase. However, this facility often results in connection to an answer machine message and calls are not always returned.

Having read the case study, go onto the Web and have a look around the Dell site. To what extent do you agree with the analysis presented above?

FURTHER READING

Cranfield School of Management (2000) *Marketing Management: A Relationship Marketing Perspective*, London: Macmillan Business.

Godin, S. (1999) *Permission Marketing*, New York: Simon and Schuster.

Kasanoff, B. (2001) *Making It Personal: How to Profit from Personalisation without Invading Privacy*, Chicester, UK: Wiley.

Peppers, D. and Rogers, M. (2001) *One to One B2B*, New York: Doubleday.

QUESTIONS

Question 6.1

Do you foresee any problems with the idea of involving customers in staff development?

Feedback – It seems an interesting idea, but is this really a role that many customers would seek? How would staff feel about the prospect of being assessed by customers in such a way? Depending on the prevailing organizational culture, it could be perceived as an opportunity or a threat.

Question 6.2

Implementing relationship marketing sounds very logical and straightforward on paper. From your reading so far, why do you think so few companies get it right?

Feedback – It is not easy to get a unified view of customers' activity when they make contact by telephone one day, and PC or WAP internet the next. Also, many different parts of the organization may have to work together if the customer buys a range of products and the company is structured by product range rather than by customer activity. Think, for example, of the challenge to a retail bank in obtaining an inclusive view when a single customer may have a mortgage, a branch current account, an internet account, a pension, a loan, a business account . . .

Question 6.3

Can you think of any problems that might arise with the use of 'double opt-in' policies?

Feedback – This is an emerging paradox. There is increasing pressure on companies to increase the size of their email lists, but adherence to 'double opt-in' will keep list sizes small in order to placate privacy advocates. You might well argue that it is better to have a small list of people who have a definite interest in the area, rather than a large list of people who are less committed and who may even complain when contacted.

Question 6.4

How can Dell use its Web site to develop effective relationships with customers?

Feedback – The segmentation by customer group allows particular parts of the site to be customized to meet diverse customer needs. You might think, however, that there is a danger of the Premier Pages inducing envy and hence dissatisfaction in customers who are not singled out for such treatment. Allowing customers to customize their PCs to suit their specific requirements sets the firm apart from many of its competitors. The sheer scale of the products and services on offer sets new standards in the industry. By selling direct, Dell fosters the perception that it offers value for money in comparison with competitors with retail channels to support.

WEB LINKS

www.autotrader.co.uk
Example of an online community based on visitors' shared purpose.

www.bhf.org.uk
Example of an online community based on servicing the diverse needs of British Heart Foundation stakeholders (i.e. patients, carers, researchers, donors, fundraisers, doctors)

www.broadvision.com
A good example (with a series of case studies) of commercial software to help personalize marketing campaigns.

www.cyberatlas.com
A useful resource of Internet statistics.

www.cisco.com
Classic example of an online community based around the company's technical support function.

www.dell.com
Web site organized and customized around the needs of key customer groups.

www.esteel.com
An online community bringing together a diverse range of companies with an interest in the steel industry.

www.eggfreezone.com
A community site set up by Egg to canvass customer feedback.

www.1to1.com
The Peppers and Rogers Web site with a number of personalization case studies.

www.thepetchannel.com
Example of a community site set up to meet the needs of a particular interest group.

www.untied.com
A 'vigilante' site set up by customers critical of the customer service provided by United Airlines.

Chapter 7

Multi-channel marketing

LISA HARRIS

MINDMAP

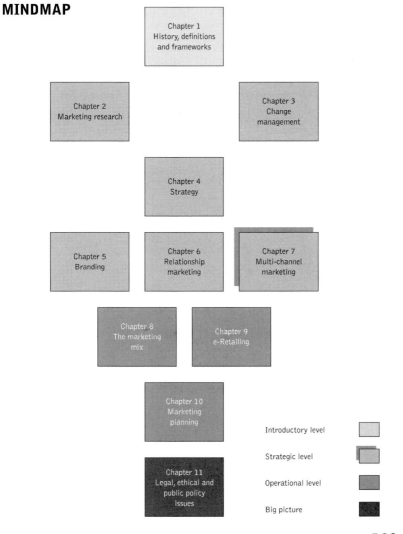

LINKS TO OTHER CHAPTERS

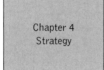

Chapter 4
Strategy

Chapter 8
The marketing
mix

Chapter 9
e-Retailing

- Chapter 4 – Strategy
- Chapter 8 – Marketing mix
- Chapter 9 – e-Retailing

KEY LEARNING POINTS

After completing this chapter you will have an understanding of:

- The scope of recent technological developments such as the mobile Internet and their emerging marketing applications
- The new challenge of integrating PC, mobile and digital television platforms as part of a multi-channel marketing strategy

ORDERED LIST OF SUB TOPICS

- New Internet channels
  - Interactive radio
  - The mobile Internet
  - Digital television
  - The future
- Challenges of multi-channel marketing
- Chapter summary
- ❖ Case study: Marketing to drivers with Onstar
- ❖ Case study: Genie Internet
- ❖ Further reading
- ❖ Questions
- ❖ Web links

NEW INTERNET CHANNELS

As introduced briefly in Chapter 4, recent technological developments mean that the choice for businesses is no longer merely 'online' versus 'offline'. Increasingly, multiple platforms need to be supported. For example, W. H. Smith Online (www.whsmith.co.uk) offers customers PC, mobile and digital television access to its products. As Chaffey (2002) notes, possible benefits of such multi-channel strategies include:

- enhanced brand image;
- early mover advantage;
- learning about the technology from experience;
- customer acquisition;
- customer retention.

Other Internet access platforms at early stages of development include home appliances (Electrolux), vending machines (Maytag) and cars (General Motors' Onstar), which is the subject of a case study later in this chapter.

In general terms, recent online strategic developments can be summarized as in Figure 7.1, which is adapted from a presentation by IBM. Specific recent developments in interactive radio, mobile Internet and digital television will now be considered in turn.

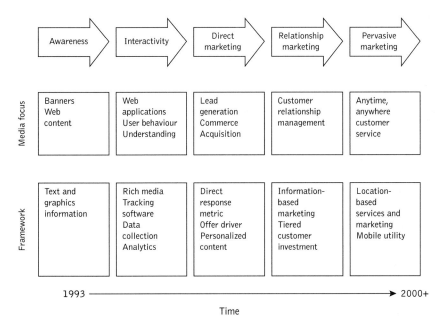

Figure 7.1 The evolution of interactive marketing

Source: Adapted from IBM seminar presentation, 2001

Interactive radio

Smith and Chaffey (2002) note that there are currently two types of interactive radio:

- Digital radio allows two-way communication and is transactional. At the moment, it requires a separate receiver, but streaming technology is not too far off.
- Web radio is traditional radio delivered over the Internet. Once you log onto a station, you can keep surfing while still listening to the radio.

Both types offer good brand-building opportunities. Listeners are already used to interacting with a favourite radio station through voice or email, and the facility to make an instant purchase in response to an advertisement offers significant added value. On the negative side, it is still very early days for these services, and audience fragmentation is likely to occur as the number of stations increases.

The mobile Internet

Review of recent developments

As Figure 7.2 illustrates, the growth of the mobile Internet now exceeds that of the PC version. Mobile communications offer considerable potential to marketers because of their unrivalled combination of:

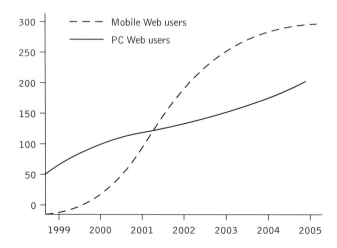

Figure 7.2 Mobile v. PC Internet access: worldwide trends

Source: Ovum, September 2000

192

- instant response;
- personalized content (as each customer has a unique telephone number);
- scope for geographical location tracking.

The potential for mobile networks is particularly high in developing countries that do not have an established wired telephone network and hence no established PC-based Internet services. In the Philippines, for example, SMS messaging (see p. 194) has recently taken off rapidly, and mobile Internet services therefore offer huge marketing opportunities in these emerging markets.

There has been a lot of hype recently about the potential of location-based technology in particular. However, current services are very basic, and it is important to remember that there is some way to go before they become sufficiently reliable and useful to have a broad appeal. For example, variations on the scenario whereby a customer is called on their phone and advised of a special breakfast offer just as they walk to work past a Starbucks outlet, have been heralded as the ultimate in personalized promotional campaigns. There are a number of practical difficulties, though, such as customers' reluctance to be bombarded with intrusive advertising messages and the challenge of communicating effectively with the wide range of mobile devices and standards currently in use.

The usefulness of wireless devices has recently been improved by new standards such as Jini and Bluetooth that connect wireless devices to other electronic products:

- Jini (www.jini.com) allows mobile phones, PCs and personal digital assistants (PDAs) to collaborate as part of an intelligent network, without the need for the correct device driver to be added to the operating system before a new device can be used.
- Bluetooth (www.bluetooth.com) is particularly useful for linking mobile devices because it does not require any wire connections. For example, it could allow a user on a mobile in a car to transfer data from an office PC directly to a home printer.

Keynote systems (www.keynote.com) recently launched a mobile performance measurement service to compare the services offered by all the major UK networks. It can measure delivery times, network comparisons, handset performance and geographic availability, thereby allowing content providers, networks or manufacturers to judge how successful their services have been. It also allows consumers to benchmark performance and make informed purchase decisions. In addition, for a detailed comparison of the characteristics of different mobile technologies, see Smith and Chaffey (2002: ch. 5).

Mobile phones are now rapidly evolving and becoming 'pocket portals' that provide a range of personalized services including email and text messaging with just one monthly bill. Before discussing some of the recent and pending innovations in this area, we shall review developments over the past two or three years.

The first mobiles to offer Internet access, using Wireless Application Protocol (WAP), were introduced in 1999. The information displayed had to be especially formatted for a small screen area, and the limited functionality fell well short of the often extreme levels of industry hype. The telecommunications industry broke one of the central rules of marketing, which states that promotional campaigns should 'under-promise' and 'over-deliver' rather than the other way round. Users found that navigating between pages on a mobile phone could be an extremely laborious process, for which they were paying by the minute for connection charges. During 2000, many early users abandoned mobile commerce after disappointing experiences. While mobile commerce is useful for 'distress' purchases such as parking, actually browsing the Web on a mobile phone is hardly a straightforward and stress-free experience. However, there have been successes to date, notably with mobile banking and gambling services.

'Second-generation' mobile phones introduced early in 2001 offer faster connection speeds and are starting to carry advertising (mobile marketing promotions will be discussed in more detail in the next section of this chapter). High response rates are currently enjoyed by advertisers (perhaps owing to the novelty factor!), and the most successful campaigns have been run by companies such as the *Sun* newspaper, which has used the mobile channel to advertise competitions being run in the paper itself. In other words, the *Sun* is using online advertising to drive its traditional core business – which is offline newspaper sales. Mobile advertising still represents a very small percentage of company promotional spend in comparison with more traditional media such as radio and television, but the figure is increasing. Business services via mobile channels are currently few and far between, but early experiments are under way with order placing, stock-checking availability and order tracking to facilitate supply chain integration.

The much-hyped but still awaited third generation of mobile communications (3G) is expected to deliver sound and images and be 'always on'. Auctions held in 2000 for the licences to operate 3G services netted the UK government over £20 billion, but since then the share prices of the 'successful' telecommunication firms that purchased them have been severely dented.

The technology competing with WAP is called Short Message Systems (SMS), and it is currently by far the more successful in terms of user numbers. SMS is a derivative of numeric paging technology, which has been in existence for many years, updated for two-way communication. To illustrate the rapid growth of SMS, consider the following figures:

- In 1998, mobile phones had a 20 per cent market penetration in the UK and some *1 million* text messages were sent.

- In 2001, market penetration increased to 60 per cent and *1.4 billion* text messages were sent.

Although business applications of SMS are growing, the service has particular appeal in the B2C sector to children and students. According to research by the Yankee Group (www.yankeegroup.com) the European SMS market is expected to be worth £31 billion by 2006. The success of SMS relative to WAP indicates that customers currently regard one-to-one communication services as more important than the ability to download information from Web-based content providers. So in order to make money, mobile operators will need to focus on increasing revenues from mobile traffic by enhancing communications services such as email rather than relying on charging for content provision or mobile commerce. Of potential here is group-based text messaging, which allows individuals to communicate with a group of people via a single message. If operators offer a reduced fee for such services, the increase in volume of messages sent can more than offset the lower per-message fees charged.

Enhanced Messaging Services (EMS), which integrate logos, ring tones and text in a single message, are starting to come onto the market at the time of writing (early 2002). Such capabilities offer increased scope for advertisers to make an impact with their brands. Multimedia Messaging Services (MMS), which incorporate pictures and sound, are promised for the summer of 2002 in Europe, but such services are already big business in Japan. MMS is also likely to boost voice traffic, as according to research by Nokia (as reported in *The Economist*, in October 2001), seven out of ten picture messages sent actually generate a phone call in response (The Economist 2001a).

On the business side, PDAs, which incorporate diary, word-processing and email facilities, are developing into a valuable communication tool. The market leader is Palm, which now provides Internet connection software as standard in all its PDAs. A recent survey by Motient (www.motient.com), an Internet communications and mobile provider, reveals that 'always on' wireless two-way email is quickly becoming a top-priority requirement among PDA users. New features are emerging on a regular basis, and it is clear that mobile phones and PDAs are rapidly converging. By summer 2002, colour screens will be standard in all new devices as will the capability to display, and transmit digital pictures.

In summary, the rate of growth of the mobile Internet has been far quicker than that of earlier technologies, as Figure 7.3 demonstrates. Current opportunities for marketers presented by recent mobile developments centre upon:

- interacting with customers through personalized content provision and associated advertising;
- online shopping and the processing of transactions (m-Commerce);
- internal communications such as distribution of information to a remote workforce.

195

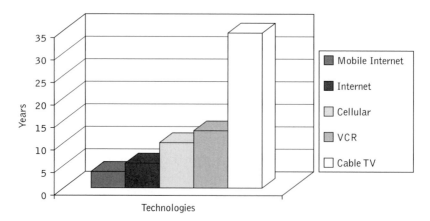

Figure 7.3 *Growth of various means of accessing the Internet.*
Source: Jupiter Research Strategies

As with the growth of the PC-based Internet, it seems that communications with staff and customers are currently adding most value at this early stage, while the widespread acceptance of mobile transactions is still some way away. One must also bear in mind (as discussed with regard to Internet strategy as a whole in Chapter 4) that not all these applications will be relevant to all companies all the time, and in most cases they will complement rather than replace existing channels. The key skill for marketers is to focus on the particular aspects of mobile marketing that will add value to customers in their specific industry contexts. We will now examine each of these areas in turn, drawing upon a number of examples to illustrate this important point.

Content provision and advertising

Figure 7.4 demonstrates that mobile advertising is expected to grow exponentially following a slow start in the difficult economic conditions of 2000–1. The long-anticipated 3G technology will offer far more scope for creative advertising than the small black and white text-only screens that have dominated the market until recently.

It seems to be commonly accepted that busy professional people do not want their important business interrupted by marketing messages on their mobile phones. However, we all at least tolerate advertisements while watching movies . . . so firms that specialize in placing advertisements on mobile firms are at the moment focusing their advertisement placement on mobile entertainment services rather than on business ones. Placing adverts in mobile games that users are playing when they have time to spare is likely to be more acceptable than if a

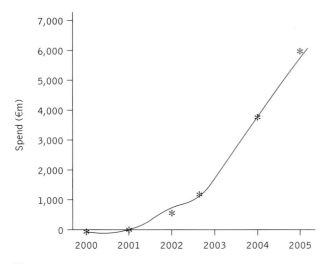

Figure 7.4 *Projected European mobile advertising spend*
Source: Ovum, September 2000

user is interrupted while trying to link up remotely to a company for business purposes. In exchange for the entertainment value in the game, it is reasonable to expect that the customer will tolerate (and, companies of course will hope, respond to) the advertising message. For example, Stone (2002) reports that Mobliss, a US-based wireless marketing agency, worked with Tribune Media in turning its 'Jumble' brand (a scrambled-word game) into a multi-player wireless game. It was also an effective advertising tool because the words used in the puzzles could be directly related to the advertiser's company or product. The advertisements can be displayed as either graphical images or text and themed to correlate with the creative campaign that the advertiser is running offline. In either case, with mobile Internet access, customers also have the ability to click a button and be connected directly to the advertiser's call centre.

Mobliss has also launched a snow report system at www.mysnowreport.com where customers can go online and build in their preferences for particular resorts. Then a text message detailing snow conditions can be sent to the customer's phone. By forming partnerships with companies like the travel agency Moguls that are trying to reach the skier demographic (high income, high expenditure), a customer is able to check out the snow conditions at a resort, and then follow an advertiser's link that is offering a discounted package trip to that resort. Then another link will connect the customer to the call centre to speak to a ski-travel agent. In these circumstances, the customer is more likely to perceive the advertisement as a benefit rather than as just a nuisance. Targeting is very effective because if a user is enquiring about snow conditions, then almost by definition they are themselves a skier. In addition, the fact that the overwhelming majority of people currently using mobile Web services are males aged 20–39 with incomes over £30,000 is of course very appealing to advertisers.

Traditional magazines have been experiencing a fall in advertising revenues over the past couple of years due to the global economic slowdown. The ability to offer interactivity through SMS can make a publication more appealing to companies seeking to place advertisements, while at the same time winning new readers for the magazine itself. So, for example, a company seeking to run a mobile advertising campaign to promote its brand could:

- first, rent a database of readers of a particular magazine that fit the demographic profile of their target group;
- second, send text messages promoting a competition linked to the brand that is set out in the paper-based magazine.

Stone (2002) reports that a few companies have begun sending coupons as messages to wireless devices in order to unload 'perishable' services such concert seats or restaurant tables. He describes the example of PlanetHopper, a small company based in New York, which is focusing upon the entertainment industry. It has partnered General Cinemas, theatres and Shecky's guide to bars and clubs to provide the wireless coupons. By advertising in cinemas and in some 200 New York bars and restaurants, it drew some 20,000 users who opted in to get the promotional messages.

As was discussed in Chapter 6, the key to success is 'opt in' messaging, as people's tolerance of spam messages falls. *The Economist* (2001) recommends that to avoid giving offence, mobile advertisements must:

- be optional (meaning actively requested by users);
- be personalized;
- be moderate in volume;
- be free to the recipient;
- offer a means to unsubscribe.

The article goes on to report on a recent initiative by a mobile advertising company called the Mobile Trial, in which advertisements as text messages had an average response rate of 10–20 per cent. This is much higher than usual rates for direct mail (3 per cent) and Internet banner advertisements (less than 1 per cent).

Mobile commerce

Mobile commerce – meaning the actual purchase of items from the mobile Internet – is expected to grow rapidly over the next few years. Forrester Research (www.forrrester.com) suggests that worldwide revenues could reach $200 billion by 2005. Be warned that we have heard wild projections before – in connection with the potential revenues likely to be generated by dotcoms, for example – so do not read too much into these figures. Before getting carried away in another round of Internet euphoria, think about the recent high level of negative publicity about mobile theft, which highlights the problem of security. Steps have recently been taken by the major market players to address this issue. In early 2002, a common database of stolen phone numbers was established so that the handsets could be disabled to prevent unauthorized purchases being made. Remember also that many people are still reluctant to undertake PC-based commerce, let alone transact through a mobile phone.

Growth in mobile commerce is likely to be driven by alliances between banks and telecommunications companies. Both parties have particular strengths which if brought together can add considerable value. Banks have a banking licence, credit verification skills and an established retail network. Mobile operators provide a modern brand image and the infrastructure of a mobile network. Both have a large customer base upon which to draw. While some companies (notably Vodafone) have made public their objective to provide financial services when restrictions on the allocation of banking licences are lifted (in 2002), others believe that the partnership route is the way forward. So far, banks have taken a cautious approach and built their mobile capabilities for small numbers of customers on a trial basis. They now face the challenge of scaling up the infrastructure to cope with larger volumes of users. Abbey National, for example, offers e-Banking via the Genie mobile portal, which can be accessed by WAP phones over any service network. According to Bansal (2001), the bank's strategy is to develop partnerships that enable it to offer electronic banking across all technology platforms. These alliances offer customers the security of dealing with an established brand, which can be significant in building the necessary trust for mobile banking to really take off.

Internal communications

Remote workers can use wireless devices to access office systems and marketing information held on the corporate intranet. Such services are useful for logistics companies needing to keep track of their drivers' location and also to send SMS messages with reminders and alerts, for example of schedule changes or traffic problems. Salespeople operating in the field can update customer records or request specific information automatically. Although the potential for the mobile Internet to enhance communications between staff or between staff and customers is considerable, adapting the corporate security systems to allow access through the mobile environment can be a significant headache, as can the practicalities of integrating mobile channels with existing IT systems more generally.

Mobile challenges

Leung and Antypas (2001) note how the current mobile landscape resembles the first-generation Internet in the mid-1990s in terms of the key business challenges:

- *Bandwidth*. Many innovative services such as real-time video streaming will not be feasible, given the limited bandwidth currently available, and will remain what the authors refer to as 'pipe dreams' for the foreseeable future. The problem may be eased somewhat – although by no means fully addressed – by the arrival of 2.5G and 3G handsets promised for 2002.
- *Interperability*. Cellular carriers currently have different systems and standards that are not compatible with each other. GSM (Global Service for Mobile), TDMA (Time Division Multiple Access) and CDMA (Code Division Multiple Access) are available on different carriers in different areas, meaning that communications with customers may need to be channelled through each carrier for its specific area.
- *Equipment*. The mobile cannot compete with the desktop in terms of display, computing power and keyboard facilities. The displays are currently available only in black and white, and support very limited animation. There are no cookies to recognize passwords and personalize greetings, and if the Internet connection is broken, then access cannot be resumed from where it was last used because the application will restart.

Mini case study:
THE MOBEY FORUM

The Mobey Forum, (www.mobeyforum.org) was established in May 2000 to develop and promote mobile technology in financial services, in search of a secure and customer-friendly solution to the issue of mobile payments. The Forum aims to ensure that users will be able to pay for goods and services as easily with their phones as they can with credit or debit cards today. Its mission is to encourage the use of mobile technology for services such as remote banking and share-dealing. The Forum advocates a 'dual chip' phone, one for the mobile service and one for banking transactions. This means that the financial services provided will be independent of the telecom provider. Users are expected to treat the phone as they would a wallet, as it will encompass facilities for:

- receipt storage;
- electronic ticketing;
- promotional coupons;
- making payments.

A series of trials are currently under way. By working closely with European standardization bodies, the Mobey Forum aims to avoid fragmentation of the mobile commerce market by a multitude of competing standards. It is also putting across the message that if mobile payment services are to thrive, the key customer needs of security, convenience and usability must be central to developers' agendas.

Mini case study:
IS THE FUTURE OF E-COMMERCE MOBILE?

In Japan, most business people have to commute every day and will spend a good part of their working days in densha or chikatetsu, the Japanese public transport system. As a result, mobile communication devices such as PHSs (Personal Handyphone System), mobile phones and pagers have become very popular and are being supplied in a wide variety of models. The PHS, developed by Japan's NTT, is a lightweight portable wireless phone that can function as a cordless phone at the user's home and as a mobile phone elsewhere. It can handle voice, fax and video signals. Users can send and receive email and even develop their own Web pages on tiny mobile handsets.

At the Information Technology Conference in Taiwan held in June 2000, Tadashi Sekizawa, the CEO of Fujitsu, claimed that the mobile Internet – defined as an intelligent transmitting system that can link with any Internet-accessible hardware or satellite system – will gradually replace personal computers as the most important application in the electronic commerce era. Japan is an exceptional player in the mobile field, having developed its own unique hardware system. The service is not delivered via desktop personal computers, laptop computers or digital televisions, but by using mobile phones and PDAs.

NTT Mobile Communication network, Japan's leading mobile phone operator, and its competitors Nippon IDO Tsushin and DDI Cellular Group, are already providing mobile data services such as home banking, news headlines, restaurant guides, weather reports, cinema schedules and fortune-telling to the Japanese market.

NTT DoCoMo, one of the most advanced companies in the telecommunication's industry today, is currently introducing the first 3G mobile phone service. The 3G mobile phone service will be the first step for Japan into the 'Evernet' (a Japanese term for universal access to the Internet, irrespective of place, time and equipment). NTT DoCoMo is using a technology called FOMA (Freedom of Mobile Multimedia Access) which will provide more freedom in terms of speed and quality than the WAP technology developed in the West. The company has already begun offering its hit 'i-mode' wireless Internet service to the US market through its partner AT&T Wireless. The service will be tested first in the Seattle area before

201

being expanded nationwide early in 2002. It will allow US users to exchange email, check stock prices and find restaurants, movies and other information from their cell phones.

NTT DoCoMo is set to expand rapidly, having bought a 16 per cent stake in AT&T Wireless in 2000, as well as minority stakes in KPN Mobile NV of Netherlands, Hutchinson 3G UK Holdings, Taiwan's KG Telecom and Hutchinson Telecom of Hong Kong. Kiyoyuki Tsujimuru, Managing Director in charge of global strategy, was confident the i-mode would be a hit overseas: 'Cell phones in the United States and Europe are still like 13-inch black and white TV sets. There is a huge gap in technology. People see colour displays and are stunned.' US users will be able to access a wide variety of i-mode sites such as CNN for news or Disney for their characters. There are already 40,000 i-mode sites operational in Japan. The variety and the quality of the information displayed makes NTT DoCoMo one of the first in the world able to offer advanced forms of wireless technology allowing for video, audio and other data-rich transmissions.

Sources: *Global Views Monthly* (July 2000); Tadashi Sekizawa, CEO of Fujitsu, at the World Information Technology Conference, Taiwan; *eCommon Wealth* (February 2001); Japanese Evernet, Taiwan; Yuri Kageyama, AP News, 14 March 2001.

Digital television

Interactive Digital Television (iDTV) looks similar to PC-based Internet but is delivered through a television set and can be operated using a remote control. From a standing start in 1999, market penetration by 2002 is currently around 40 per cent of UK households and is projected to rise to 95 per cent by 2010, according to a Netpoll survey. Leading providers include Sky Digital, ON Digital, Telewest and NTL. One of the key drivers for this surprisingly rapid growth has been the provision of free set-top boxes by these platform providers. Services currently provided include home shopping, email, video, banking and travel. Forrester Research (2001) predicts that more people will access the Internet through a television than through a PC by the end of 2004.

Advertising through this mechanism can be interactive, as viewers can respond immediately to request further information or to sign up for a promotion. Digital television has helped increase the fragmentation of viewers, as there are over 200 channels now available in the UK. This means that advertising can be easily targeted to tighter niche audiences, for example through exposure on sports, cooking or health channels. Advertisers can develop their own television channels in order to incorporate content provision and communicate with their customers less intrusively. For example, the PC version of Boots' digital health channel,

Wellbeing, is also automatically accessed if you type in 'www.boots.co.uk'. Specialist digital television channels also provide more focus for sponsorship deals. Domino's Pizza, which is represented on satellite, cable and the Web, is one of the early success stories of iDTV. e-Commerce transactions represent 4 per cent of its total business. Management credit the firm's sponsorship of *The Simpsons* as pivotal in building Domino's iDTV business. This activity has given Domino's a brand recognition figure of 98 per cent in multi-channel homes.

The UK government is currently pushing for total digital television penetration, and there has been talk of switching off the analogue signal by as soon as 2010. By the end of 2001, the number of digital television owners in the UK reached the same level (36 per cent) as the number of Internet users in the country for the first time, according to e-MORI's Technology Tracker (www.e-mori.co.uk). While the number of new users seeking Internet access is levelling off, digital TV ownership more than doubled in 2001. In social groups AB and C1, PC-based Internet access far outweighs digital television ownership, but the ratio shifts in social groups C2 and DE, in which twice as many households have digital television as have Internet access via PC. The relationship between social class and choice of Internet access mechanism is illustrated in Figure 7.5. Fewer than half of digital television owners have so far used interactive services such as shopping, banking, gaming or email. This is because PCs have been traditionally

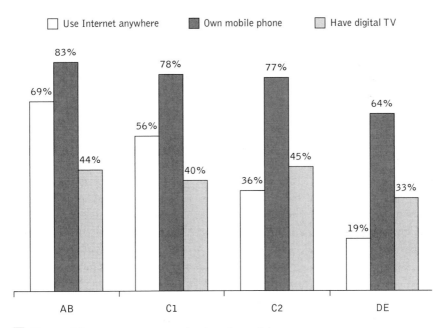

Figure 7.5 *Internet access mechanisms by social group*

Source: www.e-mori.co.uk (accessed February 2002)

viewed as information tools and are a logical choice for accessing the Internet and using online consumer services. The television, however, is viewed as an entertainment tool, and the biggest driver for digital adoption so far has been improved picture quality and a greater choice of channels, with little attention being paid by consumers to the advantages of interactive services.

Smith and Chaffey (2002) note the following advantages of iDTV to marketers:

- direct-response mass-market advertising;
- highly targetable;
- moving buyers through the complete buying process;
- audience engagement through interaction;
- brand-building and positioning reinforcement;
- brand-building through community-building;
- customer service – reduction of bottlenecks;
- security – less risk associated with TV than Web sites;
- controllable – highly measurable;
- cost savings.

These authors go on to recommend five key steps to making iDTV work in practice:

1 Start small; test out advertisements first on a small scale and see what reaction is gained.
2 Develop your own content area or micro Web site linked to iDTV.
3 Design for the lowest common denominator to maximize the number of people who can make use of your service.
4 Grow your offer over time to include purchasing or personalization.
5 Form partnerships or build a team for the future to ensure that the necessary skills are available.

However, despite the rapidly increasing volume of viewers, actual purchase transactions have been slow to take off. Forrester Research notes that many retailers currently using iDTV as a channel to market are planning to pull out when their contracts come up for renewal. The main reason for their dissatisfaction is weak sales. The Forrester Research report points to a poor visitor-to-purchase ratio of only 2 per cent. Also problematic is the location of transactional sites within 'walled gardens', which are dedicated interactive channels that are separate from programme content. The challenge is to find ways and means of driving consumers to these interactive channels and encouraging them to carry out transactions. Although a shake-out of unprofitable business is probably inevitable, the iDTV medium is slowly evolving, costs are falling and interactivity becoming less 'clunky', suggesting that opportunities will present themselves to companies prepared to take the longer view.

The future

'Push' technology is the name given to a broad spectrum of products that automate the delivery of information to the user. Many Web sites are currently based upon 'pull' models, whereby users seek out the information in which they are interested. In contrast, push technologies create automated communications relationships whereby products can be aimed at users who have expressed an interest and given permission to be sent targeted material. This shift in focus has significant implications for marketers which were discussed in Chapter 6.

V-Commerce (short for 'voice') allows users to conduct self-service transactions alternately using the web and the telephone. This initiative is being led by the V-Commerce Alliance, which consists of a number of Internet and telecom companies. For example, a consumer would be able to make an airline reservation over the Web, and then later call a specific number to obtain departure gate or frequent-flyer information – or, before ordering a new computer online, speak to a customer service representative to check which model would be most suitable for their requirements.

Speech recognition is becoming increasingly common in US call centres, particularly in the banking and airline industries. It is also being adapted as a 'hands-free' input device for cars in Europe and Japan, as the motor industry recognizes that voice is the safest way for drivers to interact with in-car technologies (The Economist, 2001b). Nissan already sells a premium model that uses voice instruction to control audio, temperature, navigation and lighting. The new technologies promise to deliver access to information and services on a permanent basis anywhere that there is a telephone connection. It is only in the past year or so that the necessary computing power has become small and cheap enough to fit into mobile devices in a cost-effective way. In addition, the (admittedly slow) spread of broadband access to the Internet in public places is fuelling the demand for instant information. What is also generating interest is the way in which speech recognition is improving the quality of information services by eliminating the need for telephone queuing and badly designed menu-driven voicemail systems. The *Economist* report goes on to note the advantages that have accrued to Charles Schwab, a US discount stockbroker that was one of the first firms in the world to introduce a speech-based system, in 1996:

> That year, the number of new accounts with the company increased by 41 per cent, and its call centres took 97 million calls. The new system was installed by leading speech-recognition supplier, Nuance of Menlo Park, California. At

Schwab, the automated attendant can understand 15,000 names of individual equities and funds; takes up to 100,000 calls a day; and is 93 per cent accurate in identifying queries the first time they are made. Customers get immediate access to quotes and trading, even during busy periods. Costs have been cut from $4–5 per call to $1.

(2001b: 96)

Apart from call centres, other opportunities for telephone-based services using speech recognition include:

- self-service banking;
- catalogue ordering;
- weather and stock market reports;
- email collection;
- virtual personal assistants (VPAs).

In order for the telephone and the Internet to be merged effectively, common industry standards need to be achieved so that Web pages can handle voice. In October 2001 the World Wide Web Consortium (www.w3.org) – a voluntary organization that sets international standards – released a draft version of VoiceXML for this purpose. At the same time, however, a new platform was created by such key players as Microsoft, Intel and Philips to develop a rival standard called SALT (Speech Application Language Tags). It remains to be seen which of these will prevail.

Virgin plans a new service (www.virginunlimited.com) that aims to sell everything from cars and toasters to holidays at big discounts. It will offer postcode-specific advice on financial services and household utilities at the lowest prices. In order to provide this service, the company has established partnerships with a number of consumer durable wholesalers and also providers of specialist niche products. Consumers will be able to ask product providers to compete for business by stating their requirements. The company that offers the best price and terms will win the order.

Consumers are often frustrated at having to deal with different service providers for each channel, which necessitates separate billing arrangements, passwords and email addresses. Consequently, they will migrate to services that allow them to personalize a single service for use on multiple devices. Looking ahead, Java TV (still at a very early stage of development) will bring together television and computing technologies to enable broadcasters to deliver value-added services to a range of Java-enabled devices. This means that the Internet will be rendered 'device independent' and customers will be able to switch their viewing from television to PC or mobile – anywhere and at any time – as their circumstances dictate. However, as was noted in Chapters 4 and 6, the organizational challenges associated with developing and integrating effective multiple channel operations should not be underestimated.

ACTIVITY

To check out the progress of some predictions, see 'The virtual world begins to get real' in the *Financial Times*, 25 August 1999 (available from www.ft. com). Chapter 5 of Smith and Chaffey (2002) is also worth reading for its interesting investigation of such new applications as wearable (yes, really!) computers.

Challenges of multi-channel marketing

Figure 7.6 illustrates how the usage of various Internet access mechanisms has developed over the past few years. At this early stage, companies need to address a number of challenges when considering the development of multi-channel strategies that allow customers to access online content from a range of devices:

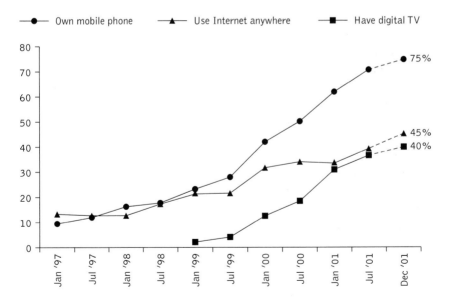

Figure 7.6 *Market penetration of Internet access mechanisms*

Source: www.e-mori.co.uk (accessed February 2002)

- The extent to which they should invest in these relatively untried technologies, with little indication of likely customer demand or long-term prospects for making money.
- The need to 'repurpose' content for each tool (Smith and Chaffey 2002). For example, trying to display a Web site on a WAP screen means that graphics and pictures are lost, and different coding is required. Smith and Chaffey also note that switching between PC and iDTV is problematic because Web sites are designed to be viewed in 'lean-forward mode' from two feet away, but iDTV in 'laid-back mode' from more like eight feet away. Navigating with a mouse is also very different from navigating with a remote control device.
- The unique properties of each medium in terms of the user experience delivered. For example, mobile transactions are likely to be for low-value or distress purchases, because the amount and quality of information that can be displayed to the customer on screen is limited. In contrast, the PC allows huge volumes of data to searched and displayed, and so is best suited to situations where the customer wants to carry out extensive research before making a purchase. Digital television offers yet another dynamic; although it is still in its infancy, early usage suggests that purchases may take place in a more collaborative, impulsive and social context than through the other channels.
- Whether they should offer all their products or services across each medium (and if so, the extent to which customization is necessary and/or appropriate) or 'mix and match' according to the characteristics of each channel and the specific message to be delivered.
- The need for *integrated* online and offline marketing campaigns. Smith and Chaffey (2002) describe how MTV asked viewers to send in SMS text messages to provide comments and vote for their favourite video. MTV then played the winning video together with the comments live. The event was promoted through offline magazines read by the target audience, and the paper-based advertisement demonstrated a text message on a phone explaining how to take part.
- How to manage the necessary internal information processing that will allow the company to achieve a unified view of customer activity across all channels. For this to work, a central database is necessary to provide up-to-date customer details to all channel operators. Remember that customers' expectations are continually rising and they may expect to use a combination of channels to effect just one single purchase . . .

It should be clear from this brief discussion that the technical ability to offer multi-channel access is just the starting point. Considerable investment needs to be made in the back-office computer systems and business process integration

208

necessary to actually make it work in practice. The difficulties are even greater for small firms with limited financial resources, or those with legacy computer systems that cannot be easily integrated. However, for those that succeed, the potential for combine multi-channel offerings with *personalized* content (as discussed in Chapter 6) provides an enormous marketing opportunity.

ACTIVITY

Activity – Look up the Argos Web site (www.argos.co.uk) and evaluate its scope. Argos set up an iDTV service in 2001 and is currently working on a mobile offering. The company is now facing the challenge of how to tailor a catalogue of over 9,000 products to electronic platforms that will present the information in very different ways.

Despite the difficulties highlighted above, IBM is staking its future on 'next-generation e-Business'. Figure 7.7 illustrates the company's view of the new economy as 'powered by connectivity'.

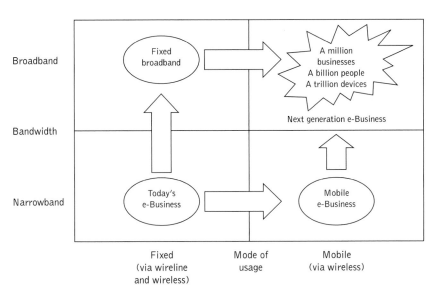

Figure 7.7 *The new economy is powered by connectivity*

Source: Adapted from IBM seminar presentation, 2001

Mini case study:
ECKOH

In June 2001, 365 Corporation (www.365corp.com) launched Europe's first comprehensive voice portal, Eckoh, which can be accessed over the internet at www.08701101010.com or from any standard telephone – mobile or landline. Eckoh uses voice-activated dialling technology to allow the user to:

- send and retrieve emails and SMS messages;
- go shopping;
- listen to the latest news, sport and entertainment;
- set up conference calls;
- check and create diary appointments;
- update diaries.

Through partnerships with content providers such as Travelmaster and the Press Association it is able to offer sports, travel and entertainment news. Alliances with William Hill, Teleflorist and Domino's Pizza allow consumers to make transactions via voice. All partners pay to be included in the service, and 365 also receives a percentage from calls made, which are charged to customers at national rates. Advertising and sponsorship possibilities are also being explored, with the possibility of crediting the user's phone bill for having to listen to advertisements. Future plans also include premium-rate services allowing users to talk directly to professionals such as vets, lawyers and doctors. To ensure customers are able to navigate effectively around the portal, a choice of 'personal assistants' is included. Customers can select a character to guide them through the services offered, and will even be able to vote different characters on or off the service in *Big Brother*-style elections.

365 Corporation and Virgin Mobile have recently formed a partnership to launch the UK's first mobile voice portal. 365 Corporation's voice services division, called Eckohtec, has partnered with Virgin Mobile to provide the latter's 1.25 million customers with voice-activated information, entertainment and commerce services. The voice portal will operate as part of Virgin Mobile's VirginXtras brand, and will be powered by the Eckoh voice platform. The partnership is for a minimum of two years and gives Eckohtec both application development and maintenance fees and an ongoing revenue stream based on usage. Eckohtec will host the service on its 4,000-line Interactive Voice Response (IVR) platform, giving Virgin Mobile access to a rapidly growing market. Virgin Mobile customers will access the voice portal service via a four-digit shortcode number and navigate around the system using speech recognition technology. Users can listen to news and sport and other audio content, as well as use the service to go shopping.

Source: Adapted from www.ft.com, 21 November 2001

CHAPTER SUMMARY

Multi-channel marketing is a rapidly developing area offering enormous scope for creativity, brand-building and competitive advantage. Mobile channels in particular can offer personalized content and transactional capabilities to customers, and targeted advertising opportunities. They also permit effective internal communications such as the distribution of information to a remote workforce. Considerable 'hype' currently surrounds the mobile industry, and the examples discussed in the chapter demonstrate not only the significant business opportunities but also a reminder that the technical ability to offer multi-channel services is just the starting point. Considerable investment needs to be made in the back-office computer systems and business process integration necessary to actually make it work in practice. The difficulties of multi-channel marketing are even greater for small firms with limited financial resources or those with legacy computer systems that cannot be easily integrated.

Case study:
MARKETING TO DRIVERS WITH ONSTAR

Onstar has been developed by General Motors to provide functions that guide drivers and summon help in case of an emergency. Using cellular technology and a receiver that picks up signals from the satellites of the Global Positioning System, a subscriber's car can report its location to a command centre, and the driver can communicate with an operator or with a voice-recognition system through a hands-free microphone and the car's speakers. Additional services are built around small screens on the dashboard that display maps and other information.

General Motors ran a successful television advertising campaign in 2000 for its Onstar service that generated worldwide publicity and curiosity about the increasingly diverse applications of wireless technology. The commercials focused on Onstar's capability to help stranded motorists or provide directions to the service's 1.5 million subscribers. As Onstar equipment makes it technically possible for the system to know a car's location at any time, information could be used to deliver highly specific advertisements pointing the driver to a convenient local restaurant or store. The dangers centre upon distracted drivers compromising road safety and the Onstar brand being damaged by a barrage of marketing ploys that outweigh the benefits of the system to the driver. (The wireless phone industry will soon confront the same dilemma, as the US government pushes it to add tracking features to phones for safety reasons.)

211

However, Onstar seems more interested in advertising that is tied to content, rather than to a subscriber's location. Since May 2001, owners of some GM models have been able to subscribe to Onstar's 'Virtual Advisor'. The $399 yearly service gives access to investment accounts, sport scores, horoscopes, weather reports, stock quotes, customized news and other personal information. Subscribers obtaining stock quotes from the service are told that the information is sponsored by Fidelity Investments. If they have a Fidelity account, they can connect to an automated Fidelity system and trade stocks while they drive.

In 2002, developers of these 'telematic' services hope to reach beyond the Onstar image to include a wide array of information services and mobile commerce initiatives benefiting from the technology. For example, Chrysler now offers hands-free cell phone access as an option on its cars, which will be incorporated as a factory-installed accessory by 2003. Using Bluetooth wireless technology to communicate with any cellphone both in and out of the car, the unit includes a dashboard-mounted receiver and a microphone embedded in the rear-view mirror and phone. While the system works with any carrier and phone number, AT&T Wireless was picked as Chrysler's preferred provider. Despite the safety and privacy concerns mentioned above, participating companies are coming under increasing pressure to recoup some of their significant development costs. Consequently, they are starting to add advertising and 'mobile commerce' to the mix, while claiming that their subscribers will not be subject to the dashboard equivalent of junk email and annoying pop-up ads. Wingcast, for example, a joint venture of Ford Motor and Qualcomm, plans to offer a 'gas station locator' feature soon after its service is introduced in mid-2002. Subscribers can set up a personal profile on the service's Web site, then designate their preferred petrol station chains. When fuel is running low, a computerized voice will notify the driver and offer directions to the nearest station. Other services might let the driver know which petrol station in the area has the lowest prices, whether a favourite department store is having a sale or when a specific new CD is available at a music outlet nearby. Services like Wingcast could potentially charge companies for the right to send marketing messages to their customers, or get a cut when a transaction takes place.

Of course, drivers already listen to unsolicited commercial messages every day on their car radio. Philip J. Rowland of the consulting firm McKinsey and Co. predicts a shift from traditional radio to digital audio services for drivers. This might mix personalized information such as local traffic reports with advertising messages that the subscriber has *agreed* to receive. Mr Rowland said the increased automation of telematics services, using voice recognition and other technologies, should lower the cost significantly, and growth could also be driven by loyalty programmes for petrol stations and airlines. For example, a service might let a driver know about a chance to earn frequent-flier miles by shopping at a store nearby.

Source: Adapted from Walser (2001)

212

Case study:
O2 AND THE GENIE INTERNET PORTAL

Background

In order to set the context for this case study, it is important to bear in mind that mobile phones now have a 60 per cent market penetration in the UK, and usage increased by over 1,500 per cent between 2000 and 2002. The rate of industry growth and product innovation therefore has been – and continues to be – phenomenal.

O2 is the holding company for the BT division formally known as Cellnet. It began trading in November 2001 and has 100 per cent ownership of mobile network operators in four countries:

- the UK (BT Cellnet);
- Germany (Viag Interkom);
- the Netherlands (Telfort Mobiel);
- Ireland (Digifone).

Additionally, O2 has operations on the Isle of Man (Manx Telecom) and a leading European mobile internet portal business, Genie (www.genie.co.uk). O2 was the first company in the world to launch and roll out a commercial GPRS (or '2.5G') network, and has secured third-generation mobile telephony ('3G') licences in the UK, the Netherlands and Germany. The company expects to apply for a 3G licence in Ireland when the application process commences. O2 has approximately 17 million customers and some 15,000 employees, with revenues for the year ended 31 March 2001 of £3.2 billion. Data now represents over 10 per cent of O2 service revenues and, with the recent launch of new devices and services as well as future developments, it is expected to increase to 25 per cent contribution within three years.

In January 2002, O2 announced that it had signed a group-wide agreement with Handspring to distribute and market Handspring's Treo family of compact wireless communicators throughout O2's operating businesses. Handspring is a leading innovator in personal communication and handheld computing. Targeted principally at the mobile professional and SME markets, Treo is the first integrated Palm OS wireless communicator product to be launched on O2 networks, providing customers with a pocket-sized solution for combined voice and data services. With telephone, organizer, Web and messaging applications combined in a small and lightweight device, Treo will initially take advantage of O2's broad GSM networks, but will upgrade to GPRS upon availability of GPRS software.

The company is now in the process of rebranding its consumer services, which will trade under the O2 banner from spring 2002. An extensive advertising campaign encompassing both digital and traditional channels and rumoured to be costing £150 million is currently at the planning stage. Agency Republic has been appointed to

213

manage the O2 brand across the web, mobile phones and interactive television, and digital advertising is to be fundamental to the rebranding campaign. Traditional advertising has not been forgotten – on the significant date of 2 February 2002 (020202), double-page spreads in the UK quality press kick-started the rebranding exercise.

The Genie mobile Internet portal

Genie was launched in 2001 as the world's first exclusively online mobile service. Genie's UK mobile service operates on the BT Cellnet network and is therefore now part of O2. BT Cellnet is one of the largest UK mobile networks, with over 8 million customers, and offers 99 per cent coverage of the UK population. Genie is the UK's leading mobile Internet company, with over 3 million registered users of the Genie Internet portal. It provides free text messaging and free access to WAP. The mobile Internet is the technology that allows users to view information, play games and manage personal email via a WAP phone. WAP stands for Wireless Application Protocol and is the worldwide standard enabling WAP mobile phones to access the Mobile Internet. Genie Mobile Internet provides a number of services available on WAP phones:

- email – the ability to read, reply and forward emails;
- m-Commerce – you can now buy books and CDs;
- information – the latest sports scores, current news and gossip;
- enquiries – flight times, cinema times;
- entertainment – games, competitions and reviews.

Mobile phone and Internet services are integrated so that customers can access information on a PC or via mobile phone.

The Genie portal itself runs at significant loss, but its services appeal to the key market segment of early-adopter mobile phone users. Members of this group are predisposed to purchasing new gadgets, understand the rapidly developing terminology and issues surrounding mobile developments, and also happen to spend the most money on mobiles. Any mobile user can register on the site – they do not necessarily have to be using O2 networks. By permission-based marketing to these registered Genie visitors, special deals can be offered to get them to switch to the O2 network. At this stage of market development, the key selling points as far as users are concerned relate to content (in the form of information and alerts about share prices, skiing conditions, sports results, etc.) rather than transactional commerce.

The Genie brand has high awareness ratings despite low advertising spend. According to *Campaign*'s dotcom weekly awareness survey (30 November 2001), Genie is ranked tenth in the UK, with an awareness rating of 27 per cent, just behind the Easy Group on 32 per cent and ahead of Wellbeing on 20 per cent. Genie is promoted on the major portals such as Google, MSN and Yahoo!, and pays for prominent placements on search engines so that a banner is invoked should a surfer conduct a search for 'mobile phone', for example.

Genie aims to leverage value from its mobile services by offering customers special deals through partnerships with banks and ISPs as part of a 'closed' network. This business model is superior to many 'open' network portals because partner firms will either pay for preferential access to Genie customers or at least provide content for free. Genie customers who want to access services from companies outside the partner network have to pay extra for the privilege. To illustrate how this works, consider the example of mobile banking. Genie provides secure links to eight leading banks to enable customers to access their bank accounts via their mobile phones on the O2 network. Within the next twelve months, customers will also be able to trade stocks in this way. Hence there is scope for the major stockbrokers to be 'plumbed in' to the partnership to make the entire contact, share purchase and payment transaction from the bank account a seamless and immediate process for the customer. If such a service is available, why would a customer want to look elsewhere for a stockbroker? Stockbrokers, therefore, will pay for a preferential placing in the Genie portfolio, and indeed several may compete with each other – with the best positions on the listing commanding the highest fees.

From the partner firms' perspective, there are three key drivers for associating with Genie:

- to obtain additional revenue from existing customers by offering an alternative channel to access the company;
- to expand the customer base by appealing to new market segments (for example people who use their mobile phone to bet with Ladbrokes through the Genie gateway have a very different demographic profile from that of Ladbroke's traditional customer base relying upon the firm's network of betting shops);
- to reduce the costs of servicing their customer base. This is the key driver for banking partners, for example.

To illustrate the potential of mobile services to reduce costs (and in some cases change the partner firm's entire business model), consider the example of a recruitment agency for temporary staff. In the past, such a firm would rely upon a team of office-based employees to make telephone calls to perhaps hundreds of registered individuals to advise them of newly received employment opportunities and sign people up as required. This could be an expensive and time-consuming exercise if large numbers of staff were required. By sending a text message simultaneously to the entire labour pool database requesting those interested to call in and sign up for the job, the entire cost structure of the business is altered. The staff employed to recruit would only have to answer calls from people accepting the work, rather than make a large number of outgoing calls touting for business. In the near future, the acceptance procedure will also become Web based, thereby reducing the need for human intervention still further.

FURTHER READING

Haig, M. (2002) *Mobile Marketing*, London: Kogan Page.
Lindstrom, M. (2001) *Clicks, Bricks and Brands*, London: Kogan Page.

QUESTIONS

Question 7.1

What do you think are the potential opportunities of these messaging services for advertisers looking for a suitable channel through which to promote their brands?

Feedback – There seems to be particular scope for companies looking to target the teenage market segment. According to NOP Research (www.nop.co.uk), in early 2002, about 50 per cent of children in the UK aged between 7 and 16 have mobile phones, sending on average three text messages per day. Broadcasting companies such as ITV have recently launched campaigns using text messages as trailers for programmes in order to reach key demographic viewing groups. The confectionery group Mars expects to make one of its advertising tunes available as a free mobile ringtone delivered as a text message.

Question 7.2

Although the technical developments appear very exciting, to what extent do you think marketers can effectively convey brand personality through wireless media?

Feedback – It is unlikely that many promotional campaigns will rely solely on mobile channels. Opportunities for innovation arise by combining a number of online and offline channels to develop an integrated promotional strategy. For example, the car manufacturer Audi has used a combination of:

- television for brand-building;
- newspapers for providing performance data;
- WAP for invitations to new model launches and test drives;
- PC-based Internet for feature specification;
- the established dealer network for face-to-face discussions with salespeople.

Each element of the campaign can therefore address a different aspect of the buying process.

Question 7.3

Why do you think the response rates to early mobile advertising campaigns were so high?

Feedback – Mobile advertising is still so new that the novelty factor may well apply. In the early days of the Internet, banner advertisement 'click-through' rates were high, but viewers soon learned to filter out unwanted promotions.

Question 7.4

Although many of the new project ideas such as wearable computers discussed in this chapter seem very exciting, what factors do you think might constrain the rate of growth and scope of these products and services?

Feedback – It is easy to get carried away by the possibilities inherent in the Internet and related products. Do not forget that issues such as security and inadequacies of the existing telephone network in the face of ever increasing demand leading to slow or interrupted access are real problems that have yet to be fully addressed. It is also difficult to determine at this stage just how much customers will be prepared to pay.

Question 7.5

McKinsey estimates that telematics (as discussed in the Onstar case study) could be a $100 billion business in the United States, Western Europe and Japan by 2010. This seems incredibly optimistic – what do you think?

Feedback – While the technical possibilities are obviously exciting, it is important to bear in mind the challenges posed by services of this nature. The key seems to be that marketing messages will be acceptable to drivers only if they are based upon *permission*. In other words, the driver agrees to receive certain messages (and only those messages) that are directly relevant to his or her specific interests (see Chapter 6 for a full discussion of 'permission' marketing). In addition, there are important privacy concerns about the potential for misuse of a system that can track the movements of an individual in this manner.

Question 7.6

From your reading of the Genie case study, why do you think such an expensive rebranding exercise was deemed necessary?

Feedback – There has been a lot of negative publicity after early WAP services promised more than they could actually deliver, so it would be reasonable to assume that the new branding offers the opportunity for a 'new start'. It is also possible that the previous connection with BT means that customers make unwelcome associations with 'old-economy' traditions such as slow-moving, bureaucratic organizational structures.

WEB LINKS

www.ukdigitalradio.com
The latest developments in digital radio.

www.tnbt.com
Features on the latest developments in new technology.

www.howstuffworks.com
Clear explanations of technical issues and terminology.

www.m-commercetimes.com
Useful articles on recent mobile developments.

www.w3.org
The World Wide Web Consortium, which is a voluntary body responsible for
developing new technical standards for the Web.

www.jini.com
A new technical standard that allows a range of hardware devices to communicate as
part of an intelligent network.

www.bluetooth.com
A new technical standard that allows a range of hardware devices to communicate
without physical connections.

www.keynote.com
Offers a service to measure and compare the performance of different mobile service
providers.

www.whsmith.co.uk
A good example of multi-channel marketing in action.

www.yankeegroup.com
A consultancy specializing in mobile developments.

www.mysnowreport.com
A recent example of a personalized mobile information service detailing the latest
snow conditions at specified resorts.

www.e-mori.co.uk
UK-based research into the latest 'e'-related trends.

Chapter 8

The marketing mix

CHARLES DENNIS

MINDMAP

	Chapter 1 History, definitions and frameworks	
Chapter 2 Marketing research		Chapter 3 Change management
	Chapter 4 Strategy	
Chapter 5 Branding	Chapter 6 Relationship marketing	Chapter 7 Multi-channel marketing
	Chapter 8 The marketing mix	Chapter 9 e-Retailing
	Chapter 10 Marketing planning	
	Chapter 11 Legal, ethical and public policy issues	

Introductory level

Strategic level

Operational level

Big picture

LINKS TO OTHER CHAPTERS

Chapter 6
Relationship
marketing

Chapter 9
e-Retailing

- Chapter 6 – Building relationships with customers
- Chapter 9 – e-Retailing

KEY LEARNING POINTS

After completing this chapter you will have an understanding of:

- What the marketing mix is and its importance as a framework for planning e-Marketing strategy
- The elements of the traditional 4Ps of the marketing mix (Place, Product, Price and Promotion) and how businesses use them to help achieve e-Marketing success
- A more customer-orientated approach: the 4Cs equivalent to the traditional 4Ps (Convenience, Customer benefit, Cost to the customer and Communication respectively)
- An extension to the marketing mix: three more Ps (People, Process and Physical evidence)

ORDERED LIST OF SUB TOPICS

- What is the marketing mix?
- Place (Convenience in the 4Cs)
- Product (Customer benefit in the 4Cs)
- Price (Cost to the customer in the 4Cs)
- Promotion (Communication in the 4Cs)
- Bringing the marketing mix together
- Conclusions

- ■ Chapter summary
- ❖ Case study: WebPromote
- ❖ Further reading
- ❖ Questions
- ❖ Web links

WHAT IS THE MARKETING MIX?

This chapter considers tools and techniques for marketing the e-Business – the 'marketing mix'. The idea of the marketing mix has been around for many years – well before an 'e-' came in front of Marketing or anything else. As far back as the first half of the twentieth century, the job of the marketer was described as a 'mixer of ingredients' (Culliton 1948). Marketers devise strategies and tactics aimed at providing satisfaction and adding value for customers. The various elements are blended into a 'marketing mix' – a phrase first coined by Neil Borden (1964) of Harvard Business School.

The marketing mix can be defined as the blend of tools and techniques that marketers use to provide value for customers. It is most widely known as E. Jerome McCarthy's (1960) '4Ps': Place, Product, Price and Promotion. 'Place' is not quite self-explanatory, but refers to the routes organizations take to get the benefits of the product or service to the intended customers – channels of distribution. 'Product' means both tangible product and also 'service' and all the ways in which an organization adds value. 'Price' means not just the price charged, but also all aspects of pricing policy, including, for example, distributor margins. 'Promotion' is not just the more specialized 'sales promotion', but also every way in which a product is promoted to customers – from print advertising to Web sites.

The 4Ps are used as an approach to marketing planning that, according to later editions of McCarthy's still-popular *Basic Marketing*, has worked for millions of students and teachers. The prominence of the 4Ps derives largely from Kotler's and colleagues' (e.g. 2003, 2001) focus on these as central to marketing strategy (*Marketing Management* and *Principles of Marketing* texts – the early US editions of which were widely accepted as the basis of marketing teaching).

In recent decades, there have been numerous attempts to update and revise the marketing mix. For example, Jefkins (1993: 37) pointed out that the concept of 4Ps is no more than a simplifying convention that 'loses sight of the chronological sequence'. He devised a more realistic twenty-element mix that attempted to describe the marketing process sequentially, starting from conception, through pricing, product, distribution and sales to maintaining customer interest and loyalty.

221

Some marketers assert that there are '5Ps' of marketing, with the fifth being 'People'. 'People' has two meanings in this context. First, customers are people, often buying according to emotion and whim. Without these fickle customers, we have no business. Second, people make it happen. Without people to put marketing plans into operation, nothing happens.

Booms and Bitner (1982) proposed that for marketing services, the marketing mix should be extended to seven, by adding 'Process' and 'Physical evidence' in addition to 'People'. For a service, where there is no tangible product, the process of providing the service is all-important. Similarly, a service cannot be sampled. The provider needs to present evidence of the quality of the process.

With an increasing 'service' element in the added value of most production activities, the '7Ps' approach is becoming more widely accepted. The e-Retailing book in this series will return to the '7' approach. For simplicity we shall use the better-known '4' here as a framework for examining online marketing operations. The operational aspects of the other three will be incorporated where relevant.

In recent years, what marketers actually do has changed radically. Some authors (e.g. Gronroos 1997) have questioned whether the old idea of the marketing mix can still be valid. The challenge is based on a shift of emphasis towards relationship marketing and customer relationship management (CRM), as was discussed in Chapter 6 – aspects which are fundamental to marketing the e-Business. The CRM approach has many advantages, but in this chapter we focus on the well-tried 4Ps as an aid to classifying marketing tactics, e- or otherwise.

One development has merit as being descriptive of the way marketers think about the customer. The '4Cs' (Lauterborn 1990) imply more emphasis on customer wants and concerns than do the Ps. 'Place', rather than implying managements' methods of placing products where they want them to be, can be thought of as 'Convenience for the customer', recognizing the customers' choices for buying in ways convenient to them. 'Product', rather than being something that a company makes, which then has to be sold, can be thought of as a 'Customer benefit' – meaning satisfactions wanted by customers. 'Price' may be what companies decide to charge for their products, but 'Cost to the customer' represents the real cost that customers will pay, including, for example, their own transport costs. Finally, 'Promotion' suggests ways in which companies persuade people to buy, whereas 'Communication' is a two-way process also involving feedback from customers to suppliers. In the sections that follow, we consider the operational aspects of marketing the e-Business. While using the better-known 4Ps for our headings, we draw attention to differences in approach implied by the 4Cs.

Box 8.1:
TYPICAL MARKETING DECISIONS CLASSIFIED BY THE 7PS FRAMEWORK

Place

Channels of distribution

Service levels

Logistics

Channel segmentation

Product

Tangible products

Psychological attributes

Quality

Services

Benefits and features

Packaging

Styling

Image

Branding

Customer service

After care

Guarantees

Image

Price

Selling price

Price positioning

Distributor margins

Credit

Discounts

Payment methods

Price promotions

Discriminatory and variable pricing

Promotion

Advertising

Web sites

Direct marketing – including email as well as direct mail and telephone marketing.

Public relations (PR) and publicity

Personal selling

Sales promotion

People

People are our customers – often acting unpredictably, with a right to their own opinions even in the face of conflicting evidence

Customer contact staff

People make it happen. Our marketing is only as good as our marketing people

Recruitment, selection, training, salaries and other human relations issues

Process

Focus on customers

Quality assurance procedures and audits

Making all the systems work efficiently

Research and development

Physical evidence

Guarantees, warranties

Testimonials from satisfied customers and well-known personalities

Logos, uniforms and corporate branding

223

Box 8.2:

THE 4CS – A MORE CUSTOMER-ORIENTATED VERSION OF THE MARKETING MIX THAN THE 4PS

For	Place,	read:	Convenience
	Product		Customer benefit
	Price		Cost to the customer
	Promotion		Communication

PLACE

'Place' (**Convenience** in the 4 Cs) means the elements of the marketing mix that marketers use to enable customers to access the benefits of a product or service. Traditionally, this has meant 'channels of distribution' through (e.g.) various wholesaler and retailer combinations. Viewing from the 'convenience for the customer' (4Cs) perspective gives a more customer-orientated focus. This is a vital decision area for the e-Business for three reasons. First, relatively small local companies can widen their market and even export (e.g. Botham (www.Botham.co.uk), to be described further in Chapter 9). Second, many e-Businesses aim to gain competitive advantage by using e-Systems to de-layer the distribution chain. For example, Dell (www.dell.co.uk) supplies customers directly, rather than through distributors, wholesalers or retailers. Third, distribution is an area where some e-Businesses have been severely criticized for failing to deliver customer service (see Chapter 9 for more details).

Place elements of the marketing mix have been changing rapidly over recent decades, and these changes impact in many ways on the marketing operations of the e-Business. First, the growth of retailer power has involved major retailers taking more control of their supply chains. The involvement of wholesalers has been reduced, tending to give way to contract logistics (under retailer control). At the same time, supply chains have become more efficient, with computer network links between suppliers and retailers – many still based on EDI. Pre-dating the Internet, EDI is based on privately owned third-party computer networks. Stock levels have been reduced using techniques such as JIT and Enterprise Resource Planning (ERP). Control of the physical distribution, ordering, invoicing and payment systems, particularly for major retailers, is often still carried out using EDI networks such as Tradanet (www.gegxs.com/gxs/products/product/traser). Increasingly, though, retailers such as Tesco are allowing Internet access to their suppliers for real-time electronic point-of-sale (EPOS) data. Trusted supplier partners can thus respond more quickly to changes in customer demand.

Mini case study:
DISTRIBUTION AT WALMART

Now the world's largest and most profitable retailer, only two decades ago Walmart was a small retailer in the southern states of the USA. Growth has been founded on a belief in the importance of IT systems in building an efficient operation. Much of Wal-Mart's success has been ascribed to its stockless warehouse JIT distribution system. Goods delivered to the regional distribution depots are immediately picked for reshipment and sent on to stores. Economies of scale mean that Walmart can purchase full truckloads from suppliers, gaining a critical 3 per cent cost advantage over competitors.

The system is based on a private satellite EDI communications network that sends EPOS data to 4,000 suppliers. Employees, management and suppliers have access to real-time sales, stock and order information plus buying patterns.

In the UK, Walmart is utilizing its US expertise to improve the already efficient systems operated by ASDA prior to merger. Walmart (Asda Walmart in the UK; www.asda.co.uk) uses these slick distribution systems to e-Retail a wide variety of electronics and other non-food products direct to consumers.

Source: Adapted from Chaston (2001b)

EDI networks are expensive for small businesses to install, costing at least hundreds of thousands of pounds. Therefore, there is a growing trend towards the use of the Internet for B2B, particularly for smaller businesses (suppliers and customers) and smaller order quantities.

Mini case study:
BOEING SPARE PARTS

Aircraft manufacturer Boeing supplies spare parts by EDI to the top 10 per cent of its customers (representing 60 per cent of parts sales by value). In 1996, Boeing introduced its PART page on the Internet, to open up access to e-Buying to smaller customers. Customers anywhere in the world can check availability and prices, order from a catalogue of around half a million spare parts, and track the order status. The service is used by most of Boeing's customers, and handles half a million transactions per year.

Access to the Boeing PART page requires a password, but for more information go to the Boeing home page and enter PART in the search box: www. Boeing.com.

Source: Adapted from Chaffey *et al*. (2000)

THINK POINT

Given that Internet commerce is becoming more secure and is much cheaper than EDI, what do you think will be the long-term future trends for private EDI networks?

Improving efficiency has led to what formerly would have been warehouses becoming almost stockless regional distribution depots. Major retailers such as Tesco or Asda Walmart thus control a distribution chain typically consisting of:

Manufacturer $\rightarrow$ Regional distribution depot $\rightarrow$

Retail superstore $\rightarrow$ Customer

From the customers' 'convenience' point of view, there has been a trend towards 'one-stop' shopping at superstores, hypermarkets and shopping centres. This trend has had the side effect of a reduction in the number of small, independent and perhaps less efficient retail outlets.

High distribution efficiency is largely behind the success of 'bricks and clicks' retailers such as Tesco. Conversely, lack of established, efficient distribution channels has been a major factor in the failure of a number of pure-play dotcoms that have concentrated on 'Promotion' at the expense of 'Place' and the rest of the marketing mix.

The tendency has been towards a de-layering of channels of distribution – termed 'disintermediation'. e-Commerce has, of course, accelerated that trend by enabling mechanisms for businesses to trade directly with end customers rather than through intermediaries. Traditional functions of intermediaries such as breaking bulk and physical distribution still have to be performed, though. This is true even for the pure-play e-Business supplying directly to the consumer. Therefore, cutting out the intermediary does not necessarily save as much cost as might be expected. For example, Amazon has an efficient distribution system and consequently offers low prices. The low prices, though, are not a true reflection of efficiency, as Amazon, like many e-Businesses, has taken a long time to come into profit. Effectively, the low prices have been largely subsidized by shareholders, rather than reflecting increased efficiency. To emphasize the point, in the UK, Amazon is using its distribution expertise to carry out distribution services on contract for bricks retailers such as W. H. Smith and Toys 'R' Us. Such contract operations account for a substantial part of Amazon's profit.

Although recent trends have led to a decline in the numbers and influence of traditional intermediaries such as wholesalers, the Internet has spawned a variety

Box 8.3:
E-INTERMEDIARIES

Directories such as uk.yahoo.com

Search engines such as www.google.com

e-Malls such as www.buckinghamgate.com/bgate

Virtual resellers that own stock and sell directly, such as www.cdnow.com

Financial intermediaries handling payment, such as www.ecashservices.com

Virtual communities of fan clubs and user groups, such as Blake's 7:
www.ee.surrey.ac.uk/Contrib/SciFi/Blakes7

Evaluators that review and compare offers, such as www.thisisboating.com

Electronic trading exchanges such as www.timberweb.com.

Source: Adapted from Chaffey (2000), originally based on Sarkar *et al.* (1995)

of new intermediaries, from e-Malls to electronic trading exchanges. The growth of e-Intermediaries has been termed 'reintermediation'.

Apart from major 'bricks and clicks' retailers, many of the e-Businesses offering the most efficient distribution and customer convenience efficiency are established mail-order businesses. For example, Quill and Screwfix (office supplies and tradesperson supplies respectively) operate established mail businesses via a paper catalogue. Orders can be placed by telephone, post, fax, Internet and email twenty-four hours a day – usually for next-day delivery. Deliveries are reliable, and any unwanted or faulty goods can be returned simply. These organizations base their success on their focus on convenience for the customer.

Mini case study:
SCREWFIX

Screwfix (www.screwfix.com) is primarily a trade wholesale supplier, but also sells for DIY. Products include not only screws, bolts and nails, but also fixings, adhesives, tools, hardware, lighting, plumbing and cleaning products – the claim is 'Everything for the trade and DIY – next day.' The home page has many examples of good practice, for example:

- **Register/Login**: Optional registration makes ordering quicker and easier.
- **Special Offers**: A number of good deals are always available.
- **Recommend a Friend**: Get a reward when they order for the first time.
- **Open a Business Account**
- **Express Shopping**: If you have the catalogue, simply type in the quantities and catalogue number, or alternatively
- **Use Search** to find what you want.

Screwfix provides a useful example of the additional 3Ps:

- **People**: A freephone telephone number is available twenty-four hours a day, plus fax and email options, offering improved personal interaction.
- **Process**: To test the service, we ordered a long, complex list of equipment and fittings at 4.00 p.m. on a Sunday. The complete, correct order was delivered on the Monday morning.

Physical evidence

- **Testimonials**: 'I have just received my order and felt I must congratulate you on an excellent service. Your site is well designed. The products are well laid out and the order processing excellent.' 'Your Web site is brilliant, the designer needs a big pat on the back. Well laid out, and to order online is so easy.'
- **Award**: Winner of best use of supply chain management at the 2001 Internet Business Awards.

PRODUCT

'Product' is equivalent to **Customer benefit** in the 4Cs. In fact, people do not buy 'products' as such, but rather solutions to problems, or good feelings. The oft-quoted example is of a company selling the 'product' of an 8-mm drill bit. What the customer actually buys, though, is 8-mm holes. The customer is not interested in features of the drill such as the grade of steel used, only in whether it will solve the particular problem: drilling through plaster, mortar and brick, for example. Online catalogues selling B2B might well describe this as 'tungsten carbide tipped' in the realistic expectation that trade customers will fully understand the purpose. When selling B2C, a description more in line with customer wants should be used, say 'for drilling masonry for wall plugs and similar'. When buying online, customers are far less likely to request help than they are in the store, cash-and-carry, buying via telesales or even when placing a formal written order. Rather, when buying online, customers who need help in understanding a product are more likely to abandon the transaction and find an alternative supplier, or even buy through a different channel. e-Businesses, therefore, need to be particularly careful about describing products clearly in customer benefit terms.

The second reason why customers buy products – to get good feelings – is also apt for the e-Business. Other channels such as the retail store or the face-to-face salesperson are often much better at identifying and satisfying customers' emotional needs and wants. The physical store uses atmospherics in the attempt to change mood and give shoppers a pleasant emotional experience when buying. Emotional cues may include visual (decor), olfactory (perfume), touch (smooth and cool or soft and cuddly) and oral (music) cues. Similarly, the sales representative selling face to face has the opportunity of using verbal and non-verbal (body language) communication to build personal relationships with customers, enhancing the emotional value of products.

In trying to replicate the physical buying experience, the e-Business is at a disadvantage. On the other hand, with transaction data ready-digitized, the e-Business is well placed to enhance product value using CRM techniques. For example, data-mining can be used to build a picture of products most likely to be wanted by individual customers. Products tailored specifically can be offered proactively. Amazon (www.amazon.co.uk), for instance, uses such a system to match new books to existing customers likely to be interested in them.

The Internet, though, has the advantage in selling information-based products, including market information, business application and games software. For example, to find information on size and trends of consumer markets, there is no need to purchase a heavy paper-based report; the information can be downloaded from suppliers such as Mintel (sinatra2.mintel.com).

PRICE

'Price' is equivalent to **cost to the customer** in the 4Cs. Pricing decisions generate revenue, whereas the rest of the marketing mix involves costs. Pricing decisions are particularly critical for the e-Business as there is a customer perception that prices should be lower online than otherwise. Many organizations (e.g. Eurotunnel; www.Eurotunnel.com for car crossings from England to France) apply a standard discount for online purchase.

In some cases, customers can make much bigger savings buying online. For instance, to buy tickets from a travel agent in the UK for the Calgary Stampede rodeo in Canada (www.calgarystampede.com/stampede) is likely to be expensive, as the agent will probably sell these only as part of a package. Tickets can be booked directly via the Internet at a substantial saving.

Some e-Businesses sell almost solely on the basis of price. For example, emagazineshop (www.emagazineshop.com) sells a wide range of the magazines

229

normally available at newsagents'. Subscription prices are normally lower than newsagents, but emagazineshop offers lower prices still. The most popular magazines are discounted by at least 20 per cent, more specialist ones 10 per cent. This is a rare example of a pure-play dotcom, founded in 1997, that has survived the dotcom crash and is growing steadily, now employing 25 people.

Despite the Internet facilitating de-layering of intermediaries, it is still not automatic that costs will be less for selling online. Someone still has to carry out functions such as breaking bulk and physical delivery – and for online sales these can be even higher than for offline (many small orders delivered to individual customers rather than fewer, larger deliveries to a store), with consequent loss of advantages of economies of scale. Hence, many suppliers selling on the basis of cheap prices, even successful ones like Amazon (www.amazon.co.uk), struggle to make a profit on their e-Operations. Again, this is an area where the success of emagazineshop is an exception.

Not all prices are lower on the Internet. As already mentioned, the cost to the customer includes not just the selling price, but all the costs of buying. To buy from a (bricks) grocery supermarket incurs transport costs, and also the notional cost of the value of a customer's travel time. Tesco (www.tesco.com) is able to make a charge for home delivery, which its many e-Customers must consider represents good value.

Box 8.4:
PRICE COMPARISON SITES

Price comparison sites provide shopping engines that allow customers quickly and simply to compare prices across a range of Internet suppliers. For example, Easy Value (www.EasyValue.com) provides price and delivery comparisons for flights, books, CDs, videos, DVDs, games and handheld computers. Director James Rothnie claims that 'people know the products and price is driving them'. Customers can be confident that they are buying brands they can trust, and all suppliers must conform to security and service standards.

Shopsmart's approach is broader (uk.shopsmart.com). Each of its sites has been rated for not only price but also ease of use, service, returns policy, order tracking and online experience quality. Chief Executive Daniel Gestetner says, 'Customers do not automatically buy from the cheapest retailer; they are looking at other things. The companies that will do best are those that invest in the back-end infrastructure to deliver on all their promises.'

Source: Summarized and adapted from Clawson (2001)

The Internet is an ideal medium for operating a mechanistic market. For the customers, this means quick and easy access to the 'best' deals. For sellers, this should in theory mean a level playing field, where products offered at a competitive price sell, regardless of issues such as the size of the organization; hence the suitability of the Internet for electronic trading exchange (see Chapter 4). The level playing field idea, though, has hit some snags when translated to practice, and price-based services have achieved no more than modest success to date. A number of buying services are available such as Shopsmart (uk.shopsmart.com), the leading consumer price comparison site, and ComputerPrices (www. ComputerPrices.co.uk), which finds the cheapest computer kit in the UK. Priceline (www.priceline.com) is an alternative price-based service that creates a market or reverse auction. Enter the price you want to pay for a wide range of services like flights or hire cars and the system searches for suppliers willing to sell at that price – but the customer cannot choose the (say) airline for their flight. The company does, however, guarantee that it will be one of the top airlines. Most UK customers, though, prefer to have more control over what they get, rather than buying purely on price. For most e-Businesses, pricing remains as for non-electronic strategies; that is, based on the complex interaction of all elements of the marketing mix and value. Marketing pricing is still what it was, the price that customers are willing to pay, based on considerations such as the company, brand, reputation and product. The difference that e-Commerce makes is that pricing and competitor information is faster and more transparent, meaning that market forces also tend to act faster and perhaps more efficiently. There is thus a tendency for prices to converge at lower levels.

Mini case study:
TIMBERWEB

TIMBERweb (www.timberweb.com) is the international electronic trading exchange for sustainable timber. The site is independent – not affiliated to any participant. The 600-plus 'certified sellers' across the world are carefully screened. Buyers and sellers meet to make timber contracts, and promote their businesses in a personalized, secure environment. Members benefit from immediate access to real-time timber, lumber and wood market requirements, plus the latest news, trading methods, technical and market information. Since launch in 1997, the site has had 1.5 million hits per month from 20,000 businesses.

231

PROMOTION

'Promotion' is equivalent to **Communication** in the 4Cs. First thoughts on promoting the e–Business must be that it is unnecessary – the business can rely on its super Web site. Having built that Web site, it can sit back and wait for customers. Of course, we quickly realize that there is more to it than that. Why should visitors come to our Web site? If surfers do find it, are they our potential customers? In practice, it is likely that we will have to be more proactive in promotion, integrating e- with other communications channels. For many businesses, selling predominantly both on- and offline, the Internet is just one of a wide range of communication channels. The 'process' of integrating the communication tools is vital.

Box 8.5:
OFFLINE ADVERTISING

Include a URL on all brochures, letterheads, stationery, plus the label and packaging of your product (whether sold on- or offline).

Place advertisements in the offline media for your business. For example, if your product is teddy bears, advertise in Teddy Bear Club International.

If you are selling a general product of interest to most people, try advertising in Internet magazines such as *It's On The Net* – readers probably shop online.

Place advertisements in the 'click here' sections of the general press (e.g. *Sunday Times, Daily Mail*). These are a lot cheaper and likely to be more cost-effective than large colour advertisements.

Source: Adapted from Lundquist (1998)

'People' play a vital part in the marketing communication process, even (or perhaps especially) for the e-Business. Customers want human contact, and those businesses that can provide a real human to interact with a customer quickly – whether online, via email, over the telephone or even face to face – are more likely to succeed than some of the faceless, e-only operations that have been getting a reputation for poor service. Similarly, though, those e-Businesses with customer-friendly systems that effectively mimic human interaction (such as Google (www.google.com) and Amazon (www.amazon.com)) tend to be more popular than the more mechanistic sites. The People aspect is also important for e-Businesses in tailoring offers to the individual customer. For example, Amazon emails details of new books to customers whose profile makes them likely customers.

Incorporating the last of the '7Ps', 'Physical evidence', also into 'promotion', many customers remain suspicious of e-Business. Customer resistance to buying by Internet can be partly broken down by the use of testimonials from satisfied

Box 8.6:
MAKING BANNERS WORK

Recently, a perception has arisen in the marketing world that banner ads are not cost-effective. Despite this, online advertising expenditure is still growing, and has now reached well over £150 million per year (£30 million more than cinema advertising, for example).

The interstitial, a pop-up that interrupts browsing to show an ad, is a much more active form of advertising. Some people using the Web for a specific purpose find these irritating, though. Online advertising company RealMedia (www.uk.realmedia.com) is using a less intrusive system called adPointer. This generates an ad when the cursor has not moved for a specific time.

Schemes that provide users with incentives to look at advertisements have been around for some years, but in the UK, Bananalotto.com (www.bananalotto.com) has raised the stakes by offering the chance to win £1 million as you click the banner ad. KPE, the media and entertainment consultancy, developed around ten games for its clients. Managing Director Paul Zwillberg says, 'So much of the Internet has been characterized by repurposing things that worked well in print or on TV. "Advergaming" is . . . a new combination that's made for the medium. . . . You take one of the most popular uses of interactive content and marry it with tried and tested advertising models like brand association, trial or data capture and you get something really wonderful.'

Source: Summarized and adapted from *Marketing Business*'s 'e-Business' supplement

customers and/or endorsements from celebrities. For example, Europe's largest direct sales yachting equipment company, Compass (German based, www. compass24.com), successfully launched in the UK with endorsement from Robin Knox-Johnston, the famous ocean rower and yachtsman.

BRINGING THE MARKETING MIX TOGETHER

The 4Ps are a useful framework for designing e-Marketing strategies – and have the benefit that they are clear and familiar to most managers. Successful e-Businesses bring together the elements of the marketing mix into an integrated offer representing value to the customer. This can be illustrated, for example, by outlining aspects of the 4Ps of the marketing mix of the office supplies company Quill (www.quillcorp.com).

Place

Customers are offered the convenience of easy ordering – not just by Web but via many other routes, with expert personal assistance readily available by telephone. We have personally tested the service and found it fast and reliable. A particular benefit is the UPS (courier service) order tracker so that customers can track the delivery status of their order.

Product

Quill offers a wide range of office and computer supplies, furniture and speciality products. The main selling point is the very wide range available from stock – almost everything imaginable for the office. This is a 'hypermarket'-type approach, offering customers far more choice than would be expected from most traditional suppliers.

Price

Competitive, discount prices can be offered. Low price levels are sustainable because of the e-Efficiency of the business, and also the economies of scale arising from successfully selling large volumes.

Promotion

Quill is promoted by a wide range of integrated marketing communications of which an affiliate programme and e-Newsletter are central.

Box 8.7:
WAYS TO GET MORE TRAFFIC TO YOUR WEB SITE

- Get indexed by the major search engines
- Use metatags in html files
- Use a descriptive title
- Buy an advertisement on a top site such as Yahoo!
- Get into strategic partnerships – links to and from other busy sites
- Use offline publicity and advertising
- Be active on discussion groups, bulletin boards, chat rooms and Usenet
- Look for more information on specialist sites such as Yahoo! and Web-Promote

Source: Adapted from Lundquist (1998)

CONCLUSIONS

The concept of the 4Ps of the marketing mix may have a slightly old-fashioned ring to it in the current climate of 'new' marketing. Nevertheless, the approach is still as useful as ever as a framework for planning marketing strategy for the e-Business. Researching customers' wants, satisfying those wants with appropriate products and services, distributed conveniently, priced to reflect value, and communicating with customers about the benefits remains central to marketing planning.

CHAPTER SUMMARY

The marketing mix is the blend of tools and techniques that marketers use to provide value for customers. It is most commonly simplified to 4Ps: Place, Product, Price and Promotion. Sometimes three extra Ps are added: People, Process and Physical evidence – although in marketing planning these can be included under the 'Promotion' heading. The marketing mix may also be expressed as the more customer-orientated 4Cs.

Place is a shorthand nickname to classify the elements of the marketing mix that marketers use to enable customers to access the benefits of a product or service (Convenience in the 4Cs). Successful e-Businesses use IT-based systems to achieve this. The Internet puts the technology within the capability of small and medium-sized e-Businesses, rather than needing the very substantial investment in more traditional EDI. Selling by the Internet allows e-Businesses to cut out intermediaries such as wholesalers and retailers – disintermediation. On the other hand, many e-Businesses are using a range of new e-Intermediaries such as directories, e-Malls and electronic trading exchanges.

Product is a shorthand nickname to classify the elements of the marketing mix that marketers use to provide a 'bundle of satisfactions' for customers. 'Product' in the marketing mix embraces not just tangible products but also intangible services and augmented value (Customer benefit in the 4Cs). The pure-play e-Business is at a disadvantage, owing to the difficulty of providing sensory cues such as olfactory and touch. On the other hand, the Internet has the advantage in selling information-based products such as market data where there is no need for a physical product.

Price is a shorthand nickname to classify the elements of the marketing mix that result in the costs to the customers of obtaining the benefits of a product (Cost to the customer in the 4Cs). The Internet makes for more transparency of price information, and as a consequence, prices are tending to converge at lower levels. In practice, there are still only a few examples of suppliers that sell primarily on the basis of price, and price-based buying services, succeeding in achieving long-term profitability.

Promotion is a shorthand nickname to classify the elements of the marketing mix that marketers use to communicate with customers – both to make known the benefits of a product or service (e.g. advertising) and to gather information (e.g. marketing research) (Communication in the 4Cs). Three extra Ps – People, Process and Physical evidence – can be incorporated into Promotion. Successful e-Businesses often use offline advertising such as trade magazines and 'click here' sections of newspapers integrated with online marketing communications. Online methods include banner ads and pop-ups (often incentivized); paid-for listings in search engines and directories; and affiliate programmes. People issues are addressed by, for example, customer knowledge, enabling personalized communications about new products; and provision of alternative interactive personal communication such as by telephone. Process considerations are paramount in overcoming e-Businesses' problems with order fulfilment and delivery. Finally, physical evidence can help the virtual business to become more established, for example by using testimonials from customers and celebrities.

Case study:
WEBPROMOTE

WebPromote (www.webpromote.com), founded in 1996, publishes a weekly newsletter packed with useful information on promoting Web sites. It is one of the largest Internet marketing newsletters, with 170,000-plus double-opt-in subscribers. WebPromote provides free information on the latest online promotion and marketing development opportunities. Four years of past issues are available in the archives section.

One example included five predictions for trends in Internet marketing, forecast by marketing consultant Chee Wee:

1 Pay-per-click advertising will increase dramatically

Pay-per-click (PPC) engines like Overture and FindWhat are performing extremely well. Sites displaying Overture's listings include America Online, Yahoo! Lycos, Hotbot, AltaVista, Netscape, InfoSpace, Dogpile and Excite. Overture's partnership with Yahoo! ends in June 2002, when Yahoo! is likely to roll out its own PPC system. More search engines are expected to adopt the PPC model or offer co-branded Overture listings. If you are advertising on Overture, expect gradual increases in traffic from most keywords.

2 Ads will grow BIGGER

Yahoo! has begun displaying larger banner ad units that are 720 × 90 pixels in screen size. More sites are expected to follow. The standard 468 × 60 pixel banner size may be replaced with a larger one. Sites that depend largely on advertising for their revenues are likely to roll out more of these large ad units. When Web users become immune to these ads, will content publishers try even larger ads?

3 Rich-media ads will increase in prominence

Ads with animation, sound and interactivity will become more common. Flash ads are already gaining a foothold on the Internet. They work well to capture visitors' attention. Best of all, they do not need to be large and intrusive – just creative.

4 More email marketing

Permission-based email marketing will increase. The response rates to opt-in email campaigns are significantly higher than for other online ads; the cost per acquisition is lower; turnaround time is faster; and results can be accurately tracked. More companies are expected to move their offline direct mailings online. Unfortunately, spam is likely to increase. More aggressive spam filters will be developed.

237

5 Viral marketing will grow

More companies are forecast to use viral marketing campaigns (introduced in Chapter 5) to promote and brand their products and services. These campaigns are likely to come with more sophisticated tracking of open, click-through and success rates.

The WebPromote site carries many useful tips for promoting Web sites. The comprehensive guide to link popularity is particularly useful.

How to increase link popularity

Search engines use 'link popularity' in locating and ranking sites – the term refers to both the number of other sites linking to the measured site and, especially, the importance and relevance of the linking sites. Improving link popularity raises a site in search engine rankings. To measure your own site on AltaVista, Google and Hotbot, visit www.linkpopularity.com.

View a comparison of your site's link popularity relative to those of your competitors and to other well-known sites at www.marketleap.com/publinkpop.

Build a matrix of linking sites

Instead of having a single site that covers many different keywords, separate each product or service into groupings. Use related specialist sites that all link to the 'mother site' and to each other. Each should cover its own niche based on a core theme. The sites should be about the same size, say around five pages. Ideally, locate each on a different ISP. A sample matrix can be viewed at www.marketingchallenge.com/chronicles/278/matrix.gif.

Get a listing in Yahoo!

Obaining a listing in Yahoo! can be difficult to achieve, but a paid listing may be worthwhile: deadlock.com/promote/search-engines/yahoo.html.

Get a listing in the Excite/LookSmart paid inclusion programme

As with Yahoo!, other search engines managers consider that if you are listed in LookSmart, your site must be worth listing. A single step submits your page to both, and also supplies results to AltaVista, MSN and iWon: http://listings.looksmart.com/?synd=none&chan=lshomebus.

Get a listing in top directories

An example is the free Open Directory Project: www.dmoz.org/add.html.

Get a listing in relevant databases

Get a listing in relevant databases in SEARCH ENGINE GUIDE: www.search engineguide.com/searchengines.html

Start an affiliate programme

Affiliates earn a commission when a visitor to their site clicks the link to your sales page and then makes a purchase. Concentrate on related sites.

Get links to and from similar high-traffic, quality sites

Look for sites that serve the same audience as your site but are not competitive. Also, contact sites that link to your competition. For more information, see www.directhit.com and www.about.com.

Write articles

Become known as an expert in your field by writing articles that you post to your site. Submit these to other Web sites and e-zines. Include hyperlinks back to your own site.

Source: Summarized and adapted from www.webpromote.com. The link popularity section was originally from *Internet Marketing Challenge*.

FURTHER READING

Chaston, I. (2001) *e-Marketing Strategy,* Maidenhead, UK: McGraw-Hill. A comprehensive textbook on Internet marketing.

Lundquist, L. H. (1998) *Selling On Line for Dummies,* Foster City, CA: IDG. Written for US readers, this is a simple guide to promotion and all aspects of selling online.

Randall, G. (2001) *Principles of Marketing*, 2nd edition, London: International Thompson. This is a concise, up-to-date textbook introducing the principles of marketing, including the marketing mix.

Wilson, R. (2000) *Planning Your Internet Marketing Strategy: A Doctor Ebiz Guide,* New York: Wiley. Written for US readers, this is a practical guide to Internet marketing strategy.

QUESTIONS

Question 8.1

Why do you think the 4Cs are considered more customer orientated than the 4Ps?

Feedback – The 4Cs are phrased around the customer: the customer's convenience, benefit, costs and two-way communication. On the other hand, the 4Ps seem to imply a company-centred approach: how the company distributes the products that it makes, how products are priced and how they are sold.

Question 8.2

The additional 3Ps were devised for an extended marketing mix for services. Why are they also useful for an e-Business selling tangible products?

Feedback – 'Service' is becoming an increasingly essential element of any business's success. In addition, customers may be more suspicious of the less tangible e-Business than they are of an established 'bricks' business. An emphasis on the real people aspects, and presenting physical evidence of reliability, can help overcome this customer resistance. Getting the process right is also essential in order to build customer confidence.

Question 8.3

If the 4Cs and the 7Ps are superior to the 4Ps, why are the 4Ps still in extensive use as a strategy and planning framework?

Feedback – Because most managers are familiar with the 4Ps. Anyway, the 4Ps can easily be used in a customer-orientated way without calling them 'Cs'. The additional 3Ps can be incorporated into 'Promotion' rather than ignored.

Question 8.4

Why are prices sometimes lower and sometimes higher for Internet shopping compared with 'bricks'?

Feedback – Some services can be distributed much more efficiently by selling directly to customers via the Internet rather than through intermediaries; for example, information services, tickets and travel. On the other hand, the functions of intermediaries still have to be carried out: breaking bulk, delivery, and so on. For physical products that e-Businesses have to deliver in small orders to a customer's address (such as groceries), transport costs are higher than for bulk deliveries to a store.

Question 8.5

Why should an e-Business carrying out supply and promotion via the Web and email need to advertise in conventional media?

Feedback – Many customers will not be aware of the business unless it uses more general advertising. Surfers who find the site by chance may not be interested in buying. Conventional advertising builds confidence that a business is reliable and established.

WEB LINKS

sol.brunel.ac.uk/~dennis
Follow the links for an introduction to marketing, the marketing concept and the
marketing mix.

www.bananalotto.com
Free lottery site that claims to generate 15,000–20,000 clicks per day for
advertisers.

www.Ecademy.com
Free membership for anyone interested in e-Business. Networking with members,
DailEnews, finding companies, reports, training courses, services and products. Free
book when you join. Links to the '12 Ecademy Principles™', a step-by-step guide.

www.webpromote.com
Packed with advice and information on promoting Web sites.

www.wilsonweb.com
Thousands of articles on Web marketing, and a sample chapter from *Planning Your
Internet Marketing Strategy: A Doctor Ebiz Guide* by Ralph Wilson. This page also
has links for subscribing to the e-zines *Web Marketing Today* and *Doctor Ebiz* (free)
plus *Web Commerce Today* (paid subscription).

e-Retailing

CHARLES DENNIS

MINDMAP

	Chapter 1 History, definitions and frameworks	
Chapter 2 Marketing research		Chapter 3 Change management
	Chapter 4 Strategy	
Chapter 5 Branding	Chapter 6 Relationship marketing	Chapter 7 Multi-channel marketing
Chapter 8 The marketing mix	Chapter 9 e-Retailing	
	Chapter 10 Marketing planning	
	Chapter 11 Legal, ethical and public policy issues	

Introductory level

Strategic level

Operational level

Big picture

242

LINKS TO OTHER CHAPTERS

- Chapter 8 – The marketing mix

KEY LEARNING POINTS

After completing this chapter you will have an understanding of:

- What e-Retail is, advantages and disadvantages for retailers and consumers
- The success factors for e-Retail
- The growing importance of multi-channel retailing
- The e-Retailing strategic options for retailers
- The trade-offs between high street/shopping centres and e-Retail.

ORDERED LIST OF SUB TOPICS

- What is e-Retail?
- Disadvantages and advantages of e-Retailing for retailers
- Disadvantages and advantages of e-Shopping for consumers
- Is the product suitable for e-Retailing?
- Strategic options for retailers
- Success factors in e-Retail
- Growth of and prospects for e-Retailing
- e-malls v. high streets and shopping centres
- Non-computer e-Retailing
- Conclusions
- Chapter summary
- ❖ Further reading
- ❖ Questions
- ❖ Web links

WHAT IS E-RETAIL?

e-Retail is the sale of goods and services via Internet or other electronic channels, for personal or household use by consumers. This formal definition encompasses all the activities of B2C. Despite the dotcom crash of 2000, e-Retailing has been steadily growing, particularly for the 'top seven' products which account for three-quarters of all European sales: books, music, groceries, software, hardware, travel and clothes.

DISADVANTAGES AND ADVANTAGES OF E-RETAILING FOR RETAILERS

Disadvantages

Retailers have been slow to take up e-Retailing. This is to some extent understandable in the light of the many disadvantages and problems. Retailers, for example, may lack the technical know-how, the substantial investment required or the order fulfilment capabilities. Set-up costs start from around £20,000 for a small site, up to £500,000 for a large operation. And set-up costs are only the start: Datamonitor estimates that high street retailers are spending more on ongoing costs than on setting up new sites.

There can be legal problems. For example, if purchaser and supplier are in different countries, there may be conflict between the laws of the two countries.

A further disadvantage is that e-Selling is less powerful than face-to-face selling (it is easier to say 'no' to a computer). This viewpoint is linked to a concern of

Box 9.1:
DISADVANTAGES OF E-RETAILING FOR RETAILERS

- May lack know-how and technology
- Substantial set-up, investment and ongoing costs
- Complex logistics of fulfilment
- e-Selling less powerful than face-to-face – uptake slow for goods selected by taste or smell
- Fewer impulse purchases
- Legal problems
- Less role for traditional high street retail expertise
- Pressure on margins and prices in-store
- After-sales care difficulties

traditional high street retailers that e-Retailing offers a diminished role for their expertise. For example, there are obvious difficulties with products sold by 'atmosphere' – touch, feel, smell – and with impulse purchases. In addition, consumers have a perception of lower prices online. This puts pressure on margins for e-Retailing, and can lead to shoppers expecting consistent low prices in store. Finally, after-care can be difficult, especially if the shopper is overseas.

Advantages

On the other hand, there are a number of advantages for retailers. First, location is unimportant. According to some textbooks, adapting an old saying, the three most important elements in retail are 'location, location and location'. The best high street locations are therefore expensive. The e-Retailer, though, can sell equally well to anywhere in the country, and even overseas. Second, size does not matter: small e-Retailers can compete on equal terms with large ones, and reach a larger audience than the high street – and be open twenty-four hours a day. For example, the independent bakery Bothams of Whitby in northern England has been a pioneer of e-Retailing and become one of the best-known UK case studies.

Mini case study:
BOTHAMS OF WHITBY

Bothams, a family-run craft bakery (www.botham.co.uk) in the ancient port of Whitby on the North Yorkshire (UK) coast is a benchmark of best practice and an e-Retailing pioneer. Products are from original recipes, using the 'finest ingredients, skilfully combined to produce biscuits, plum bread and cakes of the highest standard'. The site is packed with interesting information about the products, with frequently updated interest content such as 'meet the family' and 'kids' pages'. This independent local business has built a reputation for UK and worldwide delivery of hampers and cakes.

There are many other advantages. The socio-demographic profile of e-Shoppers is attractive to many retailers, with higher-than-average education, employment and disposable income levels. In theory at least, online selling saves on the wages costs of face-to-face salespeople and the costs of premises. The savings may be less than expected, though, as there are still costs in Internet customer contact, and packaging and delivery can be more expensive to provide. Perhaps a more substantial advantage is the ease with which e-Retailing integrates with CRM and

245

Box 9.2:

ADVANTAGES OF E-RETAILING FOR RETAILERS

- Location is unimportant
- Size does not matter
- Saves on the wages and premises costs
- Reach a larger audience
- Higher disposable income profile than average
- Accepts orders 24 hours a day
- More opportunities for CRM, micro-marketing, cross- and up-selling
- If we don't, our competitors will

micro-marketing systems – identifying and treating the customer as an individual. This, together with the easier provision of product information, leads to greater opportunities for cross-selling and selling up. Finally, the late entrants into e-Retailing are largely being driven by the thought that 'if we don't, our competitors will'.

Other retailers, though, are put off e-Retailing by what they perceive as consumer resistance. According to e-Research company Forrester, nearly 40 per cent of UK homes are now connected to the Internet, but estimates vary from only 12 per cent (Verdict) up to 20 per cent (Forrester) of UK adults shopping

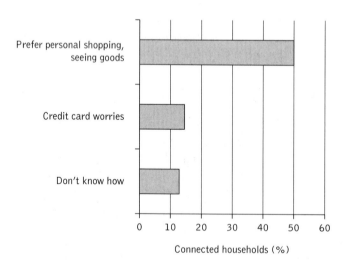

Figure 9.1 *Why Internet-connected consumers do not e-Shop*

Source: Doidge and Higgins 2000

online. This contrasts with the faster take-up of e-Business for B2B, with 25 per cent of businesses ordering online (Chartered Institute of Marketing).

DISADVANTAGES AND ADVANTAGES OF e-SHOPPING FOR CONSUMERS

Disadvantages

Consumers, too, have been slow to embrace e-Shopping. Back in 1996, the UK's largest e-Consultancy, Cap Gemini, carried out an employee survey. The main disadvantages for shoppers, in ranked order were 'Availability'; 'Can't be in to receive delivery'; 'Premium charged for delivery'; and 'Can't see or feel the merchandise'. With years more experience, many e-Retailers still do not have satisfactory answers to these problems. Typical shopper comments have included 'They left it in the garden and didn't tell me'; 'It's a twenty-four-hour shopping service but only a six-hour delivery service' and 'Returning unwanted products is when it all goes low-tech' (consumer surveys from Vincent et al. 2000).

Another survey reported, in ranked order, reasons why Internet-connected shoppers do not e-Shop: 'Prefer personal shopping, seeing goods'; 'Credit card worries'; and 'Don't know how' (Doidge and Higgins 2000 – see Figure 9.1). In 2001, the retail researcher Verdict confirmed security fears as the number one barrier to more consumers shopping online. Our own pilot mini-surveys have indicated that (real) shopping centres still have the edge over e-Retail on 'Quality of the stores', 'Customer service' and 'Positive image' (Dennis et al. 2002). The respondents for the survey results illustrated in Figure 9.2 were sixth-form students – the shoppers of tomorrow – but our results for adults were similar. When shopping online, the sixth-formers used their parents' credit cards. This

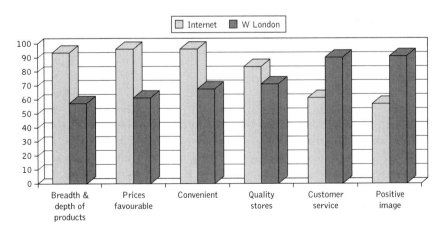

Figure 9.2 Comparing ratings: the Internet versus a west London shopping centre

Box 9.3:
DISADVANTAGES OF E-SHOPPING FOR CONSUMERS

- Credit card and security worries
- Lack of personal and social interaction
- Can't see or feel the merchandise
- Don't know how
- Can't be in to receive delivery
- Premium charged for delivery
- Difficulties with returning goods for refund

is an obvious security worry for parents, but also a nuisance, restricting the e-Shopping activities of young people. Credit cards are offered only to those of 18 years of age and above, although alternative 'plastic cash' is available for children, with transactions authorized (in the example of the Solo card (www. solocard.co.uk)) only up to what is in the bank account. The disadvantage is that so far these cards are accepted by only a tiny fraction of e-Retailers.

The disadvantages are typical of those that faced mail order traders a few decades ago. Given time, as sales grow, sellers work to overcome the customers' concerns, and consumers become more confident. In the USA, L. L. Bean (www.llbean.com) could claim to be the pioneer of mail order, selling goods to rural farmers since way back in the mid-nineteenth century. Today the company has put its reputation for customer responsiveness, helpfulness, cheerfulness and reliability to use in becoming world leader in e-Retailing outdoor equipment and clothing, with an efficient, award-winning site.

Advantages

Counterbalancing the disadvantages and the slow responses of many UK e-Retailers to addressing them, there are a number of advantages for shoppers. First, in ranked order from the Cap Gemini survey are the responses 'Convenient/ easy'; 'Saves time'; and 'Fits in with other activities'. Other commonly cited advantages, typified by responses to our own pilot mini-survey, include 'Breadth and depth of products'; 'Prices favourable'; and 'Convenient' (Dennis *et al.* 2002 – see Figure 9.2). According to Verdict, 'cost effectiveness' (rather than just low prices) is the key reason for shoppers to buy online, followed by convenience and ease of purchase.

There are considerable potential benefits for consumers from personalization of the presentation and merchandise. For instance, shoppers can see how they will look in the clothes. The successful US retailer Lands' End (www.land-send.com) provides a virtual 'dressing room' where 'you put it all together. The site features a virtual model you can tailor to your size, shape and hair colour before dressing it up – you can mix and match items and change their colors'.

In Levi stores there is an interactive kiosk where customers can input measurements and have 'custom fit' jeans made up in a week or two. If a pair of jeans is simply a replacement, why should the customer have to visit the store? Levi has tested the concept on the Internet, but does not sell directly to consumers (www.levistraus.com).

By visiting a 3-D scanning booth such as the Hamamatsu (www.hamamatsu.co.uk), you can have your body shape stored digitally. At the time of writing, there are around half a dozen 3-D scanners in the UK, including those such as the London College of Fashion, involved in the National Sizing Survey. When e-Retailers offer the service, you will be able really to see how you will look, and clothes can be made to measure – 'mass customization'.

Consumers are fast catching on to the benefits with the UK second only to the USA in e-Shopping.

Box 9.4:
ADVANTAGES OF E-SHOPPING FOR CONSUMERS

- Cost-effective
- Convenient
- Easy
- Saves time
- Fits in with other activities
- Breadth and depth of products
- Easy search of many alternatives
- Personalization of presentation and merchandise
- Prices favourable

IS THE PRODUCT SUITABLE FOR E-RETAILING?

How important is e-Retailing for various classes of products? Which high street retailers are going to be most affected by the growth of e-Shopping? Can some products be sold just as effectively by e-Retail as by conventional retail? Are some products unsuitable for e-Retailing? Michael de Kare-Silver has developed the 'ES' (e-Shopping) test aimed at estimating the proportion of the target customers who will be likely to buy the product online. De Kare-Silver claims that the approach can be applied to any product or service in any industry sector. The test consists of three dimensions: (1) product characteristics; (2) familiarity and confidence; (3) consumer attributes. Products with 'likely high ES potential-scoring' include basic groceries, household items and clothing, plus drinks, financial services, travel, hotels and books (de Kare-Silver, 2001).

Box 9.5:
THE ES (ELECTRONIC SHOPPING) TEST

The ES test has been designed to quantify the likely e-Retailing potential of a product. The three-step test considers:

1. *Product characteristics.* The more virtual a product's appeal, the higher the score; the more physical, the lower. The main appeal can be scored from 'intellect' scoring 10 at the 'virtual' end of the scale, through 'sight' and 'sound', down to 'smell', 'taste' and 'touch' scoring 0 at the physical end.

2. *Familiarity and confidence.* This dimension is measured by considering previous use, satisfactory use and branding or reputation, again on a 0–10 scale.

3. *Consumer attributes.* Consumers' attitudes can outweigh the first two steps, so this factor is accordingly weighted higher, with a 0–30 scale. The essential test is the percentage of the target consumers responsive to e-Retail offers. Are the target consumers mainly 'habit-bound diehards' and 'social' shoppers, unresponsive to e-Retail? Or are there a high proportion of e-responsive 'convenience' shoppers? The scale runs from 0 (no e-responsive shoppers) to 30 (90 per cent e-responsive).

The scores for some sample products are shown in Table 9.1.

The evaluation should be repeated regularly to track trends. Any score over 20 represents substantial e-Shopping potential.

Source: Adapted from de Kare Silver (2001)

Table 9.1 Sample products with likely high electronic shopping (ES) potential scores

Product	1 Product character- istics (0–10)	2 Familiarity and confi- dence (0–10)	3 Consumer attributes (0–30)	Total
Basic grocery	4	8	15	27
Basic household	8	8	15	31
Basic clothing	4	7	8	19
Drinks	4	8	15	27
Financial services, e.g. car insurance	10	5	8	23
Travel	10	6	15	31
Hotels	7	6	15	28
Books	8	7	23	38

STRATEGIC OPTIONS FOR RETAILERS

If a retailer's products or services have a potential for e-Retailing, what courses of action are available? De Kare-Silver lists ten options, which can be arranged on a scale from 'no e-Retail operations' to 'switch fully', in order of increasing e-Shopping responsiveness, paralleled with increasing commitment to e-Retailing.

No e-Retail operations

Having no e-Retail operations is the defensive option, based on revitalizing the 'experience' and 'social' aspects of shopping as in towns and shopping centres. Consumers, though, expect every organization to have at least an information Web site and an email address.

Information only

Reluctance to tackle the disadvantages of e-Retailing leads some well-known high street retailers (e.g. Monsoon (www.monsoon.co.uk)) to use the Internet purely as a marketing communication channel rather than for online sales.

Box 9.6:
TEN STRATEGIC OPTIONS FOR RETAILERS – IN ORDER OF INCREASING COMMITMENT TO E-RETAILING

- No e-Retail operations
- Information only
- Export
- Incorporate into existing business
- Add another channel
- Set up a separate business
- Pursue all fronts
- Mixed system
- Best of both worlds
- e-Retail only

Source: Adapted from de Kare Silver (2001)

Export

The approach of using the Internet only for export sales is aimed at protecting the business of the high street stores while widening the potential customer base with the e-Channels. De Kare-Silver cites the example of bookseller Blackwells (bookshop.blackwell.co.uk), which has eighty-two outlets in university towns and campuses across the UK, but its listing of 1 million specialist and academic titles is now available worldwide on the Web.

Incorporate into existing business

The option of incorporating e-Retailing into existing business seeks to protect the existing stores by using an 'order and collect' system. By coming to the store to collect the order, the shopper is more likely to think of extra purchases or to pick up impulse buys. In the UK, the supermarket chains Safeway (www.safeway.co.uk) and J. Sainsbury (www.jsainsbury.com) have implemented this system but have not gained the popularity of market leader Tesco; Sainsbury is now introducing home delivery, based on warehouse picking centres rather than stores, and Safeway has dropped its e-Retailing service.

Add another channel

Retailers such as Next (market leader in online clothing sales, according to Verdict) use e-Retailing as an extra route to reach more of their target customers. Retailers in this category are often represented on an e-Mall, saving much of the setting-up cost of a dedicated e-Retailing operation.

Mini case study: NEXT

Next (www.next.co.uk) is a top name in UK high street fashion, and since 1987 has built a successful mail order business, Next Directory. The expertise in order handling, fulfilment and customer care has proved invaluable, taking the business to the number one spot in UK clothing e-Retailing. The entire Next Directory is available online, including formalwear, casual wear, accessories, shoes, swimwear, lingerie, menswear and children's wear. To shop online, you have to set up an account, which can take a day or two to arrange. There is a small charge for next-day delivery, and a courier picks up returns free.

Set up a separate business

The idea of the separate business is to offer competitive e-Shopping benefits without alienating the existing customers for the high street operation, who probably pay higher prices. The separately branded direct operation has been popular for financial services; for example, Abbey National's e-Bank, Cahoot (www.cahoot.co.uk).

Pursue all fronts

The National Westminster Bank multi-channel system is based on making every possible channel open to the customer: high street branches, direct mail, ATMs, telephone, interactive television and Internet (www.natwest.co.uk).

Mixed system

A mixed approach recognizes that strong brands are essential to successful e-Retailing. Brand strength is showcased in flagship stores in major cities; for example, Virgin Megastore (www.virginmega.com).

Best of both worlds

Is it possible to retain all the high street operations while at the same time being state-of-the-art in e-Retailing? This is probably practicable only for a clear market leader in a sector, and represents a high-investment strategy, making it more difficult for competitors to catch up – the Tesco approach.

e-Retail only

Few retailers are brave enough to close all high street outlets and operate only virtual shops. Pre-dotcom crash, though, a number of e-Retail-only operations were developed, the best known and most successful being Amazon.com. At the time of writing, even Amazon appear to be looking for some 'real' presence, with a joint venture with US discount retailer Target. Only those operations high in e-Shopping potential, such as travel, and with big budgets to build the brand (e.g. Lastminute.com (www.lastminute.com)), are likely to be leaders with Internet-only operations.

SUCCESS FACTORS IN E-RETAIL

According to research company Forrester (www.forrester.com), two-thirds of e-Shopping transactions are aborted after the shopper has already placed goods in the shopping basket, and nine out of ten buyers do not make a repeat purchase. e-Retailers need to make the purchasing process reliable, easy to use and efficient, removing the reasons for abandoning purchases. Human contact needs to be available to sort out problems – at least by email, but preferably also with a phone option. A software device such as HyPhone from Byzantium allows 'phone-through' without dropping the Internet connection (www.byzantium.com during office hours for a live demonstration).

A US survey correlated Web site characteristics with customer satisfaction. The conclusion was that success followed the content. A further important discriminator between high and low customer satisfaction was the 'chat' aspect (Feinberg 2001). Other US studies have found that the strongest predictor of consumers' intention to e-Shop was 'hedonic'; that is, the pure enjoyment of the experience (Childers *et al.* 2001; Dholakia and Uusitalo 2001). The importance of the enjoyment and human communication aspects is borne out by, for example, eBay (a US auction site (www.ebay.com)), with its emphasis on community interests such as chat rooms and bulletin boards, 'one of the few Internet start-up companies to be avoiding financial pain' (Reynolds 2000).

In-store, male and female behaviour have been demonstrated to be different, with females tending to value the social and experiential aspects, males being more purposeful shoppers. e-Shopping, though, is poor at providing the social

254

Box 9.7:
DOS AND DON'TS OF E-RETAILING

Don'ts

- Save your best page till last
- Use too many graphics (long download)
- Fill each page, leaving no 'white space'
- Use too much narrative and long-winded wording
- Have too many sequential click-through pages

Dos

- Make it easy to buy ('three clicks')*
- Provide good service and aftercare*
- Provide membership incentives*
- Human communication, chat rooms and bulletin boards*
- Make e-Shopping an enjoyable experience – especially for female shoppers. Design the 'Webmosphere' for enjoyable shopping: video, audio, graphics and virtual store layout*
- Open with a strong introduction – great home page
- Design creative visual images
- Create a company image that makes your Web site stand out
- Avoid a clustered visual image (too many banners, too much information)
- Reinforce brand image and build brand strength
- Use short, concise phrases
- Vividly describe product benefits
- Offer speed-navigation to known points
- Build in customer interactivity
- Provide expert information
- Update displays regularly
- Price competitively
- Provide loyalty incentives
- Include testimonials from satisfied customers and, if possible, well-known personalities
- Offer a clear guarantee

Sources: Adapted from Tiernan (2001), except points marked * – sourced from research referenced in the text

and experiential benefits, but good at finding the best deals quickly – the male purposeful style (Dennis *et al.* 2001; Lindquist and Kaufman-Scarborough 2000). Male and female shopping behaviour tend to be much more similar on the Web than in-store, meaning that females are losing out on social and experiential benefits. According to US surveys, two-thirds of Web site visitors 'will not buy online until there is more human interaction', and women in particular want a 'sense of personalized relationship' (Harris 1998; McCarthy 2000). e-Retailers should make the buying process more personal and interactive, especially for female shoppers.

GROWTH OF AND PROSPECTS FOR E-RETAILING

Despite the disadvantages and the dotcom crash, the advantages are driving a growth in e-Shopping in the UK, at least in certain categories. Sales had reached £3.3 billion by 2001. It was forecast that 'most people' will buy groceries, books, CDs and even clothes by e-Shopping, making up 10 per cent of total shopping by 2009. Figures 9.3–9.5 indicate the growth and the main categories of purchases. It has been forecast that 94 per cent of e-Retailing will be at the expense of the high street, with only 6 per cent arising from incremental growth (Gibson 1999; Prefontayne 1999; RICS Foundation 2000; Verdict 2000, 2001, 2002).

According to Verdict, in 2001 grocery would account for half of all e-Sales – £1.3 billion, which sounds massive, but accounts for only 5.6 per cent of groceries. The market leaders in their sectors were Amazon (books, plus CDs

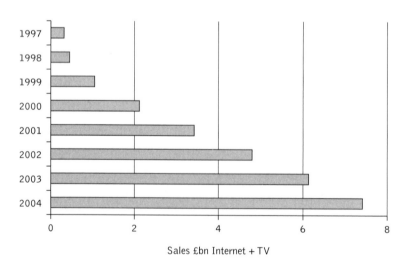

Sales £bn Internet + TV

Figure 9.3 *Growth of online shopping: surveys for 1997 to 2001, forecasts for 2002 to 2004*

Source: Verdict (2000, 2001, 2002)

256

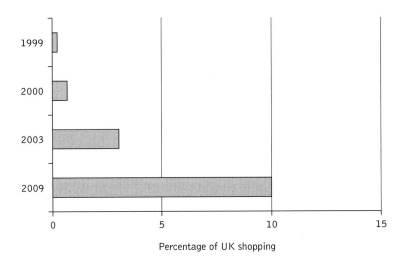

Figure 9.4 *e-Retailing as a percentage of total shopping in the UK*
Source: Verdict (2000); Gibson (1999)

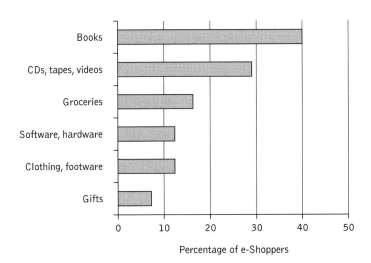

Figure 9.5 *What e-Shoppers buy*
Source: Doidge and Higgins (2000)

and videos), Tesco (groceries), Dell (computers) and Next (clothing). Average spend has risen faster for men (+15 per cent) than women (+5 per cent), leading Verdict to comment that 'the proliferation of female-orientated sites . . . have failed to motivate women to shop significantly more'. The proportion of e-Shoppers preferring to shop from e-Sites run by high street retailers rather than Internet-only is soaring (up from 22 per cent in October 2000 to 33 per cent in April 2001). The main service is travel, and the main virtual product is sex (pictures and stories) – often absent from published statistics, but accounting for around 10 per cent of e-Retailing. In the words of *The Virgin Internet Shopping Guide*, 'However much you may despise the sex industry, it has been almost solely responsible for driving forward the revolution in online shopping.'

THINK POINT

If people can e-Shop easily, why should anyone use the high street?

Mini case study:
AMAZON

The US-based company Amazon is well known as the world's biggest e-Retailer of books, head to head with Barnes and Noble for the title of the world's largest bookstore, even though Amazon sells online only. From a start-up in 1995, annual sales have grown to more than $1 billion and the company has 2.5 million customers – but reported its first profit only in 2002. Other products include CDs and videos. The UK site (www.amazon.uk) was formed in 1998 by the takeover of Bookpages, and the UK is now Amazon's biggest market outside the USA.

Amazon.co.uk followed the US parent's example of using heavy (non-electronic) advertising to promote brand awareness. Traffic to the site is encouraged using the affiliate system. For example, popular search engines such as AltaVista offer links to books related to the key words. The site is user-friendly, enabling e-Shoppers to find books quickly by title, author or subject. Users can find their title in seconds from a few keywords. Synopses and contents lists are provided, along with a list of other relevant books. Amazon keeps a record of customers' preferences and advises when new books likely to be of interest are published. One of the main selling propositions is a discount of up to 40 per cent – but such deep discounting made it hard for the company to reach profitability.

Amazon is renowned for customer service, security and fast delivery.

Mini case study: DELL

Dell (www.dell.com) has been a pioneer in telemarketing and direct selling since the late 1980s, demonstrating that a complex product like a computer could be sold without face-to-face contact. Much of the success has been due to investment in staff training and customer service systems: 'We will use our employees to deliver the personal touch that many customers desire – you do not need physical contact to do that.' The company was one the first e-Retailers and is the market leader worldwide for computer hardware. Dell does not use high street stores, but remains dual channel: via telesales and the Internet.

Source: Adapted from de Kare Silver (2001)

E-MALLS V. HIGH STREETS AND SHOPPING CENTRES

Even on modest projections, e-Retail will take a 5 to 10 per cent share of total retail sales within five to ten years. This may seem a small percentage, but it represents around £8 billion in annual sales. High street banks, other financial services and travel agents are most at risk (British Council of Shopping Centres 2001). Some forecasters predict the eventual disappearance from the high street of any businesses that work better as e-Businesses: banks, travel agents, bookshops, music shops and electronics shops.

> Clothes shops will persist because the experience of shopping for clothes is too deeply ingrained, especially in women, to be abandoned. Also specialist, up-market retailers that require expertise and offer the consumer a specific experience will flourish. The high street will be freed of its ranks of the same old stores and become a more interesting place.
>
> (Bryan Appleyard, writing in the *Sunday Times Magazine*, 22 July 2001).

The winners in the high street are likely to be well-branded retailers offering service and added value. Indications so far are that most e-Retail success too is going to existing, well-branded retailers which are likely to have efficient supply chain and fulfilment systems (Verdict 2001) – a trend likely to continue for the next five years (according to College of Estate Management research: British Council of Shopping Centres 2001). According to a *Computer Weekly* survey, the top three rated e-Retailers for customer satisfaction and service are Marks and Spencer, Littlewoods (www.littlewoods.co.uk) and Iceland (www.iceland.co.uk).

Mini case study:
MARKS AND SPENCER

Marks and Spencer (www.marksandspencer.com) was once well known as the most successful retailer in Europe. The company's high street operation may have been slow to regain its sparkle following poor results in the late 1990s, but the e-Retail site is a model of good practice. It is easy to navigate, with a good selection of clothing and underwear, plus home furnishings, gifts and flowers – but not food. Two-day delivery is free at the time of writing. Returns can be made either to a Marks and Spencer store or with the post-paid label provided.

Source: Adapted from the *Sunday Times* Doors 'Webwatch' site test

---

THINK POINT

The traditional slogan for the (telephone directory) Yellow Pages was 'Let your fingers do the walking' – use the 'phone to save trudging round the shops. Now, to solve a problem we tend to turn first to the Web: 'Let your fingers do the clicking.' Why should retailers pay to advertise in paper directories if consumers hardly use them?

UK shopping centres appear to have been slow to embrace e-Commerce, although some towns and shopping centres do have Web sites (e.g. the south-west England resort of Newquay (www.newquay.com – site designed and maintained by a Brunel University student)). Eighty-eight per cent of US shopping centres currently have Web sites compared with 10 per cent of UK ones (British Council of Shipping Centres, 2001). In the USA, Myshoppingcenter (www.myshoppingcenter.com) provides low-cost market-tested platforms getting shopping centres onto the Web. Shoppers can find shopping centres in a particular geographical area and download coupons for special offers. In the UK, Zagme (www.zagme.com), currently on trial at the regional shopping centres of Bluewater (Kent) and Lakeside (Essex), may be an indicator of things to come. It is entirely a permission-marketing system; shoppers can receive text messages with special offers from participating retailers.

There are now, though, a handful of successful UK e-Malls. An e-Mall, e-Shopping centre or virtual mall brings together a number of separately owned e-Retail sites to a single virtual location, the e-Retailers paying rent – commission and/or annual fee – to the centre management. The e-Mall provides unified guarantees and an easy route to a wide range of e-Shops. Usually, for convenience, shoppers can carry their shopping basket from one e-Shop to another in the mall. For example, after a slow start with BarclaySquare (in 1995), Barclays has now relaunched its e-Mall as IndigoSquare (www.indigosquare.com). As far as we are aware, only one 'bricks' shopping centre also offers 'clicks' shopping. Nevertheless, according to the British Council of Shopping Centres (2001), so-called 'wired leases' will develop, further enabling shoppers to follow links from a shopping centre Web site to buy online from the tenant retailers.

NON-COMPUTER E-RETAILING

It has been forecast that a high proportion of e-Shopping will be by other than desktop computer means, for example using interactive television and TV Internet. The biggest growth area is likely to be in m-Commerce following the launch of third-generation mobile devices, as discussed in Chapter 7. m-Commerce has been forecast to reach 25 per cent of all Internet transactions by 2003. In Japan, i-mode m-commerce technology has already taken off exponentially: 70 per cent of the population have a mobile, 60 per cent of those have i-mode (14 million subscribers) – and e-Retail in Japan is already at 10 per cent of total retail sales. Users can program their likes and dislikes – very popular for meeting people, but also successful in generating m-Shopping business (Yoshida 2001). In the UK, AvantGo (www.avantgo.co.uk) is the market-leading content provider, with a wide range of information and m-Shopping, including books, CDs/videos, computers travel, electronics and clothing.

THINK POINT

Interactive digital television enables e-Shopping without a PC, potentially doubling the e-Shopper customer base. Could this development spell the end for the high street retailers most vulnerable to e-Retail competition?

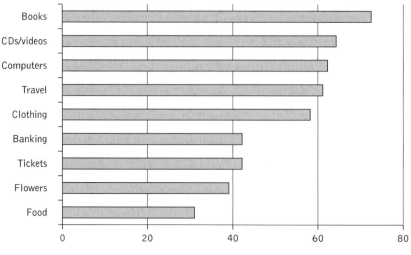

Figure 9.6 *What m-Shoppers buy*

Source: AvantGo Demographic Survey for the six months to February 2001

m-CRM (customer relationship management via mobile devices) is the driver that makes m-tailing cost-effective compared to traditional high street retailing. Zagme is a permission-based example: 'I know you're passing, why not pop in for . . .?' According to AvantCo, retail special offers redeemed by electronic bar code are achieving astonishing 5 to 8 per cent response rates.

CONCLUSIONS

While many will regret the passing of the old-fashioned high street, change is inevitable. With the technical security issues now largely resolved, consumers are steadily overcoming their reservations concerning e-Shopping. Beyond the hype that was prevalent pre-dotcom crash, and the pessimism that followed, e-Shopping has resumed a steady growth. Market forces in action mean that the e-Retailing survivors and leaders are the strong brands that are successfully addressing the customer service and fulfilment issues. Given the unstoppable progress of e-Retailing, traditionalists can at least take comfort in the current e-Retailing success of the high street multi-channel retailers – which one hopes will preserve at least some vibrant 'bricks' shopping alongside the growing proportion of 'clicks'.

THINK POINT

For each of these e-Retailers: Bothams, Next, Amazon, Marks and Spencer, Boots and Tesco, consider the reasons for their success (or otherwise) as e-Retailers.

CHAPTER SUMMARY

e-Retail is the sale of goods and services via Internet or other electronic channels, for personal or household use by consumers. Success factors in e-Retail include making it easy for consumers to buy, providing good service, making e-Shopping an enjoyable experience and including human communication. The 'don'ts' include having too many graphics, too much narrative and too many click-through pages.

Retailers must choose an e-Retailing strategic option based on degree of commitment and responsiveness to e-Shopping. Multi-channel retail (high street plus e-Retail) is becoming more dominant. High streets and shopping centres still have the edge on aspects such as customer service and experiential shopping, but e-Retail is ahead on range of products, prices and convenience.

Case study: TESCO

Tesco (www.tesco.com)is Britain's biggest grocery retailer and has been active in telesales (at pilot locations) since 1996. The initial telesales pilot, at Ealing, west London, was developed from Tesco's home delivery service to less mobile consumers, subcontracted from the local authority. This low-tech operation was developed into the pilot for e-Retailing – built on the proven delivery system and hand-picking from the shelves of the grocery stores. Tesco still uses this tried and reliable system for groceries in preference to a heavy investment in warehouse picking centres (although non-food items such as books are now handled from a non-store facility). Customers can purchase any of the 20,000-plus product lines available from the stores, for next-day delivery for UK customers within delivery distance of a store (which includes most of the UK's population). A more limited product range is available for delivery worldwide. As an alternative to composing your shopping list online, Tesco sends shoppers a monthly

CD-ROM and information on special offers by mail. Using the CD-ROM can speed up and simplify the ordering process, and you can store your shopping list so you do not have to go through a long order process each time. This is a big 'convenience' benefit, as 80 per cent of grocery shopping is replenishment. Tesco follows the maxim 'Make it easy for your customers to buy', accepting orders by Web, CD-ROM, TV Internet, fax, phone, home delivery or collect, and of course shop in store. You can buy books, music, clothes, PCs and Internet services. There are regular paper mailings and special offers, including non-food promotions such as 'The top 50 books 10 per cent cheaper than Amazon'. Addressing the need for more social interaction, particularly for female shoppers, the Tesco site links to iVillage, providing information and chat rooms. With an e-Turnover of around £300 million per year, Tesco claims to be the UK's biggest e-Retailer and the world's largest e-Grocer.

FURTHER READING

These texts were written pre-dotcom crash, so parts may seem overenthusiastic now.

Collin, S. (1999) *The Virgin Internet Shopping Guide*, London: Virgin. This is a good, concise introduction and directory for UK e-Shopping.

de Kare-Silver, M. (2001) *e-Shock: The New Rules*, Basingstoke, UK: Palgrave. This UK book includes an in-depth analysis of the effect of e-Shopping on strategies for both retailers and manufacturers.

Lundquist, L. H. (1998) *Selling On Line for Dummies*, Foster City, CA: IDG. Written for US readers, this is a good introduction to the basic nuts and bolts of e-Retailing.

Tiernan, B. (2000) *e-Tailing*, Chicago: Dearborn. This is a definitive text on e-Retailing, written for a US audience.

QUESTIONS

Question 9.1

What do you think would be disadvantages of e-Retailing for an independent baker like Bothams?

Feedback – A small firm might be put off by high set-up, investment and ongoing costs, plus the level of know-how and technology needed.

Question 9.2

What do you consider are the main advantages of e-Retailing for a small independent baker like Bothams?

Feedback – Location is unimportant; size does not matter; and e-Retailing reaches a larger audience.

Question 9.3

Why do you think Abbey National's e-Bank is separately branded as 'Cahoot'?
Feedback – High street customers might consider they were being unfairly treated if e-Customers of the same bank received a better deal.

Question 9.4

Which of these companies' products would you expect to be most and least suitable for e-Retailing: Bothams, Next, Amazon, Marks and Spencer, Boots, Tesco.
Feedback – According to de Kare Silver's test, the most suitable should be Amazon followed by Tesco – both high on consumer attributes, having a high proportion of e-Responsive convenience shoppers; with Amazon rated higher on product characteristics; that is, more virtual appeal of the product. Least suitable would be Next and Marks and Spencer, both low on consumer attributes, having a high proportion of social and comparison shoppers.

 WEB LINKS

Adapted from *The Virgin Internet Shopping Guide*.

Try these sites to taste the flavour of e-Shopping

www.amazon.co.uk
Busy, friendly and informative; Amazon is the market leader for books plus music and much more

www.animail.co.uk
Animail offers masses of goodies for pets.

www.blackstar.co.uk
Blackstar is the top choice for videos and CDs.

www.dell.co.uk
Dell is the market leader for computer sales.

www.fao.com
F.A.O. Schwarz offers a fantastic range of thousands of toys.

www.landsend.com
Lands' End offers simple, cotton clothes in a clean and airy site.

www.softwareparadise.com
Software Paradise has a wide range of software.

www.tesco.com
Tesco is the top grocery supermarket online as well as in-store.

www.unbeatable.co.uk
Unbeatable offers great prices on electrical goods.

www.wallpaperstore.com
Wallpaper store has a huge range of wallpaper styles.

www.winecellar.co.uk
Winecellar has a good range of wines.

Price-comparison sites

These sites allow comparison of the prices of the same item from different e-Retailers.

www.buy.co.uk
Finds the cheapest electricity, gas or other utility – and has a directory of e-Shops.

www.ComputerPrices.co.uk
Finds the cheapest computer kit in the UK.

www.priceline.com
Creates a market or reverse auction. Enter the price you want to pay for a range of services such as air travel and car hire. The system searches for suppliers willing to sell at that price.

www.shopsmart.co.uk
The leading price comparison site.

Directories of UK shops

www.british-shopping.com

www.buy.co.uk

www.enterprisecity.co.uk

www.shops.imrg.org

www.ishop.co.uk

www.Lycos.co.uk

www.shopguide.co.uk

www.shoppingcity.co.uk

Auctions

www.ebay.co.uk
In the USA, e-Auctions are the most active and popular way of e-Shopping, with eBay the leader for fun (and risk?).

www.qxl.co.uk
Unlike most auction sites, the UK-based QXL sells products itself, as well as allowing the public to sell in personal auctions.

More e-Retail and e-Mall links

www.verdict.co.uk
For links to e-Retailers.

sol.brunel.ac.uk/~dennis
For links to 'case studies' and (via 'search'), e-Shopping and e-Malls.

Chapter 10

Marketing planning

LISA HARRIS

MINDMAP

	Chapter 1 History, definitions and frameworks	
Chapter 2 Marketing research		Chapter 3 Change management
	Chapter 4 Strategy	
Chapter 5 Branding	Chapter 6 Relationship marketing	Chapter 7 Multi-channel marketing
Chapter 8 The marketing mix	Chapter 9 e-Retailing	
	Chapter 10 Marketing planning	
	Chapter 11 Legal, ethical and public policy issues	

Introductory level

Strategic level

Operational level

Big picture

LINKS TO OTHER CHAPTERS

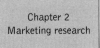

Chapter 2
Marketing research

Chapter 3
Change
management

Chapter 4
Strategy

Chapter 8
The marketing
mix

- Chapter 2 – Marketing research
- Chapter 3 – Change management
- Chapter 4 – Strategy
- Chapter 8 – The marketing mix

KEY LEARNING POINTS

After completing this chapter you will have an understanding of:

- The principles of Internet marketing planning
- How the issues discussed throughout the book can be integrated into an effective mechanism for developing, implementing and evaluating online marketing activities in a systematic way
- How the range of online marketing strategies available can be customized to suit specific industry contexts and business priorities

ORDERED LIST OF SUB TOPICS

- What is a marketing plan?
- The marketing planning process
  - Marketing audit
  - Objectives
  - Formulation and choice of strategy

- Implementation through the marketing mix
- Evaluation and control
■ Example marketing plans
  - A market-leading multi-channel retailer
  - A traditional retailer
  - A small toy shop
  - A B2B provider of Internet services
■ Chapter summary
❖ Further reading
❖ Questions
❖ Web links

WHAT IS A MARKETING PLAN?

A marketing plan is an operational planning device detailing both the initial development and implementation of the chosen strategy and how the associated marketing activities can be integrated in order to meet the stated objectives.

It is important not to confuse the planning *document* (see examples later in the chapter) with the planning *process*, which is described below.

THE MARKETING PLANNING PROCESS

The principles of marketing planning apply just as much to online marketing as they do to more traditional marketing activities. Planning forces a proactive approach which involves:

- defining objectives;
- assessing the operating environment;
- reviewing alternatives;
- selecting the best approach based upon effective matching of skills and resources with identified market opportunities;
- evaluating progress towards meeting the defined objectives.

Only by setting realistic objectives and assessing whether they have been achieved can a firm evaluate the contribution its online marketing is making, and then use this information to guide the choice of future strategy and its implementation. In this chapter, we will be focusing on outline plans, but a model guiding the planning process in extensive detail has been developed by McDonald (1999) if you wish to examine this topic in more depth.

The planning cycle can be represented as follows:

- stage 1 (the marketing audit) addresses the question 'where are we now?';
- stage 2 (segmentation, targeting, positioning, setting objectives) addresses the question 'where do we want to be?';
- stage 3 (choice of strategy) addresses the question 'what is the best way of getting there?';
- stage 4 (implementation of strategy through the marketing mix) addresses the question 'how do we make it happen?';
- stage 5 (evaluation and control of strategy) addresses the question 'how do we know we have got there?'.

Once stage 5 has been completed, the cycle then begins all over again from the new starting point! We will now examine each of the stages in turn.

Planning cycle stage 1: marketing audit

The key role of research in effective marketing planning was introduced in Chapter 2. The marketing audit comprises research and analysis of the internal and external environment as follows:

- The internal audit reviews existing marketing activities and assesses their effectiveness in terms of contribution to revenue, brand enhancement, customer service, customer retention, market share or sales leads.
- The external audit considers the micro-environmental influences (customers, suppliers, partners, distributors and competitors) and macro-environmental influences (political, economic, social, technological and legal) within which the company operates, as illustrated in Figure 10.1.

The circles in the figure representing different aspects of the business environment show that from a company's perspective, the various components of the micro-environment are intimately connected with the operations of its business, but the macro-environment is one step removed. This means that a company has some degree of control over the micro-environmental influences, but cannot directly influence the 'bigger picture' of the macro-environment, which would include such issues as interest rate changes, new legislation, etc. By conducting a marketing audit, a company can at least monitor and be aware of the implications of likely changes in the macro-environment, even if it cannot directly control them.

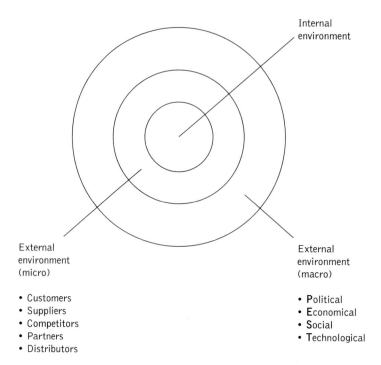

Internal environment

External environment (micro)

- Customers
- Suppliers
- Competitors
- Partners
- Distributors

External environment (macro)

- Political
- Economical
- Social
- Technological

Figure 10.1 *The relationship between different aspects of a company's environment*

Competitor analysis

An important part of the audit is competitor analysis, in which the goal is to undertake a benchmarking exercise by identifying the company's chief competitors, analysing their individual marketing strategies, and hence seeing where to position the company for maximum advantage. The first step is to identify the major players in the market. The Yahoo! Directory (www.yahoo.com) provides a comprehensive categorization of many business sectors. Zenithmedia (www.zenithmedia.co.uk) presents the main operators, split by industry sector. You can often see which companies get the most traffic by checking the Media Metrix 500 (www.mediametrix.com).

The second step is to study the top five or ten competitors carefully, as you can learn a lot from the material posted on their Web sites. Look for:

- the scope of products or services offered;
- the distribution system for products;
- the scope of guarantees, policies and other customer service procedures;
- the overall look, feel and functionality of the Web site;
- sophistication of the payment system;

- the degree of personalization offered;
- advertising campaigns and offers;
- strengths and weaknesses from the customer's point of view;
- the statement of vision or purpose;
- areas where the competitor holds a market advantage;
- vulnerabilities or gaps in what is offered.

Examining new service offerings from the Internet market leaders such as Amazon or Cisco can also give valuable insight into the latest possibilities. Some companies accord a central role to monitoring the activities of their competitors – sometimes to the extent of industrial espionage, or spying. Such competitive intelligence activities will be reviewed in Chapter 11.

Customer analysis

Wilson (www.wilsonweb.com) provides a framework that can be used to analyse customers and their changing needs (Table 10.1).

SWOT analysis

The analysis of the internal and external environment can be pulled together by means of a SWOT analysis (see examples later in the chapter).

S = strengths
W = weaknesses
O = opportunities
T = threats

This exercise allows the marketer to compare and match a company's internal strengths and weaknesses with the opportunities and threats identified in the external environment. It can therefore facilitate the choice of the most appropriate strategy for achieving the stated objectives through definitive and focused action. Speed of action is particularly important for plans that include a significant element of online activity, because competitive advantage tends to be short-lived. It is easy for competitors to monitor each other's online activities, as described above.

Table 10.1 *Customer analysis*

Geographic	Are they grouped regionally, nationally, globally?
Cultural and ethnic	What languages do they prefer to do business in? Does ethnicity affect their tastes or buying behaviours?
Economic conditions, income and/or purchasing power	What is the average household income or purchasing power of your customers? What are the economic conditions they face as individuals? As an industry?
Power	What is the level of decision-making ability and job title of your typical customer groups?
Size of company	What company size are you best able to serve? Do you determine this best by annual revenue or number of employees?
Values, attitudes, beliefs	What are the predominant values that your customers have in common? What is their attitude towards your kind of product or service?
Knowledge and awareness	How much knowledge do your customers have about your product or service, about your industry? How much education is needed? How much brand-building advertising do you need in order to make your pool of customers aware of what you offer?
Lifestyle	How many lifestyle characteristics can you name about your purchasers? Have a look at the CACI Web site (www.caci.com/Products/MSG/Databases.html). The firm has developed the fascinating ACORN system of 43 closely targeted lifestyle profiles that can be tied to specific postal codes for targeted promotional campaigns
Buying patterns	There is a growing body of information on how consumers of different ages and demographic groups shop on the Web. This is vital information for a marketing plan
Media used	How do your targeted customers learn? What do they read? What magazines do they subscribe to? What are their favourite Web sites?

Source: Adapted from www.wilsonweb.com

Marketing planning stage 2: segmentation, targeting, positioning, objectives

Segmentation

Following completion of the marketing audit, the next step is to segment customers into specific categories. This process requires considerable market research and careful analysis, but it enables much more focused marketing efforts. The marketing plan should contain a paragraph explaining how customers are segmented, indicating which products or services are most suitable for each segment. Different marketing strategies might be required for each market segment if their needs are diverse. Depending upon the characteristics of the various market segments, more or less emphasis upon online marketing may be appropriate in each case. As was emphasized in Chapter 4, no marketing strategy should *force* customers online; instead, it should offer appropriate *choice*. A flexible strategy will add to costs but maintain the focus on specific customer needs. In practice, budgetary constraints and the company's attitude to risk will probably mean that a compromise has to be reached with regard to the extent of choice offered.

Have a look at how IBM segments its markets (http://www.ibm.com). You will find this breakdown:

- IBM business partners;
- developers;
- home/home office;
- investors;
- job opportunities;
- small business.

Thus IBM has four classes of customers – enterprise, developers, home/home office and small business – and markets to each of them differently. Within each category will be the products designed for that particular class of customers, with the layout, language and emphasis of each part of the site customized accordingly.

Targeting

Once the segmentation exercise is complete, the next task is to target resources on the segments deemed to offer most potential. It is unlikely that a firm would be able to meet the needs of a diverse range of customer groups, and once again the audit results can be used to select the segments the firm is best placed to focus upon.

Positioning

Positioning is the process of designing an appropriate image and value so that customers within the target segments understand what the company stands for. It also refers to the firm's location in the market in relation to its competitors. Through competitor analysis, the firm can identify where gaps lie that it may be well equipped to exploit through careful positioning.

Objectives

Without quantifiable objectives, strategies take place in a vacuum because the degree of success cannot be measured. An example of an objective could be to raise the contribution of online sales as a percentage of total sales from 10 percent to 20 percent over the next year. The popular mnemonic SMART can be usefully applied to the objective-setting process:

SPECIFIC	Objectives must be focused
MEASURABLE	Objectives need to be quantified to aid measurement of success
ACTIONABLE	Objectives must be realistic, in other words compatible with the skills and resources of the organization
RELEVANT	Objectives should relate to core business activities
TIMED	Achievement of objectives channelled within realistic deadlines

Marketing planning stage 3: formulating and choosing appropriate strategies

Online marketing strategies were considered in detail in Chapter 4, so we will focus here on providing some practical examples taken from different industry contexts. The most important factor governing strategic direction will be the extent of the financial and psychological support given by the senior management team. Without such a commitment, new developments will lack direction and appropriate resourcing. Following the planning approach can help firms to take a long-term view, by forcing them to think about matching their competencies with identified market opportunities, how to build upon their initial commitments over time, and how they will go about evaluating success.

Which of the alternative strategies should be chosen? If the audit has been conducted thoroughly, the best 'fit' between internal strengths and external opportunities should be apparent. But the decision can rarely be taken in isolation of often constraining organizational factors, such as a desire to maintain the status quo, the funds available and the commitment to change from senior management. As was discussed in Chapter 3, if significant change is required to existing business practices, then critical roles may also be played by 'project champions' in driving effective implementation.

Kumar (1999) suggests that a firm should decide whether the Internet will primarily *replace* or *complement* other channels to market. If the former, it is important that sufficient investment is made in the infrastructure necessary to achieve this. It is a critical decision because it forces the firm to think about whether the Internet is just another channel to market, or whether it will fundamentally change the way in which the firm interacts with its customers. Kumar suggests that replacement is most likely to happen when:

- customer access to the Internet is high;
- the Internet offers a better value proposition than other media;
- the product can be standardized, and ideally also delivered over the Internet.

The attitude of the senior management team will be critical in establishing the degree of commitment to online strategies and hence the choice of most appropriate strategy given the resources available. In many cases, firms are reluctant to commit to providing Internet channels to market because of a fear of 'cannibalizing' their existing business. This means that they fear that providing alternative channels to customers will add to costs, as existing customers take advantage of the ability to switch at will between different ways of dealing with the firm, without any new business being generated by the existence of the new channel. This is undoubtedly a risk, but the alternative of not providing the channel at all may mean that customers go to competitors that do provide the choice. So while the Internet channel may not generate additional business (at least in the short term), it should at least ensure that existing customers do not defect.

Marketing planning stage 4: implementation through the marketing mix

Once a strategy has been chosen, the next step is to ensure that implementation takes place as smoothly as possible. A number of key questions need to be addressed:

- Have the costs been estimated accurately (in terms of both people and money)?
- Can the customer service facilities that the site offers be fully supported?

277

- Can delivery of goods/services take place within stated timescales?
- Can returned goods be handled effectively?
- Are responsibilities for Web site maintenance and updating clear and appropriate?
- Is technology (fancy graphics that slow the site down, for example) used to support the business needs, or is it included just for technology's sake?
- Will organizational change be necessary?
- How will the change processes be managed?
- Can traditional supply chains be maintained *alongside* new direct selling options online?
- Do online marketing campaigns complement traditional marketing channels?
- How can the success of the Internet strategy be measured and evaluated?

Strategy implementation centres upon effective management of the marketing mix (as was discussed in Chapter 8). To see the variety of ways that the mix can be employed in practice, have a look at the sample marketing plans later in the chapter.

Marketing planning stage 5: evaluation and control of strategy

Analysing the effectiveness of a site is crucial in analysing the strategy and then revising it if necessary to overcome problems. If clear, *quantifiable* objectives were set, then the evaluation process is facilitated, because it can be easily established whether the objectives were met or not. In general terms, the measurement process can be summarized as follows:

1 Goal-setting – what do we want to achieve?
2 Performance measurement – what is happening?
3 Performance diagnosis – why is it happening?
4 Corrective action – what should we do about it?

Specific tangible evaluation methods that may be used include:

- return on investment;
- operational cost reduction;
- revenue earned;
- site profitability;

- number of new customers gained;
- changes in customer satisfaction levels ascertained through market research.

Kaplan and Norton (1993) devised an integrated measurement system called the Balanced Scorecard which provides a framework with which to evaluate the success of a strategy against the objectives set. The scorecard includes:

- customer concerns such as service quality, cost, response times;
- internal measures such as staff productivity and range of skills;
- financial measures such as revenue, profitability and costs;
- learning and growth/innovation measures such as rate of new product development, availability of staff training.

More intangible measures include:

- corporate image enhancement through online PR;
- brand-building;
- building of long-term relationships with clients.

Whatever evaluation methods are used, they must be flexible enough to be adapted to the increasingly broad range of online marketing strategies that companies are pursuing. For example, if the site is not transactional, then the relevance of financial measures may be limited.

As was discussed in Chapter 2, it is also possible to measure site usage patterns electronically, which can help with the evaluation process. To remind you, here is a summary of key techniques with some practical examples:

- log file analysis (www.webtrends.com);
- panel data (www.netratings.com);
- online questionnaires (www.websurveyor.com);
- online focus groups (www.w3focus.com);
- online mystery shopping (www.emysteryshopper.com);
- benchmarking (www.gomez.com).

So once again, the key role of research here in evaluating the success of the strategy implemented is apparent.

EXAMPLE MARKETING PLANS

Proposed outline marketing plan for multi-channel retailer W. H. Smith plc

This subsection was kindly contributed by Glen Freeman, Brunel University.

Background

The traditional high street retailer W. H. Smith plc has already established new channels to market through the Internet, digital television and WAP mobile phones. The company has a huge high street presence in the UK, with 1,500 stores nationwide. It also now has stores across the globe on major transport routes at airports and railway stations, and already has over 5 million members registered with its 'club card' scheme. These are already loyal W. H. Smith customers who have experienced the company through its stores. Moving this confidence online will be far easier than trying to generate new business online.

Marketing audit

One way to analyse W. H. Smith's current Internet strategy is to examine performance in terms of the digital marketing cycle (Chen 2001):

1 Visitors are *attracted* to the ISP through in-store promotions.
2 They are *engaged* by the W. H. Smith Portal's useful content.
3 W. H. Smith sends fortnightly emails to *retain* customers.
4 Data are gathered when the customers sign up, allowing the company to *learn* from its customers.
5 Either the product or the marketing effort is *customized* and tailored to one consumer at a time

SWOT analysis

See Table 10.2.

Objective

W. H. Smith's objective is to provide a seamless service across all channels through 'my W. H. Smith' in order to improve customer relationships and generate additional revenue per customer. Specific objectives can be summarized as shown in the following list:

Table 10.2 *SWOT analysis for W. H. Smith*

Strengths	Weaknesses
● Well-established brand and customer base	● Lack of a link between offline and online operations
● Club Card membership	● Separate departments
● ISP	● e-Commerce not a company-wide consideration (stores have little contact)
● Customer trust and loyalty	
● Links to e-Intermediaries	
● Warehousing	
● Offline stores	

Opportunities	Threats
● Large offline database to bring online	● Cannibalisation of offline business by online competitors
● Build customer relationships and increase sales through provision of a choice of integrated channels	● Weakening economy
	● New data protection legislation

- sign up one-third of Club Card Members to 'My W. H. Smith' within two years;
- increase spend per Club Card customer by 15 per cent within one year.

In order to build the trust necessary for CRM to be effective, Sawhney and Zabin (2001) recommend 'presenting a seamless face to customers, regardless of what they buy, where they buy, and how they choose to interact with the firm'.

Strategy

By providing an integrated multi-channel service, W. H. Smith can pursue both market penetration (selling more to existing customers) and market development (attracting new customers) in terms of the Ansoff (1957) model.

Amazon's example of a successful CRM campaign has set a precedent, with average spend per customer rising 25 per cent between 1998 and 2000. According to Gardner (2000), 56 per cent of Amazon customers have remained active over this period.

Implementation of strategy through the marketing mix

- The initial stage is to introduce Club Card members to the product 'My W. H. Smith' (an online customer relationship marketing scheme) by sending a welcome pack containing the 'My W. H. Smith' CD and a new, updated Club Card.

- The 'My W. H. Smith' product is free to all customers.
- Potential members will be offered a Welcome Pack in the firm's retail stores.
- In a seamless multi-channel environment people must be able to sign up via all possible channels (high street stores, travel stores, WAP phones, digital television, the Internet). They should have to register only once to use them all. Once a customer has signed up, they will be able to use their email address or W. H. Smith Net ID plus a password to access any channel.
- On Internet channels, customers will be offered the option to store a cookie on their machine to identify them. The company should use cookies only with the customer's authorization. The company's policy on cookies should also be detailed in the privacy statement.
- The customer can order goods from any channel. They can have goods delivered to their desired destination or arrange to collect them at their nearest store. Customer services and return facilities should be available through both online and offline channels.
- The customer should be able to maintain control of the relationship at all times. In order to achieve this, they should be able to change the terms of the relationship as required.
- Personalized permission-based emails can be used to promote special offers and inform the customer how many club card points they have acquired.

Evaluation and control

The success of this project will be monitored by the following values:

- 'My W. H. Smith'/Club Card ratios (reviewed monthly);
- annual revenue contribution (reviewed bimonthly by moving average);
- spend per Club Card customer (weekly targets, reviewed fortnightly).

The targets will be set at each review and adjustments made to promotions and site structure if required in order to achieve objectives.

- Store managers will be set targets for signing up new customers.
- It is also important to keep a monitor on the amount and type of customer queries received. This will allow the feedback pages to contain answers to popular questions.

Internet marketing plan for a more traditionally focused retailer, currently with 'brochureware' Web site: River Island

This subsection was kindly supplied by Laura Pegg and David McLaverty, Brunel University.

Background

River Island currently occupies 300 high street stores, with 200 of these situated in the United Kingdom. This fashion-conscious chain of retail stores has as its target market both males and females aged 18–35. It is a privately owned company that currently relies on high street sales, encouraged by the River Island Account Card and a limited paper catalogue published twice-yearly. Currently River Island works with a company called Zendor, which supplies all the core end-to-end fulfilment services such as warehousing, distribution, call centres and returns management. The company Web site is basic and does not currently support e-Commerce transactions.

River Island's main competitors are Next and Topshop, which collectively cover the same segments of the retail market. Both of these major fashion retailers have fully enabled e-Commerce Web sites. Next has also developed a sub-brand called Next Directory, which is a well-established mail order catalogue.

Objective

River Island aims to catch up with its major competitors, which have been quicker off the mark in establishing multi-channel operations. The benefits of being a market follower in this respect centre upon the ability of the firm to learn from the mistakes of early adopters of e-Commerce.

The company also aims to integrate a store-wide intranet that will provide staff with the latest information regarding the products, mark-downs, sales, memos and previews of next season's fashions. The rationale for this is that effective internal communications will boost staff confidence and morale, which in turn will translate into a better service to customers.

Strategy

River Island's chosen online marketing strategy is to develop and implement a fully functional transactional Web site within a year in order to match the achievements of its major competitors in this area and boost brand image and hence sales by offering customers a choice of online and offline channels.

283

Marketing mix

River Island's marketing mix (Table 10.3) aims to define the methods and tools needed to ensure that the marketing objective is achieved. Both online and offline operations need to function in tandem to allow the marketing objective to be achieved successfully. For example:

- Traditional media such as local radio, newspapers, magazines and posters will not be forgotten.
- Store card customers will be mailed with the Web site address and specific promotional offers.
- All bags, stationery and receipts will carry the Web site address.
- Competitions will be run via in-store leaflets that require customers to access the Web site to enter.
- Online banner advertisements and affinity marketing will be commissioned with complementary sites such as Boots, Handbag and New Women.
- Offline PR will focus on providing press releases to specialist magazines and newspapers.
- An 'opt-in' online newsletter will provide registered customers with special deals such as invitations to sale previews.

Evaluation and control

Continuous monitoring and analysis of the site will take place to ensure that all areas of the Web site are functioning properly, eventually leading to site customization, providing opportunities to make the site more efficient.

It is also important to monitor emerging technologies that could prove useful additional channels to market. Possibilities include support for m-Commerce and General Packet Radio Services (GPRS), which could further expand the customer base, or SMS support, which could be used for notifying customers of new stocks or special deals. VOIP (Voice Over Internet Protocol) is another interesting technology that may prove useful, enabling customers to contact the company with a query in real time while still online. PDA support is another possible growth area.

Outline marketing plan for Yuri's Toys, a small but long-established family business

This subsection was kindly supplied by Yuri Gandamihardja, Ketan Makwana and Alan McGuinness, Brunel University.

Background

Yuri's Toys is a 'bricks and mortar' toyshop situated in Notting Hill, a fashionable part of London. It is a small, independently run family business that has been trading for over fifty years. The Web site is currently just brochureware with a very basic email facility.

Table 10.3 *Marketing mix for River Island*

Product	Quality	The Web site must ensure functionality and offer customers a simple and uncomplicated shopping experience
	Image	The style of the site must complement and provide consistency with the shop image
	Branding	The brand will be extended through the use of this medium, creating an e-Brand
	Customer service	Customer support, email feedback, logistics, order tracking, returns and FAQs all work together to make the shopping experience more enjoyable and easier
Price	Discounts	10 per cent discount and additional benefits for members will create customer incentives to use the e-Commerce site
	Credit	Traffic can also be driven to the site through use of the store card, which can also be applied for online
	Payment methods	All major credit cards will be accepted along with the store card; security measures will be taken to protect customers
Promotion	Marketing communications	Permission marketing will be an opt-in feature to provide customers with a newsletter, informing of new ranges, discounts, etc.
People	Training and skills	Staff need training in the use of the intranet along with training in customer and IT support/telephone support departments to ensure that customer queries can be dealt with successfully
	Staff support	In-store staff will have easily accessible support and information via a company-wide intranet
Processes	Customer focus	The fulfilment of customer demands is essential in this customer-orientated market
	IT support	Maintaining site and database is essential to ensure that customers have an enjoyable shopping experience and that customers are not lost through a failing site

▨ Table 10.4 Summary audit for Yuri's Toys

Customer environment	The firm has a loyal, but localized customer base as a result of its established 'bricks and mortar' business. There are few similar businesses in the Notting Hill area
Competitor environment	Yuri's Toys faces greater competition on a national level from major market players such as Toys 'R' Us. Online activities can reduce the disparity between large and small firms because size and geographical location are less important online
Supplier environment	Yuri's Toys is a member of Youngsters, a collaborative grouping of toy stores. Youngsters is formed so that supplies can be bought in bulk, which results in economies of scale

Summary audit

A summary audit is presented in Table 10.4.

Objective

The firm wishes to develop online operations that will change the business from 'bricks and mortar' to 'clicks and mortar'. The ability to offer customers a choice of channels and stock a wider range of products should permit an objective of a 20 per cent increase in total revenues over the next year.

Strategy

A strategy of both product development and market development will be pursued initially in order to achieve the objective stated above. Revenue growth will be achieved by developing a transactional Web site and offering a wider range of toys online than is currently stocked in the shop.

The second phase of online development will focus on customer relationship-building through the creation of an online community portal. This service will incorporate a certified learning environment, whereby targeted age groups can participate in an educational online quiz run by a teacher. The winner of the educational quiz will be entitled to discount vouchers to spend at Yuri's Toys.

The third phase will focus on the exploitation of latest technology in order to make the site an interactive and innovative experience for visitors that will generate 'stickiness'. This will be achieved primarily through audio replication of toys that generate sound. By demonstrating that Yuri's Toys are at the cutting edge of new developments, brand image can be enhanced and competitive advantage gained. Currently no major competitor has focused on this aspect of online marketing.

Table 10.5 *Marketing mix for Yuri's Toys*

Marketing mix element	Offline	Online
Product	Products sold in store	Store products and additional products offered for sale
		Customer reviews of product performance can be displayed
		Gift wrapping service can be provided
Price	Recommended retail price (RRP) pricing strategy	Special offers on toys not available in-store
Promotion	Shop-window advertising	Offer promotions on additional products that are not available in-store
	Advertising in local newspaper	
	Promotions on ex-display toys	Promote online community, including e-Learning, chat room and themed products of the month
	Seasonal promotions during Christmas, school holidays, etc.	
	Monthly themed promotions of popular products	Offer e-mail promotions to community members and to potential customers who opt-in for email alerts
		Advertise via banners in local area portals
Place	Physical presence of store	Internet ordering
		Courier delivery
		Order tracking and returns management

As a small business with limited financial resources and IT skills available, it is important that developments are staged over time so that the company does not make the mistake of trying 'too much too soon'.

The marketing mix

There are a number of practical issues to consider in connection with the marketing mix (Table 10.5), such as the financial and human resourcing for Web site development. Staff will need to be trained how to use and update the site, and it is likely that new jobs will be created, or at least existing responsibilities changed. The organizational structure may need to be redesigned so that the online operations can be effectively integrated with the traditional business.

Evaluation and control

A combination of traditional marketing research and Web measurement tools can be adopted in order to obtain information on whether or not the objectives have been achieved. Specific measures will include analysis of:

- monthly sales figures;
- customer satisfaction ratings;
- participation in an online portal;
- number of 'hits' on the Web site relating to specific promotions;
- number of customers signing up for email alerts.

Outline marketing plan for Asuk Creative Limited a B2B provider of Internet services

This subsection was kindly supplied by Craig Martin and Spencer Tarring, ASUK Creative and Brunel University respectively.

Background

ASUK Creative Limited (www.asuk.com) was formed in 1998 to provide a complete set of services, from consultancy to hosting, in the business-to-business Internet industry. After introducing a small range of low-cost dedicated servers in 1999, this small Internet design company began to make an impact on the market. Its servers were the cheapest in the UK, and potential clients flocked to find the catch. At first, progress was slow, but Web-hosting guides and directories quickly picked up on the low prices, and market penetration began. Although ASUK Creative manages to compete successfully on price, it struggles to compete with the big players and the more established brand names such as Fasthosts (www.fasthosts.co.uk) and Dellhost (www.dellhost.co.uk) in the field of support and reliability. Growth over the first two years was steady, but at the end of 2001, ASUK faced a declining growth rate. ASUK's corporate Web site focuses on other parts of the business, such as Web integration consultancy and database programming, that are in decline. This is stunting the growth of the dedicated server product, while the market is growing rapidly. ASUK Creative Limited needs to take advantage of this growth by improving its marketing output.

Audit

Initially, an analysis of where ASUK stands can be achieved through a SWOT and PEST analysis as shown below:

SWOT

- **Strengths**
  - competitive pricing on products;
  - no minimum contracts, whereas other competitors demand 12 months minimum;
  - quality and performance;
  - flexibility in product variations;
  - friendly service;
  - offers twenty-four hours, seven-day support;
  - existing loyal customer base;
  - recognized brand.

- **Weaknesses**
  - small company in comparison to competitors;
  - low capital;
  - lack of product resilience;
  - poor support response times;
  - budget network operations centre;
  - only the English language supported by the sales and support teams;
  - online documentation thin and outdated;
  - under-staffed.

- **Opportunities**
  - fast-growing international markets;
  - poor competitor services, bad reputations;
  - large growth in dedicated server market;
  - partnership opportunities with automated administration developers, opening the market to less experienced users.

- **Threats**
  - competition increasingly dropping prices;
  - market saturation: many companies are trying to take advantage of the increase in market worth;
  - technological advances cause hardware to devalue quickly;
  - failure of suppliers to deliver mission-critical services;
  - decrease in bandwidth costs means more companies can afford in-house operations, eliminating the need for hosting companies.

PEST

- **Political**
  - law in regard to copyright: since dedicated servers are not controlled by ASUK, it must ensure all users understand the law;
  - government actively encouraging use of Internet.

■ **Economic**
- worldwide recession looms;
- introduction of the euro;
- fraud: the increase of credit card fraud has had two effects. First, ASUK receive more fraudulent orders; and second, real customers are less willing to give out card details.

■ **Social and cultural**
- Language barriers: ASUK supports only English.

■ **Technological**
- bandwidth usage; that is, easier access by users means that bandwidth levels are increasing;
- speed of hardware redundancy (depreciation).

After carefully assessing ASUK's position and its strengths and weaknesses within its existing market, the owners came to the conclusion that it would be in ASUK's best interest to differentiate the dedicated server market from the other services it provides. This would entail establishing a separate entity, which in effect would require the building of a new brand. After they had conducted a survey of existing clients, it became apparent that the following features were needed:

- the ability to manage services online;
- the ability to upgrade services online;
- more reliable technical and telephone support;
- easier server management software for inexperienced users.

In order to build this brand, ASUK must eliminate these weaknesses identified by the survey, and add additional value to the service under the new brand. To encourage consumption and recognition of the new brand, the company needs to offer some value-added incentives. After assessing the existing market, ASUK identified three fundamentals employed by the industry that could also help obtain a competitive advantage;

1 thirty-day 100 per cent money back guarantee (risk reversal program);
2 UK price match;
3 no minimum contract.

With the newly developed brand, ASUK will have the mechanism to penetrate fresh high-growth market areas such as Asia. For example, in India, dedicated server sales will hit $43.1 million by 2004; together with an annual growth rate of 146 per cent for the Application Service Provider (ASP) market, this gives opportunity and potential for ASUK to diversify into new market sectors.

Objectives

The objectives are each built around the SMART criteria (specific, measurable, actionable, realistic and timed).

- *Increase market share*. ASUK Creative Limited currently holds 2 per cent (200 servers) of the UK dedicated server market (approx immediately 10,000 dedicated servers). ASUK should plan to increase this steadily to 16.7 per cent after four years. Since the market share has risen from 0 to 2 per cent in one year without increased marketing, this is a realistic target.
- *Streamline ordering processes*. The new web site called DediPower.com should incorporate online facilities for order processing, upgrades and support. The development of these features can continue over time but a fully featured site should be ready for launch.
- *Increase brand awareness/brand building*. By launching a new site, ASUK can take advantage of a fresh start but still use all the advantages of an established company. A brand image of power and quality, yet competitive prices should be established through intensive marketing and excellent CRM. The company plans to have a powerful brand name within six months of launching the site.
- *Create self-contained entity for possible initial public offering (IPO) or trade sale*. ASUK can aim for an IPO within three years, being sold either to a competitor or to a diversifying larger company. The sell value is currently £300,000. A target should be set to have this at £1.5 million within three years.
- *Expansion into international markets*. The launch of DediPower means that foreign clients will become more accessible. The improved site will have support for international sales.
- *Improve CRM and customer support*. By improving these fundamentals, ASUK aims to sell additional products to its current clients. Currently, 25 per cent of clients have bought additional services, and the aim is to increase this to 55 per cent within a year.

Strategies by target markets

- *Current customers*. By rebranding, enforce customer loyalty and improve service level. Also provide an easier product upgrade path. Better support and customer self-service should also be provided.
- *Domestic*. Build brand as a high-quality service with lower-value pricing. Offer three core incentives to show confidence in the product: thirty-day money back guarantee, UK price matching initiative, no minimum

291

contract. ASUK will be the first company in the UK industry to offer all these incentives together in a genuine fashion.

- *International.* Key strengths to marketing include sustainability and experience. The product will be positioned in the market as a high-end service, offering good performance for companies that have interests across Europe.

The marketing mix

- *Price.* Although prices should be offered on a price match guarantee within the UK, they should be based around a product-line pricing strategy; that is, each customer can start with a basic product and build layers on top to create their custom product.
- *Product.* The product is to be sold individually, but a discount should be offered for multiple sales and/or prepayment packages. Customer loyalty could be rewarded with additional free services.
- *Promotion.* ASUK should base the promotion around an online marketing strategy, using online targeted banners and search engines, complemented by increased exposure on the major Web hosting guides. Publication to online and offline trade magazines of press releases and adverts will reinforce the respectability of the brand.

Evaluation and control

- *Monitor market share and company growth rate.* Frequently obtain market share statistics. An estimate can be made by obtaining the total number of dedicated in the market segment and calculating the percentage of them that ASUK holds.
- *Occasional customer surveys to ensure support satisfaction is increasing.* ASUK already has the facility to conduct customer surveys online. These should be conducted half-yearly to ensure that satisfaction objectives are met.
- *Demographic analysis of buyers and potential buyers.* To determine whether ASUK is penetrating all potential markets sufficiently, customer account details should be collated and analysed to produce maps of customer distribution.

CHAPTER SUMMARY

This chapter has pulled together the contents of the book as a whole by discussing how the principles of marketing planning can be applied as an effective mechanism for developing, implementing and evaluating online marketing activities in a systematic way. The example plans demonstrate how the increasingly broad range of online marketing strategies available can be customized to suit specific industry contexts and business priorities. The final chapter will provide a broader understanding of the macro-environment by considering some of the 'big picture' issues that apply right across the online business spectrum.

FURTHER READING

McDonald, M. (1999) 'Strategic marketing planning: theory and practice', in M. Baker (ed.) *The CIM Marketing Book*, 4th edition, Oxford: Butterworth Heinemann.

QUESTIONS

Question 10.1

How do you account for the wide-ranging scope of online marketing that is illustrated in the example plans?

Feedback – You can see from the examples in the chapter that the scope of the plan can be very different according to the size of the business, its focus (on B2B or B2C) and the industry context. Consequently, the particular focus of online activity may be upon accepting transactions, building brands, improving customer relationships or building online communities, etc. (as was discussed in Chapter 4). Further examples of outline marketing plans can be found on the very useful student-centred Web site www.marketingteacher.com.

Question 10.2

Why do you think some organizations may be reluctant to undertake formal marketing planning, particularly for online activities?

Feedback – Staff may be hostile and resistant to making the changes that they anticipate will made. The planning process may lack high-level support, or be regarded as just a 'one-off' activity. If internal communications are poor, it will be difficult to acquire the necessary information for planning to be effective. Another common reason for avoiding planning is because of the rapid changes taking place in this area, which quickly render plans obsolete.

WEB LINKS

www.yahoo.com
Contains the Yahoo! Directory, which provides a comprehensive categorization of many business sectors.

www.zenithmedia.co.uk
Presents the main operators split by industry sector, which gives a useful resource for competitor analysis.

www.mediametrix.com
Includes the Media Metrix 500, which compares the volume of traffic visiting a range of Web sites as an aid to competitor analysis.

www.wilsonweb.com
Gives detailed guidance on the preparation of marketing plans, although aimed at a US audience.

www.marketingteacher.com
A useful student resource with examples of marketing plans for a range of industry sectors and business priorities.

www.ibm.com
A good example of a site that is segmented according to the needs of key customer groups, for example small firms.

Chapter 11

Legal, ethical and public policy issues

LISA HARRIS

MINDMAP

Chapter 1
History, definitions
and frameworks

Chapter 2
Marketing research

Chapter 3
Change
management

Chapter 4
Strategy

Chapter 5
Branding

Chapter 6
Relationship
marketing

Chapter 7
Multi-channel
marketing

Chapter 8
The marketing
mix

Chapter 9
e-Retailing

Chapter 10
Marketing
planning

Chapter 11
Legal, ethical and
public policy
issues

Introductory level

Strategic level

Operational level

Big picture

LINKS TO OTHER CHAPTERS

Chapter 1 History, definitions and frameworks	Chapter 6 Relationship marketing	Chapter 7 Multi-channel marketing

Chapter 10 Marketing planning

- Chapter 1 – History, definitions and framework
- Chapter 2 – Marketing research
- Chapter 6 – Relationship marketing
- Chapter 10 – Marketing planning

KEY LEARNING POINTS

After completing this chapter you will have an understanding of:

- The interrelationship between many legal and ethical issues pertaining to online marketing
- How marketers can generate competitive advantage through ethical behaviour
- The wider implications of Internet developments for society as a whole

ORDERED LIST OF SUB TOPICS

- Overview of legal developments
  - Copyright protection
  - Contractual agreements
  - Data protection
- Overview of ethical issues:
  - Introduction to ethical theories

OVERVIEW OF LEGAL DEVELOPMENTS

Although this chapter is divided into one section dealing with 'legal' and another with 'ethical' issues, it should become clear as you read through that the two areas are very much interrelated.

A comprehensive international legislation system that applies to global online trading does not exist at present and is not expected in the foreseeable future. Even within the USA, which is comparatively advanced in its use of the Internet, legal issues such as the validity of digital signatures have caused significant disagreements. While waiting for federal legislation, many states have set up their own laws, which have differed widely from state to state. Organizations such as the United Nations or bodies dealing with international trade law have been actively calling for global co-ordination of appropriate legal structures.

Copyright protection

Because the copyright legislation on the Internet is complex and vague, many Web site operators are reusing information from other sites. Comparison-shopping sites such as www.moneysupermarket.com, for example, rely heavily on aggregating information existing on other sites and presenting it in a comparative format. While this is acceptable in the USA, which allows data to be extracted and compiled in this way, there are indications that Europe may impose certain restrictions on what one site can do with another's information.

Another contentious issue concerns domain name conflict. There have been a number of cases whereby individuals (known as 'cybersquatters') have registered domain names that resemble established brands or generic terminology and then attempted to sell the right to use that name to the company concerned. For example, Chen (2001) notes that the address 'business.com' was sold for $7.5 million and 'wine.com' for $3 million. The author goes on to describe the case of *Marks and Spencer* v. *One in a Million Limited and Others*, in which Marks and Spencer sued for infringement of its trademark after the defendant registered the domain name marksandspencer.com and demanded money in exchange for handing it over. The courts found in favour of Marks and Spencer, and One in a Million was prevented from using the name or trying to sell it to anyone else. Chen also describes the problem of character string conflicts that arise when there is more than one legitimate user of a certain combination of letters. Finally, remember the case of www.untied.com that was described in Chapter 6? This site was set up by an online 'vigilante' to publicize the customer service failings of www.ual.com (United Airlines), and accurately mimics the logo, style and layout of the original site, as illustrated in Figures 11.1 and 11.2.

This example also illustrates that copying anything from a Web site is very easy – merely a matter of cutting and pasting the code – so that protection of any intellectual property is very difficult. A famous example concerns the ongoing dispute over the piracy of music on MP3 sites, which are file compression formats allowing songs to be freely transmitted over the Web and downloaded to an individual's computer. Peer-to-peer (P2P) sites such as www.napster.com allow

Figure 11.1 United Airlines' home page

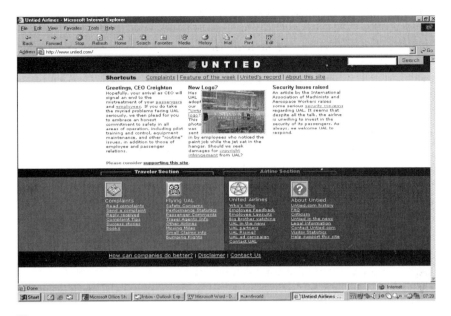

Figure 11.2 *The www.untied.com 'vigilante' site*

users to share the content of their computers, hard drives, and this technological innovation makes the worldwide sharing of music files even easier.

While legislation continues to lag behind technological developments, one of the few protections currently available to businesses is to patent innovative techniques that they have devised. In the case of *Amazon* v. *Barnes and Noble* in 1999, Amazon won a lawsuit against Barnes and Noble, which had tried to copy the famous 'one-click' ordering system pioneered by Amazon.

Contractual agreements

Electronic contractual agreements are part and parcel of e-Commerce. The registration procedure is part of the purchasing process and requests the buyer to scroll through a set of contract terms. The purchase sequence is completed only when the buyer has clicked his or her agreement to the terms and conditions presented. The validity of such an electronic contract has been tested already through the US courts, but it is not certain that it is globally acceptable. Consumer protection laws vary from country to country and the global operator must be aware of differing obligations that could impact on the validity of the transaction performed.

The importance of keeping track of changes in legislation that will affect e-Business cannot be underestimated. Certain legislation such as the law passed recently by the European Union regarding email marketing could have far-

299

reaching consequences. Effective from 1 March 2001, this law states that if a dispute occurs between a consumer and an online retailer in any of the fifteen countries of the EU, the consumer may file a suit in his or her own country. Small firms that have thrived from the freedom the Internet is offering may well find it harder now to maintain control over their direct email marketing campaigns in this increasingly legislative environment.

Mini case study:
THE CASE OF DMITRY SKLYAROV

On 13 August 2001, www.ft.com reported on the Russian hacker Dmitry Sklyarov, who faces trial in the USA for allegedly violating new copyright legislation. He was detained by FBI agents on his way back to Moscow from a hackers' conference in Las Vegas, where he had explained how to circumvent a security system on software sold by the US company Adobe. His Moscow-based company, Elcomsoft, sold a program that broke Adobe's code which prevented users copying documents published in Adobe format. Sklyarov's detention caused outrage across the cyber community, and special Internet sites and banners proclaiming 'Free Dmitry Sklyarov' and attacking Adobe were rapidly created. Adobe was surprised by the outcry and asked the US authorities to drop the charges. However, prosecutors have resolved to pursue the case, which will be a pioneering test for the 1998 Digital Millennium Copyright Act (DMCA), which makes it illegal to evade copyright-protecting technology.

Sklyarov has been released on bail, but faces a fine of up to $500,000 if found guilty. Elcomsoft argues that its program highlighted weaknesses in Adobe's security, and was not designed to allow infringement of copyright. The mainstream Russian media have followed the case extensively, and the interior ministry has said that it will not prosecute Sklyarov on his return. In the USA, libertarian groups such as the Electronic Frontier Foundation (EFF) have also argued in his defence. The case has other implications that could paradoxically lead to the potential for widespread computer damage from hackers. There is a long-standing tradition within the US technology community of 'white-hat hackers' whose hobby is finding security weaknesses within computer systems used in business applications, then publicizing them to allow computer companies to plug the security holes. Internet legal experts have expressed concern that advances in technology, together with legislation such as DMCA, is granting copyright holders too much power.

ACTIVITY

By the time you read this book, the Sklyarov case may well have been settled one way or the other. What can you find out about it on the Web?

Data protection

The UK's Data Protection Act 1984 (and later amendments) focuses on the information that companies hold on customers and how individuals can access it and ensure it is correct. Although of course this act pre-dates the Internet, the principles involved are exactly the same. More detail about the implications of recent changes in the Data Protection Act is available at www.dataprotection.gov.uk. Basically, there are eight key principles of good practice enshrined in the Act which can be summarized as follows:

Data must be:

1 fairly and lawfully processed;
2 processed for limited purposes;
3 adequate, relevant and not excessive;
4 accurate;
5 not kept longer than necessary;
6 processed in accordance with the data subject's rights;
7 secure;
8 not transferred to countries that do not have adequate protection.

The Information Commissioner's Office has produced four free introductory seminars to help both individuals and organizations that hold personal information (data controllers) to understand the Data Protection Acts. Each seminar consists of a voice-over recording accompanied by a power-point presentation. The seminars can be downloaded from www.dataprotection.gov.uk/seminars. htm.

CPExchange (www.cpexchange.org) offers an independent and open standard that allows approved customer data to be shared between disparate computer systems. This means that different areas of an organization, reliant on separate data sources and even whole computer systems, are able to obtain an integrated picture of customer information that complies with data collection criteria to be used for marketing purposes.

OVERVIEW OF ETHICAL ISSUES

Introduction to ethical theories

Ethics is about understanding right and wrong. The increased reliance by business on computers in recent years means that there are a number of contentious and evolving issues relating to ethics in cyberspace. Decision-making in business tends to focus on profit maximization, but it is increasingly being recognized that sustainable profit over the long term may best be achieved by taking careful consideration of the consequences that decisions may have for trust between stakeholders such as employees, competitors, suppliers, customers, local community and shareholders. Ethical decision-making is called 'enlightened self-interest' – business managers take 'ethical' decisions because of the positive impact on the financial bottom line.

Illegal activities can still be regarded as ethical; think, for example, of the destruction wrought by animal rights protestors. Unethical activities might still be legal; think of tobacco manufacturing, for example. The very nature of ethical debate centres upon the 'grey area' between the legal and the illegal. In the realm of the Internet, many of the ethical issues are still finding legal precedent. In the global context of e-Commerce, the law simply does not yet provide sufficient guidance on how business should behave.

Spence (2002) notes that there are a number of theories on business ethics that can be drawn upon to aid understanding of the Internet trading context.

Ethical egoism

Ethical egoists act to further their own self-interest. For example, faced with the possibility of copying a competitor's Web page design, the ethical egoist will weigh up what the likely outcomes of doing this might be. One option is that he or she could face legal charges of violating copyright; another is that he or she could save time and trouble while still fulfilling work obligations. Which of the outcomes is considered most likely will govern which decision is taken.

Utilitarianism

Utilitarianism is the notion of achieving maximum happiness for society (or avoidance of pain and pursuit of pleasure). The person acting ethically according to utilitarianism will weigh up carefully which act will result in the most positive outcomes for individuals compared with the most negative (a kind of cost–benefit analysis for happiness!). For example, when deciding whether to undercut the prices of high street booksellers, an Internet-based business would consider all the positive and negative impacts on individuals of not undercutting price, and all the positive and negative impacts on individuals of undercutting price. Although a price cut might result in some job losses and reduced dividends for share-

302

holders, the weight of advantage for many customers might outweigh this. Consequently, price undercutting on the Web may be regarded as ethical.

Kantianism

Kantianism is concerned with duty, meaning that the consequences of an act do not matter. It follows that it is our ethical duty not to lie, cheat or steal, to keep promises, and not to use others, even if the results may appear to justify such actions.

Discourse ethics

Discourse ethics theory focuses on the process by which a decision is reached. Ethical actions are those that are reached by full, open discussion that includes all those who are connected in any way to a decision. For a business, this means including all stakeholders actively in decision-making. This is impractical in some instances, and is not always culturally readily achievable, since some groups are more disposed to working towards consensus than others.

The very nature of ethical debates means there are no easy solutions. Consider the case of loyalty cards. Like many retail chains, Tesco (Club Card) and Boots (Advantage Card) use loyalty cards to encourage repeat visits of shoppers and to gather detailed information about the shopping habits of individuals. This enables highly targeted practice in terms of relationship marketing (as was discussed in Chapter 6) where individual needs are known from records of previous purchases, and special offers and new products of interest to the customer are sent directly to the individuals concerned. Marketers consider this to be ethical because customers are provided with precisely the information they want and need. Some consumer groups consider the collection of information on purchasing habits through loyalty cards (and its subsequent use to generate sales) to be a misuse of information and an abuse of customer loyalty and privacy.

The ethics of online marketing

We will now consider more specifically the benefits and drawbacks of ethics to online marketing:

Ethical benefits

- Online marketing has the potential to remove prejudice and barriers, as transactions are carried out via disembodied computer screens.
- The lack of need for a physical presence in a particular place allows the inclusion of people whose physical needs make working in an office environment difficult.

303

- Internet-based business activities are opening up markets, thereby improving information provision and freedom of speech about different products, including non-corporate information (see Hamelink 2000: 139–164). For example, typing 'Nike' into a search engine also finds sites about Nike products alleging human rights abuses by the company.

Ethical drawbacks

- Technology and law have so far been unsuccessful in controlling what is available on the Internet. This means that inaccurate claims made in relation to products or services are difficult to control.
- As systems of protection for intellectual works such as patenting and copyright were designed for tangible products, there is currently no clear protection for electronic data, or understanding of the limits of ownership. Such issues are compounded by the potential for mass dissemination via the Internet and email. The potential for the dissemination of incorrect information is significant.
- The increasing prevalence of computers in the workplace has focused the minds of employers on the use of organizational equipment for non-organizational tasks, such as booking holidays on the Internet. The most difficult area to discern is the intersection between use and abuse, meaning the area where personal use may have some positive workplace implications, and work use may have some personal implications. For example, Internet surfing for hobby interests will hone the IT skills of employees who use those same skills for work tasks.
- Electronic monitoring has enormous potential for infringing on the privacy of employees and customers. The archiving aspect of computer-mediated communication means that monitoring of employees in the workplace can be done at unprecedented levels of detail. This is a particular problem in call centre work in which people may be paid according to the number of calls handled in a particular time. It can be very demotivating when even the length of toilet breaks is measured!

Hamelink goes on to demonstrate how Internet communications have some important and distinctive ethical characteristics:

- Communicating to many anonymous people simultaneously is very easy. For example, sending an unsolicited email to a group can be construed as 'spamming'.
- The disembodied nature of electronic communication – communication is in text, and hence does not convey tone of voice or other non-textual clues, although 'symbols' are increasingly used to convey, for example, a

joke or happiness :-) = ☺, or sadness :- (= ☹. It is easy, therefore, for the 'meaning' of the message to be misinterpreted.

- Where a common language is understood, communication of images, documents and complex ideas can be made across the world as long as the technology is available.
- Cyberspace is not secure. This means that transactions on the Web can be accessed by those not party to the transaction. Security is improving, however, and of course terrestrial transactions are not 100 per cent secure either.
- The 'borderless' nature of the Internet makes control extremely difficult. Attempts at national controls, such as prohibiting the purchase of Adolf Hitler's *Mein Kampf* over the Internet in Germany, have failed.
- Communication in cyberspace has extraordinary archiving capabilities. Internet sites accessed are recorded and firms can also track the cyberspace activities of those who have visited their Web site. There are clear implications here for consumer privacy.
- Those who control the technology become very powerful, witness for example recent court cases over the monopolistic behaviour of Bill Gates's Microsoft Corporation.

From this brief list you can see that the ability to communicate quickly and easily with people across the world through the Internet has a number of ethical implications. Another, related new phenomenon is the advent of 'flaming', where individuals send offensive email messages to individuals or sometimes groups. However, it is important to recognize that few of these problems are *fundamentally* new to the Internet. Whysall (2001) notes that many of the issues discussed above can be paralleled in conventional business ethics.

Privacy

Privacy policies

In recognition of the increasingly strategic importance of privacy issues, in December 2000 IBM announced a new senior management position: Chief Privacy Officer. The company followed this appointment up in November 2001 with a large research initiative on privacy and the formation of an advisory body consisting of public- and private-sector representatives from a range of industry backgrounds. IBM has over 3,200 researchers and eight research and development centres around the world. According to a report by Foremski (2001) in the *Financial Times*, 'significant numbers' of these individuals will be redirected to work on technologies that allow large companies to implement privacy policies. The article quotes IBM's Chief Privacy Officer as saying:

There is a need for IT tools that can help enterprises deal with the many legal and other aspects related to data privacy. We are clearly in a time where deliberations over maintaining the balance between privacy and security are going to intensify in many aspects of society.

The rise of the Internet, which permits companies to get information about customers more easily than ever, has brought privacy issues to centre stage. Consumer protection groups fear that businesses will use the opportunity to capture information about people who visit their Web sites. By merging these data with a wide range of publicly available information such as credit histories, phone calls and medical records, companies can accumulate vast databases of knowledge about their customers. While this information can quite legitimately be used to develop relationships with the customer based on serving their specific needs, the data could also perhaps be sold on to other interested parties for a significant fee. Greening notes:

The value of knowing who is visiting your site, which people are generating the most revenue, and which advertisements are working most effectively can often generate profits and savings far exceeding the cost of expensive analysers.

(July 1999, www.webtechniques.com)

This imperative is supported by Prabhaker, who claims:

It is unrealistic to expect profit-driven businesses not to infringe on consumer privacy in an environment that makes it increasingly profitable and a technology that makes it easier than ever to collect and share personal information.

(2000: 162)

Kelly and Rowland (2000) report that three privacy groups (Electronic Privacy Information Centre, Junkbusters and Privacy International) were able to force Intel, the world's largest computer chip maker, to allow consumers to switch off the user-identification features built into Intel chips. Although Intel claimed that its technology enhanced security on computer networks, critics claimed that it allowed merchants to build up electronic dossiers on customers and their transactions to a level of unacceptable detail. They also describe another online privacy controversy concerning GeoCities (www.geocities.com) in which the Federal Trade Commission (FTC), in the first enforcement of its regulatory powers in the area of online privacy, ordered the company to change the way it collected and distributed information about its customers, particularly children. The FTC alleged that GeoCities sold customer information to Web advertisers in violation of its own privacy policies, and the settlement required GeoCities to post a notice stating exactly what information is collected, to whom it is disclosed, and how customers can access and remove their own data.

Kelly and Rowland note that there are a number of ways in which companies can gather information about visitors to their sites:

- They can allow access only to registered users.
- The online ordering and payment process allows credit card numbers, addresses and telephone numbers to be collected. Order histories allow profiles to be built up of the nature and volume of goods ordered by individuals.
- Tracking software enables companies to establish visitors' country of origin, the ISP they use, the type of operating system and browser, and the referring Web address from which they access the site (by clicking on a hypertext link).
- Using 'cookies' (as discussed in Chapter 2 and 6), which are devices tracking the behaviour of visitors to Web sites by attaching to their hard drives and recognizing them when they visit the site again.

To demonstrate to customers that they take their moral obligations seriously, firms can:

- include a clearly displayed privacy policy on the Web site, explaining what information will be collected about the customer and how it will be used, and stating clearly that customer lists will not be sold on to third parties;
- prevent unauthorized access by providing a secure section of the site within which collection of data and transactions can occur;
- give customers the option of opting out or correcting information that is held about them;
- sign up with an organization such as www.truste.org, which audits a Web site's privacy policies and provides a 'kitemark' to those meeting specified criteria.

A full list of privacy issues is covered by *Which?* Web Trader Code and can be found at www.which.net/trader.

Codes of conduct

Computer Professionals for Social Responsibility (1996) suggest that:

Each employer should provide and act on clear policies regarding the privacy implications of the computing resources used in the workplace. The policies should explicitly describe:

- Acceptable use of electronic mail and computer resources, including personal use;
- Practices that may be used to enforce these policies, such as the interception and reading of electronic mail or scanning of hard disks;
- Penalties for non-compliance with these policies.

ACTIVITY

Look up the Web site www.privacy.net and try the following demonstrations:

- The 'Privacy.net tracking demo' hotlink shows how cookies are placed on your system.
- The 'Web site log files' hotlink shows what types of visitor information can be captured.
- The fictional network of twenty-seven sites illustrates how your online activity is tracked across the entire network and linked to your identity

Codes of conduct can be criticized on the grounds that they may be there only for public relations purposes and just add to bureaucracy, that they ignore context and that they deny individual responsibility and moral diversity. They do, however, have the advantage of offering some guidance in a chaotic Internet environment that so far lacks any common understanding of appropriate use.

Spence (2002) notes that a good code of conduct:

- is negotiated with stakeholders and acceptable to them;
- comprises clear and well-founded ethical rules;
- is internally consistent and coherent with other policies and strategies;
- should balance rights and duties and the interests of stakeholders;
- allows for exceptions (and shows how to deal with them);
- anticipates conflicts (and shows how to deal with them);
- respects individual freedom;
- would not be used to indoctrinate;
- is easy and inexpensive to apply;
- is part of a process with regular review.

Electronic monitoring

Those against electronic monitoring argue that:

- It constitutes an invasion of privacy. Being paid by an organization does not mean that it owns you.

- Monitoring implies suspicion of misbehaviour. This undermines the trust, goodwill and loyalty of the employee.
- Monitoring results in the setting of unrealistic targets, because employees cannot keep up their fastest rate constantly. The result is increasing stress, absenteeism and, ultimately, employee turnover.
- In a climate of increasing empowerment, monitoring erodes independence of the individual to work in a way or at a time that is congenial.
- Electronic monitoring is more suited to measuring quantitative factors than qualitative, hence it is more likely that the number of phone calls rather than the effort spent building relationships with potential clients will be measured.

Employers may defend the use of electronic monitoring in the workplace as follows:

- It is necessary for security – CCTV can protect against theft and violence.
- Employers pay employees to do a particular job. It could be argued that employers have a contractual right to check that employees are doing what they are paid to do.
- Monitoring of employees stops abuse of work time and increases productivity.
- Electronic monitoring is simply an electronic version of 'managing by walking about' that saves management time.
- Electronic means of measurement mean that performance appraisal of employees is backed up by precise statistics and is unbiased.
- Electronic monitoring provides data quickly and frequently.
- It ensures realistic targets are set.
- It acts as a deterrent to stop inappropriate workplace behaviour, in the same way that a speed camera without a film can still influence motorists to keep to the legal speed limit.

Mini case study:
THE E-WALLET WARS

Shoppers wanting to get their caffeine fix online at www.starbucks.com now have only one path to take when they pay for their beans. If they are already registered with Passport, Microsoft's new identity-verification program, they can use it to complete their purchase. If not, they are directed to a site where they can sign up for Passport. Passport is being marketed as a 'one-click' solution to obtaining access to Web sites requiring registration and to make purchases over the Internet.

309

This means that shoppers cannot buy their coffee without letting Microsoft be part of the transaction. Starbucks used to let shoppers pay for their purchases by credit card, but in May 2001 it joined fifty other affiliated sites and switched to Passport. Now the personal information of every Starbucks.com buyer is stored in Microsoft's vast database.

Privacy advocates are waking up, and they don't like the smell. In August 2001 the Electronic Privacy Information Centre (EPIC) filed a complaint with the FTC alleging that Passport collects personal information deceptively. It fears that Microsoft might make use of the potentially vast amounts of data on Internet shoppers to develop a monopoly position in online payment systems and hence e-Commerce itself. EPIC also wants Microsoft to be ordered to make changes to its pending Windows XP operating system so that users are able to conceal their identities when using the Internet. Microsoft denies that it plans to turn the data over to third parties, or that it forced Starbucks.com to make Passport an exclusive payment arrangement. Starbucks claims the Passport-only policy applies only on a 'test basis' and will be re-evaluated later in 2002.

Source: Adapted from Cohen (2001)

Spam (sending persistent annoying messages)

Unsolicited electronic junk mail known as 'spam' now makes up about 10 per cent of all email throughout the world. The practice of sending it is heavily frowned upon in the online community, and offenders are known to be vulnerable to bulk retaliation that can be large enough to crash their systems. Email, of course, can be quickly and cheaply distributed to a large number of people simultaneously. The EU's Distance Selling Directive (1997) allows consumers to 'opt out' of unsolicited emails, but no protection is given to business recipients, and financial service contracts are also exempted, even in the B2C arena. Technological solutions to this problem are now emerging. For example, Hotmail (www.hotmail.com) has a filtering service that redirects junk mail to a separate folder. A US ISP called Community Connexion has developed a free product called the Anonymizer (www.anonymizer.com) that allows users to remain anonymous while surfing the Web.

ACTIVITY

Think about how you feel when receiving spam. How is your impression of the brand affected when you receive unwanted emails of this nature?

Security

One of the biggest concerns about online activity is the issue of security. Developing the ability to protect information resources from unwanted access by hackers or viruses is a major headache for many organizations. The growth of the mobile Internet (see Chapter 7), whereby employees are increasingly able to access company databases and other internal information while on the move, has piled additional pressure on security systems. At the beginning of the chapter we discussed some high-profile cases of security breaches. From a customer's perspective, the main worry involves the risk of credit card fraud if an individual's details are stored electronically, although this risk is little different from that associated with other forms of credit card transactions. Research by Jupiter Communications (2000) found that reassurance over security was the primary factor in turning online browsers into buyers.

Competitive intelligence

Competitive intelligence is the term given to the gathering of information on business rivals through legitimate means such as via published data and interviews. The practice has its own representative body, the Society of Competitive Intelligence Professionals (SCIP), and is now taught on some courses as a key business skill. Proponents claim that competitive intelligence focuses on understanding competitive dynamics and helps in planning future change. The Internet, of course, provides a comprehensive and easily accessible source of data about competitors. So the challenge these days is less about *collecting* information than it is about *analysis* and *focus*. Useful information might include news about an imminent product launch or the appointment of a new chief executive. The best competitive intelligence relates to what a competitor is going to do, rather than what it actually is doing at that time. The knowledge gained then has to be disseminated throughout the organization (a process known as organizational learning) so that it is available for possible use by other people in the company at a later date.

According to Curtis (2001), there are three principal factors driving increased investment in competitive intelligence:

- the Internet;
- globalization;
- higher customer expectations.

From an ethical perspective, the concern is the boundary across which competitive intelligence becomes industrial espionage, or spying. In 2000, software giant Oracle admitted hiring detectives to rifle through rubbish for information on rival Microsoft in a case that became known as 'Garbagegate'.

311

SCIP's ethical code means that its representatives cannot lie about who they are, but they can be as vague as possible, and usually claim to be conducting market research when contacting staff in the target company for information. Trying to obtain trade secrets (the most famous is the recipe for Coke) is against the ethical code. Competitive intelligence professionals claim that 'most' information a competitor could need is either already in the public domain or can be obtained without actually breaking the law. Whether the practice is ethical, of course, is another question entirely.

According to research by The Futures Group (www.tfgi.com), 60 per cent of companies have an organized system for collecting competitive intelligence, while 82 per cent of those with revenues of over £7 billion make comprehensive use of such a system. The researchers ranked the eight leading users as:

1 Microsoft;
2 Motorola;
3 IBM;
4 Procter and Gamble;
5 General Electric;
6 Hewlett-Packard;
7 Coca-Cola;
8 Intel.

The Futures Group recommends the following strategies for effective intelligence-gathering:

- Debrief the sales force.
- Attend conferences and trade shows.
- Examine the background and private interests of newly appointed executives.
- Keep track of patents.
- Look for hidden messages in marketing material.
- Ask what you would do if you were equipped with the same tools as your competitor.

There are a number of disparate information sources that can be drawn upon; for example:

- product samples;
- partner companies;
- rumours;
- open product demonstrations;
- product launch plans;
- advertising campaigns.

Companies such as those listed above that take competitive intelligence seriously tend to give the function a strategic rather than an operational role within their organizations. This means that the person in charge of competitive intelligence will be a senior employee and report directly to the board of directors. The intelligence gathered is then used to support executive decision-making. If competitive intelligence is treated merely as a subdivision of the marketing department, then there is little to distinguish it from 'everyday' market research.

To summarize, competitive intelligence is about not making mistakes, and reducing unnecessary risks. Consider the following examples of companies that missed out:

- Sears did not spot the potential competition from discount retailers such as Walmart
- Levi Straus' did not appreciate the growing threat from other specialist brands such as Timberland.
- Compaq did not anticipate that Dell would undercut prices by selling computers direct to consumers.

The digital divide

As the reach of the information superhighway grows, assumptions about equal access to its benefits are increasingly made. These range from the expectation that students have used email and surfed the Internet, to claims that the Internet overcomes global disparities between more and lesser economically developed countries. Companies from all over the world can compete for the same business via the Internet, with sites that do not necessarily reflect company size, longevity or financial success.

In fact, at a local as well as a global level, access to the Internet is far from universal. In 1999, it was estimated that 170 million people had Internet access. This is a minute 4 per cent of the world's population, and 50 per cent of the global population have yet to make a telephone call, let alone access the Internet. More than 80 per cent of those with Internet access are in North America and Europe (Hamelink 2000: 81). So rather than being a social leveller, the Internet is yet another divide between rich and poor, the 'haves' and 'have-nots', the networked and the non-networked. Furthermore, the gap between the advantages associated with being online and the disadvantages of not being online is continuing to diverge.

The 'digital divide' is confirmed by a report from the US Digital Divide Task Force (NTIA 2000), which notes that:

- Disabled people are only half as likely to have Internet access as the able-bodied.

- Access is less common in households with low income levels.
- There are large differences in penetration rates between different ethnic groups.
- No significant differences exist between male and female users.

ACTIVITY

Go to the Web site for the full supporting statistics to this research. What problems does such information pose to marketers?

Whysall (2001) shows that national statistics in the UK demonstrate significant differences in Internet access between geographical regions. Rates of 35–40 per cent in the South East contrast with 25 per cent in the North East, 24 per cent in Scotland and 20 per cent in Northern Ireland. Timmins (2000) notes that when income levels are taken into account, just 3 per cent of the poorest groups have access, compared with 48 per cent of the richest.

There are positive aspects to the digital divide. Look up www.thehunger-site.com (see Figure 11.3) and add your 'click' to help feed the world's poor.

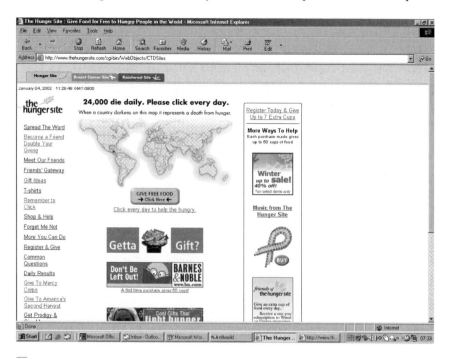

Figure 11.3 *Using technology to help the hungry: the Web site of www.thehungersite.com*

This site is sponsored by large global corporations that pay fees to the charity according to the number of visitors received. In other words, the greater the number of people exposed to the advertisements, the more the charity benefits.

Inappropriate Web site content

In the USA in 1996, the Communications Decency Act attempted to prohibit the online publication of 'indecent' material. The lack of success of this legislation is evident in the fact that some of the most frequently visited and effectively marketed Web sites in the world are pornographic in content. Legislation recently proposed in the USA seeks to force schools to use Web-filtering technologies that will prevent children viewing such material by restricting funding to those schools that do not comply. However, civil liberty organizations objected, claiming that parents should take responsibility for supervising their children's viewing. After all, one of the key drivers behind the early development of the Internet was the ability to share information freely and without censorship. For example, www.netnanny.com (as shown in Figure 11.4) allows parents to restrict access to particular sites and prevent credit card or contact details being given out by children in chat rooms by automatically breaking the Internet connection if

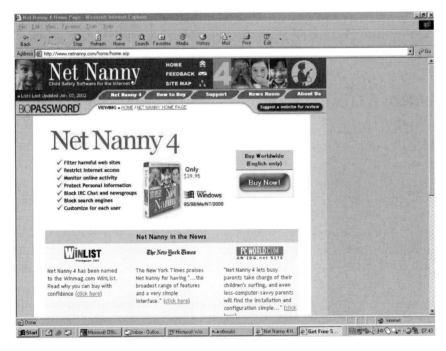

Figure 11.4 *Net Nanny allows parents to control what their children see and buy online*

prohibited actions are instigated. It also keeps a record of all activity undertaken on the computer for monitoring purposes.

Waldmeir (2001) reports in the *Financial Times* that a US judge has ruled that Yahoo! can ignore a French court ruling restricting the auction of Nazi memorabilia on its Web site. This case is critical because it indicates that national laws (in this case French anti-hate speech laws) cannot be applied more broadly on the Internet. The judge ruled that the French order violated Americans' constitutionally protected right to free speech. The case highlights the tensions involved in regulating cyberspace, given that the Internet can be accessed globally.

Chen (2001) notes a number of cases of government action taken in an attempt to control Internet content; for example:

- The Chinese government has installed software to filter foreign Web sites in order to remove any anti-communist information.
- In the United Arab Emirates, the state telecommunications company Etisalat censors Web sites deemed to breach local moral values by disconnecting offending customers

THINK POINT

How would you feel if your online activity was monitored or censored in some way?

Globalization

Another series of social and legal problems arise from the global reach of the Internet, meaning that many jurisdictions may be involved in governing online trading. Globalization involves the transfer of an existing business system to other countries or the management of another business system in other countries. By accepting online orders from overseas, a company faces a minefield of cultural and legal differences. Chen (2001) reports that a survey of major US corporations by KPMG showed that taxation-related issues were an even greater obstacle than cultural differences in global trading.

It is important that an online sales effort should also take into account the variety of currencies and country-linked value added tax (VAT) systems. Prospective customers may be reluctant to commit to an online transaction in a 'foreign' currency owing to the uncertainty presented by the daily fluctuation of exchange rates. A simple solution is to add an interactive currency calculator to the site, which will give the customer a rough idea of the cost of the product or service and an indication as to whether it is worth proceeding with the purchase.

A better solution would be to offer a payment system that not only performs currency calculations but also calculates VAT by country and product or service category. The best systems currently available automatically update the currency conversion and tax rates (relieving the Web site operator of a daily burden), and can be used with any payment system on the market. An example of such a multi-currency payment system is WordPay, which offers the Web site operator the facility of offering products or services in more than 100 currencies. By having the exchange rate updated daily, the customer will see the real value of purchases and be able to make a meaningful comparison with local stores.

The EU in its present form has a larger population than the USA. Nevertheless, most of the producers and consumers live and work in a radius of 800 km, equivalent to just 12 per cent of the land area of the USA. However, in the past, this opportunity has been compromised because transportation within European countries was been burdened with rules and regulations. For example, a trucker transporting goods from Glasgow to Athens used to spend 30 per cent of his or her time on border crossings, waiting and filling out up to 200 forms. These inefficiencies are mercifully now a thing of the past. In order to move goods between EU member states, only one simplified transit document is required, and many of the custom formalities have been eliminated. Payment systems within Europe are now also being standardized with the recent advent of the euro. These developments are encouraging more firms to take advantage of the Internet's market development capabilities, meaning the ability to extend their geographic reach at relatively low cost and risk.

Mini case study:
'LIGHTS GO OUT ON A DOTCOM REVOLUTION'

In December 2000, 10,000 dotcom employees lost their jobs in California. In the year as a whole, about 2,000 companies and $1.5 billion in funding went to the bottom of the sea. The collapse started in March. Up until then, and given enough hype, almost any dotcom company could start up, obtain funding and float on the stock exchange for a massive profit. Companies with no customers, huge losses and little to no chance of breaking even were valued at hundreds of millions of dollars, based solely on the income they would be generating if all went well. With everyone else making a killing, no money manager could afford not to invest.

However short-lived, the boom to the San Francisco economy was not universally welcomed. The two areas of the city most popular with dot-commers soon found themselves at the heart of a growing anti-dotcom movement. Local people could no longer afford property, and a group called the Yuppie Eradication Project took to burning smart cars.

317

But then reality set in. It soon became apparent that valuing companies on revenue potential alone was not a sound business practice. Companies that were not making any money because they were growing their customer base in a niche market turned out to be no more than bad businesses. A lack of customers did not show that a company was positioned snugly ahead of the zeitgeist, it just meant that nobody wanted its products or services. As the funding ran out, employees waited to be logged off the payroll. Redundancies were often badly handled, with people sacked by email, locked out of their offices or their belongings packed up in black sacks. Perhaps the final shock to bring the dot-commers back to reality happened on 11 January, when California ran out of electricity. Several days running, with less than 1 per cent of capacity remaining, power companies were obliged to impose a rolling series of blackouts to protect essential services. The culprit is an economy based on vast banks of power-hungry computers, and an abysmal policy of energy deregulation. It is a bizarre situation for the world home of high technology. With energy demands up by more than 25 per cent since 1995, and environmental concerns preventing the building of new power plants, every new PC, and every dotcom firing up its servers, caused the utilities to lose cash. Meanwhile, researchers are trying to work out just how much of the USA's power is used by the Internet. Server farms – the large climate-controlled rooms of computers used to run e-Businesses, are said to need as much electricity as a large factory.

It would be wrong, though, to imagine that the world's economy is in a downward spiral because of the dotcom crash. The effects will remain localized. PCs are not selling because nearly everyone who wants one has one. More than half the families in the UK are online now. Like first-year university students, San Francisco and its dotcom community binged on every new experience, and tried getting high in every conceivable manner.

Source: Adapted from Hammersley (2001).

Social responsibility

In recent years, the concept of social responsibility has received considerable attention in a marketing context. According to Kotler *et al.*,

> The *societal marketing concept* is a management orientation that holds the key task of the organisation is to determine the needs and wants of markets and to adapt the organisation to delivering the desired satisfactions more effectively and efficiently than its competitors in a way that preserves or enhances the consumers' and society's well-being.

(2001: 62)

This means that companies have realized that competitive advantage can be gained by behaving (or in some cases being seen to behave!) in an ethical way. For example, in the UK, the National Westminster Bank has run an advertising campaign emphasizing the abandonment of its branch closure programme. This follows considerable negative publicity accusing banks of disadvantaging the elderly or disabled by shutting branches in rural areas. The new policy indicates that NatWest is accepting a wider social responsibility by not taking branch closure decisions solely on economic grounds, and at the same time differentiating itself from its competitors. Mahoney (1994) notes that such policies can pay off in economic terms, because the value added to the brand and additional business gained from customers impressed by the company's standpoint can more than offset the costs of implementing socially responsible policies. So companies may well act in a socially responsible manner in order to make a profit. While this is not exactly an 'ethical' reason to 'go ethical', at least it should ensure a virtuous circle if companies recognize that ethical practices can be financially rewarding.

Table 11.1 *Attitudes towards social responsibility*

Model 1	Amoral	Seek to maximize profit at all cost
Model 2	Legalistic	Believe that being ethical means obeying the law
Model 3	Responsive	Recognize that good community relationships are important
Model 4	Emerging ethical	Make explicit recognition that the costs of being ethical may involve a trade-off with profits. Ethics are mentioned in mission statement or code of conduct
Model 5	Developed ethical	Clearly expressed value statements are accepted by everyone in the organization

A company's attitude towards the varying degrees of social responsibility that may be observed can be categorized as shown in Table 11.1. These models are based on three implicit assumptions:

- Consumers' wishes do not always coincide with their long-term interest or those of the public at large.
- Consumers prefer organizations that show real concern for their satisfaction and well-being.
- The most important task of the organization is to adapt itself to the target markets in such a way as to generate not only satisfaction, but also individual and collective well-being in order to attract and keep customers.

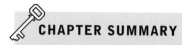

CHAPTER SUMMARY

This final chapter has considered the broader macro-environmental issues that affect all companies seeking to develop online marketing activities, including the wider implications of Internet developments for society as a whole. It is important to recognize the interrelationship between many legal and ethical issues pertaining to online marketing and to appreciate that in many as yet untested cases, both the legal and the ethical position remain uncertain. We have demonstrated that customers are increasingly demanding the highest standards of ethical behaviour from companies with which they will do business, and so being seen to be 'ethical' can lead to competitive advantage in many markets, such as retail banking.

Case study:
ETHICAL DEBATES IN B2B ONLINE BANKING

In this case study, on the ethics of e-Banking are considered by focusing on the marketing activities of one company in the wholesale banking sector.

Background

The financial services industry has been through 'structural and operational tumult' since the mid-1990s (Kalakota and Whinston 1996: 181). Innovative use of new information technology, electronic commerce and the associated cost reductions are driving ongoing changes in banking. New technology brings benefits and risks, and new challenges for human governance of the developments (Hamelink 2000: 1). One of the new management perspectives that will contribute to long-term success in electronic commerce is the associated moral responsibility of banking organizations and their stakeholders. Press and academic attention to the subject of online banking tends to focus on consumer products (B2C) and the threat they pose to traditional branch operations if concerns about privacy and security can be adequately addressed. Writers have so far largely ignored ethical issues instigated by the enormous potential of the Internet in facilitating inter-bank transactions (B2B) in the wholesale market by reducing costs.

Because online banking is still developing and is rapidly changing, there is very little experience or agreement on its related ethical issues (Turbin *et al.* 2000: 33). In any transaction, trust plays a key role. Face-to-face transactions allow for the assessment of trust on the basis of physically observed information. This is not normally part of an electronic exchange. Trust may also be based on previous experience of successful transactions with predictable outcomes. This is not normally yet established online. Where there is no personal experience, the transaction partner might rely on reputation. The best the bank can hope for is to trade on its terrestrial brand. High-profile risks of online trading such as security and privacy (Kelly and Rowland 2000), the media and popular myths all act to confound the attempts of business to operate in cyberspace, not to mention the genuine imperfection of existing technology. Building high ethical standards and systems in which transaction partners can trust is an imperative management requirement of the sustainable ethical enterprise.

International trade has grown significantly in the post-Second World War period, and with it the associated monetary flows. More recently, deregulation and globalization have led to a spectacular growth in the value of non-trade-related financial transactions. Every transaction, whether trade- or non-trade-related, gives rise to obligations that need to be settled through a transfer of money between the parties involved. Settlement of non-trade-related and large-value trade transactions is increasingly based on the electronic large-value payment systems that have been developed since the 1960s. Together these have led to a major expansion in payment and settlement systems, which now handle payment volumes on a daily basis that collectively dwarf economic output in the main industrial countries.

Electronic banking started with the use of proprietary software and private networks, but was not particularly popular until the emergence of the Internet created new commercial opportunities for networked commerce (Turbin *et al.* 2000). Development of an Internet electronic payment system provides opportunities for the creation of completely new sets of global and national trading relationships. The Internet offers the possibility of 'open-systems' payment and settlement systems that operate in parallel to existing, more traditional bank-based networks. This requires new institutional structures as well as changes to existing outdated legal, commercial and ethical systems. Harnessing the technology necessary for e-Banking is just the first of the challenges faced by the sector. Equally important is the development of the necessary management skills to ensure the sustained success of the new processes. Intertwined in the functional perspectives of marketing, human resource management and strategic planning are the ethical perspectives.

ABC Bank

The ABC Bank Group is active worldwide, with around 1,500 branches and over 50,000 employees in more than seventy countries, including all the major financial centres. Ranked by total assets, market capitalization and size of customer base, ABC Bank is one of Europe's leading banking groups. This case study focuses on Investment Banking, which is one of the bank's four main divisions, and in particular the business area of foreign exchange trading. As noted earlier, press and scholarly attention to the subject of online banking has tended to focus on consumer products (B2C), while the enormous potential of the Internet in facilitating inter-bank transactions by reducing costs (B2B) is largely ignored.

There are 8 million people in the world who are classified as being of 'high net worth', meaning they have more than $300,000 in liquid assets. All banks are chasing this business, from which they can earn high fees for arranging and managing investments. It is estimated that ABC Bank earns some 40 per cent of its profits from just 12 per cent of capital usage in this area. There is absolutely no incentive for the bank to offer this group of customers Web-based services that will cut out the bank's intermediary and advisory role and hence reduce income by cannibalizing the existing lucrative business. Prospective online projects in this business area therefore stand little chance of internal acceptance and the associated financial support. Projects that are likely to result in job losses within the bank through their automation of paper-based tasks also require support from sufficiently powerful factions if they are to go ahead, and tend to result in considerable tensions between areas of the bank reliant on traditional processing and the electronic commerce development teams. In order for such a project to be financially supported, it must:

- demonstrate the potential to generate a positive return;
- be deemed necessary to keep up with competitor innovation in the area concerned;
- not tread on too many toes internally.

One project that met these criteria was the development of a Web site that offers customers access to and information about the most important Internet applications concerned with investment banking. The service provides the latest news together with selected charts and useful links. Online trading in currencies is already possible, and additional transaction applications dealing with bonds, shares and derivatives will be online very shortly. Customers have their own personalized access to the world's capital markets online, and can see and respond to changes in global currency prices in real time. The system customers are tapping into is the same as that used by ABC Bank for trading in the markets on its own account; in other words, it is a multi-million-pound investment in state-of-the-art technology with the latest security protections.

The bank has focused upon the foreign exchange transaction as its 'flagship' online product because such activity forms a natural starting point for capturing related business from customers. Very few international banking services do not involve the purchase or sale of currency, so from handling a customer's foreign exchange transactions it is relatively easy to cross-sell other products or services. In many cases, foreign exchange trading is offered to customers as a 'loss leader' because of this potential. Although start-up costs are incurred in 'plumbing in' customers' systems to that of the bank, by settling transactions online the trading costs incurred by ABC Bank are more than halved. Fewer trading staff are required and the customer is 'locked in' through the system plumbing in process, so it is therefore more likely to use the same bank for subsequent related investment banking services. If the anticipated volume of trading is high enough, ABC Bank can offer to plumb in a customer free of charge and still save money.

However, the real potential of such online trading does not lie merely in automation, but in the 'white-labelling' of the foreign exchange service. This means that the online trading facility is made available to the clients of ABC Bank's customers, branded as if the service actually belonged to the client. For example, if the customer is an Italian regional bank, then foreign exchange transactions can be exchanged between ABC Bank and all the Italian bank's clients worldwide. From the end customer's perspective, the system it uses for trading appears to belong to the Italian bank, because it will be 'badged' appropriately. (The principle is the same as that applied to ASPs 'renting' access to sophisticated computer systems and security facilities to smaller firms that would not be able to afford to purchase such expensive infrastructure outright.) The advantage to ABC Bank is the extension the facility affords to its customer base, as money-laundering regulations prevent an investment bank from accepting transactions from individuals in this area, so the Italian bank forms a useful intermediary. For the Italian bank, the attraction is the ability to 'piggyback' access to an expensive and sophisticated online system, thereby incurring prestige but none of the set-up costs.

A potential problem with this system lies in the allocation of credit limits. If ABC Bank sets a ceiling of £20 million per transaction, based on its assessment of the risk involved in dealing with the Italian bank, then the online trading system affords the same luxury to each of the Italian bank's customers, which may be far less creditworthy. Consequently, ABC Bank developed an 'add-on' system that allows the Italian bank to set appropriate sub-limits for each of its customers that are using the system. The system was developed in consultation with the bank's credit managers and designed to replicate both the qualitative and quantitative judgements that were previously made manually. The expensive credit manager role within investment banks is now threatened because of the success of the online system, which is now also being applied to the bank's own account trading.

Source: Adapted from preliminary findings of an ongoing research project by Lisa Harris and Laura Spence, Brunel University

---

FURTHER READING

Akdeniz, Y., Walker, C. and Wall, D. (eds) (2000) *The Internet, Law and Society*, Harlow, UK: Pearson Education.

Beauchamp, T. L. and Bowie, N. E. (1997) *Ethical Theory and Business*, 5th edition, London: Prentice Hall.

Hamelink, C. (2000) *Ethics in Cyberspace*, Sage: London.

Herschel, R. and Hayes Andrews, P. (1997) 'Ethical implications of technological advances on business communication', *Journal of Business Communication*, Special issue: Ethics of Business Communication, 34 (2), 160–171.

Langford, D. (ed.) (2000) *Internet Ethics*, Basingstoke, UK: Macmillan.

Zonghao, B. (2001) 'An ethical discussion on the network economy', *Business Ethics: A European Review* 10 (2): 108–112.

QUESTIONS

Question 11.1

How might a firm turn its online ethical policies to competitive advantage?

Feedback – In view of the fact that Internet security has been identified as a major inhibitor to the growth of e-Commerce, companies that are proactive and demonstrate how seriously they take such issues may well be rewarded with increased customer loyalty. They may also persuade people to transact online who have thitherto been reluctant to do so. Have a look at Amazon's privacy policy, which is clear and comprehensive (www.amazon.co.uk). There are also some interesting case studies on www.howpersonal.com.

The famous US retailer L. L. Bean (www.llbean.com) has a very clear and comprehensive privacy policy that clearly demonstrates the value of effective communications in this area. Note the prominence of the endorsement by TRUSTe and the clear explanation of cookie usage to help alleviate customers' concerns about the privacy of their data.

Question 11.2

The collection of information about customers is not a new activity, so why do you think there is so much concern about online privacy?

Feedback – Businesses have always kept records of customer preferences and purchasing behaviour, although of course they had to keep paper-based records until relatively recently. Many would argue that such information allows them to provide a better quality of service to their customers. What is new is the level of detail that can be routinely captured by increasingly sophisticated technology and the extent to which it can be combined and integrated to build up personal profiles, leading customers to feel they have lost control over how and where their data is used.

Question 11.3

What do you think the impact on employee behaviour of introducing widespread electronic monitoring into a workplace might be?

Feedback – There should be a trade-off between monitoring and respect for privacy. Just because it is possible to monitor employee activity, there is no automatic right to do so. At the very least, employees should know whether their actions are being monitored. Context is important here, because in some industries (factory workers are one example), employees have been monitored for years, but professionals value their independence highly and expect a greater degree of trust.

Question 11.4

How can multi-currency payment systems like WordPay add value to both buyer and seller?

Feedback – These proactive customer-sensitive methods are likely to reduce the number of order cancellations or returned goods, as well as building trust as the customer is fully informed of the local currency cost implications and cannot claim to have been misled.

Question 11.5

What are the advantages to ABC Bank (see the case study) of the 'white labelling' policy?

Feedback – Although the provision of foreign exchange services in this way is costly and may be regarded as a loss leader, it has the advantage of extending the customer base while allowing other (potentially more lucrative) sources of business between the two banks to be pursued. This is done through analysis of the nature, destination and frequency of the foreign exchange transactions made through the system. System links create 'lock-in', meaning that it requires a lot of effort for business then to be taken elsewhere. Together with the automation of the 'credit limits' system, it also means that the need for manual processing staff is reduced.

Question 11.6

What do you think are the key ethical issues raised in the ABC Bank case?

Feedback – From a utilitarian viewpoint, it could be argued that 'the greatest good for the greatest number' criterion has been met. White labelling also allows equality of opportunity for smaller organizations, and the automation of the credit approval process standardizes decision-making and renders the process transparent. On the negative side, it could be argued that a customer's freedom of choice is reduced and that staff are not trusted to make objective decisions when considering credit limits. There is also a deception issue: the Italian bank is misleading its customers by 'piggybacking' off the reputation and resources of another institution. It is in this respect that transparency is so critical for ethical e-Banking. Cyberspace offers fantastic opportunities for disguise. This can be used for overcoming prejudices (Rogerson 1999), but also for misleading either customer or supplier as to who you are and what you are offering.

WEB LINKS

www.bcs.org.uk
Web site of the British Computer Society. Includes the BCS Code of Conduct.

www.ccsr.cse.dmu.ac.uk
Web site of the Centre for Computing and Social Responsibility. Comprehensive Web page covering a wide range of information relating to computer ethics. Takes the perspective of the responsibilities of information systems professionals.

www.cpsr.org
Web site of the Computer Professionals for Social Responsibility: a public interest alliance of computer scientists and others concerned about the impact of computer technology on society.

www.cyber-rights.org
Web site of a not-for-profit civil liberties organization, Cyber-Rights and Cyber Liberties (UK).

www.dataprotection.gov.uk
Provides details of the latest legislation covering the types of customer information that companies can hold with and without permission. The free seminar provides practical guidance.

www.digitaldivide.gov
Includes the full text of 'Falling through the net: digital inclusion report 2001'. The Commerce Department's National Telecommunications and Information Administration (NTIA) has established this site to publicize the US government's activities regarding access to the Internet and other information technologies.

www.findlaw.com
Information resource on legal issues, with section on cyberspace law (US based).

www.ispa.org.uk
Web site of the the Internet Services Providers Association. Includes a code of conduct.

www.netnanny.com
Site allowing parents to monitor and control their children's Web surfing.

www.privacy.net
Provides demonstrations of how cookies are set and a user's surfing behaviour monitored.

www.thehungersite.com
Charity site that harnesses the power of the Web to raise funding and attract corporate sponsorship.

www.truste.org
Provides an audit of a site's privacy policies and allocates a 'kitemark' to those meeting specified criteria.

www.untied.com / www.ual.com
The 'vigilante' site and the 'offending' original, United Airlines.

www.which.net/trader
A full list of privacy issues covered by *Which*? Web Trader Code.

www.wipo.com
Web site of the World Intellectual Property Organization, which aims to harmonize intellectual property legislation and procedures.

www.w3.org
The World Wide Web Consortium (W3C) develops inter-operable technologies (specifications, guidelines, software and tools) to lead the Web to its full potential as a forum for information, commerce, communication and collective understanding.

Conclusion

The amount of rhetoric dedicated to the 'Internet revolution' in recent years means that it is tempting to regard it as a unique challenge, acting both as a driver of change and as a provider of the tools of change. Throughout this book, we have dug deeper than this to demonstrate the enduring value of core marketing principles and emphasize the key role of the Internet in *integrating* rather than *replacing* more traditional business activities. To conclude, we would like to remind you about some of the historical examples introduced in Chapter 1 that support this key point.

Hanson (2000) notes some uncanny parallels between the Internet and the growth of radio in the 1920s. He demonstrates that change is always with us, however radically we might think the Internet is 'altering' marketing practices at the moment. His description of radio developments highlights that they made a huge impact on the society of the 1920s. Hanson reminds us that radio 'so captured the public's imagination that commentators claimed it would revolutionise culture, education and commerce' (2000: 2). Jardine (1999) looked further back into history, and claimed that the emergence of the printed book in the fifteenth century was equally radical in its impact on contemporary life. Interestingly, she notes that it took some fifty years for the printing business to become profitable, with a number of prominent early market entrants going out of business along the way. If a common pattern from these historical examples is not yet obvious, the following quotation from Charles Fraser (written in 1880, reproduced in www.economist.com in 2000) should clinch matters: 'An agent is at hand to bring everything into harmonious co-operation, triumphing over space and time, to subdue prejudice and unite every part of our land in rapid and friendly communication . . . and that great motive agent is *steam*.'

In their study of the social influences upon technology, MacKenzie and Wajcman (1985) claim that a new technology is created in the context of existing systems. It appears to be radically different from what has gone before only with hindsight, because the benefit of a historical perspective filters out less successful alternatives. They criticize the idea that a technology can be 'invented' as a single inspiration in isolation of the influence of existing practices, by noting that the only hindsight allows a particular invention to be traced back to a single inspirational source. In reality, competing projects may have overlapped and been developed concurrently, but only the story of the 'winner' survives the passage of time. As we noted in the Introduction, it has been suggested that as much as 72 per cent of all IT developments are centred upon improving the efficiency of *current* operations rather than creating new ones.

We tend to assume that contemporary changes are the most significant because we are closest to them and do not have the clarity accorded by distance from the phenomenon. It is evident that earlier innovations have had radical impacts on society, but perhaps not always in ways expected at the time. The perspective lent by distance is necessary to comprehend the full extent of the changes taking place over a significant period of time. The value of such historical thinking for marketers centres upon the additional insights it provides to analysis of the current business environment. Our capacity to plan for the future can be enhanced by understanding how earlier innovations appeared at the time, so that we do not apply the standards of the present to the past through the rosy glow of hindsight. We would like conclude by observing that if the existing process is a significant building block for innovation as noted above, then perhaps as marketers we should not be too quick to abandon traditional business principles in our enthusiasm for new ideas, but rather to 'mix and match' as customer needs and market conditions dictate.

Glossary

Ad Short for 'advertisement'

Audit An analysis of a company's current position with regard to both its internal operations and its micro- and macro-environments. Used as a basis for choosing future strategies

Bandwidth Specification of the rate at which electronic data are transferred using a distinctive network medium

Banner Small advertisement embedded into a Web page

Brand awareness The extent to which customers and sometimes the public as a whole are aware of the existence of a brand and what it stands for

Brand convergence The need for companies to ensure consistency of branding and service quality across multiple-channel contact points with customers

Brand equity The extent to which the value of a brand can be quantified so that the company as a whole is worth more than the sum of its more traditional assets

Brand essence The central feature of the brand that gives it a distinctive appeal

Brand extension Extension of the image and values associated with the brand to other types of product or service

Brand preference The extent to which a brand can inspire loyalty from customers over and above competitors' offerings

Brand stretching Extension of the images and values associated with a brand to encompass related products

'Bricks' ('high street') Refers to the sale of goods and services from real shops in streets and shopping centres

Business to business (B2B) Markets in which companies trade with one another

Business to consumer (B2C) Markets in which companies trade with consumers

'Clicks' see *e-Shopping*

Co-branding The putting of their brand name on the same product by different companies in order to generate synergy

Consumer franchise Preference of a particular band by customers to the extent that the brand is not affected by aggressive promotional strategies by competitors

Cookie File placed on the computer of someone who visits a Web site in order to retain or gather information about that person

Corporate branding The distinct image and value in the minds of customers of a company as a whole

Customer relationship management (CRM) Using individual customer data to ensure that a company offers each an optimum product proposition. The CRM philosophy should permeate through each aspect of customer service and at every point of customer contact.

Data collection method A technique used to gather data or information. Such techniques can include face-to-face interviews, telephone questionnaires, email and focus groups

Data mining The process of retrieving and analysing data from a data warehouse – in order to personalize a promotional campaign, for example

Data protection Providing a secure environment for consumer information and ensuring that information about consumers does not get into the wrong hands or incorrectly passed on to third parties

Data warehouse A storage location for vast amounts of data, such as those recorded through loyalty programmes from sales transactions

Digital divide The growing gap between those people who have access to the Internet and those who do not

Digital signature An electronic technique for authenticating an Internet user as the person he or she is claiming to be

Digital television A television set on which material is received and displayed using binary code (0s and 1s)

Disintermediation The process by which intermediaries are cut out of the value chain, for example by companies selling goods directly to the public rather than through wholesalers

Diversification The development of new products for new markets

Dotcom (*Pureplay*) A business that conducts all business via electronic (rather than conventional) channels

Dotcom crash The loss of investor confidence and fall in share prices affecting the technology sector, particularly Internet start-up companies, in 2000

e-Business An approach to business in which digital and Internet technologies are integrated through the entire spectrum of business functions

e-Commerce The transaction of goods and services via digital media

e-Intermediary (also called a cybermediary or new intermediary) An Internet-based intermediary between suppliers and customers, offering services such as searching, evaluation or a marketplace

Electronic contract An electronic contractual agreement; not yet fully tested in law

Electronic Data Interchange (EDI) A system pre-dating the Internet for the transfer, via digital media, of large quantities of information, in the form of standardized documents, between buyers and sellers. Usually operated by a third-party contractor

Electronic point-of-sale (EPOS) system A retail till system that operates electronically, currently from bar codes. The data can be fed directly into, for example, Electronic Data Interchange or Just in Time systems to control stocks and reordering. (Electronic funds transfer point of sale (EFTPOS) systems also enable payment via debit or credit cards)

Electronic trading exchange (also called e-Marketplace or virtual marketplace) An Internet-based intermediary that allows buyers and sellers to trade together

e-Mall (also called e-Shopping centre, virtual mall or cybermall) A grouping of separately owned e-Retail sites at a single virtual location. The e-Retailers pay rent –commission and/or an annual fee – to the centre's management

Employer branding A company's marketing of itself as a 'good place to work', in terms of the quality of training provided or the working conditions and benefits offered to staff, in order to attract high-calibre staff by virtue of this reputation

Enhanced Messaging Services (EMS) A more sophisticated service than Short Message Systems, incorporating logos, ring tones and text

Enlightened self-interest Attracting custom through reputation for ethical trading (the Co-operative Bank is a good example)

Enterprise resource planning (ERP) software Software that can link databases from, for example, marketing, production, logistics, accounting and buying, enabling real-time analysis of activities

e-Retail The sale of goods and services via Internet or other electronic channels, for personal or household use by consumers

e-Shopping ('clicks') The purchase of goods and services by consumers using e-Retail channels

Extranet Web site that can only be password-accessed by specified users such as business partners or suppliers; it is closed to the public

e-zine A magazine or journal published only in electronic format

Flaming The sending of offensive email messages

Focus group A small group of people invited into an organization to help design and refine product offerings through group discussion

FTP (File Transfer Protocol) A standard means by which files can be moved across the Internet

Globalization The transfer of an existing business system to a number of other countries

Internal branding The process whereby staff are treated as 'internal customers' in recognition of the importance of their role as the 'face' of the organization in satisfying customer needs

Internal marketing The process of treating employees as internal customers (for example, to encourage 'buy in' to change programmes, and in recognition of the importance of employees' role as the 'face' of the organization in satisfying customer needs) by means of effectively targeted communication

Internet A physical network linking computers worldwide. It consists of an infra-structure of network servers and communication links that enables the transfer of information, messages and transactions

Internet marketing The application of digital and Internet technologies to add value to marketing strategy

Internet Service Provider (ISP) A company that provides computer users – in homes and businesses – with a gateway to the Internet

Interstitial A pop-up advertisement that interrupts browsing

Intranet A password-protected network enabling internal access to company information

Just in Time An IT-based system requiring flexible, efficient processes for ensuring that goods are available where and when wanted, with minimum order quantities and stock levels

Kitemark A badge of compliance, for example through external validation of a site's privacy policy

Legacy system A customized computer system that has evolved over time and cannot be easily integrated with Internet technologies

Link popularity (a) The number of other sites linking to a measured site, and (b) their importance and relevance. Used by search engines in locating and ranking sites

Loyalty programme A scheme to reward frequent shoppers by means of discounts or special offers that also allow the company to build up individual profiles of customer spending

Market development The selling of existing products into new geographic markets or segments

Market penetration Increasing the volume of sales to existing customers in current markets

Marketing mix The blend of tools and techniques that marketers use to provide value for customers. It is most commonly simplified to 4Ps: Place, Product, Price and Promotion. Sometimes three extra Ps are added: People, Process and Physical evidence. It may also be expressed as the more customer-orientated 4Cs: Convenience, Cost to the customer, Customer benefit and Communication

Marketing orientation An attitude of mind within an organization that puts meeting customer needs at the top of its agenda

Marketing planning The process of optimizing marketing resources to achieve marketing objectives

Marketing research Investigation by individuals or organizations to find out the needs and wants of customers and other stakeholder groups

Mass customization A process of tailoring the product itself in order to meet individual customer needs; the producing of individually designed products and communications to order on a large scale

m-Commerce The transaction of goods and services via mobile communications devices

333

m-CRM Customer relationship management via mobile communications devices

m-Shopping The purchase of goods and services via mobile communications channels, for personal or household use by consumers

Multimedia Messaging Services (MMS) A superior alternative to Enhanced Messaging Services, including pictures, colour and sound

Mystery shopping A research method whereby researchers pose as shoppers in order to test out the quality of service provided to customers by staff

Patent A means of obtaining legal protection for innovations or intellectual property

Permission marketing Marketing addressed only to individuals who have specifically requested contact, and limited to the extent of permission granted by the customer. It is designed to build up trust

Personal Digital Assistant (PDA) A mobile business service incorporating diary facilities, word processing, email and 'always on' Web access

Personalization Tailoring of a marketing campaign to individual customer needs based on analysis of the data collected through loyalty programmes and stored in a data warehouse

Place A shorthand name to classify the elements of the marketing mix that marketers use to access the benefits of a product or service. Called 'Convenience' in the 4Cs

Positioning How a company is perceived against its competitors in the market, for example in terms of quality and price

Price A shorthand name to classify the elements of the marketing mix that result in the costs to the customer of obtaining the benefits of a product. Called 'Cost to the customer' in the 4Cs

Primary data First-hand data, such as responses from an interview questionnaire

Product A shorthand name to classify the elements of the marketing mix that marketers use to provide a 'bundle of satisfactions' for customers. 'Product' in the marketing mix embraces not just tangible products but also intangible services and augmented value. Called 'Customer benefit' in the 4Cs

Product development Selling new or refined products into existing markets

Promotion A shorthand name to classify the elements of the marketing mix that marketers use to communicate with customers – both to make known the benefits of a product or service (e.g. advertising) and to gather information (e.g. marketing research). Called 'Communication' in the 4Cs

Pureplay see *dotcom*

Qualitative research Research whose objective is to extract meanings as to why and how things occur, rather than the frequency with which they occur

Quantitative research Research focusing on the statistically significant frequency with which certain phenomena occur

Reintermediation The process by which new intermediaries in the traditional value chain provide services such as price aggregation

Retail The sale of goods and services for personal, family or household use by consumers using any distribution channel or combination of channels

Sample A selection of individuals chosen from the population of interest as the subjects in an experiment, or to be the respondents to a survey

Secondary data Data not collected at first hand, such as data from company reports, articles, newspapers, journals and the Internet

Segmentation The process by which customers are categorized into smaller groups with similar characteristics or expectations for targeting purposes

Short Message Systems (SMS) An increasingly popular text messaging system

SMART objective A target for the company to aim at that is specific, measurable, actionable, relevant and timed

Social responsibility Companies' behaving or being seen to behave in an ethical way

Spam (sending persistent annoying messages) Unsolicited junk email, or, as a verb, the sending of such messages

Spamming The opposite of permission marketing, whereby unsolicited marketing messages (known as spam mail) are sent out in bulk to an entire database of addresses

Stakeholder group The diverse range of people with a particular interest in the running of a business, such as shareholders, employees, customers, suppliers and partners

SWOT analysis A mechanism by which the findings of a marketing audit can be summarized in order to guide the choice of strategy

Targeting The process by which a company chooses which segments of its market offer the most potential and should therefore be focused upon

Viral marketing Taking advantage of the network effects of the Internet to spread marketing messages widely by customer endorsement

Virtual organization An organization whose day-to-day business operations are carried out across tempora; and spatial barriers using information and communications technologies

Webmosphere The virtual environment of an e-Retail store. It includes structural design (e.g. frames, pop-ups, one-click checkout), media (video, audio and graphics) and layout (organization and grouping of merchandise; Childers *et al.* 2001)

Wireless Application Protocol (WAP) A system that enables wireless access to information, via a wireless service platform

WWW (World Wide Web) A vehicle for distributing information on the Internet

References

Aldisert, L. (1999) 'Branding and legacy', *Bank Marketing*, November, 31 (11): 36.

Anders, G. (2000) 'Power partners', *Fast Company*, September.

Ansoff, H. (1957) 'Strategies for diversification', *Harvard Business Review*. September–October: 113–124.

Badham, R., Couchman, P. and McLoughlin, I. P. (1997) 'Implementing vulnerable socio-technical change projects', in I. P. McLoughlin and M Harris (eds) *Innovation, Organizational Change and Technology*, London: ITB Press.

Banker, The (1999) 'Bottom line', *The Banker*, June, 149 (880): 72.

Bansal, P. (2001) 'Mobile banking steps up a gear', *The Banker*, July, 151 (905): 121.

Bartels, R. and Hoffmann, A. (2001) 'e-Branding in the chemical industry', *Chemical Market Reporter*, 28 May.

Berners-Lee, T. (1999) *Weaving the Web: The Past, Present and Future of the World Wide Web by Its Inventor*, London: Orion.

Berry, L. L., Shostack, G. L. and Upah, G. D. (1983) *Emerging Perspectives on Services Marketing*, Chicago: American Marketing Association.

Bicknell, D. (2000) 'e-Commerce outpaces strategy', *Computer Weekly*, 24 February: 20–21.

Booms, B. and Bitner, M. (1982) 'Marketing strategies and organisation structures for service firms', in J. H. Donelly and W. R. George (eds) *Marketing of Services*, Chicago: American Marketing Association.

Borden, N. H. (1964) 'The concepts of the marketing mix', *Journal of Marketing Research*, June, 4: 2–7.

Boss, S., McGranahan, D. and Mehta, A. (2000) 'Will the banks control on-line banking?', *McKinsey Quarterly*, Summer: 70.

Brassington, F. and Pettitt, S. (2000) *Principles of Marketing*, London: Prentice Hall.

British Council of Shopping Centres (2001) *Future Shock or e-Hype? The Impact of Online Shopping on UK Retail Property*, London: BCSC and College of Estate Management.

Brown, A. D. (1998) *Organisational Culture*, 2nd edition, London: Pitman Publishing/ Financial Times.

Buchanan, D. and Boddy, D. (1992) *The Expertise of the Change Agent*, Hemel Hempstead, UK: Prentice Hall.

Burns, T. and Stalker, G. M. (1961) *The Management of Innovation*, London: Tavistock.

Burton, P. (2001) 'Trench warfare in the European battle to free the last mile', *Financial Times*, 17 January.

Butler, M., Power, T. and Richmond, C. (1999) *The e-Business Advantage*, London: Ecademists.

Capell, K. (2001) 'Virgin takes e-Wing', *Business Week*, 22 January, (3716): EB30–EB34.

Carnall, C. A. (1999) *Managing Change in Organisations*, 3rd edition, London: Prentice Hall.

Carr, P. (2000) *The Age of Enterprise*, Dublin: Blackhall Publishing.

Cellan-Jones, R. (2001) *Dot.bomb: The Rise and Fall of Dot.com Britain*, London: Aurum.

Centre for the Study of Financial Innovation (CSFI) (1999) 'Brands and the Web', *Bank Marketing*, January–February, (101): 8.

Chaffey, D. (2002) *e-Business and e-Commerce Management*, London: Prentice Hall/Financial Times.

Chaffey, D., Mayer, R., Johnston, K. and Ellis-Chadwick, F. (2000) *Internet Marketing*, London: Prentice Hall/Financial Times.

Chaston, I. (2001a) *Strategic Internet Marketing*, Maidenhead, UK: McGraw-Hill.

Chaston, I. (2001b) *e-Marketing Strategy*, Maidenhead, UK: McGraw-Hill.

Chen, S. (2001) *Strategic Management of e-Business*, Chichester, UK: Wiley.

Childers, T. L., Carr, C. L., Peck, J. and Carson, S. (2001) 'Hedonic and utilitarian motivations for online shopping behaviour', *Journal of Retailing* 77 (4): 511–535.

Classe, A. (1997) 'Advancing with caution', *Computer Weekly*, 24 April: 48.

Clawson, T. (2001) 'Feeling the squeeze', *e-Business*, April: 40–44.

Cohan, P. S. (2000) *e-Profit: High Payoff Strategies for Capturing the e-Commerce Edge*, New York: Amacom.

Cohen, A. (2001) 'Coming: the e-Wallet wars', *Time*, 6 August: 46.

Computer Professionals for Social Responsibility (1996) 'Electronic privacy principles', www.bcs.org.uk.

Conway, P. (2000) 'Lasting legacy?', *e-Business*, June: 62–64.

Cope, N. (2000) 'No one hears you scream on the Easy route to e-mail hell', *The Independent*, 14 August.

Cranfield School of Management, *Marketing Management: A Relationship Marketing Perspective*, London: Macmillan Business (2000).

Culliton, J. W. (1948) *The Management of Marketing Costs*, Cambridge, MA: Harvard University Press.

Curtis, J. (2001) 'Behind enemy lines', *Marketing*, 24 May: 28.

Dahlen, M. (2001) 'Banner advertisements through a new lens', *Journal of Advertising Research*, July–August, 41 (4): 23–30.

Daranvala, T. N. (2000) 'e-Financial services take place', *McKinsey Quarterly*, Summer: 6.

David, P. A. (1991) 'Computer and dynamo: the modern productivity paradox in a not-too-distant mirror', in *Technology and Productivity: The Challenge for Economic Policy*, Paris: OECD.

Day, G. S. (1998) 'Organising for interactivity', *Journal of Interactive Marketing* 12 (1): 47–53.

de Kare-Silver, M. (2001) *e-Shock: The New Rules*, Basingstoke, UK: Palgrave.

Dennis, C., Marsland, D. and Cockett, W. (2001) 'The mystery of consumer behaviour: market segmentation and shoppers' choices of shopping centres', *International Journal of New Product Development and Innovation Management*, June–July, 3 (2): 185–189.

Dennis, C., Harris, L. and Sandhu, B. (2002) 'From bricks to clicks: understanding the e-Consumer', *Qualitative Marketing Research, an International Journal* 5 (4).

Department of Trade and Industry (2000) 'Business in the Information Age: international benchmarking study 2000', www.ukonlineforbusiness.gov.uk

Dhensa, G. (2001) 'An investigation of e-Loyalty', unpublished M.Sc. thesis, Brunel University.

Dholakia, R. R. and Uusitalo, O. (2001) 'The structure and determinants of consumer intention to switch to electronic shopping formats', *Recent Advances in Retailing and Services Science*, 8th International Conference, European Institute of Retailing and Services Studies, Eindhoven.

Doidge, R. and Higgins, C. (2000) *The Big Dot.com Con*, Colliers Conrad Ritblat Erdman.

Durlacher (2000) *Business to Business e-Commerce: Investment Perspective*, London: Durlacher Research Ltd.

Dutta, S. and Biren, B. (2001) 'Business transformation in the Internet: results from the 2000 study', *European Management Journal*, 19 (5): 449–462.

Dwyer, F., Schurr, P. H. and Oh, S. (1987) 'Developing buyer and seller relationships', *Journal of Marketing*, April, 51: 11–27.

Economist, The (1999) 'You'll never walk alone', Survey: Business and the Internet, *The Economist*, 26 June.

Economist, The (2001a) 'Looking for the pot of gold: what do consumers want from the mobile Internet?', *The Economist*, 13 October.

Economist, The (2001b) 'Just talk to me', *The Economist*, 6 December.

Evans, M., Wedande, W., Ralston, L. and van't Hul, S. (2001) 'Consumer interaction in the virtual era: some qualitative insights', *Qualitative Market Research: An International Journal* 4 (3): 150–159.

Feinberg, R. (2001) 'Correlates of Internet shopping customer satisfaction', *Recent Advances in Retailing and Services Science*, 8th International Conference, European Institute of Retailing and Services Studies, Eindhoven.

Fischer, J. (1999) *Understanding the Internet Economy: A Companion Guide to the Motley Fool's Internet Report*, New York: Motley Fool.

Foremski, T. (2001) 'IBM increases focus on privacy and security', *Financial Times*, 12 November.

Forrester, *The Technographics Brief*, www.forrester.com (accessed 31 July 2001).

Forrester Research (2001) *Bridging the B2B Credibility Gap*, February.

Fournier, S., Dobscha, S. and Mick, D. G. (1998) 'Preventing the premature death of relationship marketing', *Harvard Business Review*, January–February, 76 (1): 42–49.

Fraser, H. (2001) 'Dotcoms that came back from the dead', *Daily Telegraph*, 24 March.

Freeman, R. E. (1997) 'A stakeholder theory of the modern corporation', in T. Beauchamp and N. Bowie (eds) *Ethical Theory and Business*, Englewood Cliffs, NJ: Prentice Hall.

Gandy, T. (2000) 'Clicks supersede bricks', *The Banker*, July, 150 (893): 122.

Gardner, D. (2000) TMF interview with Amazon.com, *The Motley Fool*, Alexandria, NY, http://www.fool.com/foolaudio/transcripts/2000/stocktlk001109.htm (accessed 2 January 2002).

Gates, W. (1995) *The Road Ahead*, New York: Penguin.

Gibson, B. (1999) 'Beyond shopping centres: e-Commerce', British Council of Shopping Centres Conference.

Gledhill, D. (2001) 'Dotcoms fly like dodos', *The Independent*, 17 March.

Godin, S. (1999) *Permission Marketing*, New York: Simon and Schuster.

Graham, M. B. W. (1986) *RCA and the Video Disk*, Cambridge: Cambridge University Press.

Grande, C. (2001) 'Internet surveys receive a dressing down', FT.com, 13 August.

Grassl, W. (1999) 'The reality of brands: towards an ontology of marketing', *American Journal of Economics and Sociology*, April, 58 (2): 313.

Green, S. (1994) 'Strategy, organizational culture and symbolism', in E. Rhodes and D. Wield (eds) *Implementing New Technologies: Innovation and the Management of Technology*, 2nd edition, Oxford: Blackwell.

Gronroos, C. (1997) 'From marketing mix to relationship marketing: towards a paradigm shift in marketing', *Management Decision*, March–April, 35 (3–4): 322–339.

Gruen, T. W. (1997) 'Relationship marketing: the route to marketing efficiency and effectiveness', *Business Horizons*, November–December, 40 (6): 32–38.

Gulati, R. and Garino, J. (2000) 'Getting the right mix of bricks and clicks for your company', *Harvard Business Review*, May–June: 107–114.

Gummesson, E. (1991) *Qualitative Issues in Management Research*, Newbury Park, CA: Sage.

Gummesson, E. (1997) 'Relationship marketing as a paradigm shift: some conclusions from the 30R approach', *Management Decision*, March–April, 35 (3–4): 267–272.

Hackbarth, G. and Kettinger, W. (2000) 'Building an e-Business strategy', *Information Systems Management*, Summer, 17: 78–94.

Haigh, D. (2000) 'e-Commerce = added value?', *Marketing*, March: 33.

Hamel, G., Doz, Y. and Prahalad, C. K. (1989) 'Collaborate with your competitors – and win', *Harvard Business Review* 67 (1): 133–139.

Hamelink, C. (2000) *The Ethics of Cyberspace*, London: Sage.

Hanson, W. (2000) *Principles of Internet Marketing*, New York: Thomson Learning.

Harris, K. (1998) 'Women on the Net II: the female-friendly site', *Sporting Goods Business* 31 (13): 16.

Heim, S. J. (2001) 'Hit or myth?', *Adweek*, 23 April, 42 (17): 28.

Hoffman, D. and Novak, T. (1997) 'A new marketing paradigm for electronic commerce', *Information Society*, January–March, 13: 43–54.

Hunt, J. W. (1998) 'Management and technology: escape from the shock of the new: the perils of change could be reduced with the help of a simple checklist', *Financial Times*, 18 June.

IBM Global Services (1999) *Building a Successful e-Business*, New York: Caspian Publishing.

IMT Strategies (2001) *Tactical Insights: Managing the Impact of Technology on Sales and Marketing*, Stamford, CT: IMT Strategies.

Jackson, T. (2001) 'Burning money at Boo', *Financial Times*, 1 November.

Jardine, L. (1999) 'The future began in 1455', *Spectator*, 16 October.

Jefkins, F. (1993) *Modern Marketing*, London: Pitman Publishing.

Jobber, D. (2001) *Principles and Practice of Marketing*, Maidenhead, UK: McGraw-Hill.

Jupiter Communications (2000) 'Turning browsers into buyers', www.jup.com.

339

Kalakota, R. and Robinson, M. (1999) *e-Business Roadmap for Success*, New York: Addison Wesley.

Kalakota, R. and Robinson, M. (2001) *e-Business Roadmap for Success*, 2nd edition, Harlow, UK: Addison Wesley.

Kalakota, R. and Whinston, A. B. (1996) *Electronic Commerce: A Manager's Guide*, Harlow, UK: Addison Wesley.

Kanter, R. M. (2001) *Evolve! Succeeding in the Digital Culture of Tomorrow*, Boston, MA: Harvard Business School Press.

Kaplan, R. S. and Norton, D. P. (1993) 'Putting the balanced scorecard to work', *Harvard Business Review*, September–October: 134–142.

Keegan, W. J. and Green, M. C. (1997) *Principles of Global Marketing*, London: Prentice Hall.

Keith, R. J. (1960) 'The marketing revolution', *Journal of Marketing* 24: 35–38.

Kelly, E. and Rowland, H. (2000) 'Ethical and online privacy issues in electronic commerce', *Business Horizons* 43 (3): 3–12.

Kleindl, B. A. (2001) *Strategic Electronic Marketing: Managing e-Business*, Cincinnati: South Western College Publishing.

Knox, S. (2000) 'Branding and positioning', in *Marketing Management: A Relationship and Marketing Perspective*, Cranfield School of Management, London: Macmillan Business.

Kotha, S., Rindova, V. and Rothaermel, F. T. (2001) 'Assets and actions: firm-specific factors in the internationalization of US Internet firms', *Journal of International Business Studies*, Winter, 32 (4): 76.

Kotler, P. (2003) *Marketing Management* 11th edition, Englewood Cliffs, NJ: Prentice Hall.

Kotler, P., Armstrong, G., Saunders, J. and Wong, Y. (2001) *Principles of Marketing*, 3rd European edition, London: Prentice Hall/Financial Times.

Kozinets, R. (1999) 'e-Tribalized marketing? The strategic implications of virtual communities of consumption', *European Management Journal* 17 (3): 252–264.

Kumar, N. (1999) 'Internet distribution strategies: dilemmas for the incumbent', *Financial Times*, special issue on Mastering Information Management, no. 7, Electronic Commerce (www.ftmastering.com).

Kumar, N. (1999) 'Internet distribution strategies: dilemmas for the incumbent', *Financial Times*, special issue on Mastering Information Management, no. 7, Electronic Commerce (www.ftmastering.com).

Kuo, J. D. (2001) *Dot.bomb: Inside an Internet Goliath from Lunatic Optimism to Panic and Crash*, London: Little, Brown.

Lauterborn, R. (1990) 'New marketing litany: 4Ps passé; 4Cs take over', *Advertising Age*, 1 October.

Leibovich, M. (1999) 'At Amazon.com, service workers without a smile', *Washington Post*, 22 November: A1.

Leung, K. and Antypas, J. (2001) 'Improving returns on m-Commerce investments', *Journal of Business Strategy*, September, 22 (5): 12.

Levine, R., Locke, D., Searls, D. and Weinberger, D. (2000) *The Cluetrain Manifesto: The End of Business as Usual*, Cambridge, MA: Perseus.

Lewin, K. (1952) *Field Theory in Social Science*, London: Tavistock.

Lindquist, J. D. and Kaufman-Scarborough, C. (2000) 'Browsing and purchasing activity in selected non-store settings: a contrast between female and male shoppers', *Retailing 2000: Launching the New Millennium, Proceedings of the 6th Triennial*

National Retailing Conference, the Academy of Marketing Science and the American Collegiate Retailing Association, Columbus, OH: Hofstra University.

Lindstrom, M. (1999) 'Rat race scurry', *ClickZ Network*, www.clickz.com, 2 December.

Lindstrom, M. (2001) *Clicks, Bricks and Brands*, London: Kogan Page.

Luengo-Jones, S. (2001) *All-to-One: The Winning Model for Marketing in the Post-Internet Economy*, London: McGraw-Hill.

Lundquist, L. H. (1998) *Selling On Line for Dummies*, Foster City, CA: IDG.

Lynch, R. (2000) *Corporate Strategy*, Harlow, UK: Pearson Education.

McCarthy, E. J. (1960) *Basic Marketing*, Homewood, IL: Irwin

McCarthy, S. (2000) 'Your web site is calling, please hold for your customer', *Call Center Solutions* 18 (8): 70–73.

McDaniel, C. and Gates, R. (2002) *Marketing Research: The Impact of the Internet*, 5th edition, Cincinnati: South-Western Publishing.

McDonald, M. (1999) 'Strategic marketing planning: theory and practice', in M. Baker (ed.) *The CIM Marketing Book*, 4th edition, Oxford: Butterworth Heinemann.

McIntosh, M., Leipziger, D., Jones, K. and Coleman, G. (1998) *Corporate Citizenship: Successful Strategies for Responsible Companies*, London: Pitman Publishing/Financial Times.

MacKenzie, D. and Wajcman, J. (eds) (1985) *The Social Shaping of Technology*, Milton Keynes, UK: Open University Press.

McLuhan, R. (2001) 'How DM can build consumer loyalty', *Marketing*, June: 66–68.

Mahoney, J. (1994) 'What makes a company ethical?', *Business Strategy Review* 5 (4): 1–15.

Malmsten, E., Portanger, E. and Drazin, C. (2001) *Boo Hoo: A Dot-com Story from Concept to Catastrophe*, London: Random House.

Maloney, D. (2001) 'The power behind the pony', *Modern Materials Handling*, June, 56 (7): 30–35.

March, J. G. and Simon, H. E. (1994) *Organisations*, 2nd edition, Oxford: Blackwell Business.

Markus, L. (1999) 'Survey – Mastering information management: how workers react to new technology', *Financial Times*, 22 March.

Miles, R. E. and Snow, C. C. (1986) 'Network organisation: new concepts for new forms', *McKinsey Quarterly*, Autumn.

Mintzberg, H. (1979) *The Structuring of Organisations*, Englewood Cliffs, NJ: Prentice Hall.

Mintzberg, H. (1994) *The Rise and Fall of Strategic Planning*, Englewood Cliffs, NJ: Prentice Hall.

Morgan, R. M. and Hunt, S. D. (1994) 'The commitment–trust theory of relationship marketing', *Journal of Marketing*, 58: 20–38.

Murphy, M. and Berg, M. (1999) 'Start small but get started', *The Banker*, April, 149 (878): 87.

Nadler, D. and Tushman, M. L. (1997) 'Implementing new designs: managing organisational change', in M. L. Tushman and P. Anderson (eds) *Managing Strategic Innovation and Change*, Oxford: Oxford University Press.

Nancarrow, C., Pallister, J. and Brace, I. (2001) 'A new research medium', *Qualitative Market Research: An International Journal* 4 (3): 136–149.

National Telecommunications and Information Administration (2000) 'Falling through the Net: toward digital inclusion', http://search.ntia.doc.gov/pdf/fttn00.pdf.

341

Neuborne, E. (2001) 'Pepsi's aim is true', *Business Week*, 22 January, issue 3716: EB52.

Newell, F. (2000) *Loyalty.com: Customer Relationship Management in the New Era of Internet Marketing*, New York: McGraw-Hill.

Newell, F. (2000) *Loyalty.com: Customer Relationship Management in the New Era of Internet Marketing*, New York: McGraw-Hill.

O'Malley, L. and Tynan, C. (2001) 'Reframing relationship marketing for consumer markets', *Interactive Marketing* 2 (3): 240–246.

Olins, W. (1999) *Corporate Identity*, London: Thames and Hudson.

Palmer, A. (1997) 'Defining relationship marketing: an international perspective', *Management Decision*, March–April, 35 (3–4): 319–322.

Palmer, R. A. (2001) 'There's no business like e-Business', paper presented at Business Intelligence and e-Marketing Workshop, Warwick, UK, 6 December.

Palmer, R. A. (2002) 'Bricks, clicks, mortar and porter', *Marketing Intelligence and Planning*, 20: 1.

Parker, R. (2000) *Relationship Marketing on the Internet*, Holbrook, MA: Adams Media Corporation.

Payne, A. (ed.) (1995) *Advances in Relationship Marketing*, London: Kogan Page.

Peppers, D. and Rogers, M. (1997) *Enterprise One to One*, London: Piatkus.

Peppers, D. and Rogers, M. (2001) *One to One B2B*, New York: Capstone Publishing.

Petrof, J. V. (1998) 'Relationship marketing: the emperor in used clothes' (Response to Thomas Gruen, *Business Horizons*, November–December, 40 (6): 32–38), *Business Horizons*, November–December, 41 (2): 79–83.

Phillips, F. Y. (2001) *Market-Oriented Technology Management*, Berlin: Springer.

Pickton, D. and Broderick, A. (2001) *Integrated Marketing Communications*, London: Prentice Hall.

Piercy, N. F. (1997) *Market-Led Strategic Change*, Oxford: Butterworth Heinemann.

Piercy, N. F. (2000) *Market-Led Strategic Change*, 2nd edition, Oxford: Butterworth Heinemann.

Piore, M. and Sabel, C. (1984) *The Second Industrial Divide: Possibilities for Prosperity*, New York: Basic Books.

Pollack, B. (1999) 'The state of Internet marketing', *Direct Marketing*, January: 18–22.

Porter, M. (2001) 'Strategy and the Internet', *Harvard Business Review*, March.

Prabhaker, P. R. (2000) 'Who owns the online consumer?', *Journal of Consumer Marketing* 17 (2): 158–171.

Prefontaine, M. (1999) 'Beyond shopping centres: e-Commerce', British Council of Shopping Centres Conference.

Reichheld, F., Markey, G. R. and Hopton, C. (2000) 'e-Customer loyalty: applying the traditional rules of business for online services', *European Business Journal* 12 (4): 173.

Reynolds, J. (2000) 'Pricing dynamics and European retailing: direct and indirect impacts of e-Commerce', *Proceedings of the International EARCD Conference on Retail Innovation* (CD-ROM), European Association for Education and Research in Commercial Distribution, Barcelona, ESADE.

RICS Foundation (2000) *20:20 Visions of the Future*, London: Royal Institute of Chartered Surveyors.

Rogerson, S. (1999) 'e-Society – panacea or apocalypse? The rights and wrongs of the information age', Inaugural Lecture, De Montfort University, Leicester, 26 May.

Rosenfield, J. R. (1999) 'Whatever happened to relationship marketing? Nine big mistakes', *Direct Marketing*, May, 62 (1): 30–33.

Ross, V. (2001) Review of *Permission Marketing* by Seth Godin, *Interactive Marketing*, January–March, 2 (3): 17.

Rowley, J. (2001) 'Eight questions for customer knowledge management in e-Business', paper presented at the Business Intelligence and e-Marketing Workshop, IBM, Warwick, 6 December.

Sarkar, M. B., Butler, B. and Steinfield, C. (1995) 'Intermediaries and cybermediaries: a continuing role for mediating players in the electronic marketplace', *Journal of Computer Mediated Communications* 3 (3).

Sawhney, M. and Zabin, J. (2001) *The Seven Steps to Nirvana: Strategic Insights into e-Business Transformation*, New York: McGraw-Hill.

Schein, E. H. (1985) *Organizational Culture and Leadership*, San Francisco: Jossey Bass.

Schiffman, L. G. and Kanuk, L. L. (1997) *Consumer Behaviour*, 6th edition, London: Prentice Hall.

Seth, J. and Sisodia, R. (1999) 'Re-visiting marketing's lawlike generalizations', *Journal of the Academy of Marketing Science* 27 (1): 71–87.

Seybold, P. B. (1998) *Customers.com: How to Create a Profitable Business Strategy for the Internet and Beyond*, New York: Random House.

Siegel, D. (2000) *Futurize Your Business: Business Strategy in the Age of the e-Customer*, New York: Wiley.

Simon, H. A. (1987) 'The steam engine and the computer: what makes technology revolutionary', *EDUCOM Bulletin* 22 (1): 2–5.

Smith, P. R. and Chaffey, D. (2002) *e-Marketing Excellence*, Oxford: Butterworth Heinemann.

Spence, L. J. (2002) '"Like building a new motorway": establishing the rules for ethical email use at a UK higher education institution', *Business Ethics: A European Review*, January.

Sterne, J. (2001) *World Wide Web Marketing*, 3rd edition, New York: Wiley.

Stone, A. (2002) 'Mobile marketing strategies', www.m-commercetimes.com, 11 January.

Strauss, J. and Frost, R. (2001) *e-Marketing*, Englewood Cliffs, NJ: Prentice Hall.

Stroud, D. (1998) *Internet Strategies: A Corporate Guide to Exploiting the Internet*, Basingstoke, UK: Macmillan.

Sweet, C. (2001) 'Designing and conducting virtual focus groups', *Qualitative Market Research: An International Journal* 4 (3): 130–135.

Symonds, M. (1999a) 'The Net imperative', survey, Business and the Internet, *The Economist*, 26 June.

Symonds, M. (1999b) 'You'll never walk alone', survey, Business and the Internet, *The Economist*, 26 June.

Tapscott, D. (1995) *The Digital Economy*, New York: McGraw-Hill.

Tapscott, D., Ticoll, D. and Lowy, A. (2000) *Digital Capital*, New York, Nicholas Brearley Publishing.

Tiernan, B. (2000) *e-tailing*, Chicago: Dearborn.

Timewell, S. and Young, K. (1999) 'How the Internet redefines banking', *The Banker*, June, 149 (880): 27.

Timmers, P. (1999) *Electronic Commerce*, New York: Wiley.

Timmins, N. (2000) 'Digital divide grows in UK', www.ft.com, 19 December.

343

Tunick, B. (2001) 'Life after Boo is not as we knew it', *Euromoney* 376: 90.

Turbin, E., Lee, J., King, D. and Chung, H. M. (2000) *Electronic Commerce: A Managerial Perspective*, London: Prentice Hall.

Turner, C. (2000) *The Information E-conomy*, London: Kogan Page.

Ulrich, D. (1989) 'Tie the corporate knot: gaining complete customer commitment', *Sloan Management Review*, Summer: 19–27.

Venkatram (2000)

Verdict (2000) *Verdict on Electronic Shopping 2000*, London: Verdict.

Verdict (2001) *Verdict on Electronic Shopping 2001*, London: Verdict.

Verdict (2002) *Verdict on Electronic Shopping 2002*, London: Verdict.

Vincent, A., Clark, H. and English, A. (2000) 'Retail distribution: a multi-channel traffic jam', *International Journal of New Product Development and Innovation Management* 2 (2): 179–196.

Waldmeir, P. (2001) 'Yahoo! can ignore French website ruling', *Financial Times*, 8 November.

Walser, M. (2001) 'Onstar started it all', www.m-commercetimes.com, 11 April.

Watson, A. (1994) *In Search of Management*, London: Routledge.

Weber, M. and Seibert, P. (2001) 'Connecting', *Credit Union Management*, May, 24 (5): 16–17.

Whitehead, D. (1999) 'Data warehousing: winning the loyalty game', *Telecommunications*, international edition, 33 (8): 68–74.

Whysall, P. (2001) 'Does e-Commerce create new ethical challenges?', paper presented at the Business Intelligence and e-Marketing Workshop, IBM, Warwick, UK, 6 December.

Willcocks, L. and Sauer, C. (2000) *e-Business: The Ultimate Practical Guide to Effective e-Business*, London: Random House.

Williams, K. (2000) 'Are you ready for Internet banking?', *Strategic Finance*, April: 8 (10): 23.

Yakhlef, A. (2001) 'Does the Internet compete with or complement bricks-and-mortar bank branches?', *International Journal of Retail and Distribution Management* 29 (6): 272–281.

Yoshida, E. (2001) 'e-Commerce and culture', *Recent Advances in Retailing and Services Science*, 8th International Conference, European Institute of Retailing and Services Studies.

Zwass, V. (1998) 'Structure and macro-level impacts of electronic commerce: from technological infrastructure to electronic marketplaces', in E. Kendall (ed.) *Emerging Information Technologies*, Thousand Oaks, CA: Sage.

Index

Note: page numbers followed by '*f*' refer to figures. Page numbers followed by '*t*' refer to tables.